ECONOMIC AND SOCIAL SURVEY OF ASIA AND THE PACIFIC 2005

Dealing with shocks

ECONOMIC AND SOCIAL COMMISSION FOR ASIA AND THE PACIFIC

The work is published for
and on behalf of the United Nations

ACADEMIC FOUNDATION

ESCAP is the regional development arm of the United Nations and serves as the main economic and social development centre for the United Nations in Asia and the Pacific. Its mandate is to foster cooperation between its 53 members and 9 associate members. ESCAP provides the strategic link between global and country-level programmes and issues. It supports Governments of the region in consolidating regional positions and advocates regional approaches to meeting the region's unique socio-economic challenges in a globalizing world. The ESCAP office is located in Bangkok, Thailand. Web site <www.unescap.org>

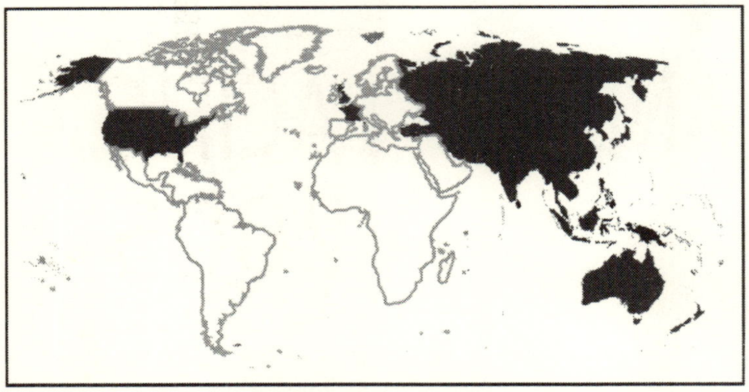

The shaded areas of the map indicate ESCAP members and associate members.

Cover design by Bryan Joseph Granados Sabroso

UNITED NATIONS PUBLICATION

The work is published for and
on behalf of the United Nations
by

ACADEMIC FOUNDATION

4772 / 23 Bharat Ram Road, (23 Ansari Road),
Darya Ganj, New Delhi - 110 002.

Tel : +91-11-23245001 / 02 / 03 / 04
Fax : +91-11-23245005
e-mail : academic@vsnl.com
www.academicfoundation.com

ISBN 81-7188-503-9

This edition is printed in India in 2006.

FOREWORD

Between the earthquake in Bam, Islamic Republic of Iran, in December 2003 and the earthquake and tsunami disaster of December 2004 – the period covered by this report – the Asia-Pacific region withstood a wide spectrum of shocks. These ranged from avian influenza to persistent high oil prices, from the spread of HIV/AIDS to cyclones, typhoons, floods and drought. The tsunami catastrophe alone is estimated to have taken more than a quarter of a million lives, while severely damaging the physical and social infrastructure of the affected countries, as well as export-oriented sectors such as fisheries, agriculture and tourism.

Yet in the same year, ESCAP economies grew at their fastest pace in four years, with broad-based growth accompanied in most cases by low inflation. The resilience of the region's economies was essentially built on exports within and outside the region, as well as on domestic demand. Capital expenditure revived in many countries, while foreign direct investment inflows increased sharply. However, prospects for 2005 have been undermined in the affected countries by the tsunami disaster and other factors.

This year's *Economic and Social Survey of Asia and the Pacific* also examines the dynamics of population ageing with a special focus on how the region, especially developing economies, can respond to this challenge. I hope the analysis and policy options outlined in the *Survey* will help member countries take bold actions in two ways: transform the challenge of ageing into an opportunity to improve living standards; and make old age productive by providing training and a flexible working environment, while encouraging the elderly to continue to participate in their communities.

Because 2005 has been designated by the General Assembly as the International Year of Microcredit, with the principal objective of promoting the role of microfinance in poverty reduction, the *Survey* also contains a special feature highlighting meaningful ways to strengthen income and employment generation, economic security and empowerment of the poor in Asia and the Pacific.

I hope the *Survey* reaches the wide global audience it deserves.

Kofi A. Annan
Secretary-General

March 2005

ACKNOWLEDGEMENTS

The *Economic and Social Survey of Asia and the Pacific 2005* was prepared under the direction of Raj Kumar and coordinated by Eugene Gherman (chapter II) and Hiren Sarkar and Amarakoon Bandara (chapter III) of the Poverty and Development Division of ESCAP.

Experts from within and outside the ESCAP secretariat contributed to various stages in the preparation of the *Survey 2005*. The team of staff members of the Poverty and Development Division who prepared the *Survey 2005* comprised: Shahid Ahmed, Amarakoon Bandara, Eugene Gherman, Fareeda Maroof Hla, Nobuko Kajiura, Muhammad H. Malik, Hiren Sarkar, Seok-Dong Wang and Marin Yari. Staff analysis was based on data and information available up to the end of February 2005. Research assistance was provided by Somchai Congtavinsutti, Kiatkanid Pongpanich and Amornrut Supornsinchai. All graphics work was done by Somchai Congtavinsutti. The logistics of processing and production, and the organization of the meetings referred to below, were handled by Dusdeemala Kanittanon and Woranut Sompitayanurak.

Andrew Flatt, Chief of the Statistics Division, provided useful comments and suggestions on data presentation in all draft chapters of the *Survey 2005*. Inputs for the *Survey 2005* also came from Aynul Hasan, Chief, and Hirohito Toda, Economic Affairs Officer, of the Least Developed Countries Coordination Unit/Millennium Development Goals Centre, Office of the Executive Secretary, and from Tiziana Bonapace, Chief, and Harish Iyer, Economic Affairs Officer, of the Trade Policy Section, Trade and Investment Division.

Major inputs for the *Survey 2005* were received from the following external consultants: Mushtaq Ahmad, Tarun Das, Ron Duncan, Muhammad Allah Malik Kazemi, Yuba Raj Khatiwada, Mohammad Kordbache, George Manzano, Ahmed Mohamed, Kamsouk Sundara and Vo Tri Thanh.

Chapter I was the anchor paper for discussion at the Meeting of Eminent Persons on Current and Prospective Economic and Social Performance in the ESCAP Region held at ESCAP, Bangkok, on 14 and 15 October 2004. The eminent persons, who attended the Meeting in their personal capacity, were: Mustafizur Rahman (Bangladesh), Pingyao Lai (China), Djisman Simanjuntak (Indonesia), Shinichi Ichimura (Japan), Ragayah Haji Mat Zin (Malaysia), Yuba Raj Khatiwada (Nepal), Seung Jin Kim (Republic of Korea), Mikhail G. Nosov (Russian Federation), John Wong (Singapore), Pisit Leeahtam (Thailand) and Vo Tri Thanh (Viet Nam). J.K. Robert England (UNDP, Bangkok), Kazi Matin (World Bank, Bangkok) and Xianbin Yao (ADB, Manila) also participated in the Meeting.

Chapter III was discussed at the Expert Group Meeting on Development Issues and Policies held at Bangkok from 8 to 10 December 2004. The experts, who participated in the Meeting in their personal capacity, were: Xiaozu Wang (China), Stephen Y.L. Cheung (Hong Kong, China), Tarun Das (India), V.R. Panchamukhi (India), Sayuri Shirai (Japan), George Manzano (Philippines), Chong Ook Rhee (Republic of Korea), Valentin Kudrov (Russian Federation), Ramkishen Rajan (Singapore) and Suthad Setboonsarng (Thailand).

CONTENTS

	Page
I. Asia-Pacific region: key developments and prospects	1
The global setting and implications for Asia-Pacific	8
Developed countries	8
Recent trends in international trade	11
Commodities	16
Foreign direct investment flows	19
Financial market developments	19
Developments, prospects and policy issues in Asia and the Pacific	23
Developing economies in the subregion	28
Developed countries of the region	33
Near-term policy issues for the region	33
Longer-term development policy issues for the region	38
II. Macroeconomic performance, issues and policies	45
Developing economies of the ESCAP region	45
East and North-East Asia	45
North and Central Asia	63
Pacific island economies	85
South and South-West Asia	109
South-East Asia	145
Developed countries of the region	197
Australia, Japan and New Zealand	197

CONTENTS *(continued)*

Page

III. Dynamics of population ageing: how can Asia and the Pacific respond? 215

Introduction 215

Population dynamics 219

Determinants of population ageing 219

Decline in mortality 220

Decline in the fertility rate 221

Scale and speed of ageing 223

Ageing of the older population 224

Is ageing a gender issue? 226

Implications of population ageing 227

Fiscal implications 228

Public pensions 228

Health care 229

Implications for the labour market 229

Savings and investment 231

Public debt 232

Impact on capital markets 232

Economic growth 233

Care of older persons 234

Poverty, isolation and discrimination 234

CONTENTS *(continued)*

Page

Policy responses 235

Pension reforms 235

Increasing efficiency in the health-care sector 237

Healthy ageing 237

Health insurance 239

Institutional arrangements for care of the elderly 239

Promotion of familial care of the elderly 239

Market reforms 241

Labour market reforms 241

Migration policy 243

Population policy 244

Fiscal policy 246

Role of the private sector 246

Conclusion 247

Special feature to mark the International Year of Microcredit, 2005 249

Microfinance in poverty reduction – Asia-Pacific challenges 249

BOXES

Page

I.1. Impact of high oil prices in the ESCAP region 5

I.2. Multilateralism and free trade areas in Asia and the Pacific 15

I.3. World Conference on Disaster Reduction and early warning systems 39

II.1. Mauritius International Meeting on Small Island Developing States reaffirms sustainable development and related issues 107

II.2. Smooth transition for countries graduating from the list of least developed countries 143

II.3. Post-tsunami reconstruction in Aceh and North Sumatra 172

II.4. Phase-out of the Multifibre Arrangement and least developed countries in the Asian and Pacific region 185

II.5. Economic implications of privatizing Japan Post 212

III.1. Growing implicit pension debt 233

III.2. Responding to rapid ageing in Australia: a strategic approach 240

III.3. Population ageing: from problem to opportunity 242

III.4. Migration policy: a cushion for the ageing process? 245

TABLES

		Page
I.1.	Selected indicators of global economic conditions, 2001-2005	3
I.2.	World trade and prices, 1991-2004	12
I.3.	Commodity price index, 2001-2004	17
I.4.	Net capital flows of developing countries and developing economies in Asia, 1997-2005	22
I.5.	Selected economies of the ESCAP region: rates of economic growth and inflation, 2003-2006	24
I.6.	Percentage of the population below the $1 per day poverty line in selected countries, 1990-2003	40
II.1.	Selected East and North-East Asian economies: growth rates, 2001-2004	47
II.2.	Selected East and North-East Asian economies: ratios of gross domestic savings and investment to GDP, 2001-2004	48
II.3.	Selected East and North-East Asian economies: inflation and money supply growth (M2), 2001-2004	51
II.4.	Selected East and North-East Asian economies: merchandise exports and their rates of growth, 2001-2004	53
II.5.	Selected East and North-East Asian economies: merchandise imports and their rates of growth, 2001-2004	55
II.6.	Selected East and North-East Asian economies: budget and current account balance as a percentage of GDP, 2001-2004	56
II.7.	North and Central Asian economies: growth rates, 2001-2004	66
II.8.	North and Central Asian economies: inflation, 2001-2004	69
II.9.	North and Central Asian economies: budget balance as a percentage of GDP, 2001-2004	71
II.10.	North and Central Asian economies: merchandise exports and their rates of growth, 2001-2004	73
II.11.	North and Central Asian economies: merchandise imports and their rates of growth, 2001-2004	74
II.12.	North and Central Asian economies: current account balance as a percentage of GDP, 2001-2004	74

TABLES *(continued)*

		Page
II.13.	Selected Pacific island economies: growth rates, 2001-2004	88
II.14.	Selected Pacific island economies: budget and current account balance as a percentage of GDP, 2001-2004	91
II.15.	Selected Pacific island economies: inflation and money supply growth (M2), 2001-2004	96
II.16.	Selected Pacific island economies: merchandise exports and their rates of growth, 2001-2004	99
II.17.	Selected Pacific island economies: merchandise imports and their rates of growth, 2001-2004	101
II.18.	Selected South and South-West Asian economies: growth rates, 2001-2004	113
II.19.	Selected South and South-West Asian economies: ratios of gross domestic savings and investment to GDP, 2001-2004	114
II.20.	Selected South and South-West Asian economies: inflation and money supply growth (M2), 2001-2004	116
II.21.	Selected South and South-West Asian economies: budget and current account balance as a percentage of GDP, 2001-2004	117
II.22.	Selected South and South-West Asian economies: merchandise exports and their rates of growth, 2001-2004	119
II.23.	Selected South and South-West Asian economies: merchandise imports and their rates of growth, 2001-2004	120
II.24.	Least developed countries in South and South-West Asia: growth rates, 2001-2004	132
II.25.	Least developed countries in South and South-West Asia: inflation and money supply growth (M2), 2001-2004	135
II.26.	Least developed countries in South and South-West Asia: merchandise exports and their rates of growth, 2001-2004	137
II.27.	Least developed countries in South and South-West Asia: merchandise imports and their rates of growth, 2001-2004	138
II.28.	Selected South-East Asian economies: growth rates, 2001-2004	150
II.29.	Selected South-East Asian economies: ratios of gross domestic savings and investment to GDP, 2001-2004	151

TABLES *(continued)*

Page

II.30. Selected South-East Asian economies: inflation and money supply growth (M2), 2001-2004 157

II.31. Selected South-East Asian economies: budget and current account balance as a percentage of GDP, 2001-2004 161

II.32. Selected South-East Asian economies: merchandise exports and their rates of growth, 2001-2004 164

II.33. Selected South-East Asian economies: merchandise imports and their rates of growth, 2001-2004 165

II.34. Least developed countries in South-East Asia: growth rates, 2001-2004 183

II.35. Least developed countries in South-East Asia: inflation and money supply growth (M2), 2001-2004 188

II.36. Least developed countries in South-East Asia: budget and current account balance as a percentage of GDP, 2001-2004 189

II.37. Least developed countries in South-East Asia: merchandise exports and their rates of growth, 2001-2004 191

II.38. Least developed countries in South-East Asia: merchandise imports and their rates of growth, 2001-2004 192

II.39. Developed countries of the ESCAP region: rates of economic growth and inflation, 2001-2004 200

II.40. Developed countries of the ESCAP region: consumption and investment as a percentage of GDP, 2001-2004 201

II.41. Developed countries of the ESCAP region: short-term interest rates and money supply growth (M2), 2001-2004 202

II.42. Developed countries of the ESCAP region: budget and current account balance as a percentage of GDP, 2001-2004 203

II.43. Developed countries of the ESCAP region: merchandise exports and their rates of growth, 2001-2004 208

II.44. Developed countries of the ESCAP region: merchandise imports and their rates of growth, 2001-2004 208

TABLES *(continued)*

		Page
III.1.	Diversity of the demographic characteristics in the region	216
III.2.	Changes in infant mortality rate and total fertility rate in developing countries	220
III.3.	Total fertility rate	221
III.4.	Population aged 60 and over	223
III.5.	Speed of ageing of 60+ population	225
III.6.	Common features of pension schemes in the Asian region and policy options	238

FIGURES

Page

II.1. Rates of GDP growth in selected East and North-East Asian economies, 2001-2004 45

II.2. Inflation in selected East and North-East Asian economies, 2001-2004 46

II.3. Growth rates in merchandise export earnings of selected East and North-East Asian economies, 2001-2004 54

II.4. Growth rates in merchandise import spending of selected East and North-East Asian economies, 2001-2004 55

II.5. Index of exchange rates against the United States dollar of selected East and North-East Asian economies, 1996-2004 58

II.6. Rates of GDP growth in North and Central Asian economies, 2001-2004 63

II.7. Inflation in North and Central Asian economies, 2001-2004 64

II.8. Index of exchange rates against the United States dollar of North and Central Asian economies, 1996-2004 77

II.9. Rates of GDP growth in selected Pacific island economies, 2001-2004 85

II.10. Inflation in selected Pacific island economies, 2001-2004 86

II.11. Index of exchange rates against the United States dollar of selected Pacific island economies and Australia and New Zealand, 1996-2004 97

II.12. Growth rates in merchandise export earnings of selected Pacific island economies, 2001-2004 100

II.13. Growth rates in merchandise import spending of selected Pacific island economies, 2001-2004 102

II.14. Rates of GDP growth in selected South and South-West Asian economies, 2001-2004 109

II.15. Inflation in selected South and South-West Asian economies, 2001-2004 110

II.16. Growth rates in merchandise export earnings of selected South and South-West Asian economies, 2001-2004 111

FIGURES *(continued)*

Page

II.17. Growth rates in merchandise import spending of selected South and South-West Asian economies, 2001-2004 112

II.18. Index of exchange rates against the United States dollar of selected South and South-West Asian economies, 1996-2004 123

II.19. Rates of GDP growth in least developed countries in South and South-West Asia, 2001-2004 129

II.20. Inflation in least developed countries in South and South-West Asia, 2001-2004 130

II.21. Index of exchange rates against the United States dollar of least developed countries in South and South-West Asia, 1996-2004 131

II.22. Growth rates in merchandise export earnings of least developed countries in South and South-West Asia, 2001-2004 138

II.23. Growth rates in merchandise import spending of least developed countries in South and South-West Asia, 2001-2004 139

II.24. Rates of GDP growth in selected South-East Asian economies, 2001-2004 145

II.25. Inflation in selected South-East Asian economies, 2001-2004 146

II.26. Growth rates in merchandise export earnings of selected South-East Asian economies, 2001-2004 147

II.27. Growth rates in merchandise import spending of selected South-East Asian economies, 2001-2004 148

II.28. Index of exchange rates against the United States dollar of selected South-East Asian economies, 1996-2004 149

II.29. Rates of GDP growth in the least developed countries in South-East Asia, 2001-2004 181

II.30. Inflation in the least developed countries in South-East Asia, 2001-2004 182

II.31. Index of exchange rates against the United States dollar of least developed countries in South-East Asia, 1996-2004 190

II.32. Rates of GDP growth in developed countries in the ESCAP region, 2001-2004 197

FIGURES *(continued)*

Page

II.33. Inflation in developed countries in the ESCAP region, 2001-2004 198

II.34. Growth rates in merchandise export earnings of developed countries in the ESCAP region, 2001-2004 199

II.35. Growth rates in merchandise import spending of developed countries in the ESCAP region, 2001-2004 199

II.36. Index of exchange rates against the United States dollar of developed countries in the ESCAP region, 1996-2004 210

III.1. Proportion of population aged 60 and over 219

III.2. Life expectancy and fertility trends 221

III.3. Distribution of 60+ population in selected economies, 2000 and 2050 224

III.4. Total 80+ population by ESCAP subregions and the rest of the world 226

III.5. Distribution of 80+ population in selected economies, 2000 and 2050 226

III.6. Share of male and female population aged 60+ and 80+ of Asian and Pacific economies in the total population, 1950-2050 227

III.7. Old-age dependency ratio in Asia and the Pacific and selected economies 228

III.8. Dynamics of the working-age population in selected economies: population aged 15-59 for selected Asian and Pacific economies as a percentage of the total population, 1950-2050 230

Map No. 3974 Rev. 10 UNITED NATIONS
July 2003

Department of Public Information
Cartographic Section

EXPLANATORY NOTES

The term "ESCAP region" is used in the present issue of the *Survey* to include Afghanistan; American Samoa; Armenia; Australia; Azerbaijan; Bangladesh; Bhutan; Brunei Darussalam; Cambodia; China; Cook Islands; Democratic People's Republic of Korea; Fiji; French Polynesia; Georgia; Guam; Hong Kong, China; India; Indonesia; Iran (Islamic Republic of); Japan; Kazakhstan; Kiribati; Kyrgyzstan; Lao People's Democratic Republic; Macao, China; Malaysia; Maldives; Marshall Islands; Micronesia (Federated States of); Mongolia; Myanmar; Nauru; Nepal; New Caledonia; New Zealand; Niue; Northern Mariana Islands; Pakistan; Palau; Papua New Guinea; Philippines; Republic of Korea; Russian Federation; Samoa; Singapore; Solomon Islands; Sri Lanka; Tajikistan; Thailand; Timor-Leste; Tonga; Turkey; Turkmenistan; Tuvalu; Uzbekistan; Vanuatu; and Viet Nam. The term "developing ESCAP region" excludes Australia, Japan and New Zealand.

The term "Central Asian republics" in this issue of the *Survey* refers to Armenia, Azerbaijan, Georgia, Kazakhstan, Kyrgyzstan, Tajikistan, Turkmenistan and Uzbekistan.

The term "East and North-East Asia" in this issue of the *Survey* refers to China, Hong Kong, China, Mongolia and the Republic of Korea.

The designations employed and the presentation of the material in this publication do not imply the expression of any opinion whatsoever on the part of the Secretariat of the United Nations concerning the legal status of any country, territory, city or area, or of its authorities, or concerning the delimitation of its frontiers or boundaries.

Mention of firm names and commercial products does not imply the endorsement of the United Nations.

The abbreviated title *Survey* in footnotes refers to the *Economic and Social Survey of Asia and the Pacific* for the year indicated.

Many figures used in the *Survey* are on a fiscal year basis and are assigned to the calendar year which covers the major part or second half of the fiscal year.

Growth rates are on an annual basis, except where indicated otherwise.

Reference to "tons" indicates metric tons.

Values are in United States dollars unless specified otherwise.

The term "billion" signifies a thousand million. The term "trillion" signifies a million million.

In the tables, two dots (..) indicate that data are not available or are not separately reported, a dash (–) indicates that the amount is nil or negligible, and a blank indicates that the item is not applicable.

In dates, a hyphen (-) is used to signify the full period involved, including the beginning and end years, and a stroke (/) indicates a crop year, fiscal year or plan year. The fiscal years, currencies and 2004 exchange rates of the economies in the ESCAP region are listed in the following table:

Country or area	*Fiscal year*	*Currency and abbreviation*	*Rate of exchange for $1 as at December 2004*
Afghanistan	21 March to 20 March	afghani (Af)	3 000.00[a]
American Samoa	..	United States dollar ($)	1.00
Armenia	1 January to 31 December	dram	485.84
Australia	1 July to 30 June	Australian dollar ($A)	1.28
Azerbaijan	1 January to 31 December	Azeri manat (AZM)	4 902.00[a]
Bangladesh	1 July to 30 June	taka (Tk)	60.74
Bhutan	1 July to 30 June	ngultrum (Nu)	43.58
Brunei Darussalam	1 January to 31 December	Brunei dollar (B$)	1.63
Cambodia	1 January to 31 December	riel (CR)	4 027.00
China	1 January to 31 December	yuan renminbi (Y)	8.28
Cook Islands	1 April to 31 March	New Zealand dollar ($NZ)	1.39
Democratic People's Republic of Korea	..	won (W)	135.80
Fiji	1 January to 31 December	Fiji dollar (F$)	1.65
French Polynesia	..	French Pacific Community franc (FCFP)	95.50[b]

Country or area	*Fiscal year*	*Currency and abbreviation*	*Rate of exchange for $1 as at December 2004*
Georgia	1 January to 31 December	lari (L)	1.83
Guam	1 October to 30 September	United States dollar ($)	1.00
Hong Kong, China	1 April to 31 March	Hong Kong dollar (HK$)	7.77
India	1 April to 31 March	Indian rupee (Rs)	43.58
Indonesia	1 April to 31 March	Indonesian rupiah (Rp)	9 290.00
Iran (Islamic Republic of)	21 March to 20 March	Iranian rial (Rls)	8 793.00
Japan	1 April to 31 March	yen (¥)	104.12
Kazakhstan	1 January to 31 December	tenge (T)	130.00
Kiribati	1 January to 31 December	Australian dollar ($A)	1.28
Kyrgyzstan	1 January to 31 December	som (som)	41.62
Lao People's Democratic Republic	1 October to 30 September	new kip (NK)	10 950.00[c]
Macao, China	1 July to 30 June	pataca (P)	8.00
Malaysia	1 January to 31 December	ringgit (M$)	3.80
Maldives	1 January to 31 December	rufiyaa (Rf)	12.80
Marshall Islands	1 October to 30 September	United States dollar ($)	1.00
Micronesia (Federated States of)	1 October to 30 September	United States dollar ($)	1.00
Mongolia	1 January to 31 December	tugrik (Tug)	1 209.00
Myanmar	1 April to 31 March	kyat (K)	5.52
Nauru	1 July to 30 June	Australian dollar ($A)	1.27
Nepal	16 July to 15 July	Nepalese rupee (NRs)	71.80
New Caledonia	..	French Pacific Community franc (FCFP)	95.50[b]
New Zealand	1 April to 31 March	New Zealand dollar ($NZ)	1.39
Niue	1 April to 31 March	New Zealand dollar ($NZ)	1.39
Northern Mariana Islands	1 October to 30 September	United States dollar ($)	1.00
Pakistan	1 July to 30 June	Pakistan rupee (PRs)	59.12
Palau	1 October to 30 September	United States dollar ($)	1.00
Papua New Guinea	1 January to 31 December	kina (K)	3.13
Philippines	1 January to 31 December	Philippine peso (P)	56.27
Republic of Korea	1 January to 31 December	won (W)	1 035.10
Russian Federation	1 January to 31 December	rouble (R)	27.75
Samoa	1 July to 30 June	tala (WS$)	2.67
Singapore	1 April to 31 March	Singapore dollar (S$)	1.63
Solomon Islands	1 January to 31 December	Solomon Islands dollar (SI$)	7.51[d]
Sri Lanka	1 January to 31 December	Sri Lanka rupee (SL Rs)	104.61
Tajikistan	1 January to 31 December	somoni	3.03[a]
Thailand	1 October to 30 September	baht (B)	39.06
Timor-Leste	1 July to 30 June	United States dollar ($)	1.00
Tonga	1 July to 30 June	pa'anga (T$)	1.91
Turkey	1 January to 31 December	Turkish lira (LT)	1 473 700.00[c]
Turkmenistan	1 January to 31 December	Turkmen manat (M)	5 200.00
Tuvalu	1 January to 31 December	Australian dollar ($A)	1.27
Uzbekistan	1 January to 31 December	sum (sum)	1 051.02
Vanuatu	1 January to 31 December	vatu (VT)	106.79[a]
Viet Nam	1 January to 31 December	dong (D)	15 764.00[e]

Sources: United Nations, *Monthly Bulletin of Statistics*, available at <http://esa.un.org/unsd/mbs/mbssearch.asp> (10 March 2005); EIU, *Country Reports,* available at <http://db.eiu.com/countries.asp> (2 February 2005); and Central Bank of Solomon Islands web site <http://www.cbsi.com.sb> (10 March 2005).

[a] November 2004.
[b] Average 2004.
[c] October 2004.
[d] January 2005.
[e] August 2004.

ABBREVIATIONS

ADB	Asian Development Bank
AFTA	ASEAN Free Trade Area
ASEAN	Association of Southeast Asian Nations
BIS	Bank for International Settlements
c.i.f.	cost, insurance, freight
CD-ROM	compact disk read-only memory
CIS	Commonwealth of Independent States
CPI	consumer price index
ECE	Economic Commission for Europe
EIU	Economist Intelligence Unit
ESCAP	Economic and Social Commission for Asia and the Pacific
EU	European Union
FAO	Food and Agriculture Organization of the United Nations
FDI	foreign direct investment
f.o.b.	free on board
FTAs	free trade agreements
GATT	General Agreement on Tariffs and Trade
GDP	gross domestic product
ICT	information and communication technology
IMF	International Monetary Fund
IT	information technology
M2	broad money supply
MFA	Multifibre Arrangement
NPL	non-performing loan
ODA	official development assistance
OECD	Organization for Economic Cooperation and Development
OPEC	Organization of the Petroleum Exporting Countries

ABBREVIATIONS *(continued)*

PPP	purchasing power parity
PRSP	Poverty Reduction Strategy Paper
PTAs	preferential trading arrangements
R&D	research and development
RTAs	regional trade agreements
SAFTA	South Asian Free Trade Area
SARS	severe acute respiratory syndrome
SMEs	small and medium-sized enterprises
SOEs	State-owned enterprises
UNCTAD	United Nations Conference on Trade and Development
UNDP	United Nations Development Programme
UNESCO	United Nations Educational, Scientific and Cultural Organization
VAT	value added tax
WTO	World Trade Organization

I ASIA-PACIFIC REGION: KEY DEVELOPMENTS AND PROSPECTS[1]

Tsunami disaster unprecedented in scale and response …

The year 2005 began with attention focused on the Indian Ocean earthquake and tsunami catastrophe of 26 December 2004, which affected a dozen countries, most of them in the Asian and Pacific region. The sheer geographical scale, suddenness and speed of the destruction were unique and were matched by equally unprecedented national and international emergency relief efforts, both private and public. Formally recorded official aid resource pledges have exceeded $6.3 billion. Despite the high estimated death toll of over 280,000, the damage to coastal areas and the loss of livelihoods, the overall impact of the disaster on the economic performance of the Asia-Pacific region in 2005 is likely to be small. However, in terms of the destruction of human, social and physical capital, as well as infrastructure, development has been severely set back in the smaller affected countries.

… but major challenges of rehabilitation and reconstruction still to come

The impact on the GDP of individual countries will vary across region, with Maldives particularly hard-hit and expected to lose 4 percentage points of GDP growth in 2005 owing to its small size and heavy reliance on tourism and fisheries. Sri Lanka is also expected to face a reduction of 1 per cent in 2005 economic growth, for similar reasons. For the larger, more diversified economies such as India, Indonesia and Thailand, the likely GDP growth loss is expected to be less than 0.5 per cent in 2005. This is because of the relatively small contribution the affected areas were making in conventional economic terms to economic output in those countries and the negligible damage to major areas of economic activity and ports. Reconstruction costs in the affected areas are still being worked out and are likely to be very significant for some countries while the process of reconstruction itself is expected to take several years. The repercussions on local communities in the areas affected, especially those reliant on fishing and tourism, have been massive, particularly where many residents were already poor with substandard housing and living conditions. Some 3 million people were initially displaced by the catastrophe, most of them in India, Indonesia and Sri Lanka. It is necessary that reconstruction and rehabilitation address the

[1] Part of this chapter consists of a revised and updated version of "Global and regional economic developments: implications and prospects for the ESCAP region", in *Bulletin on Asia-Pacific Perspectives 2004/05* (United Nations publication, Sales No. E.04.II.F.47).

broader issues of poverty reduction; otherwise, the communities affected will remain vulnerable to income disruption, malnutrition and disease, not to mention natural disasters. At the same time greater efforts, at both the regional and country levels, must be made to integrate disaster risk management into policies and programmes, including the setting up of multi-hazard early warning systems.

Fastest global economic growth in almost 30 years lifts Asia and the Pacific to best performance since 2000

Despite the subdued mood arising from the tsunami disaster in the closing days of 2004, the year produced the fastest global economic growth for almost three decades, estimated at 4.0 per cent (table I.1). Developing countries in the ESCAP region also had an impressive economic performance, with estimated growth of 7.2 per cent, the highest since 2000. As discussed further in chapter II below, Japan, the largest economy in the region, achieved the fastest rate of GDP growth in 14 years of 2.6 per cent, doubling its performance in 2003, although sustaining the recovery is proving difficult. China, the second-largest economy, performed beyond expectations and exceeded the rapid growth of 2003 to achieve a 9.5 per cent growth rate, signalling that steps to cool the overheating economy have yet to take full effect. The Republic of Korea, the third-largest economy in the region, similarly had a better performance in 2004 with a growth rate of 4.7 per cent, 1.6 percentage points higher than in 2003. In 2004, South-East Asia had its highest economic growth rate since the 1997 financial crisis, averaging 6.4 per cent, with Singapore leading with 8.4 per cent, compared with 1.4 per cent the previous year; both Malaysia and Viet Nam had growth rates above 7 per cent, while the rest of the ASEAN economies had 3.5-6.5 per cent growth rates. India, the fourth-largest economy in the region, achieved a rate of 6.9 per cent, 1.6 percentage points below 2003 performance, but above the trend rate. High commodity prices resulted in growth rates of 7.1 per cent for the Russian Federation and 9.4 per cent for Kazakhstan. Australia and New Zealand also improved on their 2003 performance. Unfortunately, for most Pacific island economies and some least developed and landlocked countries, the growth rates, while positive, were below 5 per cent, insufficient to meet their development challenges.

High oil prices initially affected growth sentiment

The impressive economic performance under conditions of generally low inflation reaffirms the resilience of the global and regional economies, in the face of a series of ongoing and new challenges. In addition to risks arising from continuing geopolitical concerns, in particular the conflict in Iraq, persistent fears of terrorist attacks and the unresolved problem of global imbalances, notably the combination of large fiscal and external imbalances in the United States of America, a new challenge came in the form of record rises in crude oil prices in nominal terms. Measured against the SDR, so as to avoid valuation effects of the decline in the United States dollar, the average price of oil in the second half of 2004 was about 50 per cent higher than the average of 2001-2003. Up to mid-2004, ESCAP developing economies enjoyed buoyant growth; in the

Table I.1. Selected indicators of global economic conditions, 2001-2005

(Percentage)

		2001	2002	2003	2004[a]	2005[b]
Economic growth (percentage change of GDP)						
World						
At market exchange rates		1.3	1.9	2.8	4.0	3.3
At PPP exchange rates		2.3	2.8	3.8	5.0	4.3
Developed economies		1.0	1.4	2.2	3.4	2.5
Japan		0.2	−0.3	1.4	2.6	1.5
United States of America		0.8	1.9	3.0	4.4	3.5
European Union		1.7	1.2	1.1	2.6	2.5
Developing economies		2.4	3.4	4.6	6.2	5.5
Developing economies in the ESCAP region		3.7	5.7	6.3	7.2	6.2
Trade in goods and services (percentage)						
World		0.1	3.3	5.1	8.8	7.2
Developed economies	Exports	−0.8	2.2	2.6	8.1	6.3
	Imports	−0.7	2.6	3.7	7.6	5.6
Developing economies	Exports	3.5	6.6	10.9	10.8	10.6
	Imports	3.3	6.0	11.1	12.8	11.9
Commodity prices (annual percentage change in dollar terms)						
Non-fuel primary commodities		−4.1	0.6	7.1	16.8	−3.9
Oil		−13.8	2.5	15.8	28.9	..
Inflation rate (percentage)[c]						
CPI in the developed economies		2.2	1.5	1.8	2.1	2.1
CPI in the developing economies		6.8	6.0	6.1	6.0	5.5
Short-term interest rates						
United States		3.7	1.7	1.2	1.3	2.8
Japan		0.12	0.06	0.04	0.00	0.20
Euro area		4.3	3.3	2.3	2.4	3.1
Exchange rates[d] (nominal units per dollar)						
Yen per dollar		121.5	125.4	115.9	108.2	95.0
Euros per dollar		1.118	1.063	0.886	0.806	0.719

Sources: United Nations, *World Economic Situation and Prospects 2005* (United Nations publication, Sales No. E.05.II.C.2); IMF, *World Economic Outlook, September 2004: The Global Demographic Transition* (Washington, IMF, 2004); and *The Economist*, 15 January 2005.

[a] Estimate.

[b] Forecast.

[c] Developed and developing economy ratios weighted at purchasing power parity.

[d] Period average.

second half of the year, momentum appeared to falter partly in response the rising price of oil. In the early months of 2005, prices continued to be high, representing an increase of over 40 per cent from January 2004 levels, as well as volatile. However, OPEC decided to maintain the prevailing production target of 27 million barrels a day and to temporarily suspend its now unrealistic target price range of $22-$28 pending a further review, which is likely to raise it.

It would appear that, on balance, the sharp rise in crude oil prices in 2004 did not significantly harm economic growth in the region despite its considerable dependence on imported energy.[2] High oil prices added to upward pressure on overall consumer prices to some degree. However, the impact was relatively modest, with consumer price indices creeping up by an additional 0.5-1.0 percentage points for most countries in the region compared with 12 months earlier, owing partly to subsidies on fuel. In addition, the weight of energy is relatively small compared with, say, food. China and India, the two largest economies in the region, faced more acute price pressures, but not all of them were due to higher oil prices (box I.1).

Rising global demand, particularly from China, and tight supply conditions cause oil price increases

Unlike previous oil shocks, where OPEC-supported supply restrictions were the main cause of higher prices, the 2004 price rises were largely the result of rapid world growth leading to rising demand for oil (an estimated 6.5 per cent increase from 2002 to 2004), including from Asia, principally China and to a lesser extent India. This put pressure on supplies in the context of low levels of spare global production and refining capacity and commercial inventories. The latter was due largely to low levels of investment in capacity expansion projects owing to persistently low real average oil prices from 1985 to 2000. Further, geopolitical concerns and possible disturbances in supplies from Nigeria, the Russian Federation and Venezuela raised questions about stability of supply. Most developed countries are probably less vulnerable to the 2004-2005 price rises than they were to the shocks of the 1970s and early 1980s because energy represents a smaller share of household purchases and business input costs, something which has yet to be achieved by emerging market economies in Asia-Pacific, where oil consumption relative to GDP is three times the 1.5 per cent ratio in developed countries.

Higher oil prices could have reversed inflationary expectations

An immediate impact of higher oil prices on the region is that they contributed to, but were not the only reason for, a reversal in inflationary expectations. Some central banks began to raise interest rates pre-emptively albeit in small steps to counter the risk of potentially higher inflation later in 2005. Many observers have interpreted such measures of

---

[2] Asian countries consume around 40 per cent of the global oil production of 82 million barrels a day, with the percentage expected to rise over the next decade.

Box I.1. Impact of high oil prices in the ESCAP region

Two previous episodes of rapid, large and relatively long-lasting increases in oil prices – known as the "oil shocks" of 1973 and 1981 – plunged the global economy into recession on both occasions. The recent high oil prices with spot prices surpassing the $50 mark and the increase in volatility do not yet merit the description of an oil shock. Output growth in the region and indeed in other parts of the world continues to remain relatively strong and price pressures, by and large, appear to have increased only marginally in most economies, for the time being at any rate. Nevertheless, there are fears that should oil prices continue at their present levels or rise higher, the adverse effects on output and prices would become more visible and more widespread across the region. From the perspective of the ESCAP region, given its size and diversity and its growing role as a driver of regional and global GDP growth, it is important that policy makers and others be aware of the potential impact of high oil prices on the economies of the region.

A high oil price acts as a tax on both production and consumption. According to the International Energy Agency, the effect of a sustained $10 rise in the price of a barrel of oil, i.e., a rise that persists for at least 12 months, would tend to reduce growth in the following year in the ESCAP region, other things being equal, by 0.8 percentage points. Other calculations suggest that higher production costs on account of oil would push inflation up by 0.5 percentage points. It should be stressed, however, that these numerical relationships are based upon the experience of the two oil shocks referred to above. In the interim much has changed, principally a decline in the use of oil as a proportion of GDP i.e., the lower energy intensity of manufacturing and services nearly everywhere but more so in the developed than in the developing countries. Hence, it is unlikely that high oil prices will automatically lead to the same adverse effects on output and prices now. Nevertheless, the effects of a long-lasting increase in oil prices would require considerable adjustment.

From the perspective of the ESCAP region, it is self-evident that the effects of high oil prices would not be uniform: one, there would be obvious differences between oil-exporting and oil-importing countries; two, there would be differences between the more developed and less developed economies in the region; and three, Governments could and, indeed, would take countervailing measures, such as changes in the taxes and subsidies that are levied on oil products in virtually all ESCAP member countries. There would be changes, too, in monetary policy to counter the inflationary effects of high oil prices. The overall impact of high prices hence becomes difficult to measure.

In the ESCAP region, although there are a number of countries that produce oil, only seven are net exporters: Azerbaijan, Brunei Darussalam, the Islamic Republic of Iran, Kazakhstan, Malaysia, the Russian Federation and Viet Nam. Indonesia, traditionally a large producer and exporter of energy, is now a net exporter of natural gas but not of oil. China is a major oil producer (3.5 million barrels per day) but is also a large oil importer (2.4 million bpd). Most other economies produce varying, sometimes significant, quantities of oil but still need to import the bulk of their requirements. Japan, the Republic of Korea and Taiwan Province of China, three of the five largest economies in the region, produce no oil. India produces 0.8 million bpd and imports 2.1 million bpd, while Singapore imports 0.7 million bpd of crude oil and exports 0.6 million bpd of oil products. Broadly speaking, the region remains a large net importer of oil and is therefore vulnerable to a sustained rise in oil prices. The consumption of oil in the ESCAP economies is estimated to be 4.5 per cent of GDP but is on a gradual downward path, particularly in the developed and middle-income developing economies although much remains to be done in improving the efficiency of energy use in the region.

In principle, oil-exporting countries would benefit both from the extra revenue that higher prices would generate and from the improvement in their terms of trade. Oil-importing countries, which constitute the bulk of ESCAP members, would, however, experience higher production costs and lower consumption and a net transfer of income to the oil-exporting countries. Between developed and developing countries, even if both are significant net importers, the effects would be markedly different: the former use roughly half as much oil per unit of output as developing countries. In addition, terms of trade losses can be recouped more quickly by developed countries than by developing countries, given the different price elasticities of their tradable goods. If oil-importing countries were to lower taxes or increase subsidies on oil products within, say, a constant tax-to-GDP ratio this would redistribute

(Continued overleaf)

(Continued from preceding page)

income from the general taxpayers to oil product users. In other words, there would be a variety of impacts depending upon the status of the particular country as an oil exporter or importer, its level of development, its resource situation and what policy measures its Government took to deal with the high oil prices. Whether the impact would be deleterious to growth in the region and to what extent is very difficult to judge but the following aspects might shed some light on the situation.

Essentially, Governments have sought to shield consumers from the full impact of high crude oil prices by either reducing the taxes and duties they levy on oil products or by not letting the final prices paid by consumers fully reflect the rise in crude oil prices that has occurred in the previous few months. But, as oil prices have remained high for several months, both approaches will prove to be a heavy financial burden on the Governments concerned. In the first instance there would be a clear fiscal cost that would have to be made up through taxes elsewhere or through higher borrowing if the Government is committed to maintaining a particular level of spending; in the second instance, the Government would need to find the resources to compensate the oil companies, whether State or private, that have not been able to pass on the full cost of the crude oil to the consumers. As an illustration, in Indonesia, oil subsidies in 2004 amounted to a staggering $7.5 billion, a huge fiscal burden on the Government. It is noteworthy that similar subsidization schemes are currently operating in a number of ESCAP member countries to protect consumers from the full extent of the rise in oil prices with varying fiscal consequences.

While the logic of subsidized oil product prices is understandable, such a policy approach is almost certainly not viable over the medium term given its high fiscal and opportunity costs. Moreover, subsidies invariably distort relative prices, discourage conservation and fuel efficiency in transport and encourage overuse of the subsidized items. Even apparently well-targeted subsidies, such as for diesel fuel, are likely to prove unsustainable over the medium term and eventually have the same negative effects as more general fuel subsidies. Moreover, with all fuel subsidies, the overall environmental impact is clearly negative.

It needs to be emphasized that the ability of subsidies to preserve a higher momentum of growth than would otherwise have been the case is likely to be true, at best, only in the short term. Eventually the higher costs of fuel would need to be allowed into the calculus of costs and benefits facing both the producers and consumers of energy and all activities in the economy would need to be evaluated on a uniform basis on resource allocation grounds. In that general context, high oil prices provide Governments with a window of opportunity to bring vital environmental issues relating to energy conservation to the forefront.

monetary tightening, modest though they are, as signalling the end of the low inflationary and interest rate environment of the last two years. Measures to deal with the twin deficits in the fiscal and current accounts of the United States and the consequent impact on exchange rate valuations will be important determinants of the future course of interest rates. The small rise in interest rates so far is not expected to have an adverse impact on short-term growth per se, but its indirect impact on business and consumer confidence may well gradually translate into negative effects on levels of demand and output over the next 12 months.

Compounding developments in the energy markets, in the United States and Japan, two important sources of external demand for economies in the region, output growth slowed somewhat in the former and there were signs of a recession in the latter in the second half of 2004. Although there were indications of a recovery early in 2005, if the external environment were to weaken during the rest of the year, this would feed back into the domestic economies of the region. Thus, while the regional economy has so far been only marginally affected by the rise in oil prices and the firming trend in interest rates, the outlook for 2005 is still uncertain and overall growth in the region could well be lower than in 2004.

Countries need to prepare for a slower momentum of growth in 2005

Any marked or prolonged slowdown in the momentum of growth, were it to occur, could generate significant social and macroeconomic repercussions for Governments of the region. Sustained buoyant growth has been instrumental in generating the increase in employment that lifted millions out of poverty after the 1997-1998 economic crisis and again after the slowdown following the end of the dot com boom in 2001. Buoyant growth also enabled economies in the region to enjoy macroeconomic stability despite increased public debt in many cases. A slowdown would therefore not only generate immediate social and economic consequences but may also damage the longer-term prospects for the region by reducing public investment in vitally needed physical and social infrastructure. On the macroeconomic front, a slower pace of growth would in all likelihood constrain the growth of tax revenues and could thus be instrumental in widening fiscal deficits once again in several economies. A more sustained rise in inflation would automatically trigger higher interest rates, which would add to the cost of servicing the public deficits, as well as affecting consumer spending. In a worst-case scenario, the region could therefore see not only a deceleration in the momentum of growth over the next 12 months but also possible setbacks in social indicators. As at February 2005 there was a degree of optimism that inflationary pressures could be contained in most economies and interest rates, although having bottomed out, were not expected to increase rapidly, or to very high levels, over the next 12 months.

In this context, it is worth noting that economic growth in the region has become more autonomous in the last few years with the rapid increase in intraregional trade; it has also become more domestically driven. Nonetheless, it still remains dependent to a significant degree on demand from outside the region, and export growth remains a crucial element in maintaining the current growth momentum. Exports depend on demand from the EU, Japan and the United States. China's rapid growth has itself generated a large increase in both global and regional trade. Although the signs in early-2005 have been encouraging, any simultaneous slowdown in China, Japan and the United States were it to emerge and continuing lacklustre growth in the EU could thus have an adverse impact on the region as a whole during 2005. Other downside risks emanate from developments in the commodity and financial markets and their impact on imponderables such as consumer and business confidence. Finally, although the risk of terrorism remains ever-present in the region, its impact is likely to be muted. However, local unrest in some countries could have an impact on investment and increase security expenditures, putting pressure on fiscal balances.

Governments should maintain the domestic momentum of growth

Depending on how energy and commodity prices behave in the months ahead, the extent of the external slowdown in 2005 and what impact, if any, these developments have on financial markets, Governments in the region will need to take appropriate measures to ensure that the domestic momentum of growth remains broadly unaffected and to simultaneously minimize any macroeconomic instability induced by external events. They will also need to ensure that long-term development goals continue to receive due attention.

In the following pages, prospects for the region and policy issues over the next 12 months are examined against the background of the current global economic setting, developments in international trade, including trends in commodities, and the amalgam of influences currently bearing on financial markets and how these might impact on consumer sentiment and corporate behaviour in the region. Finally, the balance of risks to growth emanating from these developments and the main issues that arise as a result for the Governments of the region, including some longer-term development policy challenges, are discussed.

THE GLOBAL SETTING AND IMPLICATIONS FOR ASIA-PACIFIC

This section reviews the performance of key developed countries with special reference to issues that will have an impact on the economic performance of the Asian and Pacific region. It also reviews recent trends in international trade, FDI flows and financial market developments.

Developed countries

United States economy exercises major influence in region

With a weight of 21 per cent in global output and 10 per cent of global imports, 42 per cent of which are sourced from Asia-Pacific, the United States economy continues to exercise a major influence on the region. Although the United States economy grew 4.4 per cent in 2004, the fastest rate of expansion since 1999, some loss in the momentum of growth in the second and fourth quarters have raised concerns about prospects for 2005.

The strength of the American economy in the first half of 2004 was the result of the large fiscal boost that it received in late 2003. This, combined with low interest rates, kept unemployment low and stimulated both corporate and household spending. In the latter, rising house prices have played a major role via their wealth effects. Consumer spending in 2004 grew by 3.8 per cent, the highest level since 2000. However, by mid-2004 the macroeconomic stimulus was starting to wane and nascent price pressures were beginning to emerge. In response, the Federal Reserve Board has raised its benchmark federal funds rate six times since

June 2004. Given the size of the fiscal deficit, expectations of any extra federal budgetary stimulus are considered unrealistic for 2005. Rather, the Board's current strategy is to withdraw monetary stimulus gradually. Furthermore, much of the domestic demand strength leaked into imports and the trade deficit, which swelled to its widest level ever in November 2004, subtracted around 1.7 percentage points from growth in the fourth quarter.

Another factor that underpinned the economy in 2003 and part of 2004 was the equity markets. More recently, equity prices have been relatively stagnant, as GDP growth has not been converted into rising corporate earnings on a sustained basis. Moreover, the rather slow pace of job creation appears to have dented consumer confidence and volatile oil prices have been a negative development. Thus, taking these various factors in combination the consensus of opinion now is for the American economy to decelerate to 3.5 per cent in 2005.[3] Thus, as far as ESCAP economies are concerned, the United States is likely to provide less of a stimulus to growth in 2005, compared with 2003 and 2004.

Continuing concern about growing current account and fiscal deficits in the United States

A slower rate of GDP growth is not the only potential danger emanating from the United States with external repercussions. The continued large current account and fiscal deficits in the United States have weakened the dollar and, these, superimposed upon the low domestic saving rate, suggest that the American economy will be a significant demander of global savings for some time to come. Foreigners, particularly from Japan and China, hold a large part of the federal Government's debt, which stood at a record $7.5 trillion at the end of 2004, up by $1 trillion since 2003. A firming trend in interest rates is bound to aggravate the servicing of both deficits and poses the risk of a disorderly adjustment if global financial markets have become overweighted with United States assets. With the size of the twin deficits, each magnifying the other, there is a high probability for increased risk premiums on United States financial assets. These factors can create conditions of deflationary pressure on economic activity. In such a situation, all countries could be faced with significantly increased financial market and exchange rate volatility. It should, however, be emphasized that, in the past, risks to the global economy originating in the United States have not always materialized. Nevertheless, there is agreement both in the United States and in multilateral bodies that the current macroeconomic imbalances in the United States cannot be sustained indefinitely and the country will have to strengthen confidence in its fiscal sustainability to achieve a better balance between commitments and resources.

---

[3] IMF, *United States: 2004 Article IV Consultation – Staff Report; Staff Supplement; and Public Information Notice on the Executive Board Discussion,* IMF Country Report No. 04/230 (July 2004).

Rapid growth in Japan unlikely to be maintained in 2005

The Japanese economy, too, exercises a major influence in the region. Its recent buoyancy has been an unexpected source of stimulus for several economies in the region, notably in East and South-East Asia. Despite a slowdown in the second half of 2004, the Japanese economy nevertheless registered its highest rate of growth for several years in 2004. From the perspective of the region, the question, however, is whether this faster growth is sustainable into 2005 and beyond. The evidence at this stage is rather mixed. First, on the positive side, the current upturn appears to be more broadly based than previous ones, with growing evidence of a rise in household consumption, Japan's weakest link in reviving and sustaining growth over the last decade. But the risk is that household incomes, though better than at their low point in 2002, have yet to increase and this may affect the sustainability of consumption. Second, the corporate and financial sectors have undergone fairly extensive restructuring in that many firms have shed excess capacity while banks have made considerable progress in writing off NPLs and recapitalizing their balance sheets. As a result, corporate profitability has improved and banks are in a stronger position to support the recovery. This is reflected in rising business confidence. Third, deflationary pressures may be coming to an end. Indeed, analysts expect consumer prices to start rising in mid-2005 after seven years of decline. This should have a further positive impact on corporate profits and consumer spending after a certain time lag.

At the same time, however, the export sector has been the primary driving force of Japanese growth, with sales to China especially buoyant in 2004. The United States has been another source of demand, particularly in the high-technology sector. Both economies could slow in the months ahead, the United States more so than China. Corporate restructuring still has some way to go. The enormous size of the fiscal deficit and of public debt remains an ongoing concern. Given Japan's high dependence on imported energy, the rise in oil prices represents a kind of tax on expenditure that could nip growth in consumer spending in the bud.[4] Hence, the recovery is expected to ease in the months ahead with the pace moving below Japan's long-term trend rate of growth of around 2.5 per cent per annum, with a consequent impact on the regional economy.

Continuing lacklustre growth in the EU

Outside the region, the EU is finally showing signs of a moderate pickup in activity after little growth in 2002 and 2003. In the 12 euro zone countries, growth is picking up, especially in France, even though the appreciation of the euro vis-à-vis the dollar has reduced relative euro zone

---

[4] IMF, *Japan: 2004 Article IV Consultation – Staff Report: Staff Supplement; and Public Information Notice on the Executive Board Discussion,* IMF Country Report No. 04/249 (August 2004).

competitiveness. But domestic demand, particularly in Germany, remains weak, and in 2004 was 2 per cent lower than in 2000. Furthermore, high levels of euro zone unemployment at around 9.0 per cent continue to undermine consumer confidence and spending. This phenomenon, combined with slow progress in implementing structural reforms, suggests that a significant improvement in the GDP growth rate is unlikely in the short term.

Outside the euro zone, the older members of the EU, such as the United Kingdom of Great Britain and Northern Ireland and Sweden, continue to enjoy relatively buoyant growth, while the enlargement of the EU to 25 members since May 2004 presages, at the very least, a period of consolidation as the new members learn to grapple with the EU's political and economic decision-making arrangements before enjoying the benefits of an enlarged single market. In this context, the eligibility of the new entrants to the EU for membership in the euro and the reform of the Stability and Growth Pact raise complex issues that could delay the positive impact of the enlargement on trade and output growth for some time. The EU has been increasing in importance as a trading partner of ESCAP countries, accounting for nearly 20 per cent of exports in 2003, but its economic performance is unlikely to have a large impact on growth in Asia and the Pacific in 2005.

Recent trends in international trade

The strong growth of the global economy in 2003 and 2004 was both reflected in and driven by strong growth in world trade (table I.2). Overall, global trade expanded by an estimated 10.6 per cent in volume terms in 2004 following growth of just over 6 per cent in 2003. At almost 15 per cent, developing countries dominated by China and India once again outpaced developed countries in global trade growth. The ESCAP region is the main contributor to world trade growth with both exports and imports growing faster than world exports and imports.

Trade and output growth historic relationship restored in 2004

A feature of globalization worthy of note has been that merchandise trade expanded at roughly twice the rate of merchandise production in the 1990s.[5] The early years of the succeeding decade saw a marked slowdown in the rate of growth of merchandise trade – in 2001 it actually declined – but in 2004 the historical relationship between trade and output growth of the 1990s appears to have been restored. Moreover, there is evidence now that trade in services is growing rapidly to match trade in merchandise, with travel the fastest-growing category in the former but vulnerable to the rise in oil prices.

[5] UNCTAD, *Trade and Development Report, 2004* (United Nations publication, Sales No. E.04.II.D.29).

Table I.2. World trade and prices,[a] 1991-2004

	Annual percentage changes					
	1991-2000	*2000*	*2001*	*2002*	*2003*	*2004[b]*
Trade in goods (volumes)	7.3	11.5	−0.9	2.5	6.2	10.6
Trade prices (in US dollars)						
Manufactures	−0.9	−5.6	−2.8	2.4	13.2	7.5
Oil	2.1	57.0	−13.8	2.5	15.8	28.9
Other commodities	−0.9	4.4	−4.1	0.6	7.1	16.8
Terms of trade						
Developed economies[c]	0.2	−3.1	0.3	1.1	1.3	−0.1
Developing economies	0.0	7.6	−3.1	0.6	0.0	3.2

Sources: United Nations, *World Economic Situation and Prospects 2005* (United Nations publication, Sales No. E.05.II.C.2); and IMF, *World Economic Outlook, September 2004: The Global Demographic Transition* (Washington, IMF, 2004).

[a] Goods only.

[b] Forecast.

[c] Advanced industrial economies plus newly industrializing Asian economies (Hong Kong, China, Republic of Korea, Singapore and Taiwan Province of China).

Rapid shifts in trade patterns

Within the fastest-growing categories of merchandise, some subcategories play a more dynamic role than others. In this context, the most dynamic category relevant to the ESCAP region is trade in ICT equipment and software, which after picking up in the first half of 2004 began to decelerate in some Asian exporting countries in the second half of the year. Nevertheless, together, these subcategories expanded at twice the rate of total manufactured goods over the previous 12 years. Such phenomena indicate that global trade flows are not static; over relatively short periods of time they have experienced major structural shifts and have evolved in the face of changing technology and consumer tastes and preferences. It is for individual Governments to remain alert to the changes occurring around them and assist businesses in adapting to such changes through responsive policies and the provision of public goods such as market intelligence and logistical support. They also need to maintain and promote competitiveness in particular lines in order to keep market share through targeted R&D expenditures.

An apposite illustration in this regard, for instance, is that the share of agricultural products in global trade has declined steadily over the last 15 years. This is so despite the fact that production of most agricultural commodities has increased in recent years. The relative decline in trade share is partly the result of the very rapid growth in the trade of manufactured and semi-manufactured goods, principally components, and partly because demand for agricultural goods has risen more slowly in the last two decades. The recent example of wheat is illustrative of this change. World wheat production is estimated to have risen by over 9.5 per cent in 2003/04. However, according to FAO estimates global cereal trade is set to decline sharply in 2004/05 as much of the increased production will be locally consumed and preclude the need for cross-border sales and deliveries.[6] An accompanying trend is that processed agricultural goods have risen in importance in world trade throughout the last 12 years, indicating that value is being added to commodities in the exporting countries rather than in the importing ones.

Ending of the Multifibre Arrangement provides both opportunities and challenges

Another related issue in this context arises from the ending of the 30-year-old Multifibre Arrangement on 1 January 2005, which has resulted in the removal of the quota system governing trade in textiles and clothing from developing countries to developed country markets, namely, Canada, the EU, Norway and the United States. The freeing of restrictions for clothing and apparel exports represents an opportunity for low-cost producing countries in the region to gain from global competition. The main beneficiaries are expected to be China, India and Pakistan, which have well-developed indigenous textile sectors, but a number of smaller economies in the region, mainly in South and South-East Asia, which are less equipped to cope with free competition, will be faced with major challenges. In Bangladesh, exports of garments and textiles make up over 80 per cent of total exports, while in Nepal and Sri Lanka they account for about 50 per cent. Outside South Asia, exports of textiles and clothing accounted for 87.0 per cent of exports from Cambodia, 48 per cent from the Lao People's Democratic Republic and 15 per cent from Viet Nam. However, a more important implication is the possible further decrease in apparel prices, squeezing industry profit margins, and in this regard larger producers such as China will be able to be more price competitive through economies of scale.

While large shifts in trading patterns are not expected to happen overnight and countries have had several years to prepare for this event, the ending of the quota system means that such economies could well lose out to stronger competitors, unless the affected countries themselves take measures to increase their competitiveness and seek niche areas. China itself imposed export taxes on selected categories of textiles and clothing from 1 January 2005 to achieve a gradual transition and help to placate producer lobbies fearing collapse of their industries. There are some mitigating factors that may prevent or at least slow down the perceived threat. China's transitional arrangements following WTO membership will not end until 2016, and in any case, as part of the terms of China's

---

[6] FAO, *Food Outlook,* No. 3, September 2004.

accession to WTO, members of WTO have the right to impose safeguard measures under certain conditions specifically against imports from China until 2008. Shifts in supply-demand relationships for an industry that has a long history of trade protection tend to occur only gradually. It is not clear how sourcing strategies will change and certainly China-only sourcing is deemed a risky strategy. The Governments of vulnerable countries nevertheless need to redouble their efforts to further strengthen their respective textile and garment industries and forge alliances with more competitive producers in the region at all stages of the production chain to achieve greater integration. Larger countries such as China and India have an important role to play in achieving such integration through active partnerships with smaller developing countries affected (see box II.4).

With slower growth moderate deceleration of trade likely in 2005

In tandem with an expected fall in world economic growth in 2005, the rise in international trade is expected to slow to 8 per cent in real terms, close to its average growth in the 1990s. Import demand in the developed economies is likely to slow so significantly that growth within the developing economies may not be able to fully compensate. Nevertheless, developments in China will continue to be an important determinant of trade performance for most parts of the region. China has became the world's third-largest trading nation, following the United States and Germany, with its foreign trade value hitting $1 trillion in the first 11 months of 2004, partly owing to a 50 per cent increase in exports in the ICT sector.

"July Package" raises hopes for Doha Round

The adoption of a framework agreement of 1 August 2004 – the so-called "July Package" – marked the resumption of the WTO negotiations under the Doha work programme. The "July Package" sets out five core areas: agriculture, market access on non-agricultural products, services, development issues and trade facilitation. One of the most significant gains is the agreement to eliminate export subsidies, although no road map or end date has been given for achieving the goal. The original deadline of January 2005 for completion of the Doha Round has passed. Further progress will now hinge on the outcome of the Sixth WTO Ministerial Conference, to be held in Hong Kong, China, in December 2005. It is hoped that the improved qualitative atmosphere in the negotiations will rebuild consensus to successfully conclude the round.

Meanwhile, the momentum of RTAs and FTAs continued in parallel in 2004. The prevalent view among those participating is that a country that focuses on the WTO negotiations alone while others do not risks seeing a reduction in its competitiveness, including its ability to access foreign markets and attract FDI. Hence the trade and investment strategy for a number of major exporters has been to pursue the bilateral, regional and multilateral paths simultaneously. This implies that RTAs and FTAs must add to the WTO process and not weaken it and should serve as building blocks that complement and help to facilitate the WTO process (box I.2).

Box I.2. Multilateralism and free trade areas in Asia and the Pacific

The Asia-Pacific region contains some of the most important trading nations in the world, led by China and India. The region provides outstanding evidence of the benefits of open trade and investment policies, which have doubled merchandise export value between 1992 and 2003. More recently, regionalism has become a key component of the international economic order and is likely to remain an enduring feature of the trading systems. It offers Governments an attractive complementary strategy. Currently, almost without exception, trading countries of the world belong to one, or more typically, two or three RTAs or regional integration arrangements of some kind, covering about two thirds of the trade conducted. The Asia-Pacific region is no exception.

RTAs have wide-ranging definitions. For the purposes of this box, RTAs cover free trade areas, which are defined in article XXIV of GATT as consisting of "a group of two or more customs territories in which the duties and other restrictive regulations of commerce... are eliminated on substantially all the trade". RTAs also cover preferential trading arrangements (PTAs) among developing countries referred to in the GATT Decision of 28 November 1979 as those arrangements "entered into amongst less-developed contracting parties for the mutual reduction or elimination of tariffs...on products imported from one another". RTAs could also encompass customs unions, as in the proposed ASEAN Economic Community.

Traditionally, the Asia-Pacific region has been the least "regionalized" in terms of RTAs notified to WTO. At last count, however, there were more than 50 RTAs involving Asia-Pacific economies, of which 48 had been notified to WTO. This compares with over 250 PTAs around the world notified to GATT/WTO, not to mention 70 or so that are still pending. These arrangements vary considerably in membership, style, design and effectiveness, in line with the diverse and heterogeneous nature of the political and economic landscape of the Asia-Pacific region. Some have well-developed institutionalized rules of interaction, while others have a more informal structure based on voluntary cooperation. Some are open to new members while others have placed a moratorium on new members. The breadth of coverage varies as well, with services covered in a few agreements while most do not cover services in any meaningful way. Agriculture may be wholly or partially excluded, while movement of factors of production, depth of tariff cuts, coverage of non-tariff measures and decision-making processes also vary widely. Likewise, the results achieved vary tremendously.

A variant of the many trade agreements signed over the past few years is bilateralism. Bilateral trade agreements encompass the formation of a free trade area through the reduction of tariffs and other trade barriers imposed at the "border". However, they go beyond border measures, extending into large areas of domestic policy-making. Thus, they encompass a deeper integration of trade through the harmonization of a wide range of trade practices, procedures and standards. Despite the recent rapid growth of RTAs, including their bilateral format, it is not clear in which direction regionalism is moving. The sheer number of agreements under negotiation and their disparate membership and varying coverage make it difficult to draw conclusive answers. It is not clear whether this surge in bilateralism is a short-term phenomenon or not, and to what extent this trend will continue. Broadly, two major trends can be distinguished.

The first is a trend directed at coalescing existing regional groupings into outward-oriented FTAs that bridge subregions and continents. This has the potential of laying the foundation for the eventual integration of all countries of the region into a forward-looking Asia-Pacific zone of efficient production with enhanced opportunities for world trade. It is the more promising of the two trends.

This integration is centred in East and South-East Asia. Progress in bringing about the China-ASEAN FTA has been faster than initially expected, notwithstanding a recently missed deadline of 30 June 2004. With a market of nearly 1.8 billion people, a regional GDP of about $2 trillion, international trade worth $1.2 trillion and average annual economic growth of 8 per cent, based on current trends, this will become the production base and trade and investment centre of the region. The addition of Japan, which has long worked at strengthening its economic ties with the members of ASEAN, is further boosting the integration process.

(Continued overleaf)

(Continued from preceding page)

A second, but potentially more sinister, trend can also be distinguished. This is a movement in the opposite direction: instead of amalgamating RTAs into wider, bridging initiatives, there is a splintering of RTAs into bilateral FTAs. For example, the United States Framework Agreement under the Enterprise for ASEAN Initiative in effect consists of a series of bilateral PTAs with individual ASEAN countries, the United States-Singapore FTA being the first one concluded, followed by similar agreements with Australia, the Philippines and Thailand, among others, in the pipeline. Similarly, Japan has indicated that it has concerns about the varying levels of industrial development between the founding and newer members of ASEAN and prefers to enter into a series of bilateral trade agreements with individual member countries of ASEAN, also having started with Singapore, followed by the Philippines, Thailand and others in the pipeline. China is also negotiating separate bilateral agreements with a number of ASEAN countries, as well as India and Pakistan.

Against this background the question that arises is whether the Asia-Pacific region has found a new approach in these bilateral initiatives that promises greater economic benefits than a region-wide or a WTO approach to liberalization? Further, will these initiatives reinvigorate or eventually detract from the ongoing WTO negotiations? For the time being, the answers to these questions are unclear. Nevertheless, it would appear that the current criss-crossing of bilateral FTAs could evolve into, and come to rest in, a more rational hub-and-spoke configuration. Both proactive and defensive trade strategies seem to be driving this process. On the one hand, major trading powers appear to be competing to establish trade predominance in the region. At the same time, there are a number of smaller trading countries that are equally active in forging bilateral trade deals and also appear to be competing to establish dominance as a hub. This, however, may be more symptomatic of a defensive trade strategy, designed to avoid finding themselves at the spoke end of another major hub. A multilayered constellation is thus emerging, made up of a dominant hub-and-spoke arrangement with substrata of other hub-and-spoke arrangements in which smaller economies may be trying to establish alternative hubs. The option of developing countries collectively establishing themselves through ASEAN, as the alternative hub, stands out.

In assessing what could reasonably be expected to be a development-friendly outcome, a number of long-term systemic issues also arise. They are related to how the international trade architecture should evolve over the next few decades in a manner that best serves trade and development objectives. No ready answers are available, and the issues go well beyond the current Doha Round of negotiations at WTO. Nevertheless, they are fundamental because the ultimate objective is to ensure positive cross-fertilization between developments in regionalism and in the multilateral system. Regionalism is a reality and analytical tools to evaluate its welfare and trade impacts need to be sharpened.

The confluence of economics and politics will bring to the fore new challenges that are difficult to predict. Economic performance in a region as diverse as Asia and the Pacific will vary significantly among countries but overall WTO-consistent, outward-oriented trade and investment policies have the greatest potential to provide a viable basis for sustaining economic growth. A way forward would be to regard regionalism as being here to stay and consider how to accommodate it in the multilateral rules governing economic integration.

Commodities

Commodity prices on a firmer trend since 2002

After a long period of decline, commodity prices have been on the rise since 2002 (see table I.3). Prices have increased for most commodity groups, the largest increases being in agricultural raw materials, such as vegetable oilseeds and oils, and various mineral ores and metals. Rising coffee prices have brought relief to some countries where producers have often faced ruin in the face of relentless long-term price declines. However, firmer commodity price trends appear to have bypassed some agricultural products, notably bananas and hides and skins, for which producers continue to grapple with the consequences of oversupply and weak demand.[7]

Table I.3. Commodity price index, 2001-2004

(2000 = 100)

	2001	2002	2003	2004[a]
Food and tropical beverages	91.4	100.0	99.0	106.7
Tropical beverages	87.8	112.2	108.2	126.5
Food	91.6	97.7	96.9	103.1
Vegetable oilseeds and oils	114.1	150.0	176.6	159.4
Palm oil	127.5	175.5	192.5	163.4
Soybeans	87.1	111.1	153.0	119.8
Groundnut oil	95.8	121.2	164.7	162.6
Agricultural raw materials	84.4	99.1	124.8	125.7
Cotton	65.1	83.8	111.7	72.4
Rubber	78.9	137.0	203.5	203.9
Minerals, ores and metals	85.8	90.8	116.7	145.0
Aluminium	85.9	87.8	99.3	115.9
Copper	79.5	86.2	119.0	168.7
Iron ore	104.5	103.4	112.2	131.7
Nickel	72.0	98.3	193.6	192.0
Tin	76.8	80.9	115.7	173.2
Zinc	71.3	75.5	91.1	104.2

Source: Reproduced from United Nations, *World Economic Situation and Prospects 2005* (United Nations publication, Sales No. E.05.II.C.2).

[a] Calculations for 2004 are based on October 2004 over December 2003.

Dollar depreciation adds to upward pressure on commodity prices

In general, recent trends in commodities can be explained by the rapid increase in demand that the economic recovery of the last two years has brought in its wake. The rise in demand has been most visible in the ESCAP region, particularly in China, and has come in the face of secular trends that have reduced supplies and led to a decline in stocks. To put matters in perspective, however, the recent depreciation of the dollar has to a certain extent influenced the current rise in commodity prices. As most internationally traded commodities are priced in dollars, the dollar exchange rate becomes an element in the way that prices behave. Thus, for instance, while commodity prices in general have risen by nearly a

[7] UNCTAD, *Trade and Development Report, 2004* (United Nations publication, Sales No. E.04.II.D.29).

fifth over the last two years in dollar terms, they have actually fallen in terms of the euro and have barely moved in terms of the yen; hence, demand for commodities has not been greatly affected by the rise in dollar values in the EU or Japan. But it is also true that the greater part of the increase in demand has occurred in the ESCAP region, where exchange rates have either remained on a fixed parity with the dollar, as in China, or have stabilized against the dollar over the last 18 months or so, as in much of the rest of Asia. Thus, it is demand emanating from China in particular and from the region in general that has essentially driven commodity prices upward over the last two years.

Strong influence of Chinese demand in commodity markets

The rapid growth of the Chinese economy has meant that China has become the world's largest consumer and importer of several commodities, many of them sourced from within the region. As such, it has become a key factor in the commodity markets with a critical influence on price levels. China's influence extends beyond the production and sale of the commodities themselves to shipping, freight rates and related services and its market power has been most evident in vegetable oilseeds and oils, including soybeans, cotton, rubber and iron ore. China's economic growth has also resulted in a massive increase in the demand for energy, particularly coal and oil. While China can satisfy most of its requirements for coal, increased domestic demand and lower exports from China have raised international coal prices. It is in oil that Chinese demand has had the greatest impact. China's oil needs have doubled in less than a decade and contributed to the tightness in supplies in 2004. As car ownership expands rapidly in China, the prospect for oil prices could be one of significant upward pressure in the next two or three years.

However, the depreciation of the dollar also played a part in the case of oil, providing an upward momentum to prices. At the beginning of 2004, OPEC was keeping prices in the upper part of the $22-$28 per barrel range. By mid-2004 prices had risen significantly above this range and even though OPEC increased production, the unanticipated higher demand from China, aggravated by supply disruptions in Iraq and some degree of speculative activity in the futures market, sent prices soaring above $55 a barrel in October 2004. This level represents a doubling of prices over the previous 18 months in dollar terms and raises concern regarding negative repercussions on the broader global economy.

Commodity prices in real terms remain at historically low levels

The firmer trend in commodity prices witnessed over the last two years has helped the economies of commodity-producing and -exporting countries in the region by boosting export earnings. In the case of agricultural commodities, it has also bolstered farm incomes, which have stimulated overall demand and output growth and helped in the fight against poverty. But that being the case and viewed from a longer-term perspective, commodity prices in real terms continue to remain at historically low levels, considerably below their levels of 20 years ago. This has meant that over the last two decades the terms of trade of commodity producers have deteriorated. Thus, while rising commodity prices have undoubtedly helped commodity-producing countries in terms of higher exports and lower current account deficits in the short run, they have had only a minimal impact on the underlying structural problems of commodity production in these countries. Producers often tend to operate on a small scale and have little, if any, financial strength either to diversify their production or to invest in value-adding facilities. The situation will not change if the issue of long-term deterioration in terms of trade is not addressed. This factor has played a major role in the continuation of rural poverty in the region.

Foreign direct investment flows

FDI downturn reversed, with China remaining top destination in region

In 2004, world FDI also reached a turning point. UNCTAD estimated that FDI inflows had risen by 6 per cent to $612 billion, putting an end to the global FDI downturn that had begun in 2001.[8] Developing countries now account for an estimated 42 per cent of world FDI inflows compared with 27 per cent during 2001-2003. Flows to developed countries slumped by 16 per cent to $321 billion in 2004 while those to developing countries increased from $173 billion in 2003 to an estimated $255 billion in 2004. The United States was the top recipient, with inflows amounting to $121 billion, followed by China, with $62 billion. Both Hong Kong, China, and Singapore doubled their FDI levels, to $33 billion and $21 billion respectively, from the corresponding figures of 2003. The Asian and Pacific region recorded more than $166 billion in FDI inflows in 2004, a 46 per cent rise over 2003. The flows are unevenly distributed in the region with North-East Asia, principally China and the Republic of Korea, taking the giant's share followed by ASEAN countries, principally Singapore, and South Asia, principally India. Flows to Central Asia expanded because of oil and gas investment, while the Pacific subregion saw only marginal increases. For the region as a whole, UNCTAD forecasts the increase in the flow of foreign investment to continue at least until 2007, with China enhancing its role as a significant FDI provider in addition to being the top recipient. A number of other developing countries in the region, such as India, Malaysia and Singapore, have emerged as providers of FDI.

Financial market developments

Large current account imbalances continue to characterize the global economy. The United States deficit is estimated to have exceeded $570 billion or more than 5.0 per cent of GDP in 2004 and is expected to remain broadly at this level in 2005. Smaller current account deficits are run by the United Kingdom, Italy and Spain among the developed

---

[8] UNCTAD, Press Release UNCTAD/PRESS/PR/2005/002, 11 January 2005.

countries and by some of the newer members of the EU from Eastern Europe. A number of developing countries, principally in Latin America and Africa, will also run current account deficits in 2004 and beyond. Current account surpluses are found principally in Asia but also in parts of Europe, mainly Germany, Switzerland and Norway.

Since the mid-1990s, the American deficit has more than tripled in percentage points of GDP, with Japan and developing countries in Asia accounting for the bulk of the corresponding surpluses. In the United States, strong demand growth and the high value of the dollar widened the deficits in the late 1990s. Since the beginning of 2002 the deficit has continued to widen despite the weakening of the dollar.

Funding of United States twin deficits a major cause of uncertainty in financial markets …

By definition, the marked rise in the external borrowing needs of the United States since the mid-1990s has been associated with a growing gap between American investment and saving. Before the last downturn, saving by households fell and investment as a proportion of GDP increased. These two factors drove the current account deficit up, in spite of a sharp improvement in the fiscal accounts. After the downturn, the picture changed as investment was cut back and business saving rose. Nevertheless, United States foreign borrowing continued to increase as a large public sector deficit emerged. The persistence of the American deficit and its vulnerability to shifts in foreign investor sentiment are major sources of uncertainty in the global economy today.[9]

… as is the falling dollar

A lower dollar, as is already happening, would obviously contribute to reducing the United States current account deficit. However, the speed of any adjustment depends on relative trade elasticities, which suggest that the adjustment could take some time. Moreover, an adjustment of the dollar exchange rate is bound to have implications beyond the United States, especially in the ESCAP region as the dollar falls; other currencies must rise against it. Thus far, it is primarily the euro and to some extent the yen that have appreciated. In the region, the Chinese yuan renminbi, Hong Kong, China, dollar and Malaysian ringgit maintain a fixed parity with the dollar. Other currencies, not linked to the dollar, have appreciated only marginally against it over the past 24 months.

Many economies in the ESCAP region and elsewhere have relied on American import demand as an important driver of growth; a sizeable fall in the dollar might choke off this source of growth. In addition, a fall in the dollar could also push up inflation in the United States, possibly leading to higher American and global interest rates. For now, these scenarios lie in the realm of speculation. The world's economy is in uncharted territory when its largest reserve currency has substantial levels

---

[9] BIS, *74th Annual Report, 1 April 2003-31 March 2004* (Basel, BIS, 2004).

of outstanding debt. Nonetheless, the world has to find ways to accommodate the United States current account deficit, accumulate dollar-denominated assets in the process and deal as well as possible with a gradual decline in the dollar exchange rate, which reduces the value of those assets over time. The adjustment of the current global imbalances thus poses a major challenge from the perspective of both global and regional financial markets.

Despite the firming up of interest rates in recent months, their very low levels over the past two years have encouraged the growth of a variety of alternative investment vehicles. Precious metals and real estate, especially housing, have been among the most favoured investment modes as the equity and bond markets have barely moved in 2004 after rising significantly in 2003. These alternative investment modes have generated significant capital gains and kept consumer spending high.

Growing presence of hedge funds in Asia calls for improved supervision

The growth of alternative investments merits closer attention as excessive flows of speculative funds in Asia rekindle memories of the 1997-1998 financial crisis. Other than real estate and precious metals, where borrowed funds also play a role but where the amplitude of price fluctuations is limited, alternative investments have been primarily in the form of highly leveraged vehicles, such as hedge funds, usually involving a small group of wealthy individuals prepared to trade high risk for high returns on their investments. The funds managed in Asia by some 500 hedge funds rose to about $60 billion in 2004 from $34 billion the previous year.[10] But the inherent risks of leveraging and the rather wide-ranging and in some cases esoteric nature of the uses to which some hedge funds are being put, including oil futures, strongly suggest that financial market operators need to beef up their risk-evaluation systems and thus counter the threat of a major potential upheaval in the financial markets. Such an upheaval could come as a result of excessive risk-taking by an individual fund, causing, in turn, disproportionate price volatility in the securities and commodity markets over much of the world, and conceivably lead to a prolonged, and more systemic, withdrawal of liquidity from these markets. It is worth stressing that hedge funds remain essentially unregulated and their risk profiles largely unknown from a regulatory perspective.[11]

Rising foreign exchange reserves: is the region overinsured?

Along with the emergence of global imbalances, a factor worthy of note is that developing economies in the ESCAP region have become net capital exporters in recent years as persistent current account surpluses in some countries combined with a sharp increase in net private capital flows (table I.4) have been reflected primarily in the substantial accumulation of

10 "Commentary: is the boom in Asian hedge funds a healthy trend?", *International Herald Tribune*, 6 January 2005.

11 "How hedge funds are destabilizing the markets", *Financial Times*, 28 September 2004.

Table I.4. Net capital flows[a] of developing countries and developing economies in Asia, 1997-2005

(Billions of US dollars)

	1997	*1998*	*1999*	*2000*	*2001*	*2002*	*2003*	*2004[b]*	*2005[c]*
Total									
Net private capital flows[d]	195.0	70.5	88.1	46.6	47.8	61.2	120.4	81.6	47.5
Net private direct investment	144.9	155.0	173.4	177.1	191.2	143.5	147.6	166.9	175.2
Net private portfolio flows	63.3	41.9	66.6	16.1	−91.3	−99.6	−11.0	−21.3	−23.4
Net other private capital flows	−13.2	−126.4	−151.8	−146.6	−52.0	17.3	−16.2	−64.0	−104.4
Net official flows	34.6	49.7	6.5	−27.7	15.7	1.7	−24.8	−31.0	−42.1
Changes in reserves[e]	−103.8	−33.9	−92.5	−115.6	−113.2	−197.1	−367.0	−350.1	−291.2
Developing economies in Asia									
Net private capital flows[d, f]	37.6	−52.2	8.6	−4.5	9.6	25.4	52.8	79.8	8.6
Net private direct investment	56.5	56.1	66.4	67.4	60.5	53.8	70.0	77.2	77.5
Net private portfolio flows	6.7	8.1	56.1	19.8	−56.9	−59.6	5.5	12.0	−1.8
Net other private capital flows[f]	−25.5	−116.4	−113.9	−91.7	6.0	31.2	−22.8	−9.4	−67.1
Net official flows	22.6	17.9	2.2	4.5	−1.8	−1.8	−16.3	−6.9	−8.8
Changes in reserves[e]	−36.4	−52.7	−87.2	−60.9	−90.9	−158.4	−234.2	−232.6	−158.0

Source: IMF, *World Economic Outlook, September 2004: The Global Demographic Transition* (Washington, IMF, 2004).

[a] Net capital flows comprise net direct investment, net portfolio investment and other long- and short-term net investment flows, including official and private borrowing.
[b] Estimates.
[c] Forecast.
[d] Because of data limitations, "net other private capital flows", may include some official flows.
[e] A minus sign indicates an increase.
[f] Excluding the effects of the recapitalization of two large commercial banks in China with foreign reserves of the Bank of China ($45 billion), net private capital flows to developing economies in Asia in 2003 were $97.8 billion while net other private capital flows to the region amounted to $22.2 billion.

official reserves. The region holds over $2 trillion of foreign reserves, which have doubled over a period of three years. All seven economies in the world that have over $100 billion of reserves are in Asia-Pacific[12]. Net reserves in 2004 were nearly eight times the levels prevailing in 1997, but a reduction of these levels is forecast owing to expected slower economic growth in 2005.

The growing size of foreign reserves in the Asian and Pacific region is a matter drawing considerable attention from capital market participants and policy makers. The massive increase, although providing insurance

[12] They are: Japan, with total official reserves, including gold, amounting to $810.8 billion in August 2004; China with $504.7 billion; Taiwan Province of China with $211.1 billion (2003 figures); Republic of Korea with $170.5 billion; Hong Kong, China with $118.3 billion; Singapore with $101.1 billion; and India with $117.4 billion.

against a future debt crisis and, perhaps, minimizing the likelihood of one occurring in the first place, nonetheless has its own complications. For instance, it can and has led to a build-up of excess domestic liquidity in several economies and has created quasi-fiscal costs as central banks have sought to sterilize reserve accumulation. An increase in liquidity and low interest rates have been the progenitors of asset bubbles in the past; at the very least they make risk assessment and risk management by the financial system more problematic. There is also the question of opportunity costs as the reserve-holding countries, in general, currently earn less on their reserves than what they pay out on their foreign loans. There are accordingly arguments both in favour of and against accumulating large foreign exchange reserves and judgements as to whether benefits outweigh costs are not easy.

Managing financial risks becoming an important economic activity

In increasingly globalized financial markets, the management of financial risks has become a more important aspect of economic activity. This means that problems, if and when they emerge, can have serious consequences for the real economy to a greater extent than in the past. Global events and factors, such as the volatile ITC industry, the manner of dealing with the global imbalances arising from the growing external and fiscal deficits of the United States and the large increase in liquidity available in most ESCAP economies, are bound to have major effects on domestic economies via changes in exchange rates, trading links and the relative competitiveness and profitability of individual enterprises. As ESCAP developing countries become more mainstream in the global economy, capital allocation mechanisms and decisions will inevitably take on an international perspective. In this regard, as more ESCAP developing countries move from managed to floating exchange rates and as they gradually free up the balance-of-payments capital accounts, erring on the side of caution, in terms of large foreign exchange reserves, seems appropriate at least for the foreseeable future at the minimum until regional financial supervisory mechanisms are developed to handle acute problems of liquidity, such as those evident in the 1997 Asian crisis. Nevertheless, the emergence of several ESCAP developing countries as net capital exporters, given their levels of development and need for financial resources for many years in the future, raises significant policy issues for the countries concerned as well as for the region as a whole.

DEVELOPMENTS, PROSPECTS AND POLICY ISSUES IN ASIA AND THE PACIFIC

As mentioned elsewhere, developing ESCAP economies were largely unaffected by the rising price of oil and the end of the low-interest environment up to mid-2004. Some slackening in the pace of output growth took place in the second half of 2004 but was relatively modest. Although the year ended on a tragic note in the aftermath of the Indian Ocean tsunami, GDP growth in the developing economies of the region was some 0.9 percentage points higher at 7.2 per cent in 2004 than in the previous year (table I.5). Despite rising oil and food prices, overall inflation in developing economies in the region has been stable in 2003-2004. Prospects for 2005 indicate a slowdown in GDP growth to around 6.2 per cent as the external environment weakens, with inflation slowing slightly to 4.6 per cent for this group of economies. GDP growth and inflation numbers are based on the presumption that average oil prices will be around $38 a barrel in 2005, the average level prevailing in 2003, an assumption that was looking increasingly less realistic in early-2005. As mentioned earlier, the tsunami will reduce 2005 growth in some countries quite substantially but its overall effect on the region is likely to be small.

Table I.5. Selected economies of the ESCAP region: rates of economic growth and inflation, 2003-2006

(Percentage)

	Real GDP				*Inflation*[a]			
	2003	*2004*[b]	*2005*[c]	*2006*[c]	*2003*	*2004*[b]	*2005*[c]	*2006*[c]
Developing economies of the ESCAP region[d]	6.3	7.2	6.2	6.2	4.8	4.8	4.6	4.0
East and North-East Asia	6.2	7.5	6.3	6.2	1.4	3.2	3.1	2.6
China	9.3	9.5	8.5	7.8	1.2	3.9	4.0	3.0
Hong Kong, China	3.2	7.9	5.0	6.0	−2.5	−0.3	0.3	1.2
Mongolia	5.5	6.0	6.0	5.0	4.6	11.0	4.7	..
Republic of Korea	3.1	4.7	4.0	4.6	3.6	3.6	3.0	2.9
Taiwan Province of China	3.3	5.9	4.2	4.1	−0.3	1.7	1.5	1.5
North and Central Asia	7.6	7.2	6.5	6.3	12.9	10.2	7.7	8.2
Armenia	13.9	10.1	6.5	6.0	4.7	7.0	2.6	3.0
Azerbaijan	11.2	10.2	14.0	10.0	2.2	6.7	5.0	7.4
Georgia	11.1	8.4	5.0	5.0	4.8	5.7	5.6	5.8
Kazakhstan	9.2	9.4	8.5	8.0	6.4	6.9	6.6	7.1
Kyrgyzstan	6.7	7.1	6.0	6.5	3.1	4.1	3.5	3.6
Russian Federation	7.3	7.1	6.3	6.1	13.7	10.9	8.0	8.6
Tajikistan	11.0	10.6	5.0	7.0	17.1	6.8	8.0	6.0
Turkmenistan	17.0	7.0	11.0	7.0	6.5	9.0	8.0	7.0
Uzbekistan	4.4	4.9	5.3	6.4	13.1	2.4	2.8	3.1
Pacific island economies	3.0	3.0	2.6	2.4	10.6	3.3	3.6	..
Cook Islands	3.1	2.7	2.9	..	2.4	1.9	2.4	..
Fiji	3.0	3.8	1.5	0.7	4.2	3.5	3.0	..
Papua New Guinea	2.8	2.6	2.9	2.4	14.7	2.9	3.8	..
Samoa	3.5	4.0	3.5	..	0.1	3.0	3.0	..
Solomon Islands	5.6	4.2	4.4	..	8.3	5.6	2.5	..
Tonga	2.9	1.6	2.8	..	11.6	11.0	11.0	..
Vanuatu	2.4	3.2	2.9	2.5	2.5	2.6	2.5	..

(Continued on next page)

Table I.5 *(continued)*

(Percentage)

	Real GDP				*Inflation*[a]			
	2003	*2004*[b]	*2005*[c]	*2006*[c]	*2003*	*2004*[b]	*2005*[c]	*2006*[c]
South and South-West Asia[e]	7.2	7.4	6.4	6.7	10.0	6.8	6.8	5.5
Bangladesh	5.3	5.5	5.2	5.8	4.4	5.8	6.8	5.9
Bhutan	6.5	7.0	8.0	..	1.8	1.2	..	..
India	8.5	6.9	7.2	7.3	3.9	3.8	4.0	4.0
Iran (Islamic Republic of)	6.7	7.1	7.1	7.4	15.6	14.5	14.5	11.5
Nepal	3.1	3.7	4.0	5.0	4.8	4.0	5.5	4.6
Pakistan	5.1	6.4	6.6	7.2	3.1	4.6	5.0	5.0
Sri Lanka	5.9	5.2	5.0	6.0	6.3	7.6	12.0	6.0
Turkey	5.8	9.6	4.8	5.1	25.3	10.7	9.6	6.1
South-East Asia	4.9	6.4	5.7	5.8	3.2	4.1	4.5	3.9
Cambodia	5.2	4.3	1.9	4.3	1.1	2.0	3.0	3.7
Indonesia	4.9	5.1	5.5	5.7	6.6	6.1	7.0	5.8
Lao People's Democratic Republic	5.9	6.5	7.0	7.0	15.5	11.2	7.7	5.4
Malaysia	5.3	7.1	6.0	6.1	1.2	1.4	2.2	2.7
Myanmar[f]	0.0	3.6	3.3	3.0	20.0	35.0	40.0	45.0
Philippines	4.7	6.1	5.3	5.2	3.5	6.0	6.0	5.0
Singapore	1.4	8.4	5.2	4.9	0.5	1.7	1.4	1.3
Thailand	6.9	6.1	6.0	6.3	1.8	2.7	3.2	2.4
Viet Nam	7.3	7.7	8.5	8.0	3.0	9.5	6.5	8.0
Developed economies of the ESCAP region	1.4	2.7	1.6	1.3	−0.1	0.2	0.3	0.4
Australia	3.0	3.5	3.0	3.0	2.8	2.3	2.8	2.7
Japan	1.3	2.6	1.5	1.1	−0.3	0.0	0.1	0.2
New Zealand	3.3	4.8	2.7	2.9	1.8	2.3	3.0	2.8

Sources: ESCAP, based on national sources; IMF, *International Financial Statistics,* vol. LVII, No. 10 (Washington, IMF, October 2004); ADB, *Key Indicators of Developing Asian and Pacific Countries 2004* (Manila, ADB, 2004) and *Asian Development Outlook 2004 Update* (Manila, ADB, 2004); EIU, *Country Reports* and *Country Forecasts* (London, EIU, 2004 and 2005), various issues; and web site of the CIS Inter-State Statistical Committee <www.cisstat.com>, 26 October 2004 and 3 February 2005.

[a] Changes in the consumer price index.

[b] Estimate.

[c] Forecast/target.

[d] Based on data for 38 (developing) economies representing more than 95 per cent of the population of the region (including the Central Asian republics); GDP figures at market prices in United States dollars in 2000 (at 1995 prices) have been used as weights to calculate the regional and subregional growth rates. In the case of Pacific island economies for 2006, estimates are based on figures available.

[e] The estimates and forecasts for countries relate to fiscal years defined as follows: fiscal year 2004/05 = 2004 for India, the Islamic Republic of Iran and Myanmar; and fiscal year 2003/04 = 2004 for Bangladesh, Nepal and Pakistan.

[f] Inflation at the end of the period.

With the exception of China, where domestic consumption and investment have been the main drivers of growth over the past two years, the resilience of ESCAP developing economies is essentially built around exports, within and outside the ESCAP region. Domestic demand emanating from both household consumption and corporate investment expenditure and driven by low interest rates has played a supportive role. East and South-East Asia have benefited from a strong revival in the ICT sector that began in 2003 and continued into 2004, embracing a much wider range of goods now. Higher oil prices have boosted oil-producing economies and added to regional import demand without harming oil-importing economies. The stronger commodity prices, especially of agricultural products, have increased exports and simultaneously raised rural incomes, thus providing a fillip to domestic demand. Corporations have responded to the increased demand by improving capacity utilization and committing greater resources to investment in improving competitiveness, such as new products in household electronics.

The sharp rise in oil prices has inevitably added to import spending. As a result, the current account balances of ESCAP developing economies have deteriorated. In addition, there is a risk that in 2005 the overall external environment could be weaker if a simultaneous slowdown in China, the United States and Japan occurs. In that event, the external situation could reduce export growth and narrow current account balances further. However, given the accumulation of large foreign exchange reserves over the last few years, this should not impact on overall levels of activity in the region for some time.

This broad assessment is nevertheless subject to two caveats: one, given the prevailing uncertainty regarding the future course of oil prices discussed earlier, the forecasts are prone to a somewhat higher margin of error than, say, a year ago; and, two, the different ESCAP subregions and, indeed, individual ESCAP economies are likely to respond very differently to the challenges of maintaining the present growth momentum in the coming months. These differences are highlighted in the paragraphs below on each subregion's performance and outlook and discussed more fully in the subregional macroeconomic reviews contained in chapter II. One important difference between countries in the region is the extent to which they have a degree of fiscal flexibility. While some countries are able to contemplate increasing public investment in infrastructure, say, as a means to supporting growth, others have lost this degree of freedom owing to high levels of public debt and high deficits. Efforts at financial and corporate restructuring in the region have been largely successful but an emerging issue in the past two years has been the extent of household debt. Nevertheless, the increase in internal and external financial strength within the region should enable ESCAP economies to withstand most foreseeable economic shocks, including interest rate adjustments and oil price volatility. However, other forms of shocks, such as the tsunami disaster and avian influenza, also raise significant policy issues for the region.

Post-tsunami reconstruction presents challenges and opportunities

Governments in countries affected by the Indian Ocean tsunami have the daunting task of providing survivors with housing, health and schooling in 2005 and beyond and helping them to rebuild their livelihoods, as well reconstructing entire communities and infrastructure. Tackling the underlying causes of poverty has emerged as one of the main challenges facing those countries. Tourism and fisheries, two industries that provide a large number of low-skill jobs, were particularly hard-hit. The loss of manpower, fishing fleets and infrastructure such as hatcheries and fishing ports in particular will be an obstacle to economic recovery in coastal communities in all the affected countries. However, reconstruction also provides Governments with an opportunity to ensure that future development of devastated coastal areas will embody greater respect for the environment and for human safety. Involving all parties in the affected communities in a participatory planning process will enable needs to be more clearly identified, priorities more clearly set and local ownership more clearly established, not only of the reconstruction process itself but also of the environment. An opportunity also exists to help some areas to make a quantum leap in their development. For example, illustrating the scope for South-South cooperation within the ESCAP region, Indonesia and Malaysia are jointly formulating plans drawing on the latter's experience with building its new capital city to reconstruct the devastated city of Banda Aceh in a manner that will protect it from similar disasters in the future while at the same time respecting its Islamic heritage.

In this region avian influenza is a continuing risk

As well as being responsive to financial risks, the region also has to be alert to risks arising from communicable diseases that can create both economic and social shocks as SARS did in 2002. A continuing risk in the next few years is avian influenza, or bird flu, which has the potential to lead to significant setbacks to growth in the short term. In the view of many experts, the chances of eradicating the disease are slim because it has become endemic in the region. As a result, bird flu is likely to plague the poultry industry and consumer confidence in some countries in the region for most of 2005 and beyond. This is again an area where cooperation, both regional and international, has a significant role to play, particularly South-South cooperation, in helping some of the poorer countries in the region to develop the capacity to respond to the illness. For example, Thailand has been assisting its neighbours in building up capacity to identify the bird flu virus and in techniques used to contain outbreaks. The outbreaks of avian influenza in 2004 and early 2005, while less serious and more contained than in 2003, continued to cause human deaths in South-East Asia and the future evolution of the virus remains uncertain. The risk that the disease could give rise to a major human influenza pandemic cannot be discounted.

Developing economies in the subregion

East and North-East Asia

Sustained strong growth in China

Overall growth in the subregion in 2004 climbed to 7.5 per cent, 1.3 percentage points higher than in 2003. Hong Kong, China, and Taiwan Province of China recovered very strongly while China, the largest economy in the subregion, outperformed the already robust growth recorded in 2003. Other economies maintained steady growth. In common with the other subregions of ESCAP, inflation picked up in 2004 and is expected to stay high in 2005. On the external side, the current account balances are expected to narrow in 2005 on the back of higher oil prices.

Prospects for the subregion are intimately bound up with the impact of measures that the Chinese Government is currently taking to slow down the economy in 2005 and whether, as a result, China's economy experiences a "soft" landing. The Chinese authorities have already tightened credit policy and are restricting land to cool investment since ample liquidity and low interest rates triggered a massive investment boom in the economy in 2004. Such measures are, however, likely to act only after a time lag and there has been a reluctance to raise interest rates until recently. The consensus of opinion is that China's economy should decelerate gradually to a more sustainable pace in 2005 and beyond and would thus provide ample policy space for countries and economies in the subregion, and indeed in the wider ESCAP region, to adjust. However, there is a need for authorities in China to introduce greater flexibility in establishing and implementing interest and exchange rate policies and to continue with reform measures. While the fiscal situation is not currently a matter of concern in most countries of the subregion, steps to ensure fiscal soundness may be necessary in Hong Kong, China.

North and Central Asia

Oil prices dominate the economic scene in Central Asian economies

Data for 2004 indicate that this subregion enjoyed another year of buoyant growth, although marginally slower than the pace attained in 2003. Price pressures abated although the rate of inflation remains high, while current account balances deteriorated somewhat as imports grew faster than exports. However, Kazakhstan, the Russian Federation, Turkmenistan and Uzbekistan, four economies that are large producers and exporters of oil and gas, benefited from higher world oil prices. Prospects for 2005 in the subregion are for a continuation of current trends with the probability of a moderation in output growth as oil and other commodity prices ease in the months ahead.

The energy sector has been the main driver of growth over much of the subregion, accounting for approximately one third of GDP and over one half of exports in Kazakhstan and the Russian Federation. However, a backlog of investment in pipeline and port capacity and more generally in energy infrastructure is limiting growth in this sector, at least in the short term. In addition, despite reforms in recent years, the non-oil sectors of the economy are not yet a viable alternative source of growth. A major issue of concern in this subregion, which the current phase of high oil prices has served to mask, is the slow progress in the economies in diversifying away from a dependence on oil and gas and a few other commodities. This limits the possibilities for more broad-based growth once the current phase of high energy prices draws to a close. Greater integration into the regional and global economies will be needed for success in diversification and currently six economies in the subregion are engaged in negotiations to accede to WTO while three others have joined that body. At the regional level, cooperation continues through CIS.

Pacific island economies

Higher commodity prices sustain growth in Pacific island economies

Real GDP growth continued at a modest pace in 2004 in Pacific island economies. Higher prices for commodity exports, including oil in the case of Papua New Guinea, supported positive growth. Tourism benefited from stronger growth in Australia and New Zealand, boosting the construction industry. Improved economic management has resulted in reduced budget deficits and lower public debt and, as a result, monetary management has been able to improve inflation performance greatly. The increase in oil prices could jeopardize this progress if it is maintained in 2005. The outlook for 2005 is for a slowdown in economic growth, as commodity prices decline, but for a slight pickup in inflation. Higher export receipts combined with an increased inflow of remittances, assisted in some cases by inflows of ODA, have enabled official reserves to be built up in the Pacific island economies, providing ample import cover.

A notable feature of economies in this subregion is that macroeconomic stabilization has not resulted in faster economic growth so far, principally owing to the absence of an investor-friendly environment. Political instability is a major contributor to the poor climate for investment as are corruption and law and order problems. Infrastructure costs are also relatively high in Pacific island economies and services are often poor, leading some countries to turn to privatization as a possible solution to these problems. Insufficient attention to rural development continues to undermine efforts at poverty reduction in the subregion and contributes to the rural-urban drift. Public sector reforms to improve governance have been ongoing in the Pacific for several years but results so far have been mixed. Improvements in governance are, however, also required in the private sector. Finally, policies to ensure sustainable development and prevent the overexploitation of natural resources are urgently needed, and regional cooperation, illustrated, for example, by the Convention on the Conservation and Management of Highly Migratory Fish Stocks in the Western and Central Pacific Ocean, which came into force in June 2004, offers the Pacific island economies a way to address these concerns.

South and South-West Asia

South Asian prospects remain positive despite adverse natural developments

Good weather resulted in a strong agricultural performance in South Asia in 2003. Buoyant farm incomes fed into strong growth in both manufacturing and services and gave the subregion, in particular India, one of its best growth outcomes of recent years. Less favourable weather in India, Pakistan and Sri Lanka in 2004 have undermined domestic output growth, which will now also have to absorb the higher costs of oil. In 2005, should the global economy experience a loss of momentum, exports from the subregion, too, would be adversely affected. Prospects for 2005 indicate that growth should continue at, or very close to, its current pace in most countries with the exception of Turkey. However, GDP growth is expected to be 1 per cent lower than predicted earlier in Sri Lanka owing to the tsunami. In India, in particular, growth has become more broad-based and on the evidence of 2004 the loss of momentum following the below-average rainfall in the north-west of the country is expected to be minimal.

All the economies in this subregion have benefited in recent years from structural reform programmes that have sought to stabilize and improve macroeconomic fundamentals and provide production incentives for both agriculture and manufacturing on a sustained basis. However, success in this regard has been uneven. There has been substantial progress on the external front with stable exchange rates, high reserves and improved current account positions. On the domestic side, progress has been less substantial. Fiscal consolidation has made limited headway and with interest rates now moving up the effect on the budget of a higher burden of debt servicing could be a matter of some concern. Rising inflation in some countries is another concern as it may necessitate further monetary tightening in the near future. Also, the ending of the MFA from 1 January 2005 will pose a major challenge for some countries.

Among the least developed countries in the subregion, economic growth improved modestly with the exception of Afghanistan, where it slowed considerably as a result of the adverse impact of weather on the agricultural sector. Bangladesh also suffered from the effects of flooding.

As noted earlier, Maldives was devastated by the tsunami in December 2004 and this will have a severe impact on its performance in 2005. Furthermore, political events in a number of these least developed countries are expected to influence progress in 2005. Inflation in the least developed countries of South Asia was generally lower in 2004 except for Bangladesh, partly owing to the gradual appreciation of national currencies against the dollar; the appreciation also partially buffered these countries against the sharp increase in petroleum prices.

Some measures recently implemented by countries in South Asia have facilitated their economic integration. For example, India, Bangladesh and Myanmar agreed to the construction of a pipeline that will transport natural gas from Myanmar, via Bangladesh, to India to meet the anticipated increased demand for energy. In addition to direct gains from transit fees and construction-related investment through this project, Bangladesh is also expected to gain access to markets in India's north-eastern states, to trade transit routes to Nepal and Bhutan through India and to hydroelectric power sources in Nepal and Bhutan through India's power grid. India also recently agreed to import 78 items duty-free, covering 75 per cent of categories of goods exported from Bangladesh. By creating a subregional market for exports, the agreements have enabled the countries to benefit from long-term integration. As a result of increased trade liberalization and economic integration in South Asia, both exports from and imports to these countries have grown rapidly in recent years. Despite the expiry of the MFA, the external sector is therefore expected to become an increasingly important source of economic growth particularly for the least developed countries in the subregion.

South-East Asia

Growth to ease in South-East Asia in 2005

GDP growth in South-East Asia in 2004 exceeded expectations and improved on 2003 growth by the wide margin of 1.5 percentage points. All the developing economies in the subregion, with the exception of Brunei Darussalam, where oil and gas output was affected by maintenance, and Thailand, which had performed very strongly in 2003, improved upon 2003 performance, with Singapore experiencing the sharpest rebound. Growth was broadly based in most countries and manufacturing, in particular, benefited from the upturn in the electronics cycle and strong export demand. With the exception of Indonesia, where fuel subsidies have sheltered consumers, moderate inflationary pressures have emerged in recent months in most countries as a result of higher food and energy prices. These pressures were particularly strong in the Philippines and Viet Nam. It is worth noting that while high commodity prices have boosted several economies in the subregion, with Indonesia, Malaysia and Viet Nam benefiting from the higher prices, the use of oil price subsidization in several countries, particularly Indonesia, Malaysia and Thailand, is likely to pose a difficult fiscal problem before too long.

Export demand from China, the EU and the United States has been supported by domestic demand for manufactured goods, especially cars and household electronics, and housing in the developing countries of the subregion. While these factors are, by and large, expected to continue into 2005, a weakening in the external environment could trigger a slowdown or even a reversal of the current buoyancy in corporate investment expenditures that were an encouraging feature of growth in 2004. In addition, a rise in interest rates could slow consumer spending in the area of household electronics purchased on credit. While the earthquake and tsunami disaster lowered expected growth in 2005 somewhat in Thailand, Indonesia is still expecting GDP growth to increase in the next year. For the subregion, prospects for 2005 point to an easing of the collective GDP growth rate of around 0.7 per cent. In this context, it is worth stressing that Indonesia, the Philippines and Thailand are the most vulnerable to high oil prices in the months ahead.

Current account surpluses narrowed as a percentage of GDP in most developing countries in South-East Asia and official reserves also tended to increase, particularly in Malaysia and Singapore. There is a general view that financial and corporate restructuring has been largely completed in the subregion, while budget deficits have narrowed or, as in Thailand, the budget has remained in surplus. Better job creation and faster economic growth have helped to reduce poverty incidence in the subregion but policy makers continue to be preoccupied with the task of increasing the competitiveness of their economies, in part through greater public investment in infrastructure.

In the least developed countries in South-East Asia, economic growth continues to vary widely from year to year as these countries are often adversely affected by developments in the agricultural sector. Since the agricultural sector employs a significant portion of the labour force, greater investment as well as introduction of formal land titles, formal financial services, modern farming techniques and public health services are essential in order to ensure poverty reduction, especially in rural areas. Furthermore, the expiry of the MFA is expected to affect industrial and export growth adversely in both Cambodia and the Lao People's Democratic Republic. Owing to greater exchange rate stability as well as prudent monetary policies, inflation tended to be lower in all of these countries, with the exception of Myanmar, although the rise in oil prices was beginning to feed into the general price level. As the least developed countries in the subregion have continued to develop economically, additional measures have been introduced to increase revenue from domestic sources to cover current fiscal expenditure.

Developed countries of the region

Australia, Japan and New Zealand

Improved growth in developed regional economies

After the recent revision of economic data from Japan, it seems clear that there was a shallow recovery in 2003 in that country after years of stagnation and that despite a loss in momentum in the second half of the year, growth in 2004 was very much stronger but lower than previously thought. Growth also accelerated in New Zealand while remaining substantially unchanged in Australia in 2004, supported by buoyant domestic demand and high commodity prices. All three countries experienced falling unemployment and improved business and consumer confidence in 2004 but economic growth is expected to moderate in 2005 if the external environment weakens and uncertainty remains about the sustainability of domestic demand. Deflationary pressures eased in Japan but firm evidence that deflation has ended is still awaited. The Japanese current account surplus, which has been increasing as a percentage of GDP, rose further in 2004 but the fiscal deficit continues to present a daunting challenge. Fiscal positions in both Australia and New Zealand remained strong in 2004 but monetary policy was tightened in the latter in the face of a build-up of price pressures in recent months and additional measures are expected if oil prices remain high. The boom in the housing market appears to have passed its peak in Australia and inflation was subdued but some pickup in inflation is expected in both countries in the short term. Current account deficits, which have widened in recent years, have remained uncomfortably large in Australia and New Zealand and the high oil price will thus pose a challenge for both.

Near-term policy issues for the region

Is the current slowdown mainly cyclical?

Against this overall background, the first question with significant policy connotations in the region is whether the projected slowdown in the global economy expected by most Governments and international and regional multilateral bodies in 2005 will prove to be only a brief hiatus in a longer-term upswing of the global economy or whether it might presage the onset of a longer period of adjustment aggravated by oil prices that remain chronically high into the foreseeable future. Higher oil prices, in turn, risk higher inflation and higher interest rates. The second question has to do with the future course of oil prices. Here, there is a degree of uncertainty that might of itself feed back negatively into business and personal spending decisions. Finally, given China's central and growing influence on regional economic prospects, the question whether it can successfully manage moderation of what is considered, within and outside China, to be an unsustainably fast growth rate will loom large in the judgements that policy makers might be faced with in the near-term future. It should, however, be recognized that none of the issues outlined above are directly amenable to policy action at the national level in the region; they simply represent the environment within which national Governments will have to operate in the months ahead.

Prior to the sharp convulsions in the oil markets that began in mid-2004, there was widespread confidence that the global recovery that began in 2003 would be sustained and, indeed, even gather strength, in 2004 and beyond. This optimistic view tended, on the whole, to ignore the ongoing conflict in Iraq and the uncomfortably large size of global current account imbalances. Optimism was based on the perception that the Iraq conflict that had begun in 2003 had failed to act as more than an irritant to overall consumer and business confidence. It had failed, moreover, to affect the oil markets seriously. This is no longer the case. The problem of global imbalances, meanwhile, had bedevilled the world economy for three years or more without acting as a visible drag on levels of activity in either the developed or developing economies. It was thus not unreasonable to assume that significant upheavals from the latter source could be avoided in 2004 and 2005 if the dollar depreciated gradually.

By mid-2004, however, evidence emerged that both the United States and Japanese economies were slowing down. In the United States, to the current account deficit had been added an equally large fiscal deficit. There was a new realization that the low interest rate environment was likely to end sooner rather than later and, when it happened, how would holders of household and corporate debt in the United States react? Could the dollar exchange rate further depreciate in 2005? In Japan, the recovery to date had been mainly export-driven; with slowing growth in the United States, how long could the recovery be sustained? On the domestic side, deflationary pressures were stubbornly persistent, domestic demand remained fragile and corporate and financial sector restructuring was far from complete. And, looming large behind these potential difficulties lies Japan's massive public sector debt (discussed further in chapter II) and how fiscal consolidation might impact upon the Japanese economy and private consumption demand. The broad conclusion is that the global upswing was far from being durable even before oil prices rose sharply in mid-2004. It had a number of fragile components, any one of which could fall prey to a significant outside shock, such as a prolonged period of volatile oil prices.

Dealing with high oil price volatility

In the early months of 2005 oil prices moved in the \$40-\$50 per barrel range, double what they had been in nominal terms two years previously and some \$15 more than in January 2004.[13] In March 2005, even this range had been exceeded and the price of oil approached \$55

---

[13] IMF, *World Economic Outlook, September 2004: The Global Demographic Transition* (Washington, IMF, 2004) and United Nations, *World Economic Situation and Prospects 2005* (United Nations publication, Sales No E.05.II.C.2).

per barrel. Oil prices in real terms are still well below the levels they reached in the oil shocks of 1973 and 1981, but their high levels in 2004 and at the beginning of 2005 are almost certainly going to affect global growth in due course. Many causes on both the demand and supply sides can be adduced to explain the rise in oil prices: the massive increase in Chinese demand in 2004 is one and low stocks of crude and refined products are another.

How long might this uncertainty last? A precise answer is difficult, if not impossible, but the following might provide some useful clues. Analytically, the most relevant way to look at oil prices is as a tax on producers and consumers alike. In the short run, demand for oil is not very price-elastic so that even a doubling of prices does not change consumption much. The challenge for policy makers is how best to deal with the ensuing situation in which high oil prices are instrumental in both lowering output and increasing inflation: should they counter the lower output or fight higher inflation? If nominal interest rates remain unchanged, the rise in inflation lowers real interest rates, resulting in an implicit policy-easing. While this should neutralize the risk of output reduction, it risks raising inflation further. Thus, until some way is found to stabilize oil prices, monetary policy has to confront such policy dilemmas as raising interest rates in an otherwise weakening economy. Oil prices are likely to remain volatile until these competing policy objectives are aligned and reduce the pressure on available supplies from the demand side or, alternatively, some new source of supplies can be tapped. In other words, there is no effective way of dealing with high and volatile oil prices in the short term and/or by national policy initiatives alone, other than the standard prescriptions of conservation and energy-saving exhortations. Superficially at least, there appears to be a theoretical case for Governments in the ESCAP region to cooperate to create an oil reserve along the lines of the United States Strategic Petroleum Reserve, whose practical modalities are worth investigating.

Changing role of the Chinese economy

With a spectacular real GDP growth rate of 8.2 per cent a year on average between 1998 and 2004, China's economy has played a major role in driving and sustaining growth in the ESCAP region. China has emerged as a production base for the region's exports to the rest of the world and as a final export market. Asian countries have been supplying raw materials, semi-manufactured goods and machinery to serve China's role as the manufactory for much of Asia's exports. Indeed, soaring domestic demand, fuelled by low interest rates and the easy availability of credit, has stimulated strong import growth. Imports doubled over the last three years to reach an extraordinary $561 billion in 2004.[14]

---

14 "IMF concludes 2004 Article IV Consultation with the People's Republic of China", available at web site <www.imf.org/external/np/sec/pn/2004/pn0499.htm>, 27 August 2004.

Is China's growth rate sustainable?

A question to pose is whether the growth is sustainable? During 2004 the Chinese authorities took a number of steps, largely in the form of administrative controls and a small increase in interest rates, to moderate the pace of growth. The fact that the high growth in that year was achieved under conditions of low inflation and that industrial production growth appears to have slowed seems to suggest that the administrative measures are beginning to work. The overinvestment in certain sectors, creating bottlenecks in the energy and transport sectors in particular, might take time to respond to the measures taken so far. Even if investment levels in industries such as steel and cement have been falling, headline GDP growth has remained intact, helped by rising private disposable income and consumption and exports.

A gradual slowdown is generally expected in 2005 and 2006 as the pace of fixed investment falls as part of China's cyclical adjustment. What is more important is the pace at which the Chinese economy decelerates as this can have a major impact on commodity prices and on regional suppliers of finished goods and equipment. According to an IMF study, a 10 per cent decline in China's import growth for domestic use arising from a slowdown in domestic investment can result in a 0.4 per cent drop in GDP growth for the region, although some countries would be more affected than others.[15]

Balancing inflation and growth involve difficult judgements: can inflation-targeting help?

One clear lesson from the past is that while central banks cannot prevent oil prices from giving a one-off boost to inflation they must prevent them from feeding into higher wages and prices. The cyclical position of the economy will play a critical role in the conduct of monetary policy: the less slack there is in an economy the bigger the risk that oil prices will feed quickly into higher prices. Hence, in economies operating at close to potential the case for a pre-emptive tightening of monetary policy, in the face of a sharp rise in oil prices, is very strong. This would involve difficult judgements between controlling inflation and preserving the momentum of output growth. In addition, it would be useful for Governments and central banks to have clarity of purpose with respect to inflation. Inflation-targeting, a monetary framework with a pre-defined quantitative inflation target as a guide for macroeconomic policy-making, particularly for short-term interest rate expectations, has been offered as one solution whose time is ripe. Its key attribute is that economic policy can achieve better results if the authorities can commit themselves to a pre-established set of credible policy rules. Five countries in the region, Australia, New Zealand, the Philippines, the Republic of Korea and Thailand, have adopted it in varying forms and one, Indonesia, has stated its intent to do so. Those supporting it argue that it could be

---

[15] IMF, *People's Republic of China – Staff Report for the 2004 Article IV Consultation* (Washington, IMF, 6 July 2004).

brought into play in the current low inflationary environment so that market participants are aware of the future direction and pace of interest rate changes. However, many countries are either not yet ready or hesitate to introduce it for various reasons. First, while one decade or so of its introduction in over 20 countries offers useful lessons on its implementation and conduct of monetary policy, there are still unresolved issues relating to its design and implementation, particularly in terms of flexibility in a dynamic global environment; second, there is the view that inflation-targeting ties a Government's hands in promoting growth-enhancing objectives; and, third, there are questions whether countries targeting inflation have better macroeconomic outcomes than those that use other means to achieve similar objectives. Nevertheless, its proponents argue that inflation-targeting promotes both price stability and well-anchored inflation expectations and thereby facilitates stabilization of output and employment.[16]

What are the central policy messages for Governments in the region? First, oil prices have enhanced the phase of significant volatility. Furthermore, they are likely to remain under upward pressure for some time. They thus pose a threat to inflation and the uncertainty of their future course is likely to discourage investors from making significant commitments in the months ahead. Second, there is a distinct risk of the external environment deteriorating in the months ahead. Some loss of momentum was already taking place prior to the recent upheavals in the oil markets; the latter have made the likelihood of a slowdown, albeit marginal, more rather than less probable. Third, a weakening external environment, varying inflationary pressures in the region and a depreciating dollar would together pose a major challenge to maintaining growth and macroeconomic and exchange rate stability in the months ahead. Governments would thus need to assess their individual positions vis-à-vis inflation, growth, capacity utilization and their own fiscal situation before deciding upon the most appropriate course of action.

Addressing the supply side of oil

Several Governments in the region subsidize prices of oil products. Should oil prices remain high for some time, this will pose an impossible fiscal burden on them. There is a case, therefore, for re-examining the system of subsidization, to better target the subsidies and to endeavour to phase them out over a defined time-span as some Governments have begun to do. Subsidies tend to encourage overuse of the subsidized product and are usually proven to be unsustainable in the long run. As mentioned elsewhere, action is also needed to address the supply side of the oil question. While little can be done to increase supplies in the short term, Governments in the region should look into the practical aspects of

---

[16] Ben S. Bernanke, "A perspective on inflation targeting", Annual Washington Policy Conference of the National Association of Business Economists, 25 March 2003.

maintaining higher stocks of both crude and finished products and examine whether the main oil importers in the region could take more cooperative action in this area. At least some of the volatility in oil prices might be reduced as a result.

Longer-term development policy issues for the region

Tsunami disaster showed how ill prepared the region is in disaster management

The recent Asian tsunami catastrophe underscored the development challenges facing the region, despite remarkable economic progress. In the first instance, it showed the lack of a systematic disaster management framework including disaster mitigation measures in many countries, despite progress in flood risk management in some countries such as Bangladesh. The lack of readiness goes far beyond tsunamis. During the past four decades, in addition to loss of human lives and livelihoods, economic losses from natural hazards such as earthquakes, droughts, floods, storms and tropical cyclones, wild land fires and volcanic eruptions have increased almost 10 times.[17] Studies have shown that for every dollar spent on disaster reduction about $10 is saved by limiting the needs of subsequent relief, but research also shows that of all aid received for disasters, only 2 per cent goes on prevention. Much more attention therefore has to be given by policy makers to disaster prevention and preparedness, including systematically integrating multi-hazard risk management into planning and programming. Institutional strengthening and investments in infrastructure, early warning systems and evacuation procedures can improve disaster readiness. Some specific gaps have been identified in organizational, legal and policy frameworks, risk identification and assessment, monitoring and early warning systems, as well capacity and resource needs (box I.3).

Tsunami disaster also highlights continuing challenge of poverty reduction

The tsunami disaster also underscored the continuing challenge of poverty in the region, which is home to over 700 million poor persons, some two thirds of the world's poor, and where poverty incidence remains high in some countries (table I.6). It also highlighted the importance of handling vulnerability to achieve a sustainable reduction in poverty as required by the first Millennium Development Goal. Any progress made in poverty reduction can be easily wiped out not only by an economic crisis, such as the 1997 financial crisis, when some 30 million became suddenly poor, but also by natural disasters. Indeed, according to the ADB, 2 million additional persons joined the ranks of the "new poor" in the tsunami catastrophe in addition to loss of livelihoods of people on the brink of poverty.[18] A more proactive approach is required to inform,

---

[17] Munich Re Group, "Natural catastrophes – the current position", at web site <www..munichre.com/publications/302-02354-en.pdf>, 4 February 2005.

[18] ADB, "An initial assessment of the impact of the earthquake and tsunami of December 26, 2004 on South and Southeast Asia", January 2005.

Box I.3. World Conference on Disaster Reduction and early warning systems

At the World Conference on Disaster Reduction, held in Kobe, Japan, in January 2005, countries pledged to reduce the risks facing millions of people who are exposed to natural disasters. Reducing disaster risks, poverty reduction, sustainable development and good governance are mutually supportive objectives and efforts to reduce disaster risks must be systematically integrated into development and poverty reduction policies and programmes.

Seizing the momentum of urgency for action on disaster reduction following the earthquake and tsunami disaster in the Indian Ocean in December 2004, the Conference adopted the Hyogo Framework for Action 2005-2015, calling on States to integrate disaster risk into political agendas and national policies. According to the Framework, disaster risks arise when hazards interact with physical, social, economic and environmental vulnerabilities. While natural disasters cannot be avoided, investing in disaster preparedness can reduce vulnerability and, thus, disaster risks. In view of the need to strengthen the capacity of disaster-prone countries to address these risks and invest more in disaster preparedness, the Framework set the following priorities for action:

- Ensure that disaster risk reduction is a national and a local priority with a strong institutional basis for implementation;
- Identify, assess and monitor disaster risks and enhance early warning;
- Use knowledge, innovation and education to build a culture of safety and resilience at all levels;
- Reduce the underlying risk factors;
- Strengthen disaster preparedness for an effective response at all levels.

An early warning system is an important component of multi-hazard disaster preparedness and the painful experience from the recent tsunami disaster of the consequences stemming from the lack of such a system has underlined the need for early action at the regional and global levels to institute such a system. Early warning systems require (a) prior knowledge of the risks faced by communities, (b) technical monitoring of, and a warning service for, these risks, (c) dissemination of understandable warnings to those at risk and (d) knowledge, public awareness and preparedness to act in the event of a risk occurring.[a] Early warning systems require substantial international coordination to function properly, linking existing systems with new systems still to be constructed, building on regional and global initiatives and involving all stakeholders with different expertise and responsibilities.

The role of international organizations in these early warning systems is increasingly recognized as crucial for effective and sustainable operations in such initiatives. The launch during the Conference of the United Nations International Early Warning Programme, which had been proposed at the Second International Conference on Early Warning Systems, held in Bonn in October 2003, aims to improve resilience to all types of natural hazards including droughts, wild fires, floods, tropical cyclones, landslides, volcanic eruptions and tsunamis. This global-level initiative will include more widespread information flows and emphasize the importance of people-centred early warning systems as well as community education about disaster preparedness.

In response to the tsunami disaster in the Indian Ocean, the participants in the Kobe Conference pledged their support for creating a regional tsunami early warning system in the Indian Ocean, emphasizing the importance of international and regional cooperation. The new warning system will draw on the experience of the Pacific Ocean tsunami early warning system, making use of the existing coordination mechanism of the Intergovernmental Oceanographic Commission of UNESCO. During the Ministerial Meeting on Regional Cooperation on Tsunami Early Warning Arrangements held in Phuket, Thailand, at the end of January 2005, Governments in the region agreed to support the establishment of a disaster-monitoring centre with the United Nations taking a lead role.

---

[a] "Draft common statement of the special session on the Indian Ocean disaster: risk reduction for a safer future" (A/CONF.206/L.6/Rev.1).

Table I.6. Percentage of the population below the $1 per day poverty line in selected countries, 1990-2003

	1990	*1991*	*1992*	*1993*	*1994*	*1995*	*1996*	*1997*	*1998*	*1999*	*2000*	*2001*	*2002*	*2003*
Armenia	..	..	..	..	..	..	7.8	..	12.8	..	..	..	..	..
Azerbaijan	..	..	..	..	..	<2.0	..	..	..	..	..	3.7	..	..
Bangladesh	..	..	35.9	..	..	..	29.1	..	..	..	36.0	..	..	..
Cambodia	48.3	..	..	..	..	..	36.7	38.4	39.4	41.5	43.4	43.0	45.5	42.2
China	31.5	..	..	29.0	..	..	16.4	..	16.1	17.4	15.4	14.3	12.9	11.7
Georgia	..	..	..	..	..	..	0.0	..	0.0	2.6	..	2.7	..	..
India	42.1	..	..	42.3	..	..	42.2	..	..	34.7	..	..	..	..
Indonesia	20.6	..	..	14.8	..	..	7.8	..	..	12.0	9.9	9.2	7.2	5.7
Kazakhstan	0.1[a]	..	..	1.1	..	..	1.5	..	..	..	..	0.1	..	..
Kyrgyzstan	0.0[a]	..	..	23.0	..	..	..	1.6	..	0.7	2.0	0.9	..	..
Lao People's Democratic Republic	53.0	..	48.8	..	..	..	41.3	38.4	39.6	36.7	33.9	31.3	29.0	26.9
Malaysia	2.0	..	1.5	..	..	1.0	0.8	<0.5	<0.5	<0.5	<0.5	<0.5	<0.5	<0.5
Mongolia	..	..	..	..	..	13.9	..	..	..	..	..	..	..	..
Nepal	..	..	..	..	..	37.7	..	..	..	..	..	..	..	..
Pakistan	47.8	..	..	33.9	..	..	31.0	..	..	..	..	..	..	..
Papua New Guinea	35.4	..	..	..	..	..	24.6	25.6	27.8	30.7	35.3	38.0	39.2	39.4
Phillippines	18.3	19.1	..	..	19.8	..	18.4	14.8	12.1	13.7	13.5	13.5	11.9	11.1
Republic of Korea	<0.5	<0.5	<0.5	<0.5	<0.5	<0.5	<0.5	<0.5	<0.5	<0.5	<0.5	<0.5	<0.5	<0.5
Russian Federation	0.0[a]	..	..	6.2	..	..	7.2	..	7.1	..	6.1	..	..	..
Sri Lanka	3.8	..	..	..	..	6.6	..	..	..	..	..	..	..	
Tajikistan	..	..	..	..	..	..	..	..	10.3	..	..	..	..	..
Thailand	12.5	..	6.0	..	..	..	2.2	..	3.3	3.1	5.2	3.6	2.4	1.6
Turkmenistan	0.0[a]	..	..	20.9	..	..	..	..	12.1	..	..	..	..	..
Uzbekistan	0.0[a]	..	..	3.3	..	..	..	..	19.1	..	21.8	..	..	..
Viet Nam	50.8	..	..	39.9	..	..	23.6	..	16.4	16.9	15.2	14.6	13.6	10.9

Sources: World Bank, *East Asia Update,* November 2004, <http://siteresources.worldbank.org/INTEAPHALFYEARLYUPDATE/Resources/EAPupdatesfinalNov04.pdf>, 17 February 2005; global poverty monitoring web site <http://www.worldbank.org/research/povmonitor>, 14 September 2004; and *World Development Indicators 2004* (CD-ROM).

[a] 1988 data.

motivate and involve people in all aspects of disaster risk reduction and restoration of livelihood in their own local communities. Disaster-prone developing countries, especially least developed countries and small island developing States, warrant particular attention in view of their greater vulnerability and risk levels, which often greatly exceed their capacity to respond to and recover from disasters.

Shifts in attitudes and priorities necessary to meet the Millennium Development Goals

While most countries in the Asia-Pacific region are making progress to meet the target of halving income poverty by 2015, they are nevertheless, likely to miss many of the non-income goals. Hundreds of millions of poor people still lack access to basic services. Furthermore, those services are often delivered inefficiently and inequitably and create wide disparities between social groups. For instance, 1.9 billion people in the region lack access to improved sanitation and 678 million to clean water. Malnutrition and hunger continue to make achieving the goal of halving hunger levels by 2015 difficult despite the region's dynamism in food production and growth. Meanwhile, the slow progress on health-related Millennium Development Goals, in particular child and maternal mortality, continue to compound the difficulty of achieving the goals related to poverty. Reaching the targets within and across countries will demand both more resources, national and international, as well as a radical shift in attitudes, priorities and policies for ensuring equitable, effective and sustainable basic services.

Better understanding of pro-poor growth policies needed

These developments underscore the need to strengthen pro-poor growth strategies and service delivery. Despite considerable discussions and debate, agreement on the precise nature of pro-poor growth is still lacking in the region. In general, for growth to become more pro-poor, it must have a dual character. It needs to be rapid enough to reduce absolute income poverty significantly. It should also improve the relative position of the poor by achieving greater equity in income and access to a wide range of social services. Policy makers need to be concerned not only with the rate of growth but also with its structure and quality. Indeed pro-poor policies imply that the economic and social conditions of the poor improve more rapidly than those of the rest of society because poverty has a relative dimension. Unless Governments take timely corrective action, economic growth can become lopsided and divisive.

Achievement of the twin challenges of reviving growth and reducing inequality has high priority on the policy agenda of the region. Economic growth is not sustainable without human development. For policy makers, the focus must be on strengthening the links between growth and human development. Some of the most important issues are employment opportunities, access to productive assets, public spending for the provision of basic social services, gender equality, population policy and good governance. Determined efforts are needed to avoid growth that is jobless, meaning economic growth that does not expand employment opportunities.

Sharp increases in youth unemployment

In the area of employment, an urgent issue of concern is youth unemployment, which has increased sharply both in Asia and the Pacific and worldwide over the past decade. Across the globe, some 88 million young people between the ages of 15 and 24 are unemployed, representing nearly half the world's jobless. Of this total, 38 million are in the Asian region and regional trends are further causes for worry. In South-East Asia, the youth unemployment figure of 10 million is more than double that of a decade ago and the 104 per cent increase is significantly greater than the global average increase of 26 per cent. In East Asia, the 2003 figure represents an increase of 21 per cent on the 1993 figure of 9 million. In South Asia, youth unemployment also increased 21 per cent, from around 14 million in 1993 to 17 million in 2003. The growth in the numbers of young people is rapidly outstripping the ability of economies to provide them with jobs. In the future, the challenge of creating employment will continue to depend on the rate of economic growth as well as on an improvement in its employment content, in addition to its pro-poor orientation. Indeed, for some countries high youth unemployment is a wasted opportunity for reaping the "demographic dividend", an issue taken up in chapter III.

The importance of good physical infrastructure, such as transport facilities, ports and public utilities, is well known and does not require reiteration here. With regard to social infrastructure, much neglected in the past, its importance is now increasingly recognized within the broad rubric of governance. Social infrastructure is not merely the efficient operation of key institutions of governance, such as the legal system, the financial system and education and health delivery agencies, but an underlying "social contract" that defines relations between the individual and the community and between the citizens and the State. The lack of such a social contract can gravely undermine the public good; equally, the existence of one can significantly reduce the need for more formal and quasi-legalistic arrangements that often do not work at all, or work poorly, in practice in most developing economies. The poor, for example, reduce their vulnerabilities not through insurance mechanisms but through the access they have to the informal institutions of the larger community.

It is well recognized that raising the productivity of investment, both public and private, is the key to successful long-term development. Some countries get both the levels and the composition of investment right and achieve high rates of economic growth. Other countries invest too much through the public sector and crowd out private investment. Yet others invest too little through the public sector – a problem manifested in poor educational facilities, poor infrastructure and poor public institutions generally – an approach that reduces the efficiency of overall investment in the economy and reduces its long-term growth potential. While the paucity of public resources is driving many countries to involve the private sector in the provision of public services, at the root of the problem is the choice between what is best left to public provision and what is best provided by the private sector, in other words, what are the respective spheres for individuals, markets and communities, including the State.

What is the role of the private sector in providing public goods?

Beginning with the 1980s but gathering pace since the 1990s, there has been an attempt to withdraw the State from activities where previously the public interest was equated with public ownership. With globalization and technology altering traditional distinctions between the public and private sectors, a new consensus is needed to redraw the lines between the two sectors and, indeed, to have another look at the public sector itself.

Agreeing on where markets have an enhanced role and where market failure has to be tackled seriously is therefore a critical prerequisite for forging such a consensus. To argue without qualification that the only kind of reform that is worth pursuing is some form of privatization of public enterprise negates the possibility of a proper debate on how a reformed public sector, especially in non-commercial areas, might contribute to the greater achievement of efficiency and equity in society, outcomes that are universally desired.

In the above context, it is worth stressing that markets are best regarded as a means and not as ends in themselves. There is no question that markets are good at efficiently creating productive assets but it is also true that they are less good at guaranteeing fairness. If the profit motive is the only incentive, markets will rarely provide public goods and, unless corrective measures are taken, markets will tend to widen inequality of access to public goods, like education and health, and lead eventually to greater social inequality, a recipe for chronic instability in society. It is worth remembering that any given economic system is not a discrete sphere of human activity. It is a reflection of the prevailing value system. Economic structures, in turn, generate values and outcomes that help to shape the social and political consensus. If these structures result in ever-widening inequalities, in the poor provision of public services and in a general lack of fairness, the implicit social contract will eventually break down, leading to endemic instability in society.

Role of government in improving competitiveness

Linkages between investment and productivity growth have been viewed through the lens of international competitiveness in recent years. Competitiveness can be applied at both the enterprise and the national levels. Not all countries can simultaneously improve competitiveness relative to other countries. Competitiveness is determined by both real and monetary factors. It may increase as a result of greater investment in productive assets or it may increase through a slower rise in unit labour costs, from an effective exchange rate depreciation or, more usually, from a combination of all three. The role that Governments can play in maintaining and enhancing competitiveness is either as a provider of public goods and social infrastructure or as an enabler of the process. In the latter case, Governments need to look beyond the provision of macroeconomic stability and properly functioning capital markets by encouraging innovation and investment in technology by enterprises. Whether particular activities are carried out in the public or private sector is less important than that they be performed efficiently and effectively.

Successful development is thus a multifaceted phenomenon. Achieving high rates of economic growth and high average per capita incomes is merely one part of the story; its obverse is social stability, which can only be achieved if the benefits of growth are shared equitably through the public provision of public services. In the final analysis, Governments must rely not only upon their own judgement but also equally upon the contribution that informed citizens can make in this regard. Development interventions should thus be viewed not only from the narrow perspective of output growth but also in terms of their impact on the social infrastructure. Social infrastructure does not exist in a vacuum; indeed, the nature and extent of interactions between individuals and society and between State institutions and citizens hold the key to the long-term development prospects of society.[19]

---

[19] M. Woolcock and Deepa Narayan, "Social capital: implications for development theory, research, and policy", *World Bank Research Observer*, vol. 15, No. 2, August 2000.

II MACROECONOMIC PERFORMANCE, ISSUES AND POLICIES

DEVELOPING ECONOMIES OF THE ESCAP REGION

East and North-East Asia

Subregional overview and prospects

Continued strong growth in the subregion

The economies of East and North-East Asia posted strong growth performance in 2004 (figure II.1), helped by a favourable external environment and deepening regional integration, which boosted exports. Domestic demand was also robust in all four economies of the subregion, with the exception of the Republic of Korea. China maintained robust economic growth in 2004 owing to strong export and investment demand. The rapid pace of expansion of China's $1.6 trillion

Figure II.1 Rates of GDP growth in selected East and North-East Asian economies, 2001-2004

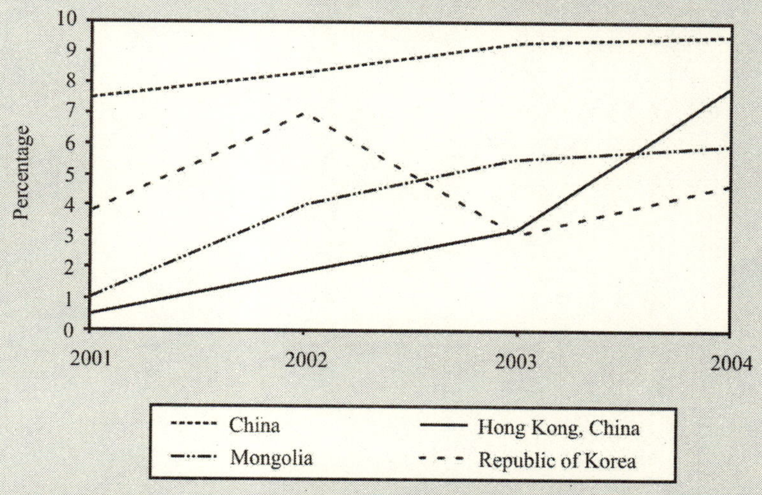

Sources: ESCAP, based on national sources; ADB, *Key Indicators of Developing Asian and Pacific Countries* 2004 (Manila, ADB, 2004); and EIU, *Country Forecasts* (London, EIU, 2004), various issues.

Note: Growth rates for 2004 are estimates.

economy raised concerns about overinvestment and led the Government to take measures to prevent overheating. Although quarterly data show some signs of softening investment, the overall upward trend in economic growth is likely to be sustained for some time. Growth in Hong Kong, China, accelerated in 2004 and the revived export performance contributed to improved business and consumer confidence, leading to greater investment and consumer spending. However, Hong Kong, China's rapid pace of economic growth is likely to slow in 2005. Mongolia also demonstrated robust economic growth in 2004, thanks to the strong performance of the mining sector, which benefited from higher world prices of copper and gold and sustained demand from China. Meanwhile, the growth rate of the Republic of Korea improved moderately in 2004 from a slump in the previous year. Despite the prolonged slowdown in private consumption and weak investment, economic expansion was sustained by exports, particularly to China. However, the overall growth rate of the Republic of Korea is expected to decline in 2005 owing to slowing exports.

Consumer price inflation was contained across the subregion in 2004, except for Mongolia, and there was a small amount of deflation in Hong Kong, China (figure II.2). All economies in the subregion maintained their budget balance as a percentage of GDP within a reasonable

Figure II.2. Inflation[a] in selected East and North-East Asian economies, 2001-2004

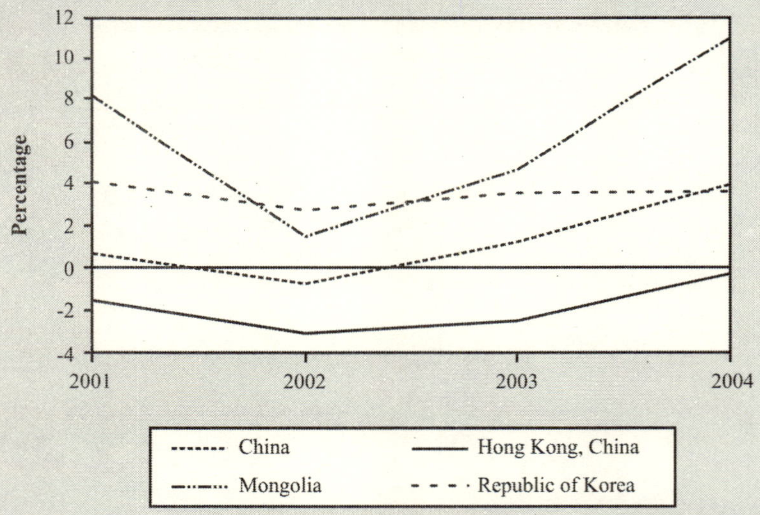

Sources: ESCAP, based on national sources; ADB, *Key Indicators of Developing Asian and Pacific Countries* 2004 (Manila, ADB, 2004); and EIU, *Country Forecasts* (London, EIU, 2004), various issues.

Note: Growth rates for 2004 are estimates.

[a] Changes in the consumer price index

range in 2004. Monetary policy was tightened in China compared with the previous year to cool down the investment boom, while easy monetary conditions were maintained in the Republic of Korea and Mongolia to stimulate domestic demand. The overall direction of economic policies in the subregion is likely to be preserved in the same way in 2005 as in the previous year. The favourable external environment in 2004 also helped all four economies in the subregion to maintain current account surpluses, with the exception of Mongolia.

GDP growth performance and outlook

Robust growth continues in China

The Chinese economy continued to perform strongly in 2004, when GDP growth reached 9.5 per cent (table II.1), higher than in 2003 and much higher than expectations, driven largely by expenditure on fixed investment and exports. After exceptionally rapid economic growth in the

Table II.1. Selected East and North-East Asian economies: growth rates, 2001-2004

(Percentage)

		Rates of growth			
		Gross domestic product	*Agriculture*	*Industry*	*Services*
China	2001	7.5	2.8	8.4	8.4
	2002	8.3	2.9	9.8	8.7
	2003	9.3	2.5	12.7	7.3
	2004	9.5	6.3	11.1	8.3
Hong Kong, China	2001	0.5	4.1	–3.7	1.6
	2002	1.9	–0.7	–3.7	3.0
	2003	3.2	2.0	–4.6	4.5
	2004	7.9	0.0	1.0	8.4
Mongolia	2001	1.0	–18.5	16.2	8.2
	2002	4.0	–10.7	5.4	12.2
	2003	5.5	4.5	1.2	8.6
	2004	6.0	..	..	..
Republic of Korea	2001	3.8	1.1	3.1	4.5
	2002	7.0	–3.5	6.4	8.0
	2003	3.1	–7.1	5.5	2.3
	2004	4.7	–5.0	9.0	4.1

Sources: ESCAP, based on national sources; National Bureau of Statistics of China, *China Statistical Yearbook 2004* (Beijing, China Statistics Press, 2004); ADB, *Key Indicators of Developing Asian and Pacific Countries 2004* (Manila, ADB, 2004); and EIU, *Country Forecasts* (London, EIU, 2004), various issues.

Notes: Growth rates for 2004 are estimates. Industry comprises mining and quarrying; manufacturing; electricity, gas and power; and construction.

last quarter of 2003 and the first half of 2004, when GDP growth was in the 9.7-9.9 per cent range, the overheated economy appeared to slow somewhat as a result of the Government's efforts to rein in the rapid pace of investment. The Government scaled back the fiscal stimulus and tightened monetary policy, using direct administrative measures aimed at restraining expansion in targeted activities. Liquidity was effectively controlled to contain inflation in the face of persistent injections from the large balance-of-payments surplus. Nevertheless, growth accelerated in the last quarter of 2004 owing to robust expansion in agriculture, catering, transport and other services, resulting in the unexpectedly high annual growth rate. The ratio of gross investment to GDP in China remains high and increased further to 45.7 per cent in 2004, exceeding the savings rate, which itself is rising fast, reaching 44.8 per cent (table II.2). A somewhat slower GDP growth rate of 8.5 per cent is expected in China in 2005.

Table II.2. Selected East and North-East Asian economies: ratios of gross domestic savings and investment to GDP, 2001-2004

(Percentage)

	2001	*2002*	*2003*	*2004*
Savings as a percentage of GDP				
China	39.4	40.7	42.7	44.8
Hong Kong, China	29.6	31.1	31.6	30.4
Mongolia	5.7	4.1	2.2	..
Republic of Korea	31.9	31.4	32.8	35.0
Investment as a percentage of GDP				
China	38.5	40.3	44.4	45.7
Hong Kong, China	25.9	23.4	22.8	23.8
Mongolia	35.8	29.0	31.1	..
Republic of Korea	29.3	29.1	29.4	29.3

Sources: ESCAP, based on national sources; ADB, *Key Indicators of Developing Asian and Pacific Countries 2004* (Manila, ADB, 2004); and EIU, *Country Forecasts* (London, EIU, 2004), various issues

Note: Figures for 2004 are estimates.

On the production side, the pace of industrial growth in China slackened somewhat to 11.1 per cent in 2004, down from 12.7 per cent in the previous year, while growth in the service sector accelerated to 8.3 per cent in 2004 after the slight slowdown in 2003. Profits of industrial enterprises, particularly in steel, chemicals, oil and communications products, grew rapidly in the first 8 months of 2004, increasing 38.5 per cent from a year earlier. The pace of earnings growth has, however, begun to ease.

Rural incomes improved in China

Agricultural production expanded by an impressive 6.3 per cent in China in 2004, after averaging 2.7 per cent annual growth in 2001-2003. There were some remarkable gains in grain production in 2004, when total output climbed to a record 469.5 million tons, reversing a five-year declining trend and exceeding the Government's output target of 455 million tons, which itself represented an increase of 20 million tons over 2003. The continuous shrinkage of grain production in previous years had raised concerns because the related shortages undermined the official goal of achieving basic national self-sufficiency in food. Promoting grain production had become a top priority for the Government, which adopted pro-rural policies to increase growing areas and provide direct subsidies to grain farmers, principally in designated major grain-producing areas. In 2004, the Government spent 11.6 billion yuan renminbi or $1.4 billion on such subsidies and the resulting increase in acreage for grain plants contributed to boosting grain output in 2004. The summer grain harvest was 4 per cent higher than in 2003, with some provinces recording growth rates ranging from 10 to 25 per cent, and the autumn harvest, which accounts for about 70 per cent of the total, appears to have been equally bountiful. Rural incomes will have benefited from both the subsidies and the higher output, and the revival of the rural economy could play an important role in rebalancing the overall economy away from investment towards consumption. About 60 per cent of China's total population still lives in rural areas and, despite low per capita income, rural residents still account for around 40 per cent of nationwide nominal private consumption.

Hong Kong, China's economy expanded rapidly as business confidence revived

The GDP growth rate of Hong Kong, China, soared to an estimated 7.9 per cent in 2004, 4.3 percentage points higher than the 3.2 per cent achieved in 2003. All expenditure components contributed to the economic acceleration. Private consumption expenditure increased by 8.5 per cent in the first half of 2004, contributing 4.9 percentage points to the GDP growth rate. Domestic consumer spending has gradually recovered since the third quarter of 2003 with a solid increase in tourism from China and in retail sales of durable goods. Following the stagnation in 2001-2002 and the recovery in 2003, buoyant growth in sales of durable goods such as motor vehicles suggests that consumers are becoming more optimistic and confident about the future. Investment expanded by 9.3 per cent in the first 6 months of 2004, contributing 2.4 percentage points to GDP growth. Investment in machinery, equipment and computer software soared to support the increased tempo of business activity but construction declined as a number of large private sector building projects and some railway projects were completed.

In recent years, growth in Hong Kong, China, has been heavily dependent on the service sector, which grew by a robust 8.4 per cent in 2004, substantially higher than in 2003. Industry managed to reverse the sharp contraction during 2001-2003 to expand by 1.0 per cent in 2004. The agricultural sector was unable to sustain the revival of 2003, when output expanded by 2 per cent, registering flat growth in 2004. Hong Kong, China's gross domestic savings ratio declined somewhat to 30.4 per cent in 2004, from 31.6 per cent in 2003, as consumer spending recovered. The gross investment ratio, which declined during 2001-2003, increased to 23.8 per cent in 2004 as business confidence returned. The outlook for GDP growth in 2005 in Hong Kong, China, is for a slowdown to about 5 per cent.

Strong performance in mining contributes to robust growth in Mongolia

A favourable external environment and progress in achieving macroeconomic stability in Mongolia benefited GDP growth, which is projected at around 6 per cent in 2004, up from 5.5 per cent in 2003 and continuing the upward trend of recent years. Higher world prices of copper and gold together with sustained demand for minerals, particularly copper, from China gave a strong boost to the mining sector, resulting in an investment boom in the minerals and mining sector that has yet to run its course. Construction benefited from the rapid development of the capital city, a trend that is likely to continue for some time. Sustained growth is also expected in the service sector as tourism recovers and demand for more sophisticated services expands with rising domestic incomes. An unchanged GDP growth rate of 6 per cent is forecast for 2005 in Mongolia.

Economic growth in the Republic of Korea moderately recovered

After a slump in 2003, the economy of the Republic of Korea began to recover in 2004. The GDP growth rate averaged 5.4 per cent year on year in the first two quarters of 2004 but a slowdown in the second half is expected to lead to overall growth for the year reaching 4.7 per cent, an improvement over the 3.1 per cent growth rate of 2003 but still well below the 7 per cent growth recorded in 2002. Sustained by export demand, industry recovered from the slowdown of 2003 and expanded at a rate of 9.0 per cent in 2004, while the agricultural sector continued its long-term decline, posting a 5.0 per cent contraction. The service sector recovered somewhat in 2004, growing at a rate of 4.1 per cent, but this was well below the 8 per cent growth of 2002.

GDP growth in the Republic of Korea was driven primarily by external demand as domestic demand continued to stagnate. Private consumption has not shown any signs of recovery yet, contracting in five out of six quarters since the second quarter of 2003. The weak performance of private consumption reflects the continuing heavy burden of a high level of household debt accumulated as a result of excessive credit card use in the past. Retail sales have been declining and demand for consumer durables remains weak. Recent growth in investment in machinery and equipment, at just over 6 per cent year on year commencing in the second quarter of 2004 after four consecutive quarters of decline, is encouraging but it remains to be seen whether this represents a sustained recovery of investment. The ratio of gross investment to GDP was little changed at 29.3 per cent in 2004 although the ratio of gross domestic savings to GDP continued the increase that began in 2003 and reached 35.0 per cent in 2004. The outlook for GDP growth in the Republic of Korea in 2005 is for a return to a slower rate of 4 per cent.

Inflation

Varied inflation performance in the subregion

The rate of increase in consumer prices in East and North-East Asia in 2004 was in a wide range between slight deflation in Hong Kong, China, and double-digit inflation in Mongolia (table II.3). In China, where deflation had once been a concern, inflation became an issue in 2004 as consumer prices increased by 3.9 per cent, or 2.7 percentage points faster than in 2003, owing mainly to sharp rises in food and fuel prices. Prices increased even more rapidly in rural areas, at a rate of 4.8 per cent, compared with urban areas, where the rate of inflation was 3.3 per cent in 2004. High oil prices and vigorous demand reflecting the economic boom led to increased prices of water, electricity and fuel while the hike in food prices partly reflected the low base of the previous year. Meanwhile, prices for clothing, household appliances and communications declined. Consumer prices softened in the second half of 2004 as food prices began to moderate but the rate of inflation is expected to remain around 4 per cent in 2005 owing to lagged effects from 2004.

Table II.3. Selected East and North-East Asian economies: inflation and money supply growth (M2), 2001-2004

(Percentage)

	2001	*2002*	*2003*	*2004*
Inflation[a]				
China	0.7	–0.8	1.2	3.9
Hong Kong, China	–1.6	–3.1	–2.5	–0.3
Mongolia	8.2	1.5	4.6	11.0
Republic of Korea	4.1	2.7	3.6	3.6
Money supply growth (M2)				
China	15.0	19.4	19.7	17.2
Hong Kong, China	–0.3	0.5	6.3	3.3
Mongolia	27.9	42.0	49.6	45.6[b]
Republic of Korea	13.2	11.0	6.7	10.0

Sources: ESCAP, based on national sources; ADB, *Key Indicators of Developing Asian and Pacific Countries 2004* (Manila, ADB, 2004); IMF, *International Financial Statistics,* vol. LVII, No. 8 (Washington, IMF, August 2004); and EIU, *Country Forecasts* (London, EIU, 2004), various issues.

Note: Figures for 2004 are estimates.

[a] Changes in the consumer price index.

[b] January-June.

Economy of Hong Kong, China, still under deflationary pressure

In Hong Kong, China, deflationary pressure still prevails, keeping nascent inflation in check. The decline in prices that commenced in November 1998 was arrested by a slight pickup in consumer prices starting in the third quarter of 2004, when the CPI rose an average of 0.8 per cent year on year. The increase in consumer prices resulted from the sustained recovery in consumer demand and higher prices for imports, as well as the effect of a property rates concession granted in the third quarter of 2003. However, despite higher electricity, gas and water and food prices, the cost of rented housing, which has the largest weight in the CPI, continued to decline, together with the prices of durable goods, and kept annual inflation in check. Consumer prices declined by 0.3 per cent in 2004 in Hong Kong, China, but as a result of the weakening United States dollar and inflationary pressures from China, consumer prices are expected to rise slightly, by less than 1 per cent in 2005.

Higher oil prices and loose monetary policy reflected in Mongolian inflation

In Mongolia, upward pressure on prices mounted significantly in 2004 owing to higher oil prices and loose monetary policy, and consumer price inflation accelerated to 11 per cent, substantially higher than the 4.6 per cent rate of 2003. The price of imported oil soared in Mongolia when the Russian Federation imposed an oil export tax in July 2004 on top of already high global oil prices and this led to second-round price increases elsewhere in the economy, particularly for transport and electricity. In addition, accommodative monetary policy also contributed to the increase in consumer prices. M2 has been growing at rates above 40 per cent since 2002 and the expansion in the money supply was 45.6 per cent year on year as at June 2004.

Consumer price inflation in the Republic of Korea moderate in 2004

The annual rate of consumer price inflation in the Republic of Korea stood at 3.6 per cent in 2004, which was unchanged from 2003 despite some acceleration of food prices at midyear owing to unfavourable summer weather conditions and the steady rise in the price of oil, of which the country is one of the world's largest consumers. However, consumer prices stagnated or declined in the second half of the year, as food prices fell. The Bank of Korea's core inflation index shows that annual inflation was broadly in check, at around 3 per cent throughout the year, suggesting little demand-led pressure on prices. The annual rate of consumer price inflation is expected to ease to around 3 per cent in 2005 as domestic demand remains weak and the won appreciates against the dollar.

The Bank of Korea loosened its monetary policy in 2004 and M2 growth increased to 10 per cent from 6.7 per cent in 2003. Contrary to the upward trend in interest rates in other leading OECD economies, the central bank cut its policy rate by 25 basis points in August and

November 2004 to 3.25 per cent in a bid to stimulate sluggish investment and consumption. The policy rate was maintained unchanged in December 2004 as the Bank waited to evaluate the impact of earlier rate cuts on demand and the possible adverse effects of further cuts on inflation.

Foreign trade and other external transactions

Foreign trade

Another blistering export performance by China

The value of merchandise exports by China expanded by 35.4 per cent in 2004, compared with a year earlier (table II.4 and figure II.3), a marginal increase from the already high 34.6 per cent for 2003. Machinery and electronic products were the major export items, accounting for around 54 per cent of total exports. Despite the uncertain external environment and rising international oil prices, China continues to attract a large volume of FDI to expand its productive capacity in the export sector. Exports by foreign-funded companies accounted for around 57 per cent of total exports in 2003-2004. The exports of privately owned enterprises showed strong momentum whereas the share of SOEs in total exports declined in 2004.

Table II.4. Selected East and North-East Asian economies: merchandise exports and their rates of growth, 2001-2004

	Exports (f.o.b.)				
	Value (millions of US dollars)	*Annual rate of growth (percentage)*			
	2003	*2001*	*2002*	*2003*	*2004*
China	438 250	7.0	22.1	34.6	35.4
Hong Kong, China[a]	223 762	–5.9	5.4	11.8	16.1
Mongolia[b]	616	–2.7	0.5	17.5	37.0
Republic of Korea	197 637	–12.7	8.0	19.3	31.2

Sources: IMF, *Direction of Trade Statistics* (CD-ROM), December 2004; China Ministry of Commerce web site <http://english.mofcom.gov.cn/>, 24 January 2005; China National Bureau of Statistics web site <http://www.stats.gov.cn/>, 25 January 2005; Hong Kong Census and Statistics Department web site <http://www.info.gov.hk/>, 7 January 2005 and Trade and Industry Department web site <http://www.tid.gov.hk/>, 7 January 2005; and Republic of Korea Ministry of Finance and Economy.

[a] Growth rate for 2004 refers to January-November 2004 compared with the corresponding period of 2003.

[b] Growth rate for 2004 refers to January-July 2004 compared with the corresponding period of 2003.

Figure II.3. Growth rates in merchandise export earnings of selected East and North-East Asian economies, 2001-2004

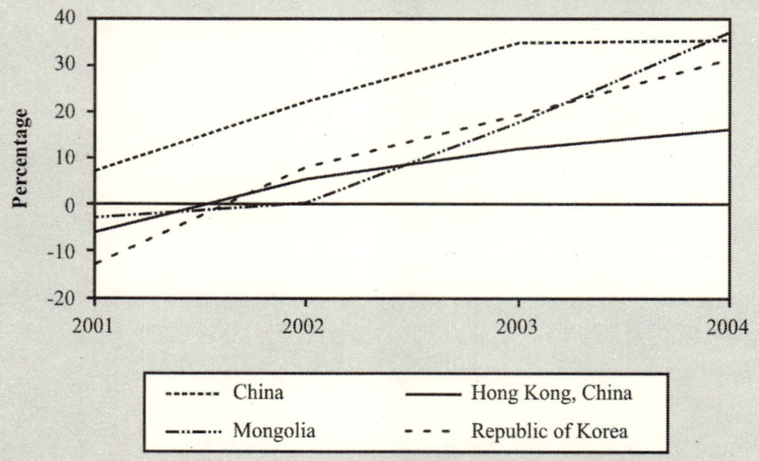

Sources: IMF, *Direction of Trade Statistics* (CD-ROM), December 2004; China Ministry of Commerce web site <http://english.mofcom.gov.cn/>, 24 January 2005; China National Bureau of Statistics web site <http://www.stats.gov.cn/>, 25 January 2005; Hong Kong Census and Statistics Department web site <http://www.info.gov.hk/>, 7 January 2005 and Trade and Industry Department web site <http://www.tid.gov.hk/>, 7 January 2005; and Republic of Korea Ministry of Finance and Economy.

Notes: Growth rates for 2004 compared with the corresponding period of 2003. Growth rates refer to the whole year for China and the Republic of Korea, January-July for Mongolia and January-November for Hong Kong, China.

China's merchandise imports soared by 36 per cent in 2004 compared with a year earlier (table II.5 and figure II.4), down moderately from the 39.7 per cent growth in 2003. Imports surged earlier in the year in response to a further reduction in tariffs implemented under WTO entry terms, but growth moderated subsequently. Crude oil imports accounted for about 6 per cent of total imports, up from 5 per cent in 2003 and 4 per cent in 2002 but appeared to be levelling off. The deceleration in import growth since mid-2004 combined with robust export growth generated a trade surplus of $32 billion in 2004. China's current account surplus declined to about 3 per cent of GDP in 2004, down from 3.2 per cent in 2003 (table II.6). The EU maintained its position as China's largest trading partner, while the United States overtook Japan to become the second largest.

Robust growth in Hong Kong, China's exports thanks to dollar weakness

In 2004, Hong Kong, China's exports of goods and services were boosted by in-bound tourism and the weakening United States dollar, to which its currency is linked. Merchandise exports increased by 16.1 per cent year on year in the first 11 months of 2004, up from 11.8 per cent in 2003 as a whole, reflecting a robust expansion of re-exports on the back of fast-growing intra-Asia trade in raw materials and semi-manufactures.

Table II.5. Selected East and North-East Asian economies: merchandise imports and their rates of growth, 2001-2004

	Value (millions of US dollars)	Imports (c.i.f.) Annual rate of growth (percentage)			
	2003	2001	2002	2003	2004
China	412 836	8.3	21.3	39.7	36.0
Hong Kong, China[a]	231 895	−5.5	3.3	11.7	17.4
Mongolia[b]	801	3.8	8.3	16.0	23.0
Republic of Korea	175 476	−12.1	7.8	17.6	25.5

Sources: IMF, *Direction of Trade Statistics* (CD-ROM), December 2004; China Ministry of Commerce web site <http://english.mofcom.gov.cn/>, 24 January 2005; China National Bureau of Statistics web site <http://www.stats.gov.cn/>, 25 January 2005; Hong Kong Census and Statistics Department web site <http://www.info.gov.hk/>, 7 January 2005 and Trade and Industry Department web site <http://www.tid.gov.hk/>, 7 January 2005; and Republic of Korea Ministry of Finance and Economy.

[a] Growth rate for 2004 refers to January-November 2004 compared with the corresponding period of 2003.
[b] Growth rate for 2004 refers to January-July 2004 compared with the corresponding period of 2003.

Figure II.4. Growth rates in merchandise import spending of selected East and North-East Asian economies, 2001-2004

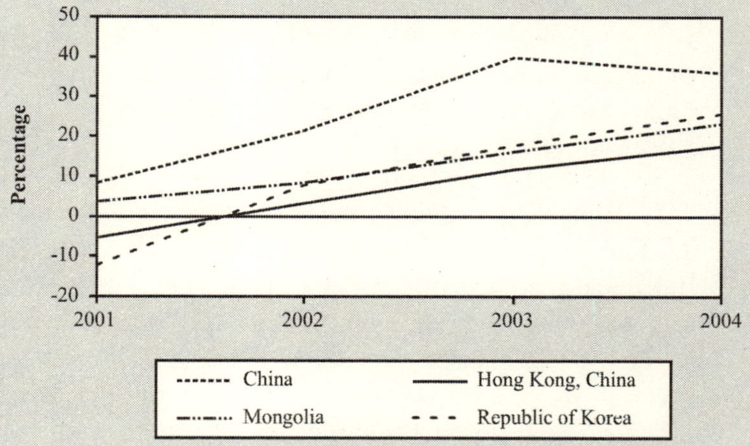

Sources: IMF, *Direction of Trade Statistics* (CD-ROM), December 2004; China Ministry of Commerce web site <http://english.mofcom.gov.cn/>, 24 January 2005; China National Bureau of Statistics web site <http://www.stats.gov.cn/>, 25 January 2005; Hong Kong Census and Statistics Department web site <http://www.info.gov.hk/>, 7 January 2005 and Trade and Industry Department web site <http://www.tid.gov.hk/>, 7 January 2005; and Republic of Korea Ministry of Finance and Economy.

Notes: Growth rates for 2004 compared with the corresponding period of 2003. Growth rates refer to the whole year for China and the Republic of Korea, January-July for Mongolia and January-November for Hong Kong, China.

Table II.6. Selected East and North-East Asian economies: budget and current account balance as a percentage of GDP, 2001-2004

(Percentage)

	2001	*2002*	*2003*	*2004*
Budget balance as a percentage of GDP				
China	−2.5	−2.9	−2.5	−2.4
Hong Kong, China	−5.0	−4.9	−4.0	−4.1
Mongolia[a]	−4.5	−6.0	−4.7	−4.0
Republic of Korea	1.2	3.3	1.1	0.3
Current account balance as a percentage of GDP				
China	1.5	2.8	3.2	3.0
Hong Kong, China	6.1	7.9	10.7	9.3
Mongolia	−16.6	−15.9	−14.9	−14.0
Republic of Korea	1.7	1.0	2.0	4.0

Sources: ESCAP, based on national sources; ADB, *Key Indicators of Developing Asian and Pacific Countries 2004* (Manila, ADB, 2004); IMF, *International Financial Statistics,* vol. LVII, No. 5 (Washington, IMF, May 2004); and EIU, *Country Forecasts* (London, EIU, 2004), various issues.

Note: Figures for 2004 are estimates.

[a] Including grants.

In 2005, merchandise export growth is expected to consolidate and return to a more sustainable pace of expansion, as economic growth slows in the United States and China. Hong Kong, China's major export markets are China, the United States, the EU and Japan with shares of 44, 17, 13 and 5 per cent of its total exports, respectively.

Hong Kong, China's merchandise imports grew by 17.4 per cent in the first 11 months of 2004, following an 11.7 per cent increase in 2003 and modest growth of 3.3 per cent in 2002. Stronger local consumption and large numbers of tourists were the principal factors behind rising imports. The merchandise trade deficit in the first 11 months of 2004 stood at $8.1 billion, almost the same as in 2003 as a whole. The trade deficit is likely to widen further in 2005 as domestic demand strengthens. The current account surplus narrowed somewhat in Hong Kong, China, to reach about 9 per cent of GDP in 2004.

Mongolia's exports surged with rising demand for copper and gold

Mongolia's export earnings soared along with the demand for copper, gold and textiles in trading partner nations. Helped by higher world prices for copper concentrate, the value of merchandise exports surged by 37 per cent year on year in the first 7 months of 2004, up from 17.5 per cent in 2003 as a whole, a significant improvement over the dismal export performance in 2001-2002. Meanwhile, merchandise imports rose by 23 per cent in the first 7 months of 2004, up from 16 per cent in the previous year. Currently, Mongolia's largest trading partners are China and the Russian Federation, with the former buying mineral products such as copper and the latter animals and animal products. Trading is expected to expand steadily with Central Asian countries such as Kazakhstan and Kyrgyzstan in the long term owing to improved transport links.

Mongolia's trade balance was in deficit to the extent of $193.3 million in the first 9 months of 2004. The current account deficit is projected to have reached about 14 per cent of its GDP in 2004, but is likely to be covered by foreign aid and FDI in the mining sector, as well as remittances from migrant workers.

The Republic of Korea's exports boosted by strong demand from China

The Republic of Korea's export earnings posted strong performance through the whole year in 2004. One of the main factors in the export boom was the demand from China, which is now the Republic of Korea's most important export market. In addition to heavy reliance on a few major markets, the Republic of Korea's exports are relatively narrowly based on a limited range of products such as wireless communication equipment, automobiles and steel. This suggests that the country's export performance is quite vulnerable to negative shocks triggered by various external factors. Nonetheless, the Republic of Korea's merchandise exports registered rapid growth of 31.2 per cent in 2004, up from 19.3 per cent in 2003 and 8.0 per cent in 2002. The major export items were passenger cars, metal goods and machinery and equipment, including electronics, telecommunications equipment and semiconductors.

Although the current account surplus widened to about 4 per cent of GDP in the Republic of Korea in 2004, rising global prices for oil and other commodities inflated the import bill. Merchandise imports increased by 25.5 per cent in 2004, up from 17.6 per cent in the previous year. The major imports to the Republic of Korea were industrial materials, fuels and capital goods, most of which were stimulated by export demand. Japan, with which the Republic of Korea's trade deficit has been rising steadily since 1999, was one of the main beneficiaries as firms from the Republic of Korea boosted imports of semiconductor manufacturing equipment and other high-end goods from that country.

Capital flows and external debt

Capital inflows to China sharply increased partly owing to speculative motives

The yuan renminbi's peg against the United States dollar (figure II.5) has been under discussion for some time in view of China's sustained current account surplus with that country. Some FDI inflows and external borrowing seem to have been partly motivated by heightened speculative interest in addition to the attraction of the strong economic performance of the Chinese economy. Gross inflows of FDI to China reached a record level of $60.6 billion in 2004, up 14 per cent from 2003. External borrowing is projected to have surged to $30 billion in 2004 from $15.5 billion in 2003. China's total external debt at the end of 2003 reached $196 billion, including $67 billion in short-term liabilities. Debt-service payments due in 2004 were $22 billion, less than 4 per cent of total exports of goods and services, indicating a broadly stable external debt situation. China's official foreign exchange reserves surged to $609.9 billion at the end of 2004, an increase of $200 billion compared with 2003, owing to substantial capital inflows and the continued current account surplus.

Figure II.5. Index of exchange rates against the United States dollar of selected East and North-East Asian economies, 1996-2004

(1996=100)

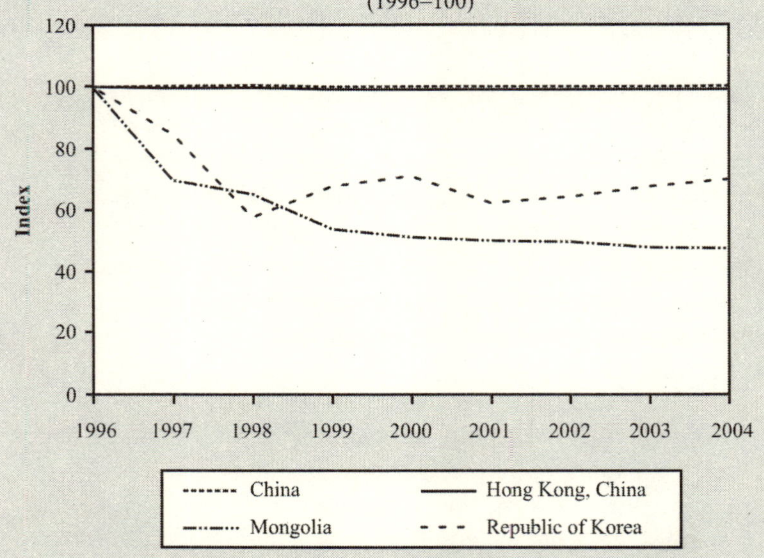

Sources: IMF, *International Financial Statistics*, vol. LVII, No. 10 (Washington, IMF, October 2004); and *The Economist,* various issues.

Note: Figures for 2004 are estimates.

Hong Kong, China, the second largest recipient of inward FDI in Asia

Hong Kong, China, was ranked as the second largest recipient of inward FDI in Asia and the eleventh in the world in 2003. FDI inflows to Hong Kong, China, increased to $13.6 billion in 2003 from $9.7 billion in 2002. Hong Kong, China, was also reported to be the largest source of outward FDI among Asian economies and the largest investor in China in 2003. The major part of the stock of investment in China is related to services. Hong Kong, China's total external debt is projected to have reached $67.7 billion at the end of 2004, up from $59.2 billion in 2003, owing partly to the prevailing low interest rate environment. Hong Kong, China's official foreign exchange reserves have increased steadily, reaching $124.3 billion at the end of December 2004, while debt service amounted to 2 per cent of export revenues. The stability of Hong Kong, China's external debt position enhances its role as a financial and logistics centre of the region.

Mongolia's external debt situation manageable

Attracted by the promise of new gold discoveries in Mongolia, FDI increased to $113 million in 2003, up 94 per cent on the previous year. Total external debt outstanding increased to $1.2 billion or 102 per cent of GDP in 2003, from 88.3 per cent of GDP in 2002, as Mongolia went through a restructuring process towards a market economy. Since most of the debt consists of loans from multilateral or bilateral sources on concessional terms, the overall debt situation appears manageable with a debt-service ratio of 5.4 per cent of exports. Mongolia's official foreign exchange reserves are projected to have reached $236 million at the end of 2003.

Inward FDI in the Republic of Korea subdued

Inflows of FDI to the Republic of Korea amounted to $4.1 billion during the first 8 months of 2004, less than half the amount received in 2000, reflecting deteriorating investor sentiment. Foreign purchases of common stock in the country reached $10 billion in the first 10 months of 2004, following an inflow of $12 billion in the previous year. Investment outflows from the Republic of Korea have themselves become substantial, with FDI outflows amounting to $2.9 billion in the first 8 months of 2004 and $3.4 billion in 2003. Outflows of portfolio investment totalled $5.8 billion during the first 8 months of 2004, up from $3.4 billion in the previous year. The trend of increasing outflows and decreasing inflows of capital suggests that the economy of the Republic of Korea might be losing its attraction as a promising emerging market and that investment funds are seeking better alternatives elsewhere.

The Republic of Korea's total external debt rose to $166.7 billion at the end of September 2004, compared with $158.9 billon at the end of 2003. Short-term external debt, mainly trade credit, was around one third of the total. The debt-service ratio has fallen since 2001 and is projected to be around 5-6 per cent of total exports in 2004. The Republic of Korea's official foreign exchange reserves were approximately $199 billion at the end of December 2004, up from $155 billion a year previously. In view of the size of its foreign exchange reserves and current account surplus, the Republic of Korea is in a relatively comfortable external position. The exchange rate of the won has been under upward pressure given the weakness of the dollar and may appreciate further in 2005.

Key policy issues

Introducing monetary flexibility while maintaining fiscal soundness in China

In China, policy has shifted from promoting growth to moderating growth, in order to bring the economy back to a more sustainable path, as perceptions of overheating and overinvestment intensified. When prices surged sharply for raw materials and bottlenecks appeared in the supply of power, symptoms of overheating were evident, especially in such industries as steel, aluminium, cement, automobiles and construction. The authorities have taken various measures to cool the economy, including increasing the bank reserve ratio, cracking down on reckless lending, dispatching inspection teams to several provinces to examine investments and terminate improper projects and cutting land allocations to sectors that have been overbuilt. Although these corrective measures slowed investment to a limited degree, the overall performance of the economy in 2004 turned out to be much stronger than expected.

The authorities in China need to tighten monetary policy in a more market-oriented way, in view of the fact that real interest rates turned negative as inflation has risen, thereby stimulating investment. Firms and banks in the private sector need to play a greater role in making investment decisions in a more market-based financial system. In this sense, more flexibility would be desirable in establishing and implementing interest and exchange rate policies.

Fiscal policy should also be supportive of the hoped-for soft landing in the short term, while fiscal reforms should be pursued in the medium term to enhance efficiency and the sustainability of revenue collection and expenditure. China's fiscal deficit declined marginally to 2.4 per cent of GDP in 2004, down from 2.5 per cent in 2003 (table II.6). Currently, China's fiscal deficit and public debt are not matters of major concern. However, maintaining fiscal soundness could become an important consideration as the economic system becomes more market-oriented and reform processes are deepened in the banking sector and in SOEs while measures are taken to narrow the widening rural-urban divide in terms of income, social benefits and standards of living.

Further reforms in financial and corporate sectors as well as labour markets in China

The combined NPL ratio of China's four largest State-owned banks and 12 joint-stock commercial banks fell by 4.6 percentage points to 13.2 per cent in 2004. In order to make the market economy function efficiently, China needs further reforms in the financial and corporate sectors as well as in the labour market. Since the banking sector will be fully open to foreign investors after 2006, China needs to improve the competency of domestic banks by strengthening supervision as well as the regulatory framework, improving accountability and transparency, refining corporate governance and building institutional capacity in such areas as risk management, while ensuring the soundness of financial institutions, especially in terms of capital adequacy. China also needs to restructure SOEs to improve performance and enhance profitability if these enterprises are to be viable. Loss-making SOEs should be considered for closure unless they meet a pressing social need. In order to accommodate laid-off workers, especially from SOEs, China needs to strengthen the social safety net, which complements the reform policy to protect the poor and the vulnerable. In order to improve the functioning of the labour market, China needs to enhance labour mobility and the quality of the information dissemination system to better match job seekers and job opportunities. China's currently underfunded pension system also needs to be revamped to become sustainable.

Stabilizing the fiscal deficit in Hong Kong, China

Hong Kong, China, faces limitations in conducting monetary policy because of the exchange rate peg against the United States dollar. So far, the weakening dollar has contributed to boosting Hong Kong, China's competitiveness. Local interest rates are largely determined by interest rates in the United States and an anticipated increase in those rates in 2005 is expected to induce a large volume of capital inflows to Hong Kong, China.

Hong Kong, China's budget deficit was around 4 per cent of GDP in 2003-2004 and balancing the budget has been a major issue facing the authorities because of the narrow tax base and the reliance on land-based revenues. The authorities need to consider reducing the ratio of expenditure to GDP while broadening the tax base to stabilize revenues. Securing a broad-based and stable revenue source such as a goods and services tax will be essential for eliminating the structural deficit problem.

As the process of global economic integration continues apace, the pressure of competition is also mounting on Hong Kong, China. Continuing to strengthen the financial infrastructure as well as the supervisory and regulatory systems will be essential if the territory is to maintain its leading position as an international financial centre in the region. The authorities need to improve transparency in the institutional and policy frameworks, as well as cross-industry supervisory coordination, as banks and other financial institutions expand the scope of their businesses. Hong Kong, China, also needs to upgrade the skills of the labour force to cope with greater competition from China and the rest of the world.

Progress on macroeconomic stability and the Millennium Development Goals in Mongolia

The fiscal deficit in Mongolia hovered between 4.5 and 6 per cent of GDP in 2001-2003 and was projected to decline to 4 per cent of GDP in 2004. Approximately 70 per cent of the deficit is covered by foreign funding, mainly concessional loans. However, as noted earlier, broad money supply has expanded very rapidly in recent years in Mongolia in response to rapid economic growth and as a result of an easing of monetary policy. Bank deposits have soared with rising confidence in the banking system, and loans have sharply increased also. However, the credit expansion has raised some concerns about the need to strengthen credit risk analysis and capital adequacy in the banking system, although interest rates have been broadly stable following the liberalization and privatization of the banking sector.

Mongolia has made good progress in achieving the Millennium Development Goals, with increased school enrolment rates, and reductions in the child mortality rate and maternal mortality ratio. Although the country has been relatively successful in maintaining macroeconomic stability in recent years, its economic structure is still highly vulnerable to the weather and to volatility in world commodity markets.

Monetary and fiscal policies eased in the Republic of Korea but impact uncertain

Boosting domestic demand has become the dominant issue for economic policy in the Republic of Korea, as consumption and investment have been depressed for a long time and the unemployment rate became a concern. As mentioned earlier, the Bank of Korea cut interest rates to a historically low level despite a higher rate of inflation in order to sustain the economic recovery. Since both long- and short-term interest rates have already reached all-time lows, the Bank of Korea's room for manoeuvre is now limited and any further stimulus will have to come from fiscal policy.

The Government of the Republic of Korea eased fiscal policy by frontloading expenditures in the first half of 2004 and enacting a supplementary budget. As a result, the budget surplus narrowed to 0.3 per cent of GDP, down from 1.1 per cent in 2003 and 3.3 per cent in 2002. Income tax cuts and an increase in tax deductions for SMEs have been proposed along with the preparation of a large public construction programme for additional demand stimulus. It remains to be seen whether the Government's stimulus policies can outweigh the factors discouraging consumption and investment, in view of the fragility of consumer sentiment and the low level of business confidence.

Although the Republic of Korea has made noticeable progress in financial and corporate sector reforms, the recent weakness of the economy requires further progress in enhancing the efficiency and capacity of the economic system. Greater flexibility in the labour market will be essential in a global environment of rapid change, as well as improvements to corporate governance. The reform measures in the labour market should include enhancing employment flexibility, improving industrial relations, raising labour productivity and promoting female participation in the labour force. To facilitate these measures, the coverage and effectiveness of the social safety net should be strengthened further and quality training programmes should also be made available. The reform measures for better corporate governance include improving transparency in accounting and management, strengthening the protection accorded to whistleblowers, ensuring independent auditors, allowing class action lawsuits for shareholders of large firms and developing risk-analysis capabilities for enterprises and financial institutions. In addition, the Government needs to reform the current pension system to ensure its sustainability, in view of the ageing population.

North and Central Asia

Subregional overview

North and Central Asian economies among the most dynamic in the region

For the past four years, several countries in North and Central Asia have been among the most dynamic in the Asian and Pacific region, with annual economic growth rates exceeding 9 per cent (figure II.6). Economic growth continued to be high in 2004 owing to a combination of soaring international prices of natural resources, strong exports and solid domestic demand. Growth in energy-exporting economies such as the Russian Federation, Azerbaijan, Kazakhstan and Turkmenistan exceeded previous forecasts. Strong demand from the Russian Federation helped to support economic growth in the subregion, for which it remained an important source of export demand and investment. Following a dramatic downturn in 2003, FDI for the construction of new pipelines to transport hydrocarbons from the subregion to international markets recovered sharply in 2004. The countries of North and Central Asia also made substantial progress on macroeconomic stabilization, pursuing prudent monetary and fiscal policies designed to contain inflation (figure II.7) and keep exchange rates stable.

Figure II.6. Rates of GDP growth in North and Central Asian economies, 2001-2004

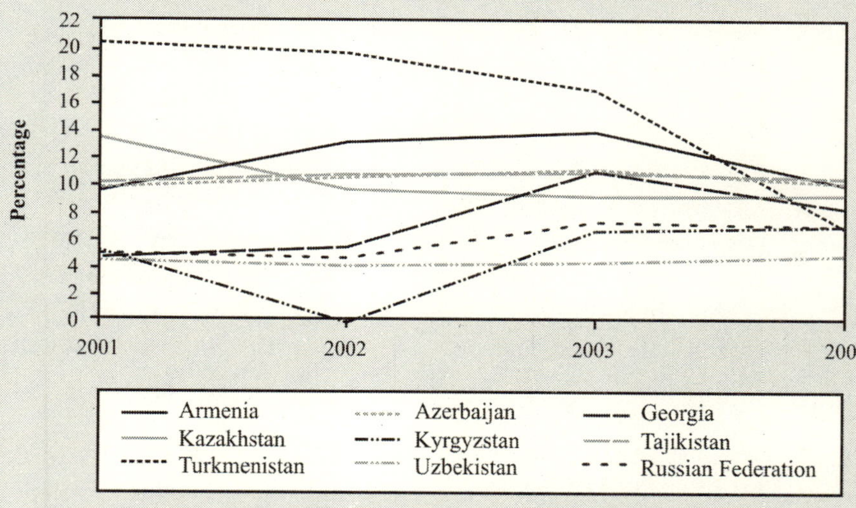

Sources: ESCAP, based on ECE, *Economic Survey of Europe 2004*, No. 1 (United Nations publication, Sales No. E.04.II.E.7); web site of the CIS Inter-State Statistical Committee <www.cisstat.com>, 26 October 2004 and 3 February 2005; EIU, *Country Reports* (London, EIU, 2004), various issues; and national sources.

Note: Growth rates for 2004 are estimates.

Figure II.7. Inflation[a] in North and Central Asian economies, 2001-2004

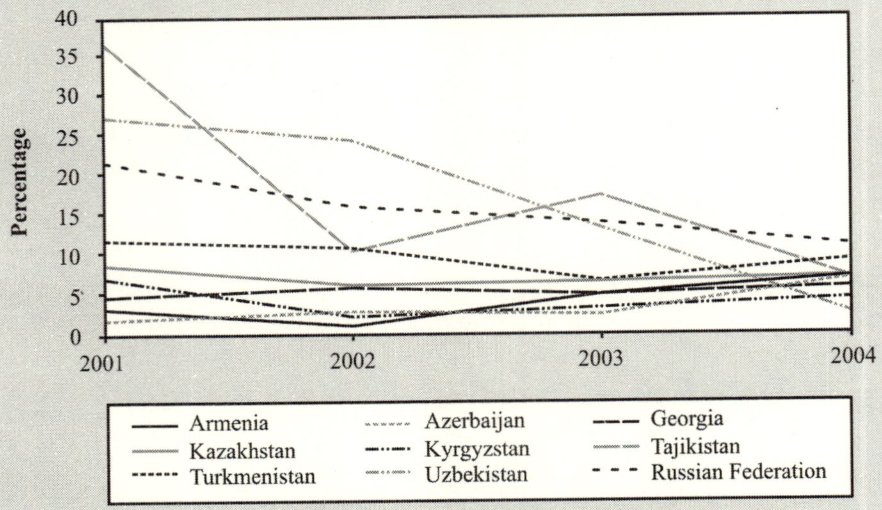

Sources: ESCAP, based on the web site of the CIS Inter-State Statistical Committee <www.cisstat.com>, 26 October 2004 and 3 February 2005; and EIU, *Country Reports* (London, EIU, 2004 and 2005), various issues.

Note: Inflation rates for 2004 are estimates.

[a] Percentage changes in the consumer price index.

Economic growth expected to fall in the medium term

The prognosis for economic growth over the next three years in the countries of North and Central Asia is based on an anticipated fall in world oil prices. Economic growth in the Russian Federation is expected to decline somewhat to 6.3 per cent in 2005 and 6.1 per cent in 2006 before recovering to 6.5 per cent in 2007. Sharper falls in GDP growth in 2005 are expected in Tajikistan and Armenia, to 5 and 6.5 per cent respectively, well below the 10-11 per cent expected in 2004. The medium-term outlook for Georgia is also for slower growth, averaging 5 per cent annually through 2008, sustained by oil and gas pipeline construction and improvements in the business climate that should foster export diversification. However, some acceleration in GDP growth is expected in Uzbekistan, to 5.3 per cent in 2005 and 6.4 per cent in 2006 from 4.9 per cent in 2004.

A gradual decline in inflation, from 8 per cent in 2005 to 3 per cent in 2008, is forecast in the Russian Federation and the pursuit of prudent monetary policies is also expected to keep inflation around 5 per cent in Tajikistan and Georgia.

Among the main policy priorities of the countries in North and Central Asia in 2004 were structural reforms to foster economic diversification so as to reduce dependence on the export of natural resources and boost economic competitiveness by improving the business climate. Greater integration into the regional and global economies will be needed to achieve these aims and a key to this is membership in WTO. In 2004, six economies in the subregion were engaged in the negotiations process with WTO, while three others, namely, Armenia, Georgia and Kyrgyzstan, have already joined that body. The countries of North and Central Asia also continued to restore and revitalize their significant economic complementarities within three economic organizations established in CIS, the Eurasian Economic Community, the Central Asian Cooperation Organization and the Single Economic Space.

Poverty reduction and improvement in the living standards of the population remain major medium-term priorities for all the countries in North and Central Asia. Economic growth in those countries has not as yet resulted in sustained poverty alleviation and the achievement of incomes above subsistence levels. Georgia is expected to reduce the share of the population living below the national poverty line from over half of the population in 2002 to about one third in 2008 and one fifth by 2015. The strategy for improving living standards in Uzbekistan envisages further reform in all spheres and continued economic liberalization. The Government of the Russian Federation intends to cut the percentage of the population living below the poverty line from over 20 per cent at present to 10-12 per cent over the next five years.

GDP performance

Sustained economic growth in the Russian Federation

Macroeconomic policies of the economies of North and Central Asia in 2004 were conducive to sustaining growth, accelerating structural reforms, containing inflation, maintaining exchange rate stability and strengthening debt management. Growth in the largest economy of the subregion, the Russian Federation, was strong owing to high oil and gas export prices and the global recovery. Domestic demand also played an important role, with fixed investment growing at double-digit rates, while strong consumer spending was sustained by rising real incomes. As a result, growth in GDP and industrial production reached 7.1 and 6.1 per cent respectively in 2004 (table II.7). The economic boom was evident in construction, which expanded 14.3 per cent in the first half of 2004, reflecting increased investment in both infrastructure and housing. Telecommunications and retailing were also among the most dynamic sectors in the economy as in 2003. Retail sales were driven by rising real incomes, which increased 12.0 per cent in 2004, in part reflecting higher revenues in the hydrocarbons sector. The economy remained heavily dependent on the energy sector, which accounted for 55 per cent of all exports in 2004. Grain production in 2004 was 16 per cent above that in 2003, with a harvest of 78 million tons, permitting exports of over 8 million tons of wheat.

Table II.7. North and Central Asian economies: growth rates, 2001-2004

(Percentage)

		Rates of growth		
		Gross domestic product	*Gross agricultural output*	*Gross industrial output*
Armenia	2001	9.6	12.0	5.3
	2002	13.2	4.0	14.6
	2003	13.9	4.0	14.9
	2004	10.1	14.5	2.1
Azerbaijan	2001	9.9	11.0	5.1
	2002	10.6	6.0	3.6
	2003	11.2	6.0	6.1
	2004	10.2	4.6	5.7
Georgia	2001	4.8	6.0	−5.0
	2002	5.5	−1.0	7.0
	2003	11.1	11.0	14.8
	2004	8.4	−6.5	3.4
Kazakhstan	2001	13.5	16.9	13.8
	2002	9.8	3.0	10.5
	2003	9.2	1.0	8.8
	2004	9.4	0.1	10.1
Kyrgyzstan	2001	5.3	6.8	5.4
	2002	0.0	3.0	−10.9
	2003	6.7	4.0	17.0
	2004	7.1	4.1	3.7
Russian Federation	2001	5.1	7.5	4.9
	2002	4.7	1.5	3.7
	2003	7.3	1.5	7.0
	2004	7.1	1.6	6.1
Tajikistan	2001	10.2	11.0	15.0
	2002	10.8	..	8.4
	2003	11.0	..	9.9
	2004	10.6	10.3[a]	14.3
Turkmenistan	2001	20.5	..	11.0
	2002	19.8	17.0[a]	10.0
	2003	17.0	..	..
	2004	7.0	20.7[a]	..
Uzbekistan	2001	4.5	5.0	7.6
	2002	4.2	6.1	8.5
	2003	4.4	4.3	6.2
	2004	4.9	10.4[b]	9.6[b]

Sources: ESCAP, based on ECE, *Economic Survey of Europe 2004,* No. 1 (United Nations publication, Sales No. E.04.II.E.7); web site of the CIS Inter-State Statistical Committee <www.cisstat.com>, 26 October 2004 and 3 February 2005; and EIU, *Country Reports* (London, EIU, 2004), various issues; and national sources.

Note: Growth rates for 2004 are estimates.

[a] January-September.

[b] January-June.

Oil production dominated industrial output in Kazakhstan

Sustained by the oil sector, Kazakhstan's GDP growth averaged 9.5 per cent in 2002-2003. This strong performance continued in 2004 with GDP growth of 9.4 per cent, reflecting a strong expansion in industrial output, owing to high volumes of oil exports and substantial FDI. Oil-related activities and new investment in infrastructure resulted in a 10.1 per cent increase in industrial output in 2004. Agricultural production increased by only 0.1 per cent in 2004 owing to a poor grain harvest that was expected to be 16 per cent below that of 2003.

Solid economic growth in Kyrgyzstan and Tajikistan

Modest growth in industrial production, which reached 3.7 per cent in 2004, also contributed to sustained expansion in Kyrgyzstan's GDP of 7.1 per cent in the same period. Metallurgy and food processing were the main drivers of industrial growth, the former accounting for around half of all industrial output. Increased investment from the Russian Federation and Kazakhstan in hydroelectricity enabled Kyrgyzstan to increase capital imports. The economic growth of Kyrgyzstan also reflected vigorous expansion in the service sector. Retail trade was up by 14.7 per cent in 2004 as real household incomes rose. Gross agricultural output grew by a more modest 4.1 per cent in 2004.

Tajikistan has experienced solid economic growth and falling levels of inflation in the last four years. The economy grew by 11 per cent in 2003 and by 10.6 per cent in 2004. The growth was largely based on the two traditional pillars of the economy – cotton and aluminium, which remained the main export items. At the same time, rapid expansion of light manufacturing, energy and services as well as private farming enabled some diversification in growth. Owing to increased inward remittances of migrant workers from Tajikistan, domestic demand was strengthened and retail trade remained robust. Industrial production expanded 14.3 per cent in 2004 and agricultural production rose 10.3 per cent in the first half of the year. However, heavy rains and landslides in the middle of 2004 affected the cotton harvest. The Government is expected to speed up land reforms in the medium term.

Considerable decline in industrial production in Armenia

GDP grew 10.1 per cent in 2004 in Armenia. This was despite a relatively poor performance of the industrial sector owing to a disruption in supplies of raw materials for diamond production and a slowdown in construction. The growth rate of industrial production declined from 14.9 per cent in 2003 to 2.1 per cent in 2004. The decline was attributed mainly to a 17 per cent decrease in diamond production, which nevertheless remains a strategic sector of the economy. In the last six years, the output of this sector has increased 10-fold and the volume of diamond processing and exports are expected to double over the next three years. Agricultural production accelerated from 4.0 per cent in 2003 to 14.5 per cent in 2004 owing to improvements to the irrigation network.

Georgia benefited from oil and gas pipeline construction

The economy of Georgia was on track to sustain the high growth observed in 2004, when GDP expanded 8.4 per cent owing primarily to new investment in construction as well as growth in other sectors such as transport and services. The construction of the Baku-Tbilisi-Ceyhan oil pipeline and the South Caucasus gas pipeline was the principal factor in the solid economic performance in Georgia in 2004. The service sector benefited from the pipeline activity, which also had important spillover effects on related sectors such as transport and communications as well as hotels and catering. Gross industrial output grew by 3.4 per cent in 2004, owing to strong growth in the extraction sector and in manufacturing. Agricultural production recorded a decline of 6.5 per cent in 2004 as farmers ran short of credit to purchase seeds and fertilizers. Implementation of the land reform initiated in 2004, which is aimed at privatizing and leasing arable land, should lead to improved performance in the sector in the near future.

Robust growth in agriculture in Uzbekistan

In 2001-2003, GDP growth in Uzbekistan was modest but steady at an annual rate above 4 per cent, sustained by robust growth in agriculture, and 4.9 per cent growth was expected in 2004. Agriculture is the dominant sector of the economy, accounting for around a third of GDP and employment, and is among the largest export earners in the country. Agricultural production grew by 10.4 per cent in the first half of 2004. The Government has reformed grain and cotton marketing and cooperative farms have been privatized. However, Uzbekistan remains dependent on wheat imports, mainly from Kazakhstan. The implementation of import-substituting industrialization and energy reforms resulted in a 9.6 per cent expansion in the industrial sector in the first half of 2004. Economic expansion in 2004 was also supported by investment from the Russian Federation and China in large projects in the hydrocarbons sector. FDI and credits also flowed to other sectors such as transport, communications, light industry, and chemicals and petrochemicals in 2004.

Hydrocarbons remained the engine of economic growth in Azerbaijan and Turkmenistan

The macroeconomic performance of Azerbaijan remained strong in 2004. Following growth of 11.2 per cent in 2003, GDP grew a further 10.2 per cent in 2004. Capital investment and construction activity linked to the development of new and ongoing oil- and gasfields and the Baku-Tbilisi-Ceyhan oil pipeline fuelled economic growth. Strong inflows of FDI into oil- and gas-related projects led to a 5.7 per cent increase in industrial production in 2004. Construction and communication services were the main beneficiary of investment inflows into the economy. Agriculture grew by 4.6 per cent in 2004 and remained the largest employer, absorbing 40 per cent of the total workforce of the country. However, the country is still not self-sufficient in food, and foodstuffs were significant import items in 2004.

The economy of Turkmenistan was expected to grow by 7.0 per cent in 2004 following a solid performance of the hydrocarbons and agricultural sectors, which continue to be the principal drivers of economic growth in the country. The strong growth was also attributed to investment in the construction of new roads and facilities in the hydrocarbons sector. The agricultural sector expanded by 20.7 per cent in the first 9 months of 2004 and the grain and cotton harvests were expected to meet the targets for the year, which have been set at their highest levels since independence.

Inflation

Inflation declined in Uzbekistan and Tajikistan …

Monetary policy in the economies of North and Central Asia in 2004 focused on containing annual inflation. Tight monetary policy contributed to the sharp drop in the rate of inflation in Uzbekistan from 13.1 per cent in 2003 to just 2.4 per cent in 2004 (table II.8). Other factors contributing to the decline in the price level were the limited cash in circulation and the low purchasing power of the population. Inflation also fell substantially in Tajikistan, from 17.1 per cent recorded in 2003 to 6.8 per cent in 2004, owing to lower food prices and relatively stable prices of basic commodities. However, higher domestic utility tariffs and increases in the prices of fuel and services could cause inflation to reach 8 per cent in 2005.

Table II.8. North and Central Asian economies: inflation,[a] 2001-2004

(Percentage)

	2001	*2002*	*2003*	*2004*
Armenia	3.1	1.0	4.7	7.0
Azerbaijan	1.6	2.8	2.2	6.7
Georgia	4.6	5.7	4.8	5.7
Kazakhstan	8.5	6.0	6.4	6.9
Kyrgyzstan	7.0	2.1	3.1	4.1
Russian Federation	21.5	15.8	13.7	10.9
Tajikistan	36.5	10.2	17.1	6.8
Turkmenistan	11.6	10.6	6.5	9.0
Uzbekistan	27.2	24.2	13.1	2.4

Sources: ESCAP, based on the web site of the CIS Inter-State Statistical Committee <www.cisstat.com>, 26 October 2004 and 3 February 2005; and EIU, *Country Reports* (London, EIU, 2004 and 2005), various issues.

Note: Inflation rates for 2004 are estimates.

[a] Percentage changes in the consumer price index.

... but increased in other economies

Inflation in Azerbaijan was in the 1.6-2.8 per cent range in 2001-2003 but increased sharply to 6.7 per cent in 2004. The acceleration in consumer price inflation was attributed mainly to strong domestic demand resulting from high oil-related investment and increased oil export revenues. Inflation was expected to fall to 5 per cent in 2005 following the sharp seasonal decline in food prices, which comprise the bulk of the consumption basket.

Following the 4.7 per cent rate of inflation in 2003, which reflected a robust expansion in the demand for money, the Government of Armenia hoped to lower inflation to 3 per cent in 2004. However, higher global food prices exerted upward pressure on bread prices in Armenia, which, together with higher utility prices, caused the rate of inflation to reach 7.0 per cent in 2004. Annual inflation exceeded government targets for 2004 in Kazakhstan and the Russian Federation. In 2004, consumer price inflation in Kazakhstan reached 6.9 per cent, exceeding the target range of 5-6 per cent. A surge in producer prices, wage rises in the public sector and strong growth in the money supply contributed to higher prices for foodstuffs and energy products. Consumer price inflation rose 10.9 per cent in the Russian Federation in 2004 boosted by strong domestic demand, largely as a result of higher oil and food prices. Rising wages and growth in the money supply exerted additional domestic demand pressures on the economy.

Inflation in Georgia accelerated from 4.8 per cent in 2003 to 5.7 per cent in 2004, driven by higher import prices for oil and wheat. A new taxation policy introduced by the Government in 2004, which increased the operating costs of industrial enterprises, was an additional factor pushing up prices as the higher costs were passed on to consumers. A tightening of monetary policy could reduce the inflation rate in 2005. In Kyrgyzstan, consumer prices rose by 4.1 per cent in 2004 compared with a 3.1 per cent increase recorded in 2003, within the central bank's target range of 4-5 per cent. Prices of food and services were relatively stable owing to adequate supplies and prudent fiscal and monetary policies in 2004. The Government of Turkmenistan continued its policy of maintaining price controls on major consumer goods and providing basic foodstuffs and some utilities free of charge. Nevertheless, there was a significant acceleration in the price level, from 6.5 per cent in 2003 to 9.0 per cent in 2004.

Fiscal policy

Fiscal performance satisfactory in most countries

Helped in many cases by the global boom in oil and other commodity prices, the fiscal situation of countries in North and Central Asia remained essentially satisfactory in 2004, with the budget balance as a percentage of GDP ranging from a surplus of 3.8 per cent in the

Russian Federation to a deficit of 2.3 per cent in Armenia (table II.9). In Armenia, the budget deficit declined from 3.2 per cent of GDP in 2003, as the Government focused on increasing revenues through reductions in VAT exemptions and reform of the profits tax and on improving customs and tax administration so as to generate greater resources for poverty reduction in the country. However, the budget deficit in 2004 was somewhat above the target of 1.9 per cent of GDP. Additional measures are needed to improve the transparency of tax and customs operations and to strengthen the overall coherence of the tax system and the management of the tax and customs agencies.

Table II.9. North and Central Asian economies: budget balance as a percentage of GDP, 2001-2004

(Percentage)

	2001	*2002*	*2003*	*2004*
Armenia	−3.8	−2.4	−3.2	−2.3
Azerbaijan	−2.0	−1.2	−1.2	−1.4
Georgia	−2.0	−2.2	−1.3	−1.3
Kazakhstan	−0.4	−0.3	−0.9	−0.4
Kyrgyzstan	0.4	−1.1	−0.8	−0.6
Russian Federation	3.1	1.7	2.4	3.8
Tajikistan	−0.6	−2.4	1.0	−0.5
Turkmenistan	0.9	−2.7	−1.8	−2.2
Uzbekistan	−3.6	−0.8	−0.4	−0.4

Sources: ESCAP, based on IMF, *International Financial Statistics,* vol. LVII, No. 8 (Washington, IMF, August 2004); and EIU, *Country Reports* (London, EIU, 2004), various issues.

Note: Figures for 2004 are estimates.

Implementation of tax reforms to simplify the tax structure, broaden the tax base and eliminate tax exemptions led to fiscal stability in Georgia in 2004. The Government was able to improve tax collection, eliminate domestic expenditure arrears and increase core spending on social projects and infrastructure. The budget deficit in 2004 was expected to be close to the target of 1.3 per cent of GDP, helped also by a substantial increase in non-tax revenues and foreign grants. The Government intends to introduce a new tax code aimed at reducing tax rates and encouraging further tax compliance.

Prudent fiscal policies and tight budgetary control enabled the Government of Tajikistan to reverse the budget deficit of 2.4 per cent of GDP in 2002 and achieve a budget surplus equivalent to 1 per cent of GDP in 2003. In 2004, the Government continued with fiscal consolidation, targeting a budget deficit of only 0.5 per cent of GDP, close to a balanced budget. In the first half of the year, however, the budget was in a surplus of 1 per cent of GDP owing to a 36 per cent increase in tax revenues.

The budget deficit of Uzbekistan declined from 3.6 per cent of GDP in 2001 to 0.4 per cent in 2003 and 2004 owing to expenditure restraint, modest wage increases in the public sector, lower energy subsidies and lower public investment. Robust gold and cotton prices and an increase in tax rates on natural resources supported budgetary revenues in 2004. In addition, the Government continued the privatization of the State-owned enterprises. In the first half of 2004, revenues from the sale of these enterprises were 80 per cent higher than in 2003. Broadening the tax base to boost tax collection remains an important policy issue.

Budget surpluses in oil-producing countries

The Government of Azerbaijan continued to pursue a sound fiscal policy and the budget deficit remained at a low level of 1.0-2.0 per cent of GDP in 2001-2004. In spite of reductions in a number of taxes, increased salaries in the public sector and higher capital expenditures, the budget recorded a surplus of 0.9 per cent of GDP in the first 8 months of 2004 which can be attributed mainly to solid growth in oil-related revenue. (The targeted budget deficit in 2004 was equal to 1.0 per cent of GDP, assuming annual GDP growth of 9 per cent and an oil price of $20/barrel.) The State Oil Fund of Azerbaijan contributed over 25 per cent of total budget revenues in the first 8 months of 2004. The Government was expected to implement further tax reforms in order to cut tax rates on non-oil activities so as to diversify the economy.

The budget of Kazakhstan was also in surplus in the first 10 months of 2004 owing to substantial increases in tax revenues from natural resources, especially oil. For the full year, however, the budget deficit was expected to be around 0.4 per cent of GDP even though budget revenues were likely to increase as VAT and payroll taxes related to social expenditures were cut. The federal budget has been in surplus since 2001 in the Russian Federation and the surplus was expected to widen in 2004, reaching 3.8 per cent of GDP, largely as a result of higher than expected oil prices and rouble appreciation. The Government increased oil export duties to compensate for tax losses incurred in other sectors and increase budgetary revenues. The Government was also able to reduce expenditures by one fourth in the first 9 months of 2004 following the implementation of administrative reforms.

Tax reform in Kyrgyzstan

The Government of Kyrgyzstan was expected to undertake modest tax reforms in order to reduce the budget deficit from 0.8 per cent of GDP in 2003 to 0.6 per cent in 2004. The reforms included measures to extend VAT to agricultural goods and the introduction of a property tax. The Government was also expected to adopt a simplified and more accessible tax code to reduce turnover tax on firms by one quarter as the current income tax policy has proved to be inefficient for tax collection. The budget deficit in Turkmenistan was expected to be 2.2 per cent of GDP in 2004 as a result of increased expenditure on social programmes such as the supply of gas, water, electricity and salt at no charge to the population.

Foreign trade and other external transactions

External trade

High global commodity prices boosted export earnings in most countries

The foreign trade of the Russian Federation expanded more than 30 per cent in January-October 2004. Merchandise exports increased 34.1 per cent, to $144 billion, and merchandise imports 34.3 per cent, to $60 billion, in the same period (tables II.10 and II.11). As a result, the trade balance was around 34 per cent higher than in the first 10 months of 2003, when it amounted to $63 billion. Fuel and energy commodities accounted for over 57 per cent of total exports. Other major export items were metal and metal goods (16.9 per cent), machinery, equipment and transport (7.5 per cent) and wood and paper (4.0 per cent). The rising trade surplus resulted in a higher current account surplus, which was expected to rise marginally from 8.3 per cent of GDP in 2003 to 8.4 per cent in 2004 (table II.12).

Table II.10. North and Central Asian economies: merchandise exports and their rates of growth, 2001-2004

	Exports (f.o.b.)				
	Value (millions of US dollars)	Annual rate of growth (percentage)			
	2003	2001	2002	2003	2004[a]
Armenia	686	13.4	48.7	35.8	2.9
Azerbaijan	2 592	33.0	-6.4	19.6	35.7
Georgia	482	-3.0	1.7	38.5	48.9
Kazakhstan	12 927	-5.3	11.8	33.7	48.7
Kyrgyzstan	582	-5.5	2.0	19.8	35.8
Russian Federation	133 450	-2.8	6.1	25.1	34.1
Tajikistan	798	-16.7	13.3	8.3	20.1
Turkmenistan[b]	3 632	6.0	13.1	27.2	16.7
Uzbekistan[c]	3 128	-6.1	-8.9	24.6	15.7

Sources: Web site of the CIS Inter-State Statistical Committee <www.cisstat.com>, 11 January 2005; and EIU, *Country Reports* (London, EIU), various issues.

[a] Figure for 2004 refers to January-October except for Turkmenistan and Uzbekistan.
[b] Figure for 2004 is EIU estimate.
[c] Figures for 2003-2004 are EIU estimates.

Table II.11. North and Central Asian economies: merchandise imports and their rates of growth, 2001-2004

	Value (millions of US dollars)	Imports (c.i.f.) Annual rate of growth (percentage)			
	2003	2001	2002	2003	2004[a]
Armenia	1 279	−0.5	13.0	29.6	4.2
Azerbaijan	2 626	22.4	16.4	57.7	39.6
Georgia	1 144	4.2	6.0	56.5	72.3
Kazakhstan	8 409	25.9	2.1	27.7	56.1
Kyrgyzstan	717	−15.8	26.0	22.1	33.1
Russian Federation	57 263	24.0	10.0	24.0	34.3
Tajikistan	881	1.8	5.0	22.4	64.3
Turkmenistan[b]	2 512	26.6	−3.7	18.5	17.1
Uzbekistan[c]	2 367	4.6	−14.4	8.3	23.8

Sources: Web site of the CIS Inter-State Statistical Committee <www.cisstat.com>, 11 January 2005; and EIU, *Country Reports* (London, EIU), various issues.

[a] Figure for 2004 refers to January-October except for Turkmenistan and Uzbekistan.

[b] Figure for 2004 in f.o.b. value is the EIU estimate.

[c] Figures for 2003-2004 in f.o.b. values are EIU estimates.

Table II.12. North and Central Asian economies: current account balance as a percentage of GDP, 2001-2004

(Percentage)

	2001	2002	2003	2004
Armenia	−9.5	−6.2	−6.6	−6.1
Azerbaijan	−0.9	−12.3	−28.3	−29.9
Georgia	−6.6	−7.4	−10.1	−10.6
Kazakhstan	−5.2	−2.9	−0.6	2.5
Kyrgyzstan	−3.4	−5.3	−2.7	−3.3
Russian Federation	11.0	8.4	8.3	8.4
Tajikistan	−6.9	−1.4	−0.3	−3.1
Turkmenistan[a]	−2.5	3.5	4.1	3.5
Uzbekistan	−1.0	1.2	8.9	8.2

Sources: ESCAP, based on IMF, *International Financial Statistics,* vol. LVII, No. 8 (Washington, IMF, August 2004) and *World Economic Outlook Databases* (Washington, IMF, September 2004); and EIU, *Country Reports* (London, EIU, 2004), various issues.

Note: Figures for 2004 are estimates.

[a] Calculated based on official exchange rates.

Increased world prices of gold and cotton and rising exports of natural gas resulted in Uzbekistan recording a trade surplus of $815 million in the first 9 months of 2004. The Government also imposed import duties on a number of foodstuffs and undertook measures to limit the import of small-scale goods in 2004 in order to accelerate the implementation of import-substituting industrialization and provide additional protection for domestic producers. Merchandise exports were expected to grow by more than 15 per cent to $3.6 billion in 2004 compared with $3.1 billion in 2003 while import expenditures were expected to increase 23.8 per cent from $2.4 billion in 2003 to $2.9 billion in 2004. Chemical products, machinery and equipment, metals and foodstuffs were the principal imports in 2004. Markets outside CIS were the main export destinations in 2004 but imports were largely sourced from CIS countries.

However, trade balances deteriorated in some countries

Despite the favourable international conditions for its principal exports, the trade deficit increased fivefold in Tajikistan to $392 million in January-October 2004 from a year earlier. Strong economic growth and robust domestic demand led to import expenditure increasing 64.3 per cent while merchandise exports expanded only 20.1 per cent in the same period. Aluminium and cotton continued to dominate exports and benefited from high global prices. In coming years, revenues from electricity sales to neighbouring countries are expected to increase.

The construction of oil and gas pipelines in Azerbaijan increased import expenditures by 39.6 per cent in the first 10 months of 2004, exceeding export revenues by a wide margin and resulting in a trade deficit of $45 million during that period. Export revenues grew by 35.7 per cent in January-October 2004 owing to increased demand for crude oil and refined products in the EU. Oil products remained the largest export of Azerbaijan and accounted for about 70 per cent of total export revenues in 2004. Transport equipment and foodstuffs were other important exports.

The widening of the trade deficit in Armenia was attributed to strong growth in imports of food, raw material and energy, as well as intermediate and capital goods. Exports and imports grew by 2.9 and 4.2 per cent respectively in the first 10 months of 2004. Exports increased to $582 million and imports to more than 1 billion over the same period and the trade deficit widened from $473 million in January-October 2003 to $506 million in the corresponding period of 2004. The diamond-processing sector continued to be the main source of export revenues, while the metallurgy sector is beginning to play an important role in the foreign trade of the country. Diamond and metal exports accounted for more than half the total export revenues of Armenia in 2003.

Imports of capital goods and services related to pipeline construction and other infrastructure development and energy imports for the growing industrial sector caused the trade balance to deteriorate in Georgia. The merchandise trade deficit rose from $539 million in January-October 2003 to $913 million in the same period in 2004. Export revenues grew strongly by 48.9 per cent owing to buoyant world prices of metals, which remained the country's principal exports, but, at 72.3 per cent, import growth was almost as fast. Turkey and the Russian Federation were the leading trade partners of Georgia in 2004.

High oil prices led to a 48.7 per cent increase in merchandise export revenues in Kazakhstan and, as a result, the trade surplus rose to $5.4 billion in January-October 2004 from $4 billion in the comparable period of 2003. However, economic growth and real exchange rate appreciation stimulated a 56.1 per cent increase in import expenditure in the first 10 months of 2004. The direction of trade shifted back towards CIS; exports of goods to CIS during the first 10 months of 2004 earned Kazakhstan $3.3 billion, up 42 per cent year on year. Imports from CIS suppliers amounted to $4.9 billion in January-October 2004, an increase of 57 per cent from a year earlier.

The foreign trade of Kyrgyzstan expanded rapidly in the first 10 months of 2004, with an increase in merchandise export revenues of 35.8 per cent and in merchandise import expenditure of 33.1 per cent. However, the trade deficit was on an upward trend, increasing $134 million year on year to $167 million in January-October 2004. Gold remained the principal source of the country's export revenues, accounting for almost half of total export earnings. CIS countries were the main buyers of vegetables, sugar, clothing, building materials and tobacco from Kyrgyzstan in 2004 while non-CIS countries were the main buyers of gold.

Hydrocarbons and cotton remained the most important export commodities of Turkmenistan in 2004. The trade surplus of $501 million recorded in the first 9 months of 2004 was attributable to the high world prices and increased export volumes of these two commodities. The merchandise export revenues of the country increased to $2.9 billion in the first 9 months of 2004. Spending on imports rose almost 30 per cent to $2.4 billion in the first 9 months of 2004, with imports of machinery and equipment increasing 60 per cent.

Exchange rates

Dollar weakness affected national currencies

The general weakness of the United States dollar against the euro and most other international currencies had an effect on exchange rate developments in all the countries of North and Central Asia. Countries of the subregion continued to pursue policies aimed at maintaining competitive exchange rates so as to encourage economic diversification away from oil and other raw materials.

In the Russian Federation, the nominal exchange rate of the rouble against the dollar has been relatively stable in recent years (figure II.8) but the real effective exchange rate was expected to appreciate some 8 per cent by the end of 2004 owing to high export revenues. All restrictions on hard-currency operations in the Russian Federation are to be lifted by 2007. At present, all hard-currency transactions need to be approved by the Central Bank and domestic companies are required to sell 50 per cent of their hard-currency revenues to the Central Bank. This policy has boosted the country's hard-currency reserves from under $7 billion in 1999 to over $86 billion in 2003. The strengthening of the rouble has had an impact on exchange rates in Central Asian countries. For example, Kazakhstan took steps to reduce the value of its currency, the tenge, in order to support export competitiveness, despite which the tenge appreciated 9 per cent against the dollar in January-September 2004.

Figure II.8. Index of exchange rates against the United States dollar of North and Central Asian economies, 1996-2004

(1996=100)

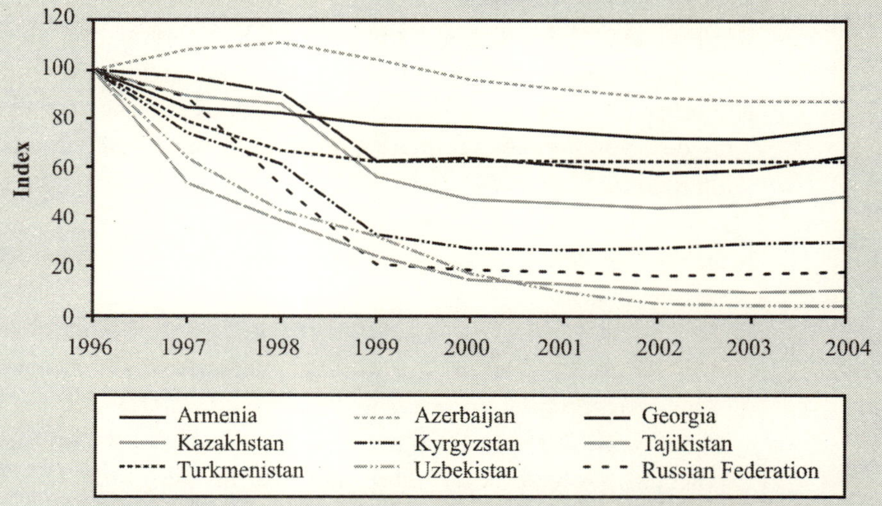

Sources: IMF, *International Financial Statistics*, vol. LVII, No. 10 (Washington, IMF, October 2004); and ADB, *Key Indicators of Developing Asian and Pacific Countries 2004* (Manila, ADB, 2004).

Note: Data for 2004 are for January-August; in the case of Kazakhstan and Russian Federation the 2004 figures are estimates.

Many currencies strengthened as FDI inflows increased

The increased inflow of FDI and foreign currency into the subregion resulted in national currencies strengthening in most countries of North and Central Asia against both the dollar and the euro in 2004. For example, the Azerbaijan manat and Georgian lari appreciated by 2.3 and 15 per cent respectively against the dollar in the first 9 months of 2004 owing largely to substantial FDI inflows related to pipeline construction in those countries. Sustained hard-currency inflows from the sale of gas and refined oil products enabled the Government of Turkmenistan to keep the exchange rate of the manat stable in 2004. The Armenian dram appreciated by 6 and 10 per cent against the dollar and the euro respectively in the first half of 2004 but the continued high rate of inflation was expected to keep the dram relatively stable during the rest of the year. The Tajikistan somoni strengthened against the dollar in 2004 owing to substantial remittances from migrant workers and rising export earnings; the Government maintains a managed float exchange rate regime.

Current account convertibility introduced in Uzbekistan

Uzbekistan introduced current account convertibility and loosened foreign exchange controls in the fall of 2003. Exchange rates were unified and the Government accepted its obligations under article VIII of the IMF Articles of Agreement. However, the unification of exchange rates reduced the volume of currency in circulation and both import and export of the national currency remain restricted. The tight monetary policy enabled the Government to stabilize the exchange rate of the sum by the third quarter of 2004. The currency had depreciated against the dollar by about 1 per cent each month after exchange rate reforms were introduced. The national currency of Kyrgyzstan, the som, depreciated 1 per cent against the dollar and 5 per cent against the euro in the first 5 months of 2004. The National Bank of Kyrgyzstan limited interventions in the foreign exchange market to smooth daily fluctuations and strengthen international reserves.

Capital inflows

Resource-based sectors received most of FDI

Most of the FDI inflows into the Central Asian subregion have been directed at bringing its oil and gas resources to Europe. At the same time, construction of an oil pipeline from Kazakhstan to China was launched in 2004. Kazakhstan is involved in three projects which were expected to lead to a rapid increase in oil production in the country. Since 1992, Kazakhstan has attracted nearly $18 billion in FDI, which has become a major contributor to the country's rapid economic growth and relative current account stability. Net inflows into the country increased almost fivefold to $1.7 billion in the first half of 2004 from a year earlier.

FDI inflows into the Russian Federation increased from $3.5 billion in 2002 to $6.7 billion in 2003. The bulk of the investment went to resource-based and service-related sectors. Given stable economic growth in the Russian Federation and Kazakhstan in the last five years, FDI flows between the two countries commenced in 2004. Oil companies from the Russian Federation intend to invest in developing oilfields on the Kazakh sector of the Caspian Sea shelf and in other oil-related projects in Kazakhstan, which in turn, was expected to invest about $1 billion in the economy of the Russian Federation in 2004.

The Russian Federation was the largest foreign investor in Armenia, accounting for over 90 per cent of $121 million additional FDI inflows in 2003. The bulk of the foreign investment was centred in three sectors of the economy, iron ore mining, telecommunications and the food industry. In the first half of 2004, FDI inflows into Armenia amounted to $93 million, compared with $23 million received in the corresponding period of 2003.

More than 80 per cent of Georgia's current-account deficit was covered by inflows of FDI in 2003, which amounted to $338 million or double the sum received in 2002 owing to the progress in constructing the oil and gas pipelines from Azerbaijan to Turkey through Georgia. The construction of the Baku-Tbilisi-Ceyhan oil pipeline brought $3.6 billion to Azerbaijan and Georgia in 2002-2004. The current revival of FDI in energy production is also driven by rising global energy consumption and new technology. Inflows of FDI into Azerbaijan increased from $1.4 billion in 2002 to $3.3 billion in 2003 and, in 2004, the ratio of FDI to GDP of Azerbaijan was around 50 per cent.

The Government of Kyrgyzstan aims to increase FDI inflows to $200-250 million by 2005 and FDI was expected to be 50 per cent higher in 2004. However, Kyrgyzstan needs to improve the business environment and strengthen cooperation in the subregion to facilitate the free flow of investment, goods and services. There is also a need to improve the country's tax legislation and make further progress on privatization and structural reforms. Two other economies, Uzbekistan and Tajikistan, need further structural reforms to attract more FDI. The levels of FDI in those countries are the lowest among the economies of the subregion owing to the poor business environment. However, there was a moderate pickup in FDI in Uzbekistan in 2003 following hydrocarbon-related investment inflows from the Russian Federation and China. Most FDI in Tajikistan in 2004 was allocated to the completion of two hydroelectric plants and development of the energy sector.

Foreign debt

External debt has been reduced owing to oil revenues

Substantial oil revenues considerably increased the domestic resources available in the oil-producing countries of the subregion, namely, the Russian Federation, Kazakhstan and Azerbaijan, to carry out development programmes without significant international borrowings in 2004. High oil prices enabled the Russian Federation to repay external debt as scheduled in 2004 and create a stabilization fund. The stabilization fund was used to refinance foreign debt. The ratio of debt to GDP fell from more than 100 per cent in 1998 to less than 30 per cent in 2003 and was expected to fall further to 21.3 per cent of GDP by the end of 2005. Kazakhstan and Azerbaijan also built up reserves of foreign exchange and high oil export earnings enabled the latter to meet debt-service costs. Azerbaijan's external debt was moderate, accounting for 22 per cent of GDP in 2003.

Debt rescheduling improved prospects for debt servicing in some countries

Tajikistan improved its prospects for external debt sustainability and the terms of debt service through debt-rescheduling agreements with its largest bilateral creditors such as the Russian Federation, Kazakhstan and Uzbekistan, effectively replacing bilateral debt with concessional borrowing. As a result, the external debt ratio declined from 82 per cent of GDP in 2002 to about 65 per cent in 2003, which is still one of the highest among the countries of North and Central Asia.

Georgia was one of the biggest recipients of development assistance among the countries of North and Central Asia in 2001-2004, in part owing to better tax effort. Debt service amounted to just under 25 per cent of export revenues in 2003 and total external debt was $1.78 billion at the beginning of 2004, and during the course of the year the Government reached an agreement with the Paris Club of leading creditor nations on rescheduling $200 million in foreign debt. The country no longer intends to borrow in the medium term except on concessional terms. Kyrgyzstan, whose total external debt is currently around $2 billion, is also expected to enter into a restructuring agreement with the Paris Club in 2005, which should result in a decline of the external debt ratio to 84.4 per cent from 91 per cent of GDP in 2004.

The foreign debt of Armenia climbed nearly 7 per cent in 2003 to reach $1.1 billion, of which almost 90 per cent was owed to the World Bank and IMF. The conclusion of a debt-to-equity agreement with the Russian Federation in 2003 reduced external debt by about $100 million. Debt servicing has not proved to be a problem for Armenia in 2004 owing to strong economic growth and increased export revenues.

Key policy issues

Poverty reduction efforts

There is a need for pro-poor growth in all countries of the subregion

Strong economic growth in the countries of North and Central Asia has underscored the need for pro-poor growth. While new jobs have been created and living standards improved in these countries, disparities between rural and urban areas and between the poor and rich remain. Rural poverty is three times higher than in urban areas in most Central Asian countries. Kyrgyzstan launched the first regional poverty reduction plan in the largest and most populous provinces of the country in 2004. The poverty rate in those regions was over 52 per cent, exceeding the average national poverty rate of 44 per cent in 2004. The main aim of the plan is to reduce poverty by more than half by 2010 through revitalizing the agricultural sector, utilizing human resources more effectively, developing the school and professional education systems further and strengthening cooperation between the central and local authorities. Real incomes of the population rose as a result of the economic expansion in Kyrgyzstan in 2004, with average monthly wages rising 4 per cent in the first 7 months of the year. However, wage levels remain much lower than average wages in Kazakhstan and the Russian Federation. As a result, there has been a sharp increase in labour migration from Kyrgyzstan and some 200,000-500,000 citizens of the country sought work in other CIS countries in 2004, particularly in the Russian Federation and Kazakhstan. The official unemployment rate declined marginally from 3.1 per cent in 2002 to 3.0 per cent in 2003 and total employment increased by 1 per cent in the same period.

Some poor countries made progress in reducing poverty …

In terms of per capita incomes, Uzbekistan remained one of the poorest CIS countries in 2004. However, the country's social indicators appear more favourable than those of other countries with similar per capita incomes. In 2004, the Government increased the minimum monthly wage from $5.5 to $6.5, the monthly pension to about $13.0 and other benefits by one third. However, over a quarter of the population of Uzbekistan is still living below the poverty line and income inequality was rising in 2004. Women make up nearly 60 per cent of the officially unemployed in Uzbekistan. The economy is expected to grow faster in 2005-2006, which will be necessary if per capita income and employment are to increase, given the rate of population growth. Despite falling birth rates, families remain large, especially in rural areas; 31 per cent of all rural families comprise 6-7 people.

Combating widespread poverty is a serious challenge facing Armenia. The Government's 12-year poverty-reduction plan seeks to reduce the poverty rate from more than 50 per cent in 2004 to 19 per cent in 2015. There were some indications of increased job creation in the country in 2004 as increased employment in labour-intensive sectors such as construction and agriculture contributed to a fall in the rate of unemployment. In 2003, 9.8 per cent of the labour force was officially registered as unemployed. The average monthly wage grew by almost a third in 2004.

… but job creation remains a challenge

The share of the population of Tajikistan living below the poverty line declined from 83 per cent in 1999 to 64 per cent in 2003. However, widespread poverty and lack of employment opportunities remain the prime social concerns of the country, which was among the poorest in CIS in 2004. In 2003, about 17 per cent of the population of Tajikistan sought jobs and higher wages in the Russian Federation and other neighbouring countries. Overseas job opportunities continued to be an important means of livelihood for many households in Tajikistan to alleviate poverty.

Incomes and salaries grew rapidly in Azerbaijan in 2004, with average monthly wages and per capita incomes increasing nearly 20 per cent and 18 per cent respectively. Workers in the oil industry and related sectors, in particular, benefited from faster growth and wages increased more rapidly. However, wages in the agricultural and social sectors remained a fraction of those in the oil sector. There was limited capacity to generate new jobs in Georgia, pipeline construction being unable to absorb the high number of newly unemployed. Reducing the share of the population living below the subsistence level from just over one half in 2003 to about one third by 2008 is one of the main goals of the Government.

Monetization of social benefits in the Russian Federation

Twenty-two per cent of the population of the Russian Federation lived in poverty in 2004 and there was a wide disparity between the rich and the poor in the country. At present, the poorest 10 per cent of the population are estimated to receive only 4 per cent of existing social benefits. To make the system fairer, a law converting certain social benefits such as free public transport and medicine into cash payments was adopted in 2004. The process of monetizing social benefits is aimed at providing the elderly with a choice between continuing to receive benefits in kind or in cash. Social benefits and assistance provided by the Government affect around 70 million people in the Russian Federation but people in rural areas suffer the greatest hardships as they are unable to take advantage of free transport and medical treatment. Cash payments are expected to give them greater direct financial support from the State and enhance choice.

Economic growth in the Russian Federation in 2004 had an impact on the labour market of the economy. The unemployment rate fell from 8.7 per cent in the first half of 2003 to 8.1 per cent in the corresponding period in 2004. Nominal wages rose 21.5 per cent in the first 10 months of 2004. Traditionally low-paid sectors continue to be health and education and, in the industrial sector, light industry and textiles. The minimum monthly wage is expected to increase from $25.7 in 2004 to almost $40 in 2006 in line with the official subsistence level. The socio-economic development programme of the Russian Federation for 2005-2008 envisages a reduction in the proportion of the population living below the subsistence level from 22 per cent in 2004 to 5.2 per cent by 2015. During this period, income inequality is expected to decline and the ratio of the average income of the top 10 per cent of income earners to the average income of the bottom 10 per cent is targeted to fall from 14.8 to 13.5 per cent.

HIV/AIDS - an emerging issue for the subregion

The poverty issues in the countries of North and Central Asia were aggravated by other social issues such as poor health and education systems and increased vulnerability to external shocks. HIV/AIDS has become a major and growing challenge for the subregion. The epidemic has been spreading rapidly in some countries where substantial increases in the number of reported HIV infections have been recorded. For example, the number of registered cases of HIV increased from under 100 in 1996 to more than 3,000 in 2002 in Kazakhstan, from 3 cases in 1995 to 1,500 in 2000 in Armenia and from a few cases in the 1990s to 402 cases in 2003 in Kyrgyzstan. In 2004, more than 3,600 people in Uzbekistan were registered as having HIV and the corresponding figure for Tajikistan was over 300. The rapid growth is a reflection of drug use and unsafe sex. According to some estimates, there were more than half a million drug users in Central Asia in 2004. Sexual transmission accounted for more than a quarter of newly registered HIV infections in the same year. Governments in Central Asian countries have adopted policies to diminish the spread of HIV/AIDS by encouraging prevention and also to improve treatment of infected persons. All countries have national AIDS centres and programmes on both health promotion and harm reduction. However, the HIV/AIDS epidemic could have far-reaching economic implications for the countries of the subregion. Long-term economic growth rates could fall by about 10 per cent in Kazakhstan and Kyrgyzstan and by over 20 per cent in Uzbekistan by 2015.

Banking and structural reforms

Consolidation of banking sectors in the Russian Federation and Tajikistan

Given the important link between structural reforms and economic growth, the countries of North and Central Asia focused on policies aimed at strengthening the banking sector, removing distortions in the energy sector and reforming natural monopolies. Banking reform in the Russian Federation included measures to consolidate the banking sector through voluntary combinations and mergers of smaller banks. There were more than 1,300 small banks in the country in 2004. As a part of this policy, the process of merging banks was simplified in order to protect the interests of creditors. All banks were expected to apply to join a deposit-insurance scheme to be introduced in 2005. Under the scheme, depositors would have the right to get up to 100,000 roubles of their deposits back in the event of a bank collapse.

In Tajikistan, the recent restructuring of commercial banks and improvements in the regulatory environment covering banking operations increased public confidence in the banking system. Kyrgyzstan, however, was not able to mobilize sufficient domestic savings for its investment needs as a result of slow banking reforms and the banking system has not played a significant intermediary role between savers and borrowers. The focus of the country's banking reform in 2004 was on developing more effective procedures for settling disputes with foreign investors, banking legislation and improving banking services for SMEs.

Natural monopolies and the energy sector also focus of reforms

The restructuring of natural monopolies was one of the cornerstones of structural reforms in the Russian Federation designed to reduce the economic influence of the State and make companies more efficient and transparent. Under the reform plan of the country's Unified Energy

System (UES), the State was expected to retain control of the transmission grid and the generation of electricity in hydropower stations. The remaining assets of power generation and distribution entities were expected to be sold to investors. The experience in reforming UES is to be used in the restructuring of one of the largest suppliers of natural gas in the world, Gazprom, in 2005. The company is an export-oriented entity responsible for the exploration, production and transport of gas. The reform of Gazprom is expected to provide access for independent gas producers to the State-controlled gas pipeline and abolish restrictions preventing foreign investors from buying the company's domestic shares to increase market capitalization of the entity.

Georgia launched an ambitious structural reform effort aimed at addressing governance issues, improving the efficiency and effectiveness of the public sector and strengthening macroeconomic fundamentals in 2004. Restoring the physical and financial viability of the energy sector was another key element of the reform agenda. Improved bill collection is expected to reduce the sizeable fiscal deficit. The power tariff methodology has been reviewed by the energy regulatory agency to facilitate cost recovery. Structural reforms in Armenia were aimed at sustaining economic growth and reducing poverty. Reforming the energy sector was one of the policy priorities for the country in 2004 and reforms included the establishment of market rules for electricity trading and privatization of distribution companies.

Apart from the banking sector, Tajikistan's structural reform agenda is extensive and includes the privatization of the energy sector and State-owned farms to enhance resource efficiency. Farms remaining in public hands are expected to be restructured and privatized by the end of 2005 through the issuance of land-use and land-share certificates. Economic policy in Azerbaijan in 2004 focused on maintaining macroeconomic stability while implementing deeper structural reforms. Recent structural reform commitments include increasing competition in the telecommunication sector and reforms in the banking and energy sectors.

Talks on WTO membership made progress but were going slowly

WTO membership is a central plank in the economic reform programmes of North and Central Asian countries. Membership is expected to enable those countries to play a full part in global trade negotiations. Talks on access to service markets, such as telecommunications and banking, were going slowly but have made progress. In 2004, the greatest progress was shown in negotiations with the Russian Federation and Kazakhstan. These two economies could eventually become members of WTO in 2005-2006. The main obstacles to the membership of other countries were State subsidies for the agricultural sector and energy pricing and access of foreign companies to markets in telecommunications and financial services.

Pacific island economies

Subregional overview

Positive though modest economic performance in 2004

As in 2003, most Pacific island economies experienced positive, though modest, real GDP growth rates in 2004 (figure II.9). Support for this positive performance has come from increases in primary commodity prices, tourist numbers and remittances. Increased cocoa, copra, palm oil, copper and gold prices have been a positive factor, particularly for countries like Papua New Guinea, Solomon Islands and Vanuatu, while increased petroleum prices have also supported the Papua New Guinea economy. Tourism expanded in Fiji, Samoa, Tonga and Vanuatu. Strong economic growth in Australia and New Zealand seems to be underpinning the growth in tourism in the Pacific and flights from those countries to Pacific destinations have been increased. Hotel construction has also picked up, giving a boost to the construction industry in several countries. Fiji is experiencing shortages of skilled workers in trying to meet its construction deadlines. Construction has also been at higher levels in Samoa and Vanuatu owing to cyclone damage.

Figure II.9. Rates of GDP growth in selected Pacific island economies, 2001-2004

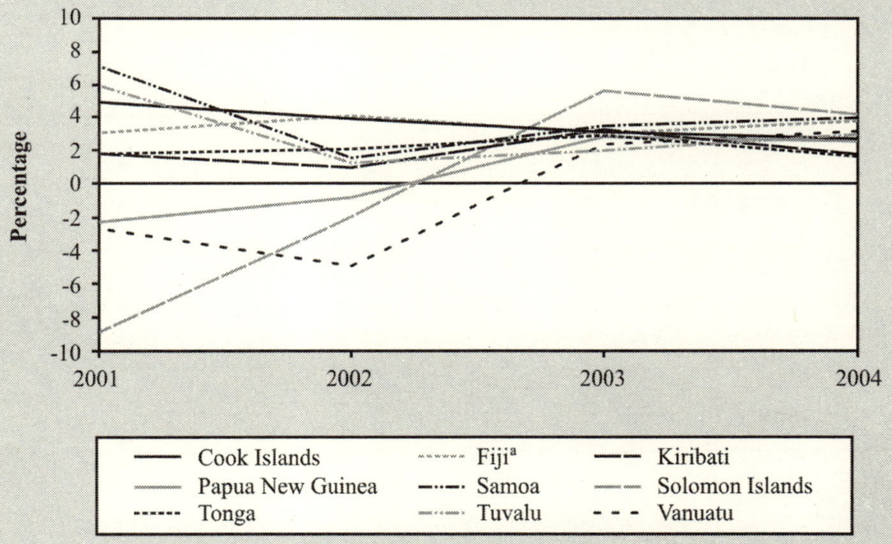

Sources: ESCAP, based on national sources; Department of Treasury and Planning, Papua New Guinea, 2005 *National Budget* (Port Moresby, 2004); and ADB, *Key Indicators of Developing Asian and Pacific Countries 2004* (Manila, ADB, 2004) and *Asian Development Outlook 2004 Update* (Manila, ADB, 2004).

Note: Growth rates for 2004 are estimates.

[a] Real GDP at factor cost.

Good macroeconomic management but high oil prices a potential threat

Across the Pacific region, improved economic management resulted in reduced budget deficits and reduced public debt and, therefore, less stress on monetary management so that performance on the inflation front has been good to excellent with the exception of Tonga (figure II.10). However, this improved fiscal and monetary performance is under threat because of the sharp increase in oil prices and the direct and indirect consequences of the high oil prices if they persist for much longer. The high prices will directly raise the costs of power and transport in Pacific island countries. Indirectly, if they lead to declines in economic growth in the developed countries, the outcome for the Pacific island countries will be reduced demand and prices for their raw material exports as well as reduced tourism. Maintaining the improved fiscal and monetary management will be critical in minimizing the damage from high oil prices.

Figure II.10. Inflation[a] in selected Pacific island economies, 2001-2004

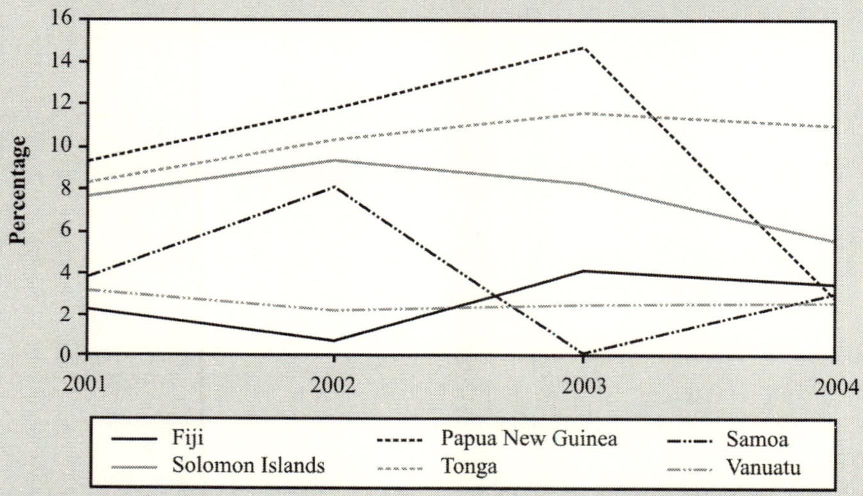

Sources: ESCAP, based on national sources; and ADB, *Key Indicators of Developing Asian and Pacific Countries 2004* (Manila, ADB, 2004) and *Asian Development Outlook 2004 Update* (Manila, ADB, 2004).

Note: Inflation rates for 2004 are estimates.

[a] Changes in the consumer price index.

Inflows of remittances increased in several countries

The inflow of remittances has given strong support to Pacific island economies. Samoa and Tonga have traditionally relied on remittances for a large share of their national income and continued to experience large inflows, mainly from long-term emigrants. However, the nature of the remittances has been changing, with short-term, offshore employment opportunities becoming more available and with other Pacific island countries such as Fiji taking advantage of these opportunities. The fact that there are so many young people in the Pacific looking for work outside their countries is a reflection of the insufficient level of investment and jobs in their own countries. Unfortunately, there is a lack of data on investment in Pacific island countries upon which to base the analysis. Only Fiji has recent data on investment and here the picture is not bright. While Fiji's investment ratio has risen in recent years, only one quarter of total investment is private. One half of total investment goes to public enterprises and statutory authorities that are mostly making losses or achieving very low returns on investments.

With the increased commodity prices, international reserves have been rebuilt to a level that provides ample import cover in most Pacific island countries. In Solomon Islands, Tonga and Vanuatu, the improvement in international reserves has also been assisted by drawings from loans and grants from international financial agencies and donors.

GDP performance and outlook

Fiji's improved economic performance in 2004 underpinned by tourism …

The recent growth in GDP in Fiji has been mainly due to continuing growth in tourist numbers, the sharp increase in remittances and government stimulation of the economy through deficit financing. In its 2005 budget, the Fiji Government projected GDP growth of 3.8 per cent in 2004 and lowered 2003 growth to 3 per cent owing to broad-based weak economic performance (table II.13). The improved growth estimated for 2004 reflects better performance by the tourism sector. Forecasts of future growth have also been sharply revised downwards and GDP growth for 2005 is now projected at 1.5 per cent owing to the expiry of the MFA and an expected decline in sugar production.

Tourist numbers again grew strongly in 2004 in Fiji, up 3.5 per cent on 2003 to a new high. Earnings from tourism are expected to be F$ 445 million in 2004, slightly higher than the F$ 431 million in 2003. The increased demand for hotel beds and additional retail and office accommodation, especially in the capital city, point to construction being a leading sector in 2005. Although they are still relatively small sectors, forestry and mining output in Fiji have grown strongly. The sharp increase in gold prices in 2004 boosted the value of gold exports as well as stimulating further investment in the industry. Landowner issues in relation to the harvesting of mahogany trees are being resolved, allowing the harvesting to proceed.

Fiji's garment exports in 2004 are expected to improve slightly on 2003, increasing from F$ 129 million to F$ 134 million. The garment industry has received a shot in the arm with the Australian Government agreeing to extend the South Pacific Regional Trade and Economic Cooperation Agreement (SPARTECA) arrangement by seven years. This extension has provided some solace to an industry that lost its preferential access to the United States market in January 2005, a predicament compounded by the appreciation of the Fijian dollar against the United

Table II.13. Selected Pacific island economies: growth rates, 2001-2004

(Percentage)

		Rates of growth			
		Gross domestic product	*Agriculture*	*Industry*	*Services*
Cook Islands	2001	4.9	−2.9	13.3	5.4
	2002	3.9	9.5	5.0	2.9
	2003	3.1	..	..	..
	2004	2.7	..	..	..
Fiji[a]	2001	3.0	−4.9	7.7	3.3
	2002	4.1	4.3	0.1	..
	2003	3.0	−3.9	3.2	9.8
	2004	3.8	3.7	3.3	7.9
Kiribati	2001	1.8	0.2	21.6	−0.5
	2002	0.9	−4.5	−7.8	3.2
	2003	3.3	..	..	..
	2004	1.8	..	..	..
Papua New Guinea	2001	−2.3	−5.3	−0.2	1.9
	2002	−0.8	7.3	−10.8	1.2
	2003	2.8	3.5	5.3	−0.1
	2004	2.6	3.0	2.1	2.0
Samoa	2001	7.1	−3.8	12.2	8.4
	2002	1.5	−6.3	−1.0	5.1
	2003	3.5	−0.6	5.6	3.6
	2004	4.0	..	..	..
Solomon Islands	2001	−9.0	−4.4	−39.7	−4.5
	2002	−2.0	5.1	0.5	−9.2
	2003	5.6	..	..	..
	2004	4.2	..	..	..
Tonga	2001	1.8	−1.1	2.3	3.4
	2002	2.1	2.1	5.5	0.6
	2003	2.9	1.4	4.0	2.4
	2004	1.6	..	..	..
Tuvalu	2001	5.9	−2.6	10.3	6.9
	2002	1.2	−9.4	6.5	2.2
	2003	2.0	..	..	..
	2004	3.0	..	..	..
Vanuatu	2001	−2.7	−3.1	−4.7	−2.4
	2002	−4.9	−3.3	−5.8	−5.2
	2003	2.4	6.2	−0.3	1.8
	2004	3.2	3.5	1.6	3.3

Sources: ESCAP, based on national sources; Department of Treasury and Planning, Papua New Guinea, *2005 National Budget* (Port Moresby, 2004); and ADB, *Key Indicators of Developing Asian and Pacific Countries 2004* (Manila, ADB, 2004) and *Asian Development Outlook 2004 Update* (Manila, ADB, 2004).

Notes: Growth rates for 2004 are estimates. Industry comprises mining and quarrying; manufacturing; electricity, gas and power; and construction.

[a] Real GDP at factor cost.

States dollar since 2002. Still, the value of SPARTECA to the Fijian garment industry can be expected to decline as tariff barriers are reduced globally via the WTO agreement. The industry will have to improve its productivity significantly if it is to be competitive with East Asian economies on the basis of unit labour costs; otherwise it will have to find niche markets that will yield higher prices. The details of the SPARTECA extension have not been worked out between the Governments of Australia and Fiji. However, a critical element must be incentives for the industry to improve its productivity.

... but the sugar industry continues to struggle

Sugar exports from Fiji are not expected to show any increase in 2004 as this highly inefficient industry labours under the Government's inability to develop a viable lease system for cane farmers. The recently announced plans for reductions in the preferential price received for African, Caribbean and Pacific sugar exported under quota to the EU also came as a shock to the industry. Much of the sugar cane land where leases were not renewed to Indo-Fijian tenants is now lying idle. Other leased land taken over by indigenous farmers, with the inducement of a F$ 10,000 grant from the Government to each new farmer, is struggling to attain the same output as previously and it may be preferable not to entice indigenous farmers into an industry that is under threat of collapse but to allow the land to be used for other purposes.

Remittances earned by teachers, nurses and military and security personnel have climbed rapidly over the past few years to reach 3.4 per cent of GDP in 2002. While the increased incomes are welcome for the families of migrant workers, and for the additional tax revenues generated from expenditure of the remittances, this resort to overseas employment is a reflection on the economy's poor capacity to generate jobs. While these short-term overseas workers are primarily indigenous Fijians, the long-term emigration of Indo-Fijians continues unabated at around 5,000 per year, resulting in a significant brain drain. Private investment is well below the level needed to generate economic growth above 5 per cent so as to provide jobs for the 9,000-10,000 young people entering the labour force each year. Although it has been increasing in recent years, total investment is only around 16 per cent of GDP and only about one quarter of this is private investment. The one half of total investment that is going into public enterprises is earning poor returns. The challenge for the Government is to create an environment in which private investment increases rapidly and the investment ratio rises to around 25 per cent of GDP; otherwise GDP growth will return to the average 2-3 per cent range of the past two decades. Success will depend primarily on there being a significant reduction in political instability and in law and order problems.

Higher mineral and oil prices sustain economic growth in Papua New Guinea

In Papua New Guinea, modest GDP growth of 2.6 per cent was recorded for 2004, a reduction from the 2.8 per cent GDP growth achieved in 2003, which itself followed three years of falling real GDP, resulting in a large loss in average per capita incomes. As in 2003, high prices of copper, gold and oil have provided the main support to the economy but the rest of the economy performed poorly. There was little change in coffee production or exports but world prices appear to be slowly recovering from their long-term slump.

Gold and copper output is continuing to decline as the Misima and Porgera mines will be closing down shortly and oil production and exports also declined in 2004. However, petroleum exports are expected to increase as the Moran field reaches full production and the high oil, copper and gold prices have stimulated exploration as have the more favourable taxation policies being followed in recent years. The optimism in the minerals sector is supported by Chinese investment in the Ramu nickel-cobalt project, the announcement that work will begin soon on the $2.3 billion gas pipeline to Australia and the commencement of production by the Napa Napa oil refinery. These activities have resulted in an inflow of $101 million in FDI into the country in 2003, almost five times the level in 2002, and equal to around 3 per cent of GDP. Most of the impact on the economy from the construction phase of the gas pipeline project will be felt in 2006 and 2007. At least a further three gold and copper mines are expected to go into production early in 2005 and GDP growth is forecast to increase to 2.9 per cent in that year.

Law and order problems continue to affect investment adversely as do high infrastructure costs. Also, recurring threats of no-confidence motions against the Government have meant that political instability persists. The Government's inability to improve the investment climate basically derives from the inability of unstable governing coalitions to implement the necessary changes in policies and in fiscal expenditure to improve infrastructure and tackle the significant law and order problem.

Budget performance improves in 2004 in Papua New Guinea

The current Government has done very well in terms of fiscal policy and is expected to end the year with a small surplus of 1.1 per cent of GDP (table II.14). According to the Bank of Papua New Guinea, the improvement was due to higher tax and dividend receipts and lower interest costs on domestic debt. The prudent fiscal management also resulted in the retirement of some Treasury bills and allowed the restructuring of domestic debt from short- to long-term. Improved fiscal management is also reflected in better control over expenditure. The increased revenue accruing to the Government as the result of high mineral and oil prices presents an opportunity to retire substantial public debt and relax pressure on interest rates. Government debt was still around 70 per cent of GDP in early 2004.

Financial reforms implemented by the previous Government have been maintained. These reforms were aimed at ensuring the independence of the central bank and placed life insurance companies and superannuation funds under its purview. The present Government has also

Table II.14. Selected Pacific island economies: budget and current account balance as a percentage of GDP, 2001-2004

(Percentage)

	2001	2002	2003	2004
Budget balance[a] as a percentage of GDP				
Fiji	−7.3	−5.6	−5.9	−4.8
Papua New Guinea	−3.7	−4.3	−1.0	1.1
Samoa	−2.3	−2.1	−0.6	−1.5
Solomon Islands	−11.9	−9.6	−1.4	..
Tonga	−0.2	1.2	−3.8	−0.7
Vanuatu	−3.7	−1.5	−1.8	0.4
Current account balance as a percentage of GDP				
Fiji	−3.0	−3.7	−5.3	−5.3
Papua New Guinea	6.9	−0.7	10.1	..
Samoa	−11.9	−7.6	−0.6	−1.1
Solomon Islands	−8.8	−6.4	12.8	..
Tonga	−19.9	14.8	−19.9	..
Vanuatu	0.8	−7.8	−11.1	..

Sources: ESCAP, based on national sources; IMF, *Solomon Islands: 2004 Article IV Consultation,* IMF Country Report No. 04/258 (August 2004); and ADB, *Key Indicators of Developing Asian and Pacific Countries 2004* (Manila, ADB, 2004) and *Asian Development Outlook 2004 Update* (Manila, ADB, 2004).

Note: Figures for 2004 are estimates.

[a] Including grants.

endeavoured to improve the performance of statutory bodies by passing a constitutional amendment under which the Public Service Commission will vet the appointment of heads of these organizations. Hopefully, this legislation will eliminate the nepotism and political cronyism that have pervaded appointments to government business enterprises in recent years. The legislation complements changes made to the Public Services Management Act in 2003, which attempt to ensure that the appointment of heads of government departments is merit-based.

As a result of the improved fiscal and monetary management, Fitch Ratings upgraded the long-term foreign currency rating of Papua New Guinea to B+ in April 2004. However, the agency expressed concern about the limited progress in critical structural reforms, which undermined the Government's efforts to offset the continuing decline in the mining and energy sectors. The agency was also concerned about the Government's heavy reliance on domestic financing of the deficit, which exposed the budget to significant interest rate and rollover risks.

In the 2005 budget, development expenditure is projected to increase by around 70 per cent over the previous year, with the bulk of the money to be spent in the provinces and districts. The emphasis of the public investment programme will be on basic education, primary health care, including increased funds for combating HIV/AIDS, law and justice, infrastructure maintenance and the promotion of export-oriented activities. The focus on the development of the rural sector is to be greatly welcomed. However, the big question mark hanging over this scenario is the capacity of the provincial and district governments to implement the programme. As elsewhere, national government control over the major sources of revenue in Papua New Guinea has meant that quality human resources tend to gravitate to the national capital. As a result, subnational authorities often do not have the human resources to design and implement projects of high quality.

Improved law and order situation and better fiscal management in Solomon Islands …

The Solomon Islands economy rebounded strongly in 2003 recording 5.6 per cent growth after contracting for the past three years and the pace of growth expected in 2004-2005 is in the 4-5 per cent range, based on continuing improvements in the law and order situation and better fiscal management. Forestry, fisheries and agriculture, particularly cocoa and copra, continue to underpin the economy. The resilience of people in rural areas and their capacity to maintain economic activities throughout the civil unrest have been a bright spot in the recent history of the country.

With most of its people living in and dependent upon rural activities, Solomon Islands has to focus on growth through increased productivity in the rural sector. In doing so, it has to diversify into areas where it has a comparative advantage. Overseas investors have shown interest in reviving the palm oil industry owing to good, long-term prospects for demand for palm oil in China and it is estimated that it will take around 18 months to rehabilitate oil palm plantations and resume production. However, available data suggest that FDI inflows into the country have been negative since 1999 and were equivalent to –0.5 per cent of GDP in 2003. Problems in ensuring secure land rights must be overcome, based upon well-designed contracts that will be backed by governments at the local and national levels. Farmers also need to get their products to markets in an efficient and reliable manner and the EU is working on a transport project to assist cocoa and copra farmers.

… but unsustainable logging continues

Management of forestry and fisheries in Solomon Islands, two of its most important natural resources, has to be substantially improved. The tuna catch has been greatly reduced by the closure of the major fishing firm during the civil unrest. However, the rate of logging was little affected by the civil unrest and continues at what is believed to be an unsustainable rate. It is estimated that, in 2003, in excess of 700,000 cubic metres of logs were felled.

The Australia-led regional assistance mission to Solomon Islands appears to be continuing on track. As part of its assistance to the economic recovery in Solomon Islands, Australia is providing substantial help in building capacity in key government departments. As a result, tax collections have strengthened and expenditure controls have been tightened. According to IMF, the budget deficit for 2003 was equivalent to 1.4 per cent of GDP, compared with 9.6 per cent in 2002, and the budget is projected to be in surplus in 2004 largely as a result of these measures.

Construction activities contributed to improved GDP growth in Samoa

According to the 2005 budget statement, real GDP in Samoa grew by 3.5 per cent in 2003, a substantial improvement over the 1.5 per cent achieved in 2002. However, Samoa has not been able to return to the 6 per cent plus GDP growth rates of 2000 and 2001. Tuna catches have been poor since mid-2002 owing to bad weather and overfishing and agricultural harvests have suffered from dry weather conditions as well as damage from a cyclone in January 2004. Construction boomed following rebuilding activities after the cyclone and helped to boost GDP growth to 4 per cent in 2004. Samoa is hosting the South Pacific Games in 2007 and the construction sector can be expected to do well in 2005-2006. Migrant remittances continue to be a mainstay of the Samoan economy although manufacturing was also a major contributor to growth in 2003, particularly exports of automotive harnesses to Australia and of garments. Tourism earnings in Samoa also increased by 4 per cent in 2003, with tourist arrivals increasing by 3.9 per cent. This is a faster rate of growth than seen in the past three years and bodes well for the future. Tourism is second only to remittances in contributing to Samoa's balance of payments and well above earnings from agricultural and fishery exports. However, the success of tourism depends on reliable air services and although the Government is committed to maintaining Polynesian Airlines, it has incurred losses over the past three years. The outlook for GDP growth in the medium term is for growth to continue in the 3-4 per cent range, if agriculture and fisheries recover.

Tonga recorded reduced GDP growth in 2004

GDP growth in Tonga in 2004 slowed to 1.6 per cent from 2.9 per cent in 2003, after the 2.1 per cent growth achieved in 2002. Agriculture, primarily squash and vanilla, fishing and tourism are the major economic activities in Tonga. Exports of squash have been increasing but the substantially lower prices received have more than offset the increase in volume. Vanilla prices have held up, leading to increases in the value of exports. The fishing industry has also been in difficulty with lower catches and lower prices. Even with the modest rates of growth, average per capita income levels continue to rise because the high level of emigration keeps population growth well below 1 per cent per year.

Private remittances, which accounted for 41.2 per cent of GDP in 2002, can be expected to continue in the region of T$ 80-90 million annually given sustained economic growth in Australia and New Zealand.

Official estimates of remittances are likely to be underestimates as much of the cash comes into the country via informal channels. In addition, there are substantial remittances in kind in the form of used clothing, furniture and other goods. As in other Pacific island countries, tourist arrivals and expenditures have been increasing in Tonga. The declining level of the pa'anga against the Australian and New Zealand currencies, as well as the safe environment offered by the Pacific island countries, appears to have encouraged visitors. Maintenance and future growth of tourism will depend heavily on the availability of reliable air services.

Recovery continued in Vanuatu helped by improved macroeconomic management

Following falls in GDP in 2001 and 2002, the economy of Vanuatu turned around in 2003 to grow at 2.4 per cent, with growth picking up further to 3.2 per cent in 2004. The upturn has been helped by sound macroeconomic management, a recovery in the agricultural sector, increased tourism and land development around the capital, Port Vila. However, high population growth relative to the GDP growth rate has led to stagnation in per capita income, and real average GDP per capita is reported to have fallen below the level of 20 years ago. The obstacles to achieving a much higher growth path appear to be continuing political instability, difficulties in mobilizing land for investment and the presence of monopolies which are mainly State-owned in key areas, particularly essential services. Vanuatu managed to attract an estimated $19 million in FDI or about 8 per cent of GDP in 2003, compared with 6.6 per cent of GDP in 2002, but the Government needs to overcome some of the obstacles already identified if economic growth is to improve.

There has been an increase in tourism in Vanuatu following more frequent airline services from Australia and New Zealand. However, the country is a high-priced destination owing to the relatively high exchange rate. In the management of the exchange rate, a critical decision has to be made whether to continue to favour existing activities or to allow other activities such as tourism and agriculture to become more internationally competitive. The value of output from the agricultural, forestry and fishing sectors in Vanuatu increased by 6.2 per cent in 2003 after a decline of 3.3 per cent the previous year. The Vanuatu Commodity Marketing Board lost its monopoly position in the export of agricultural products in 2003 when the price support scheme it was managing placed it in an unviable financial position. The licensing of private exporters has reportedly improved both efficiency and prices.

The improved economic management of the Vanuatu economy is reflected in the progress made on the fiscal front with the budget deficit narrowing from 3.7 per cent of GDP in 2001 to 1.8 per cent in 2003. A small budget surplus was recorded in the first half of 2004 and the Government's target is a surplus of 0.4 per cent of GDP for the year as a whole. However, a number of unbudgeted expenditures, such as cyclone-related expenditure and the election, may make this target difficult to hit. A longer-term concern is that frustration with the lack of a growth dividend from the comprehensive reform programme could lead to the loss of expenditure restraint. The Government's ability to promote development has been reduced by increased current spending, mainly on wages and salaries, and it has recently abolished the post of director-general of each department in an attempt to increase funds for development expenditures.

The smaller Pacific island countries also recorded uneven economic growth in 2003-2004. In the case of Cook Islands, GDP growth which has been on a downward trend since 2000 declined further to 2.7 per cent in 2004 from 3.1 per cent in 2003. The tourism sector especially hotels, restaurants and transport services witnessed moderate strengthening in 2003 following the drop in visitor arrivals triggered by the 11 September 2001 events. Kiribati's economy also declined to an estimated 1.8 per growth in 2004, compared to 3.3 per cent growth in 2003. Higher consumer spending associated with a rise in government expenditures connected with two national elections in late 2002 and mid-2003 coupled with employment in large construction projects contributed to the growth in 2004. Economic growth in Tuvalu, in contrast has been on an upward trend in recent years with an estimated GDP growth of 3.0 per cent in 2004 compared with 1.6 average growth during 2002-2003. Much of the impetus to growth in Tuvalu is attributed to government expenditure which amounted to $A 25.1 million in 2003. The increase was primarily owing to a rise in the number of civil servants and higher capital expenditures, as well as some additional extraordinary spending. Tuvalu also benefits from growing remittances from migrant seafarers, now estimated at well over $A 5 million a year, or equivalent to about 20 per cent of GDP.

Inflation

Relatively low rates of inflation in the Pacific region in 2004 ...

Except for Tonga, where the rate of inflation was in double digits, the Pacific island economies recorded low rates of inflation in 2004 (table II.15). In Papua New Guinea, annual inflation has trended sharply downwards from a rate of 14.7 per cent in 2003 to 2.9 per cent in 2004. The vastly improved inflation rate reflects, first, the increased export earnings, resulting in the build-up of international reserves and the appreciation of the exchange rate against the United States dollar (figure II.11) and, second, the expenditure restraint exercised by the Government, leading to lower budget deficits. Fortunately, wage demands have also been modest. International reserves have been rebuilt to around $600 million, passing the previous peak in 1996. The long-term decline in the nominal kina rate has been stabilized and the currency has strengthened slightly over the past two years, especially against the United States dollar. For 2005 and beyond the key issue will be how well the Government manages its good fortune in having an extended period of high mineral and oil prices. Keeping recurrent public expenditure and wages under control will be critical.

Table II.15. Selected Pacific island economies: inflation and money supply growth (M2), 2001-2004

(Percentage)

	2001	2002	2003	2004
Inflation[a]				
Fiji	2.3	0.7	4.2	3.5
Papua New Guinea	9.3	11.8	14.7	2.9
Samoa	3.8	8.1	0.1	3.0
Solomon Islands	7.7	9.4	8.3	5.6
Tonga	8.3	10.3	11.6	11.0
Vanuatu	3.2	2.2	2.5	2.6
Money supply growth (M2)				
Fiji	−3.1	7.9	25.2	14.5[b]
Papua New Guinea	1.6	4.0	−0.4	−4.5[c]
Samoa	6.1	10.2	14.0	12.3[d]
Solomon Islands	−13.6	6.0	25.4	24.8[e]
Tonga	14.9	7.8	14.4	18.7[f]
Vanuatu	5.7	−1.7	−0.8	7.7[d]

Sources: ESCAP, based on national sources; ADB, *Key Indicators of Developing Asian and Pacific Countries 2004* (Manila, ADB, 2004); and IMF, *International Financial Statistics*, vol. LVII, No. 10 (Washington, IMF, October 2004).

Note: Figures for 2004 are estimates.

[a] Changes in the consumer price index.
[b] January-August.
[c] January-March.
[d] January-July.
[e] January-May.
[f] January-June.

After averaging 2.5 per cent in the previous five years, the rate of inflation rose to 4.2 per cent in 2003 in Fiji, reflecting the imposition of a 2.5 per cent increase in the VAT rate. The growth in consumer prices eased to 3.5 per cent in 2004 but as Fiji is heavily dependent upon oil imports for power generation like most other Pacific island countries, high oil prices will push up costs of production in most activities. Already there has been a substantial increase in the prices of motor fuels. Wage pressure is also a concern, given the high level of hotel and other construction under way and the shortage of skilled workers. Achieving good fiscal management in Fiji has also been difficult, with only a small reduction in the budget deficit in 2004 to 4.8 per cent from 5.9 per cent of GDP in 2003.

The Reserve Bank of Fiji tightened monetary policy in May 2004, increasing the official interest rate from 1.25 to 1.75 per cent. The reason for the increase was the expected GDP growth of around 5 per cent, which the central bank sees as being led by consumption. However, it is more likely

Figure II.11. Index of exchange rates against the United States dollar of selected Pacific island economies and Australia and New Zealand, 1996-2004

(1996 = 100)

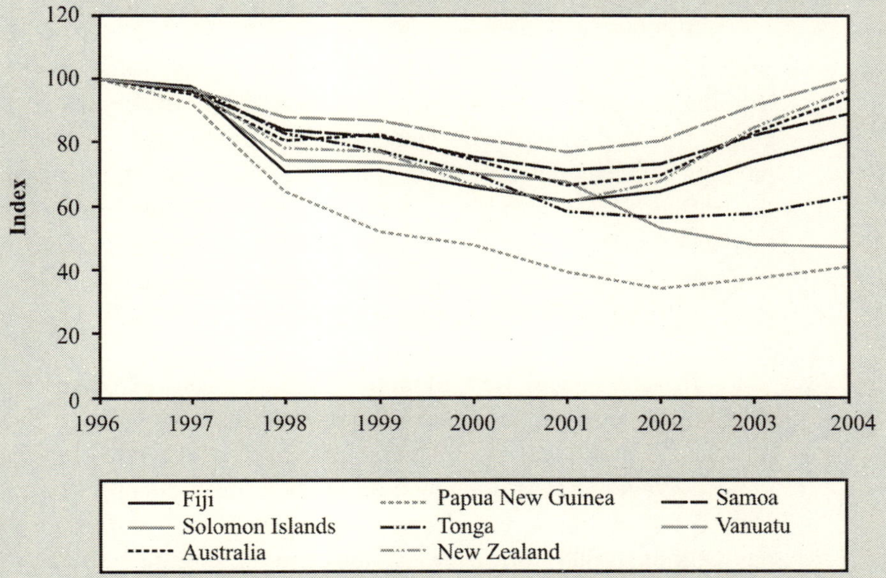

Sources: IMF, *International Financial Statistics*, vol. LVII, No. 10 (Washington, IMF, October 2004); and *The Economist*, various issues.

Note: Figures for 2004 are estimates.

that the good economic growth of recent years has been led by tourism, remittances and government-supported investments, and the increase in interest rates is unlikely to reduce the impact of these activities and is more likely to have a dampening impact on private investment. Moreover, the Government has now substantially reduced the GDP growth rates projected for 2005 and 2006. With the high oil prices and the prospect of increased wage demands, it will be a challenge for the Government's economic management to keep to the expected inflation rate of 3 per cent in 2005.

With improved fiscal and monetary management, inflation in Solomon Islands declined further in 2004 to an estimated 5.6 per cent from 8.3 per cent in 2003. Increased domestic supplies of foodstuffs as a result of the improved law and order situation are said to be partly responsible for this performance as the Solomon Islands dollar depreciated against both the United States and Australian currencies in 2004.

In Samoa, the average annual rate of inflation in 2003 fell sharply to 0.1 per cent from 8.1 per cent in 2002 owing to falling food prices. By September 2004, however, the Central Bank of Samoa reported that inflation was running at 9 per cent, having risen from 7.9 per cent in July, as the cyclone damaged food crops and the cost of oil imports increased. Recovery in agriculture should reduce food prices but the continuing high oil prices will make it difficult to reduce inflation to the expected 3 per cent level in 2004.

... except Tonga with double-digit rates

Tonga's inflation rate averaged 11.6 per cent in 2003, compared with 10.3 per cent in 2002. Monetary expansion from support provided to loss-making public enterprises that have been unable to meet their debt commitments appears to underlie the continuing depreciation of the pa'anga against the Australian dollar, resulting in import price pressure on the inflation rate. Public sector reforms currently under way appear to be leading to better fiscal management but unless there is improved management of SOEs and public sector wage demands are controlled, there will be continuing pressure on prices.

Prudent fiscal and monetary management in Vanuatu has ensured continuing good performance on the inflation front. The inflation rate was around 2.5 per cent in 2003 and increased marginally to 2.6 per cent in 2004. Wage increases were modest and the vatu appreciated against the United States dollar but depreciated against the Australian dollar, by 3.4 per cent, in 2004 following an increase in foreign reserves owing to the inflow of donor funds, including cyclone rehabilitation support, and higher export prices. The weakness of the United States dollar has offset the rise in oil prices somewhat but high petroleum prices present a challenge for economic management.

Foreign trade and other external transactions

Higher world prices for primary commodities in 2003 and 2004 have been a mixed blessing for Pacific island countries, except for Papua New Guinea. In Papua New Guinea's case the very sharp rise in oil prices and increases in the prices of gold and copper and agricultural commodities have provided an opportunity for the Government to reduce the public debt and take the pressure off interest rates. Increases in prices for cocoa, copra and coconut oil also benefited Solomon Islands and Vanuatu. The decline in squash prices has made life difficult for Tongan farmers. Pacific island countries other than Papua New Guinea rely on petroleum imports for energy production and transport and the sustained high prices for petroleum products have increased costs of production and made it difficult to control inflation and the balance of payments.

Mixed performances in export earnings despite higher commodity prices

The available data for 2004 showed that while Fiji and Tonga recorded declines in export earnings, Papua New Guinea, Solomon Islands and Vanuatu recorded large increases (table II.16 and figure II.12). Higher prices for minerals and other commodities resulted in an increase of 34.4 per cent in the value of merchandise exports, to $2.2 billion, in

Table II.16. Selected Pacific island economies: merchandise exports and their rates of growth, 2001-2004

	Value (millions of US dollars)	Exports (f.o.b.) Annual rate of growth (percentage)			
	2003	2001	2002	2003	2004
Fiji	739	-6.8	9.2	27.8	-23.5
Papua New Guinea	2 208	-13.7	-9.5	34.4	11.6
Samoa	15	9.1	-15.5	13.2	-0.2
Solomon Islands	74	-27.6	22.6	29.0	21.8
Tonga	18	2.9	67.9	-0.2	-29.5
Vanuatu	30	-24.1	1.0	48.6	25.8

Sources: Central Bank of Samoa web site <http://www.cbs.gov.ws/default.htm>, 20 January 2005; National Reserve Bank of Tonga web site <http://www.reservebank.to/pub.htm>, 14 December 2004; Central Bank of Solomon Islands web site <http://www.cbsi.com.sb/About_CBSI/eco/reports/quarterly_reports.htm>, 29 November 2004; Vanuatu Statistics Office web site <http://www.vanuatustatistics.gov.vu>, 14 December 2004; Reserve Bank of Vanuatu web site <http://www.rbv.gov.vu/QtrEconomic.htm>, 14 December 2004; Reserve Bank of Fiji web site <http://www.reservebank.gov.fj/QR_2004/quarter3.html>, 26 November 2004; and Bank of Papua New Guinea web site <http://www.bankpng.gov.pg/publications/index.htm>, 24 January 2005.

Notes: Growth rate for 2004 refers to first two quarters of 2004 compared with the corresponding period of 2003, except that for Papua New Guinea it refers to January-September, Samoa to January-November and Tonga to first three quarters. Fiscal year for Tonga.

Papua New Guinea in 2003 compared with a decline of 9.5 per cent in 2002. The value of merchandise exports from Papua New Guinea increased 11.6 per cent upto September 2004. The total value of merchandise imports increased 10.3 per cent in 2003 to $1.2 billion (table II.17 and figure II.13) and expanded by 23 per cent by September 2004. The large inflow of export revenues into Papua New Guinea has led to a firmer kina, which appreciated by 9.3 per cent against the United States dollar but depreciated against the Australian dollar by 2.3 per cent in 2004. International reserves had risen to a historically high level of $600 million at the end of August 2004, equivalent to 7.5 months of total import cover.

Declining sugar exports contribute to lower export receipts in Fiji

The value of Fiji's merchandise exports increased 28 per cent in 2003 but fell sharply in the first half of 2004 by nearly 24 per cent. Fiji's exports have been declining because of falling sugar production and exports, the loss of kava markets because of bans in Europe and the United States and stagnant fish exports. Garment exports to the United States are expected to fall beginning in 2005 and market opportunities there are expected to worsen considerably in 2006, when Fiji faces the full force of East Asian exporters. One firm that has done extremely well in developing its export market, especially in the United States, is Fiji Water, a bottler of

Figure II.12. Growth rates in merchandise export earnings of selected Pacific island economies, 2001-2004

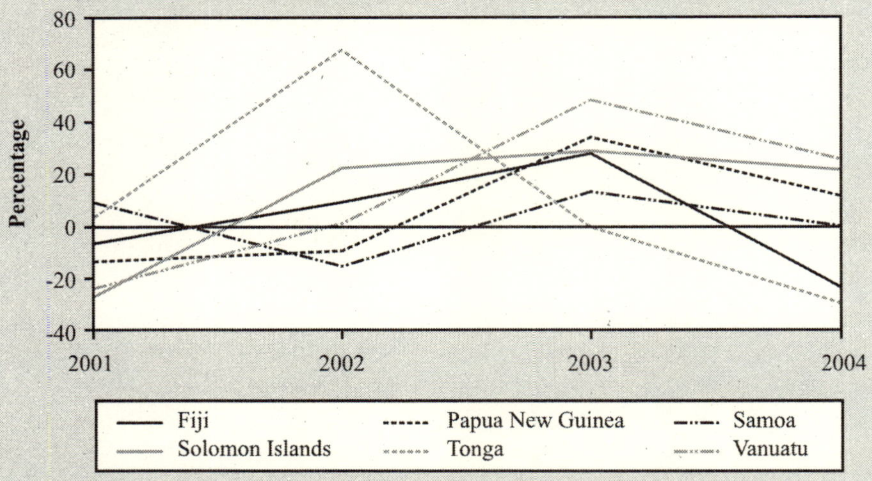

Sources: Central Bank of Samoa web site <http://www.cbs.gov.ws/default.htm>, 20 January 2005; National Reserve Bank of Tonga web site <http://www.reservebank.to/pub.htm>, 14 December 2004; Central Bank of Solomon Islands web site <http://www.cbsi.com.sb/About_CBSI/eco/reports/quarterly_reports.htm>, 29 November 2004; Vanuatu Statistics Office web site <http://www.vanuatustatistics.gov.vu>, 14 December 2004; Reserve Bank of Vanuatu web site <http://www.rbv.gov.vu/QtrEconomic.htm>, 14 December 2004; Reserve Bank of Fiji web site <http://www.reservebank.gov.fj/QR_2004/quarter3.html>, 26 November 2004; and Bank of Papua New Guinea web site <http://www.bankpng.gov.pg/publications/index.htm>, 24 January 2005.

Notes: Growth rate for 2004 refers to first two quarters of 2004 compared with the corresponding period of 2003, except that for Papua New Guinea it refers to January-September, Samoa to January-November and Tonga to first three quarters. Fiscal year for Tonga.

spring water. Exports are expected to increase from F$ 45.7 million in 2003 to F$ 60.8 million in 2004 and further to F$ 85.6 million in 2005, and the firm is expecting to triple production capacity through investment now being undertaken. The value of merchandise imports in Fiji also increased in 2002 and 2003 but fell by 23 per cent in the first half of 2004 as a result of reduced imports of intermediate and investment goods. The bright spot in respect of the balance of payments has been the sharp increase in remittances and the country's current account deficit is expected to remain unchanged at 5.3 per cent of GDP in 2004 (table II.14).

The value of merchandise exports declined 16 per cent in 2002 in Samoa, as reduced exports of fish more than offset increased garment exports, but grew 13 per cent in 2003 and remained more or less flat upto November 2004. The value of merchandise imports increased by around 7 per cent in 2002 and 2003, also remaining more or less unchanged in the first 11 months of 2004. The current account deficit improved to 0.6 per cent of GDP in 2003 as compared with 7.6 per cent in 2002, mainly as a

Table II.17. Selected Pacific island economies: merchandise imports and their rates of growth, 2001-2004

	Imports (c.i.f.)				
	Value (millions of US dollars)	Annual rate of growth (percentage)			
	2003	2001	2002	2003	2004
Fiji	1 286	−2.6	20.8	36.0	−23.3
Papua New Guinea	1 191	−6.4	14.6	10.3	23.0
Samoa	134	8.3	7.3	7.0	0.3
Solomon Islands	68	−16.5	−21.0	5.0	9.1
Tonga	76	−7.5	12.3	22.3	17.2
Vanuatu	117	1.1	−0.8	30.5	6.8

Sources: Central Bank of Samoa web site <http://www.cbs.gov.ws/default.htm>, 20 January 2005; National Reserve Bank of Tonga web site <http://www.reservebank.to/pub.htm>, 14 December 2004; Central Bank of Solomon Islands web site <http://www.cbsi.com.sb/About_CBSI/eco/reports/quarterly_reports.htm>, 29 November 2004; Vanuatu Statistics Office web site <http://www.vanuatustatistics.gov.vu>, 14 December 2004; Reserve Bank of Vanuatu web site <http://www.rbv.gov.vu/QtrEconomic.htm>, 14 December 2004; Reserve Bank of Fiji web site <http://www.reservebank.gov.fj/QR_2004/quarter3.html>, 26 November 2004; and Bank of Papua New Guinea web site <http://www.bankpng.gov.pg/publications/index.htm>, 24 January 2005.

Notes: Growth rate for 2004 refers to first two quarters of 2004 compared with the corresponding period of 2003, except that for Papua New Guinea it refers to January-September, Samoa to January-November and Tonga to first three quarters. Fiscal year for Tonga.

result of increases in net private transfers, especially remittances, and net income and services. Tourism receipts are second in importance to remittances, with tourist numbers increasing by 3.9 per cent and tourism receipts increasing by 4 per cent in 2003. The balance-of-payments surplus also increased as a result of higher inflows of capital. Net foreign reserves at the end of August 2004 amounted to $77 million, equivalent to 7 months of import cover. The Samoan tala appreciated by 7.6 per cent against the United States dollar but depreciated against the Australian and New Zealand currencies in 2004.

The value of Tonga's merchandise exports remained unchanged in 2003 after an increase of 68 per cent in 2002 but declined by about a third in the first 9 months of 2004. However, the value of imports increased by 17 per cent in the same period, after an increase of 22 per cent in 2003. Tourism has been improving, with tourist receipts in July-December 2003 increasing 32.7 per cent as compared with the same period in 2002. At the end of 2003, Tonga's foreign reserves increased to $43 million, equivalent to 5.6 months of import cover, as compared with 3.7 months of import cover at the end of 2002. The improving balance of payments was mainly due to the drawing down of external loans. The pa'anga declined against the Australian and New Zealand dollars, leading to increases in import prices.

Figure II.13. Growth rates in merchandise import spending of selected Pacific island economies, 2001-2004

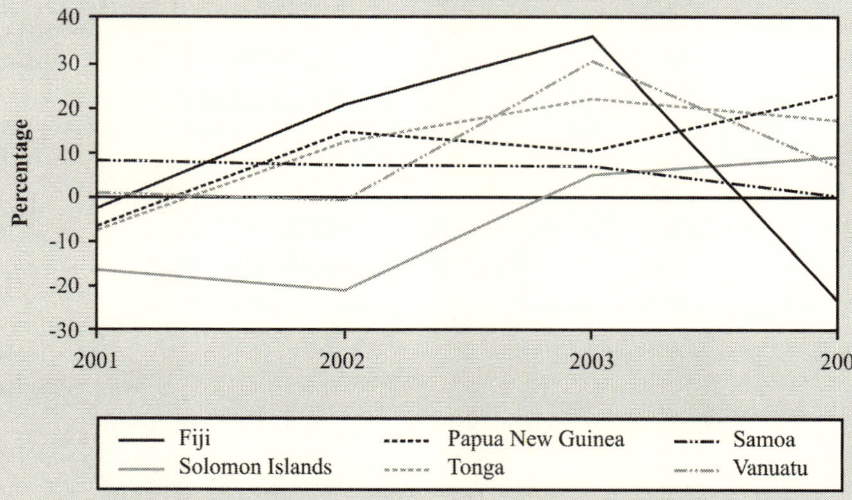

Sources: Central Bank of Samoa web site <http://www.cbs.gov.ws/default.htm>, 20 January 2005; National Reserve Bank of Tonga web site <http://www.reservebank.to/pub.htm>, 14 December 2004; Central Bank of Solomon Islands web site <http://www.cbsi.com.sb/About_CBSI/eco/reports/quarterly_reports.htm>, 29 November 2004; Vanuatu Statistics Office web site <http://www.vanuatustatistics.gov.vu>, 14 December 2004; Reserve Bank of Vanuatu web site <http://www.rbv.gov.vu/QtrEconomic.htm>, 14 December 2004; Reserve Bank of Fiji web site <http://www.reservebank.gov.fj/QR_2004/quarter3.html>, 26 November 2004; and Bank of Papua New Guinea web site <http://www.bankpng.gov.pg/publications/index.htm>, 24 January 2005.

Notes: Growth rate for 2004 refers to first two quarters of 2004 compared with the corresponding period of 2003, except that for Papua New Guinea it refers to January-September, Samoa to January-November and Tonga to first three quarters. Fiscal year, f.o.b. value for Tonga.

Agricultural exports responsible for increased export earnings in Vanuatu

The value of agricultural exports from Vanuatu increased by 66 per cent in the first half of 2004 over the same period of 2003, mostly owing to increases in export volumes of cocoa, copra and cattle. As a result, the value of merchandise exports increased 26 per cent in the first 6 months of 2004 after a jump of 49 per cent in 2003. The value of merchandise imports increased 7 per cent during the first half of 2004 after rising 30.5 per cent in 2003. Timber exports increased 54 per cent up to June 2004 as compared with the first half of 2003. The bans on kava exports to Europe and the United States are still in place; however, kava exports to other Pacific island countries are doing well, resulting in a 61 per cent increase in the first half of 2004 as compared with the same period in 2003. Kava exports to Fiji have benefited from the reduced local output in that country. In February 2004, Cyclone Ivy caused considerable damage to cocoa trees in Vanuatu. However, the cyclone led to increased harvesting of coconuts, because of the large quantities of nuts blown from the palms, at an opportune time to take advantage of the higher prices for copra and coconut oil. In September 2004, Vanuatu's international reserves had risen to $50 million, or the equivalent of 5.9 months of import cover, owing to the inflow of donor funds including cyclone relief and earthquake reconstruction funds and increased prices for exports of copra and coconut oil.

Key policy issues

Poor investment environment

As reflected in their improved performance in respect of inflation rates, budget deficits, international reserves and exchange rates, Governments in Pacific island countries have improved macroeconomic management. However, while macroeconomic stabilization has been achieved in countries such as Papua New Guinea and Vanuatu, economic growth rates remain low. As noted by international financial agencies, international ratings agencies and commercial banks, the key factor inhibiting good economic growth is the absence of an investor-friendly environment. It is suggested that both domestic and foreign investors are reluctant to invest in Pacific island countries unless expected rates of return are very high or unless they are guaranteed good returns through some form of government support (such as subsidies, tariffs and taxation allowances).

Political instability an impediment to investment …

The problems underlying the poor investment environment are numerous. One of the most important is political instability. Continuing threats of no-confidence votes arising from highly unstable coalition Governments, as in Papua New Guinea and Vanuatu, the simmering threats to the democratic process in Fiji and the insecurity of land titles in most of the countries do not give investors confidence that policies will remain stable and that contracts will be honoured. Finding ways to reduce the likelihood of unstable coalition Governments appears to be one of the biggest challenges to improving governance in the Pacific.

… as are corruption and law and order problems

Corruption appears to be widespread at all levels of the public service in Pacific island countries, both in the bureaucracy and among politicians. This was recently acknowledged by Fiji's Attorney General, who announced that his Government was considering the introduction of an independent body to combat corruption. The Auditor General's reports in Fiji and the Ombudsmen's reports in Papua New Guinea and Vanuatu also provide frequent evidence of corruption in the public sector. Transparency International's recently released report on corruption in 12 of the Pacific island countries documents the widespread nature of the problem. A thread running through the Transparency International National Integrity System reports is the difficulty of implementing controls over corrupt behaviour in small countries. The close relationship between people in the private and public sectors and, within the public sector, between people in parliament, the bureaucracy, the police and the judiciary, makes it extremely difficult for the checks and balance that are effective in larger countries to be effective in small countries. Overcoming this "small country" problem is another key challenge for those trying to improve governance in the Pacific.

Law and order is a problem area that also has to be addressed to improve the investment climate. Law and order not only means the protection of people and their property but also, in a broader sense, the protection of property rights and the enforcement of contracts. Unfortunately, there is often a vicious cycle at work in that investors are reluctant to invest because of the threat to persons and property and few jobs are therefore created. The limited number of jobs created cannot meet the needs of the growing labour force, which, in turn, leads to increased unemployment and criminal activity, adding to investment concerns. While it is important to improve the operations of the police, the courts and the prisons to cope with criminal activity, they cannot solve the problem. The solution is the creation of jobs but here Governments face a dilemma: if investors are wary because of the criminal activity resulting from high unemployment, how can jobs be created?

An aspect of law and order that is particularly troubling in Pacific island countries is the frequency of disputes over rights to land. A culture of compensation appears to have developed, which arises in part because of a lack of firmness on the part of Governments in standing behind contracts. Secure property rights and impartial enforcement of contracts are the basis for the effective operation of a market economy.

High infrastructure costs also a constraint on investment

High infrastructure costs are another constraint on investment. High-cost, unreliable supplies of water, power, telecommunications and transport services are the outcome of government-run or other forms of monopolistic enterprises. Efforts are being made in some Pacific island countries to improve these services through privatization. However, there remains a widespread belief in the Pacific that governments should operate these enterprises or that the markets are small and therefore there is only room for a single supplier. However, these ideas are outdated. The record of government operation of essential services is dismal and developments in the telecommunications industry highlight the fact that technology can make even small markets contestable.

Importance of rural sector development

Shortages of land in rural areas contributing to rural-urban migration

Another area in need of improved governance is local government. Because of the high rate of rural-urban migration and the resulting rapid growth of urban areas in all Pacific island countries (except Niue), local governments are facing great challenges. Given the continuation of existing urban growth rates, the populations of Honiara and Port Vila could double within 16 years. Rural-urban migration is not being stimulated by the availability of jobs in urban areas, as employment growth is very slow in most of these countries and well below the numbers of new entrants joining the labour force each year. Rural-urban migration appears to be due mainly to the shortage of land in rural areas in the face of rapid growth in rural populations, the low productivity of communal agriculture, the opportunities for higher education in the urban areas and the "bright lights" attractions of the urban life for young people.

Unless employment-generating economic growth is stimulated in the urban areas, it is hard to see the situation improving because local governments cannot generate sufficient funds to provide the services demanded. At the same time it is not a good idea to put in place obstacles to the movement of people from rural areas, as productivity growth in the rural sector inevitably leads to the movement of labour out of these activities.

The urban drift is leading to the growth of squatter settlements, particularly in cities such as Port Moresby, Suva, Honiara and Port Vila. The predominance of communal land ownership in the Pacific means that it is very difficult for someone coming from a rural area to find a place to live and therefore squatting largely takes place on alienated land. These people have no legal residential rights, no representation and very limited essential services. As other countries have found, moving them in bulk is not a viable option. Hence, thought has to be given to how these communities can become viable with local government representation, secure access to housing and decent access to essential services.

Decentralization does not necessary lead to improvements in the quality of governance

Decentralization of government has become popular over the past decade, along with the prominence given to governance and increased community participation in government. The reason for the link with governance is that it is believed that by bringing government closer to the people through decentralization, the local community will have a greater input into government decisions and greater oversight over the government services delivered. It is argued that corruption in the public sector will be reduced because of the closer oversight. Based on the fiscal federalism literature of economics it is also argued that if voters and capital are able to move freely within a country, decentralization should see competition between subnational governments for voters and capital and thus there will be pressure on the local governments to provide value for money. However, there is very little cross-country evidence to support the idea that greater decentralization improves the quality of governance in developing countries.

Public sector reform initiatives

Public sector reforms have been undertaken but with mixed results

Public service reform to improve governance has been an ongoing process in the Pacific for many years. Reform attempts in Cook Islands and Samoa appear to have been much more successful than in Papua New Guinea. However, the current Government in Papua New Guinea is attempting to move away from the politicization of the public service that had developed over the past decade and is implementing merit-based appointments along with performance-based contracts for the heads of departments. Fiji has recently introduced performance-based contracts for chief executive officers of government departments and a performance management system to reward staff, rather than the previous automatic cost-of-living increases.

It remains to be seen how effective the ongoing public sector reforms in Tonga will be. The Tongan economy has been labouring under heavy subsidies of loss-making public enterprises and the heavy wage demands of public servants. In most Pacific island countries, the salaries and wages of public servants are still taking too large a share of government expenditure. Ultimately, this may be a matter of the private sector and the tax base being too small, rather than the public sector being too large.

Improvements in governance also required in the private sector

Improvements in governance in the public sector are not all that is required for improved governance in Pacific island countries. The corporate sector and NGOs, including organizations running churches and schools, also have governance problems. Organizations managing funds on behalf of indigenous landowners, such as the incorporated land groups in Papua New Guinea, also have severe governance problems. Generally, what appears to be missing is an understanding of the integrity that management of these organizations should bring to their position of trust. Too often, there are reports of conflicts of interest and of the trustees, whether they are directors of companies or managers of civil society organizations or managers in charge of trust funds, acting in their personal interest rather than in the interests of their shareholders or other stakeholders.

Policies for sustainable development

Need to guide against overexploitation of limited natural resources

While it is important for Pacific island countries to promote investment initiatives, it is equally important for them to be mindful of the need for sustainable development, especially guarding against overexploitation of their limited natural resources. Unsustainable commercial logging is already happening in countries like Solomon Islands and Papua New Guinea. It is also important for Pacific island countries to ensure that they receive the maximum benefit from the exploitation of these natural resources.

The tuna fish stock is the most important physical resource for most of the Pacific island countries. However, the past three years have seen poor harvests and, as a result, some of the small countries that rely heavily on fishing access fees for government revenues have experienced difficulties. Similar to agriculture, fish harvests are weather-related and it is to be hoped that the downturn in tuna harvests is temporary. The sharply fluctuating nature of fishing revenues also poses difficulties for fiscal management in countries that are dependent upon these revenues. Therefore, it is desirable that these countries develop measures to manage these highly variable

Box II.1. Mauritius International Meeting on Small Island Developing States reaffirms sustainable development and related issues

Efforts to recognize small islands' vulnerabilities and to support their sustainable development received solid support at the International Meeting to Review the Implementation of the Programme of Action for the Sustainable Development of Small Island Developing States, held at Port Louis, Mauritius, from 10 to 14 January 2005, with the unanimous adoption of both a proactive strategy to further implement the Programme of Action, called the Mauritius Strategy, and of a political declaration, the Mauritius Declaration.

The major outcome of the Meeting was the adoption of the Mauritius Strategy, which points out that small island developing States "are located among the most vulnerable regions in the world in relation to the intensity and frequency of natural and environmental disasters and their increasing impact, and face disproportionately high economic, social and environmental consequences", as highlighted by the tragic impacts of the 26 December 2004 Indian Ocean tsunami and the destruction caused by various hurricanes, cyclones and typhoons in the Caribbean and the Pacific. It then proposes using the opportunities offered by international meetings such as the World Conference on Disaster Reduction, held in Kobe, Japan, in January 2005, to consider the specific concerns of small island developing States, including in the areas of insurance and reinsurance arrangements.

Among other things, the Mauritius Meeting called for the establishment of a global early warning system to cover not just tsunamis but also other threats, such as storm surges and cyclones. The Indian Ocean tsunami disaster in 2004 demonstrated with terrifying power the need for an early warning system, and the outpouring of support to establish one has generated several proposals.

The Pacific region already has a tsunami-warning centre based in Hawaii. This centre monitors international warning activities in the Pacific and recommends appropriate measures for members to take in the event of a natural disaster. It also monitors seismological and tidal status and instruments around the Pacific Ocean to evaluate potentially tsunamigenic earthquakes. The centre, established in 1968, is a collaborative effort involving the International Oceanographic Commission and the Governments of Australia, Cook Islands, Fiji, New Zealand and Samoa, among others. Other Pacific island countries are encouraged to consider joining the centre to take advantage of the services offered. In addition, the 59-nation, United States-led Global Earth Observation System of Systems for monitoring the Earth, which is in the process of implementation, will help to mitigate the impact of tsunamis and other disasters, as well as forecast weather months in advance and predict climate changes more effectively, including El Niño weather patterns. Legislation was introduced in Alaska and Hawaii in January 2005 to upgrade warning systems in the Pacific rim States deemed most vulnerable to tsunamis. The Tsunami Preparedness Act authorizes government agencies in the United States to boost detection and warning capabilities and upgrade a monitoring system to cover the Pacific and Atlantic Oceans, the Caribbean and the Gulf of Mexico.

With regard to climate change, the Mauritius Strategy points out that small island developing States are already experiencing major ill effects of climate change and that adaptation to adverse impacts of climate change and rising sea levels remains a major priority for them. It also promotes increased energy efficiency and development and use of renewable energy as a matter of priority, as well as advanced and cleaner fossil fuel technologies.

As for trade issues, the Mauritius Strategy recognizes that most small island developing States, as a result of their small size, persistent structural disadvantages and vulnerabilities, face specific difficulties in integrating into the global economy. It also recognizes the importance of intensifying efforts to facilitate full and effective participation by small island developing States in the deliberations and decision-making processes of WTO. For its part, the Mauritius Declaration recognizes that international trade is important for building resilience and the sustainable development of small island developing States and calls upon international institutions, including financial institutions, to pay appropriate attention to the structural disadvantages of these small island States.

(Continued overleaf)

(Continued from preceding page)

Concerning health issues, the Strategy notes that health is a key determinant of sustainable development. The strengthening and further development of small island developing States' cooperation and experience-sharing in the area of health is crucial and should be a priority. The Strategy notes the increasing incidence of such challenges as HIV/AIDS and indicates that their impact on sustainable development is a major concern in small island developing States, which are committed, with the necessary support of the international community, to addressing HIV/AIDS, as it is prevalent in many of those countries. Responding effectively to HIV/AIDS is both an urgent health issue and a development imperative.

The Mauritius Strategy recognizes that the Programme of Action for the Sustainable Development of Small Island Developing States remains the blueprint for small island developing States and it is imperative that those small States work closely with the international community to address issues of national and regional sustainable development taking account of the economic, social and environmental aspects. Small island developing States acknowledge that sustainable development is primarily a national responsibility and that there is a need for strengthened cooperation and partnership in support of such development at the national, regional and international levels. Such partnership should be broad-based and ensure the involvement and participation of the relevant stakeholders.

revenue streams. Regional cooperation offers these small countries a useful option for addressing concerns about sustainable development of natural resources. For example, the new Convention on the Conservation and Management of Highly Migratory Fish Stocks in the Western and Central Pacific Ocean, which came into force in June 2004, is expected to ensure sustainable use of these stocks through effective management.

The Mauritius International Meeting on Small Island Developing States, held from 10 to 14 January 2005, addressed sustainable development and other related issues that increasingly affect small islands, such as dwindling market access, the increasing threat from HIV/AIDS, environmental problems and threats from natural disasters (box II.1). Although in most Pacific island countries, the known prevalence of HIV/AIDS has remained relatively low, the prevalence of risk factors for HIV transfers is considered to be high, with Papua New Guinea having the highest reported rate of HIV infections in the Pacific region. In addition to its impact on individuals and families, HIV/AIDS is particularly devastating for countries with small populations and limited skilled workforces, taking a severe toll on their economies as productivity declines, income levels are reduced and the social fabric is undermined.

Pacific island countries are also very vulnerable to natural and environmental disasters and the wide destruction of life and property caused by the tsunami in several Asian countries in late 2004 reinforces the need to establish early warning systems and disaster management for all regions at risk from such disasters. Therefore, any early warning systems to be established in response to the Asian tsunami must also include these small and vulnerable Pacific island countries.

South and South-West Asia

A. Developing economies of the subregion

Subregional overview and prospects

Economic growth performance mixed in the subregion in 2004

Economic growth rates remained relatively high in the developing economies of South and South-West Asia in 2004 (figure II.14) although India and Sri Lanka experienced slower rates of growth in GDP compared with 2003. Adverse weather conditions had a negative impact on agriculture in both countries but whereas the industrial sector improved its performance in 2004 in India, in Sri Lanka growth in the industrial sector slowed. The service sector witnessed slight deceleration in both countries. In Pakistan, a strong expansion in manufacturing, wholesale and retail trade and electricity and gas distribution offset the somewhat slower growth in agriculture and GDP growth improved in 2004. Economic growth in the Islamic Republic of Iran was somewhat faster in 2004 and driven largely by higher oil revenues and the service sector, while the surge in GDP growth in Turkey in that year reflected a vigorous expansion in both industry and services, supported by strong domestic consumption and investment.

Figure II.14. Rates of GDP growth in selected South and South-West Asian economies, 2001-2004

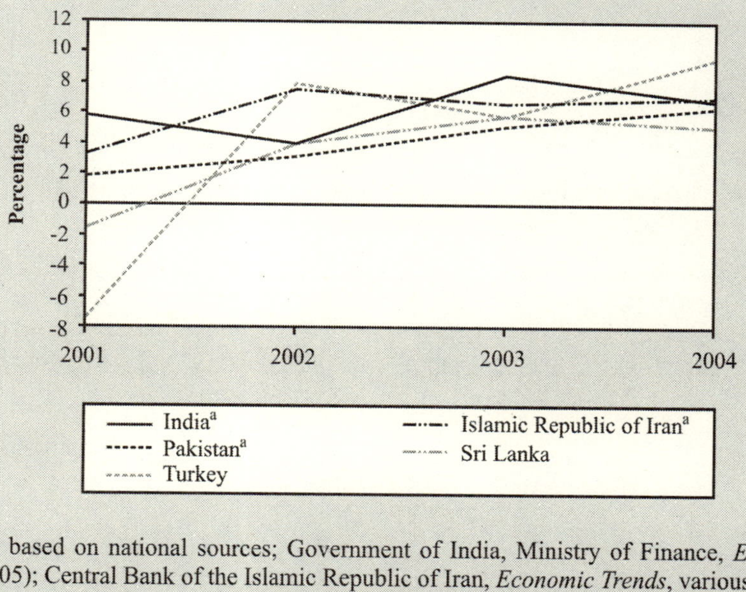

Sources: ESCAP, based on national sources; Government of India, Ministry of Finance, *Economic Survey 2004-2005* (New Delhi, 2005); Central Bank of the Islamic Republic of Iran, *Economic Trends*, various issues (Tehran, 2004); Government of Pakistan, *Economic Survey of Pakistan 2003-04* (Islamabad, 2004); Central Bank of Sri Lanka, *Annual Report 2003* (Colombo, 2004); and Central Bank of the Republic of Turkey, *Annual Report 2003* (Ankara, 2004).

Notes: Fiscal year for India, the Islamic Republic of Iran and Pakistan. Growth rates for 2004 are estimates.

[a] Real GDP at factor cost.

Higher GDP growth rates expected in 2005 for most countries

Assuming no major internal or external shocks and no political instability, India should be able to sustain real GDP growth rates in the range of 7-7.5 per cent in 2005-2007, supported by a growth rate of 2 to 4 per cent in agricultural value added, 7.5 to 8 per cent in industry and 8.5 per cent in services. India is one of the countries affected by the recent tsunami in Asia. However, the disaster is not expected to have much of an impact on the country's growth prospects given the small contribution the affected areas were making to its GDP. Pakistan's GDP is expected to grow by 6.6 per cent in 2005 but continued high oil prices could dampen growth. At the same time, persistent water shortages can damage agricultural crops and also raise the demand for imported fuel oil to generate electricity. The Sri Lankan economy is projected to grow between 5 and 6 per cent in 2005, supported by growth in all major sectors. The country was the hardest hit in the subregion by the tsunami and the growth rate may end up closer to the lower end of the projected range. The GDP of the Islamic Republic of Iran is projected to grow at 7.1 per cent in 2005, supported by all major sectors, especially industry and mining. In Turkey, GDP growth is projected to slow to 4.8 per cent in 2005 owing to a weaker exchange rate, higher interest rates and softer external demand. However, the commencement of talks in October 2005 on Turkey's entry into the EU is expected to lead to further economic stability and increased FDI inflows, boosting future economic growth.

Figure II.15. Inflation[a] in selected South and South-West Asian economies, 2001-2004

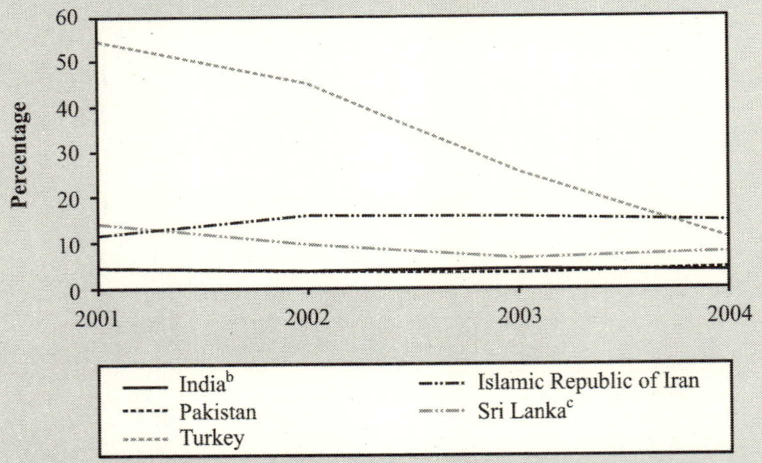

Sources: ESCAP, based on national sources; Government of India, Ministry of Finance, *Economic Survey 2004-2005* (New Delhi, 2005); Central Bank of the Islamic Republic of Iran, *Economic Trends*, various issues (Tehran, 2004); Government of Pakistan, *Economic Survey of Pakistan 2003-04* (Islamabad, 2004); Central Bank of Sri Lanka, *Annual Report 2003* (Colombo, 2004); and Central Bank of the Republic of Turkey, *Annual Report 2003* (Ankara, 2004).

Notes: Fiscal year for India, the Islamic Republic of Iran and Pakistan. Inflation rates for 2004 are estimates.

[a] Changes in the consumer price index.

[b] Consumer price index for industrial workers.

[c] Colombo only.

Re-emergence of inflationary pressures in Pakistan and Sri Lanka

Higher oil prices and the poor performance of the agricultural sector pushed inflation rates up in Pakistan and Sri Lanka (figure II.15). India succeeded in stabilizing the rate of inflation, which remained virtually unchanged in 2004. Inflation in the Islamic Republic of Iran continued to decline gradually in 2004 but remained in double digits. The relatively high rate of inflation in that country is a reflection of government policies to promote growth and employment and improve the provision of social services. Tight monetary and fiscal policies, coupled with a series of structural reforms that commenced in 2001, have helped to lower inflation substantially in Turkey at a speed exceeding the Government's target.

Foreign trade buoyant in 2004

Foreign trade remained vibrant in the subregion in 2004 as high growth rates in the values of both merchandise exports and imports were maintained (figures II.16 and II.17). India's export growth in excess of 20 per cent was the result of buoyant world demand for key manufactured exports as well as higher commodity prices and various export-facilitating measures. Strong demand for manufactured goods also enabled Turkey to

Figure II.16. Growth rates in merchandise export earnings of selected South and South-West Asian economies, 2001-2004

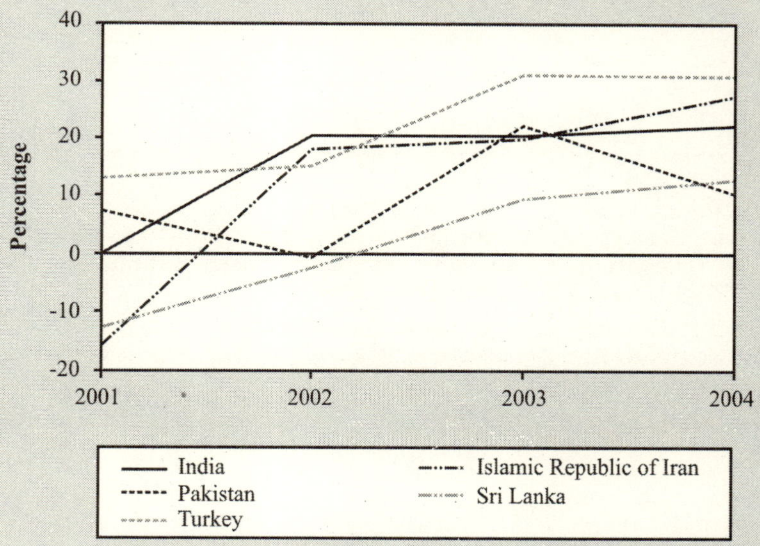

Sources: State Bank of Pakistan web site <http://www.sbp.org.pk>, 27 October 2004; Central Bank of Sri Lanka web site <www.lanka.net/centralbank>, 15 December 2004; Central Bank of the Islamic Republic of Iran web site <http:// www.cbi.ir/>, 27 October 2004; Republic of Turkey State Institute of Statistics web site <http://www.die.gov.tr/english/>, 15 December 2004; and other national sources.

Notes: Fiscal year for India, the Islamic Republic of Iran and Pakistan. Growth rates for 2004 are estimates for all countries except Turkey. The growth rate of Turkey for 2004 refers to January-October 2004 compared with the corresponding period of 2003.

maintain growth in the value of merchandise exports above 30 per cent for the second year in a row. Improved competitiveness from low unit labour costs and a decrease in the cost of finance, together with higher export prices, fuelled that growth. Higher oil prices boosted the export growth of the Islamic Republic of Iran to nearly 30 per cent in 2004. However, export growth slowed in Pakistan. In general, the average exchange rates of the domestic currencies against the dollar remained relatively stable in 2004.

Figure II.17. Growth rates in merchandise import spending of selected South and South-West Asian economies, 2001-2004

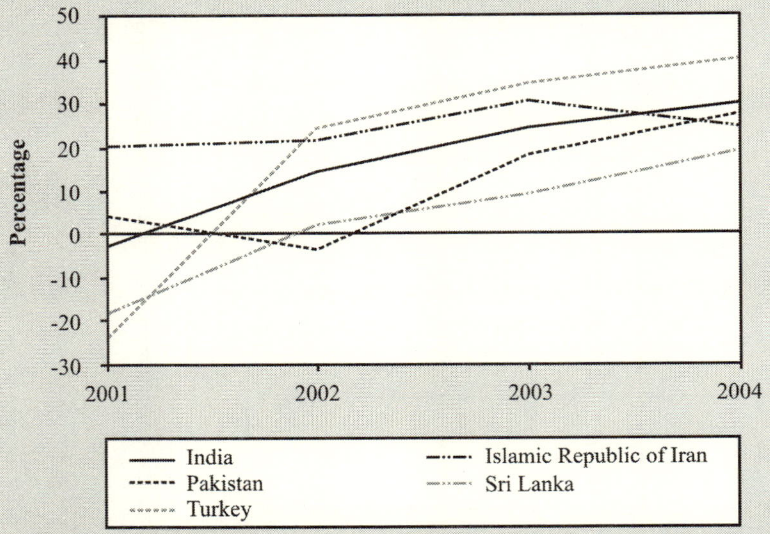

Sources: State Bank of Pakistan web site <http://www.sbp.org.pk>, 27 October 2004; Central Bank of Sri Lanka web site <www.lanka.net/centralbank>, 15 December 2004; Central Bank of the Islamic Republic of Iran web site <http://www.cbi.ir/>, 27 October 2004; Republic of Turkey State Institute of Statistics web site <http://www.die.gov.tr/english/>, 15 December 2004; and other national sources.

Notes: Fiscal year for India, the Islamic Republic of Iran and Pakistan. Growth rates for 2004 are estimates for all countries except Turkey. The growth rate of Turkey for 2004 refers to January-October 2004 compared with the corresponding period of 2003.

GDP performance

Contraction in the agricultural sector lowered growth in India

In India, GDP growth decelerated from 8.5 per cent in 2003 to 6.9 per cent in 2004 owing in large part to the slow growth in agricultural value added caused by poor weather conditions (table II.18). Rainfall was erratic as prolonged breaks punctuated the monsoon, which was also unevenly distributed over regions, flooding the north-east while leaving the north-west suffering from drought. However, industrial growth accelerated from 6.6 per cent in 2003 to 7.8 per cent in 2004 owing to stronger

Table II.18. Selected South and South-West Asian economies: growth rates, 2001-2004

(Percentage)

		Rates of growth			
		Gross domestic product	*Agriculture*	*Industry*	*Services*
India[a]	2001	5.8	6.3	3.6	6.8
	2002	4.0	−7.2	6.8	7.9
	2003	8.5	9.6	6.6	9.1
	2004	6.9	1.1	7.8	8.9
Iran (Islamic Republic of)[a]	2001	3.3	−2.3	1.9	5.7
	2002	7.5	11.4	9.3	5.5
	2003	6.7	7.1	9.2	5.1
	2004	7.1	5.3	7.3	7.3
Pakistan[a]	2001	1.8	−2.2	3.6	3.1
	2002	3.1	0.1	2.6	4.8
	2003	5.1	4.1	5.8	5.3
	2004	6.4	2.6	13.1	5.2
Sri Lanka	2001	−1.5	−3.4	−2.1	−0.5
	2002	4.0	2.5	1.0	6.1
	2003	5.9	1.5	5.5	7.8
	2004	5.2	−0.5	4.9	7.3
Turkey	2001	−7.5	−6.5	−7.5	−7.7
	2002	7.9	6.9	9.4	7.4
	2003	5.8	−2.5	7.8	6.7
	2004	9.6	3.1	10.8	10.3

Sources: ESCAP, based on national sources; Government of India, Ministry of Finance, *Economic Survey 2004-2005* (New Delhi, 2005); Central Bank of the Islamic Republic of Iran, *Economic Trends,* various issues (Tehran, 2004); Government of Pakistan, *Economic Survey of Pakistan 2003-04* (Islamabad, 2004); Central Bank of Sri Lanka, *Annual Report 2003* (Colombo, 2004); and Central Bank of the Republic of Turkey, *Annual Report 2003* (Ankara, 2004).

Notes: Fiscal year for India, the Islamic Republic of Iran and Pakistan. Growth rates for 2004 are estimates. Industry comprises mining and quarrying; manufacturing; electricity, gas and power; and construction. In the case of Turkey, construction is merged with the services.

[a] Real GDP at factor cost.

private consumption and investment, as well as more rapid export growth. The investment ratio increased further to 29 per cent in 2004, continuing the upward trend of recent years, while the savings ratio also edged upwards in 2004 (table II.19). Improved economic performance in recent years has generated demand for transport and communications, trade-related activities and financial services. In addition, a rapid increase in expenditure on public administration, social services, rural extension

Table II.19. Selected South and South-West Asian economies: ratios of gross domestic savings and investment to GDP, 2001-2004

(Percentage)

	2001	*2002*	*2003*	*2004*
Savings as a percentage of GDP				
India	23.4	26.1	28.1	29.5
Iran (Islamic Republic of)	38.4	38.5	39.9	39.9
Pakistan	17.8	18.1	17.4	17.4
Sri Lanka	15.8	14.5	15.7	16.1
Turkey	17.2	18.7	19.2	17.7
Investment as a percentage of GDP				
India	22.6	24.8	26.3	29.0
Iran (Islamic Republic of)	32.6	33.9	34.9	34.9
Pakistan	17.2	16.8	16.7	18.1
Sri Lanka	22.0	21.3	22.3	25.3
Turkey	15.9	21.3	24.1	25.9

Sources: ESCAP, based on national sources; Government of India, Ministry of Finance, *Economic Survey 2004-2005* (New Delhi, 2005); Central Bank of the Islamic Republic Iran, *Economic Trends,* various issues (Tehran, 2004); Government of Pakistan, *Economic Survey of Pakistan 2003-04* (Islamabad, 2004); Central Bank of Sri Lanka, *Annual Report 2003* (Colombo, 2004); and Central Bank of the Republic of Turkey, *Annual Report 2003* (Ankara, 2004).

Notes: Fiscal year for India, the Islamic Republic of Iran and Pakistan. Figures for 2004 are estimates.

services and defence has had a favourable impact on growth in the service sector, which averaged 9 per cent in 2003-2004, and the sector now accounts for around 52 per cent of output.

Robust performance by industry raised GDP growth in Pakistan

Pakistan's economy grew at 6.4 per cent in 2004 against 5.1 per cent in the previous year. Unlike the broad-based growth of 2003, much of the growth in 2004 was concentrated in the industrial sector, which achieved robust growth of 13.1 per cent in 2004, owing to large-scale manufacturing and electricity and gas distribution. Growth of large-scale manufacturing at 18.1 per cent was the fastest in the last three decades and was helped by an accommodative monetary policy, the global recovery, which fuelled export growth, supportive changes in government regulations and increased development expenditure. There was a substantial increase in the investment ratio to 18.1 per cent in 2004 in Pakistan, from an average of 16.8 per cent in 2002-2003. Growth in the service sector remained relatively stable at around 5 per cent in 2002-2004. Growth in the agricultural sector slowed to 2.6 per cent in 2004, as compared with 4.1 per cent in the previous year, owing to bad weather that reduced the wheat harvest and a pest problem affecting the cotton crop.

Slight deceleration in growth in Sri Lanka as agriculture contracts

Despite several adverse internal and external shocks, the slowdown in economic growth in Sri Lanka was slight, from 5.9 per cent in 2003 to 5.2 per cent in 2004. Among major domestic shocks was a prolonged drought that adversely affected agricultural crops and hydropower generation. Election-related uncertainties in early 2004 also had a deleterious effect on the economy. The major external shock came from higher oil prices but the global economic recovery had a positive impact. The agricultural sector was estimated to have contracted by 0.5 per cent in 2004 as against positive growth of 1.5 per cent in 2003. Growth in the industrial and service sectors, at 4.9 and 7.3 per cent respectively in 2004, was slower than the 5.5 and 7.8 per cent achieved in 2003. On the demand side, there was a significant increase in investment activity in 2004, reflected in the investment ratio, which reached 25.3 per cent in 2004. There was also some improvement in the savings rate. Towards the end of 2004, Sri Lanka suffered huge human and economic losses as a result of the tusnami disaster. More than 36,000 people lost their lives or are missing. The infrastructure in the affected coastal areas was severely damaged. The fishery and tourism industries suffered major damage. The reconstruction and rehabilitation costs are estimated to be over $1.5 billion. The negative impact on economic growth in 2005 may be up to 1 percentage point. The overall macroeconomic impact may remain small because none of the major sources of economic activity and exports such as garment manufacturing, the plantation sector or Colombo port were affected.

Higher revenues from oil contribute to higher growth in the Islamic Republic of Iran

In the Islamic Republic of Iran, GDP grew by 6.7 per cent in 2003, somewhat lower than the 7.5 per cent recorded in the previous year. Growth in 2003 was driven by higher oil production following increases in the country's OPEC oil production quota. Growth in the non-hydrocarbons sector remained strong, even though it decelerated to 5.9 per cent from 8 per cent in 2002. Agricultural output growth remained high after exceptionally good rainfall during the previous years. Other sectors such as manufacturing and mining expanded at double-digit rates. However, the construction and service sectors witnessed some slowdown in their growth rates. As a result of high oil prices together with a continuation of the expansionary fiscal and monetary policies of the previous year, GDP was estimated to grow at 7.1 per cent in 2004. All major sectors of the economy were expected to contribute to higher growth. The comparatively high savings and investment rates in the Islamic Republic of Iran are also sustained by its status as a major oil-producing nation.

Strong domestic demand led to higher growth in Turkey

The economy of Turkey entered a high growth period following the recession in 2001. After growing at 7.9 per cent in 2002, GDP grew at 5.8 per cent in 2003. While the agricultural sector contracted by 2.5 per cent, the industrial sector expanded by 7.8 per cent in 2003. Manufacturing grew at an even faster rate of 9.7 per cent, while the service sector expanded by 6.7 per cent. During the first half of 2004, GDP grew by 11.9 per cent, led by strong domestic demand, including both private consumption and investment, and the growth rate for the whole year is estimated at 9.6 per cent. The investment rate has risen in the past three years in Turkey, reaching 25.9 per cent in 2004.

Inflation

Inflation rate stabilizes in India

Inflation in India remained low during the early months of fiscal 2004. However, upward pressure on prices increased from August 2004 onwards. Higher prices for petroleum products, and minerals and metals and their products contributed to the increase in inflation as a result of cost-push factors driven by international prices. However, average inflation for 2004 was estimated to be 3.8 per cent, virtually unchanged as compared with 3.9 per cent in 2003 (table II.20). The Government's fiscal deficit at 4.5 per cent in 2004 remained unchanged as compared with the previous year (table II.21).

Table II.20. Selected South and South-West Asian economies: inflation and money supply growth (M2), 2001-2004

(Percentage)

	2001	*2002*	*2003*	*2004*
Inflation[a]				
India[b]	4.3	4.0	3.9	3.8
Iran (Islamic Republic of)	11.4	15.8	15.6	14.5
Pakistan	4.4	3.5	3.1	4.6
Sri Lanka[c]	14.2	9.6	6.3	7.6
Turkey	54.4	45.0	25.3	10.7
Money supply growth (M2)				
India	14.3	16.8	12.6	14.0
Iran (Islamic Republic of)	27.6	27.5	21.9	25.5[d]
Pakistan	11.7	16.8	17.5	18.1
Sri Lanka	13.6	13.4	15.3	15.0
Turkey	86.2	29.1	14.2	13.6

Sources: ESCAP, based on national sources; Government of India, Ministry of Finance, *Economic Survey 2004-2005* (New Delhi, 2005); Central Bank of the Islamic Republic of Iran, *Economic Trends,* various issues (Tehran, 2004); Government of Pakistan, *Economic Survey of Pakistan 2003-04* (Islamabad, 2004); Central Bank of Sri Lanka, *Annual Report 2003* (Colombo, 2004); Central Bank of the Republic of Turkey, *Annual Report 2003* (Ankara, 2004); and IMF, *International Financial Statistics,* vol. LVII, No. 10 (Washington, IMF, October 2004).

Notes: Fiscal year for India, the Islamic Republic of Iran and Pakistan in case of inflation. Figures for 2004 are estimates.

[a] Changes in the consumer price index.
[b] Consumer price index for industrial workers.
[c] Colombo only.
[d] January-July.

Table II.21. Selected South and South-West Asian economies: budget and current account balance as a percentage of GDP, 2001-2004

(Percentage)

	2001	2002	2003	2004
Budget balance as a percentage of GDP				
India	−6.2	−5.9	−4.5	−4.5
Iran (Islamic Republic of)[a]	−0.4	−2.2	−2.9	−3.1
Pakistan[a]	−4.3	−4.3	−3.7	−3.3
Sri Lanka[a]	−10.8	−8.9	−8.0	−8.1
Turkey	−16.0	−14.1	−11.1	−8.6
Current account balance as a percentage of GDP				
India	0.2	1.2	1.8	0.5
Iran (Islamic Republic of)	7.1	3.1	1.5	4.6
Pakistan	0.5	3.7	4.9	1.9
Sri Lanka	−1.4	−1.4	−0.6	−3.8
Turkey	2.3	−0.8	−3.3	−4.9

Sources: ESCAP, based on national sources; Government of India, Ministry of Finance, *Economic Survey 2004-2005* (New Delhi, 2005); Central Bank of the Islamic Republic of Iran, *Economic Trends,* various issues (Tehran, 2004); Government of Pakistan, *Economic Survey of Pakistan 2003-04* (Islamabad, 2004); Central Bank of Sri Lanka, *Annual Report 2003* (Colombo, 2004); and Central Bank of the Republic of Turkey, *Annual Report 2003* (Ankara, 2004).

Notes: Fiscal year for India, the Islamic Republic of Iran and Pakistan. Figures for 2004 are estimates.

[a] Excluding grants.

Inflation rate on the rise in Pakistan ...

After falling for a number of years, the rate of inflation picked up in 2004 in Pakistan. From 5.7 per cent in 1999, inflation was brought down to 3.1 per cent in 2003, the lowest figure in three decades. This low level of inflation was achieved as a result of strict fiscal discipline, the lower monetization of the budget deficit, an output recovery, a reduction in duties and taxes and exchange rate appreciation. However, the general price level came under pressure in 2004, when the inflation rate rose to 4.6 per cent, as a result of an easy monetary policy, higher oil prices and other inflationary factors, and this tendency is likely to continue in the medium term. The food and housing subgroups played a leading role in the acceleration of annual inflation. The increase in food prices can largely be attributed to artificial supply shortages of wheat that occurred in response to the realization that the Government's capacity to intervene in the market was hampered by depleted wheat stocks. Since wheat is the main staple grain of the country, a rise in its price leads to increases in the prices of other goods and services. Lower-income groups spend a higher proportion of their income on food items and suffer disproportionately from food price inflation.

... and also in Sri Lanka

In Sri Lanka, the declining trend in the rate of inflation that began in 2002 continued in the first half of 2004. However, inflation accelerated during the second half of the year and the rate for the whole year was 7.6 per cent, up from 6.3 per cent in 2003. Supply-side factors such as rising oil prices, currency depreciation and the impact of the drought on agriculture and power generation pushed consumer prices up. Monetary expansion was somewhat higher in 2003-2004 owing to credit expansion for the private sector and increased public sector borrowing. This could fuel demand-pull pressure on prices and the outlook is for inflation to rise further in 2005, aggravated by supply disruptions caused by the tsunami.

Inflation in double digits in the Islamic Republic of Iran

Inflation in the Islamic Republic of Iran averaged 15.7 per cent in 2002 and 2003 as prices of non-food items rose rapidly. Expansionary monetary and fiscal policies were partly responsible for the high rate of inflation as the Government continued to seek to stimulate growth and employment so as to overcome unemployment and address pressing social needs. The Government plans to reduce inflation gradually over the medium term and some deceleration in the growth in prices, to 14.5 per cent, was observed in 2004.

Rapid reduction in inflation in Turkey continued

In Turkey, the rate of inflation has fallen from high levels in recent years. From 45 per cent in 2002, the growth in consumer prices fell to 25.3 per cent in 2003, falling further to 10.7 per cent in 2004. The speed of the reduction in the inflation rate in Turkey has surpassed government expectations. Tight fiscal and monetary policies together with a series of structural reforms initiated in 2001 are principally responsible for containing inflationary pressures.

On 1 January 2005, Turkey renamed its currency as the new Turkish lira. The high rates of inflation of the previous few decades had necessitated the issuance of large denomination currency notes which were awkward to use. One new Turkish lira is equal to 1 million old Turkish liras, which will continue to circulate until they are withdrawn at the beginning of 2006. No significant inflationary effects are expected from the redenomination.

Foreign trade and other external transactions

External trade

India maintained high export and import growth rates

Growth in the value of India's merchandise exports remained buoyant at a rate of 20.4 per cent in 2003 owing to an increase in exports of both primary and manufactured products (table II.22). Exports expanded even faster, at a rate of 22 per cent, in 2004 sustained by strong world demand and higher world commodity prices. In addition, various measures to facilitate exports have contributed to strong growth. Exports from key manufacturing sectors such as engineering goods, chemicals, automobiles, ore and minerals, basic metals and petroleum products performed well.

Table II.22. Selected South and South-West Asian economies: merchandise exports and their rates of growth, 2001-2004

	Exports (f.o.b.)				
	Value (millions of US dollars)	Annual rate of growth (percentage)			
	2003	2001	2002	2003	2004
India	64 723	0.0	20.3	20.4	22.0
Iran (Islamic Republic of)	33 788	−16.0	18.1	19.7	27.3
Pakistan	11 160	7.4	−0.7	22.2	10.3
Sri Lanka	5 133	−12.8	−2.4	9.2	12.7
Turkey	47 253	12.8	15.1	31.0	30.7

Sources: State Bank of Pakistan web site <http://www.sbp.org.pk>, 27 October 2004; Central Bank of Sri Lanka web site <www.lanka.net/centralbank>, 15 December 2004; Central Bank of the Islamic Republic of Iran web site <http://www.cbi.ir/>, 27 October 2004; Republic of Turkey State Institute of Statistics web site <http://www.die.gov.tr/english/>, 15 December 2004; and other national sources.

Notes: Fiscal year for India, the Islamic Republic of Iran and Pakistan. Growth rates for 2004 are estimates for all countries except Turkey. The growth rate of Turkey for 2004 refers to January-October 2004 compared with the corresponding period of 2003.

Merchandise imports increased by 24.4 per cent in 2003 driven by the pickup in industrial activities and investment demand (table II.23). Imports recorded a further substantial increase of 30 per cent in 2004 mainly owing to higher imports of crude oil, intermediate goods for export and capital goods. As a result, the trade deficit as a percentage of GDP increased in 2004. Net invisible earnings were expected to grow robustly at an annual rate of 11 per cent in 2004, amounting to 4.2 per cent of GDP in 2004. The overall current account balance was once again expected to be in surplus, amounting to 0.5 per cent of GDP in 2004, albeit lower than the 1.8 per cent registered in 2003 (table II.21).

Export growth halved in Pakistan while imports soared

In Pakistan, both merchandise exports and imports registered double-digit growth in 2004. In value terms, exports reached $12.3 billion in 2004 after growing 10.3 per cent in that year as against a growth rate of 22.2 per cent in 2003. Much of the growth in 2004 was in textiles and yarn, and earnings from the four major categories, namely, cotton fabrics, knitwear, bed linen and cotton yarn, each exceeded $1 billion. Non-traditional exports also contributed to growth. The composition of Pakistan's exports has changed significantly over the years. The shares of primary and semi-manufactured exports have fallen steeply, while there has been a corresponding increase in the share of manufactured goods, which now account for around 78 per cent of merchandise exports.

Table II.23. Selected South and South-West Asian economies: merchandise imports and their rates of growth, 2001-2004

	Imports (c.i.f.)				
	Value (millions of US dollars)	*Annual rate of growth (percentage)*			
	2003	*2001*	*2002*	*2003*	*2004*
India	80 177	–2.8	14.5	24.4	30.0
Iran (Islamic Republic of)	28 795	20.2	21.6	30.7	24.6
Pakistan	12 220	4.1	–3.6	18.2	27.6
Sri Lanka	6 672	–18.4	2.2	9.3	19.2
Turkey	69 340	–24.0	24.5	34.5	39.9

Sources: State Bank of Pakistan web site <http://www.sbp.org.pk>, 27 October 2004; Central Bank of Sri Lanka web site <www.lanka.net/centralbank>, 15 December 2004; Central Bank of the Islamic Republic of Iran web site <http://www.cbi.ir/>, 27 October 2004; Republic of Turkey State Institute of Statistics web site <http://www.die.gov.tr/english/>, 15 December 2004; and other national sources.

Notes: Fiscal year for India, the Islamic Republic of Iran and Pakistan. Growth rates for 2004 are estimates for all countries except Turkey. The growth rate of Turkey for 2004 refers to January-October 2004 compared with the corresponding period of 2003.

The growth in merchandise imports accelerated to the much faster pace of 27.6 per cent in 2004 from 18.2 per cent in 2003. Machinery and metals registered the largest increases and the sharp increase in imports of machinery supports the view that the economy is on the recovery path. Pakistan's imports are also highly concentrated in a few items, namely, machinery, petroleum and petroleum products, edible oil, iron and steel, fertilizer and tea, which accounted for 76 per cent of total imports in 2003. The trade deficit widened as a result of the faster growth in imports, lowering the current account surplus from $4.2 billion in 2003 to $1.8 billion in 2004. Remittances from migrant workers, which reached an all-time high of $4 billion in 2003, maintained their momentum in 2004.

Rapid import growth outpaced export growth by a wide margin in Sri Lanka

The strong revival in merchandise exports from Sri Lanka, which expanded 9.2 per cent in 2003, further rose to 12.7 per cent in 2004. Increased exports of apparel and garments, rubber and rubber-based products, diamonds, machinery, tea, coconut and gems and jewellery contributed to export growth, helped by higher commodity prices, particularly of tea and rubber.

In response to the domestic recovery, the value of merchandise imports grew at a much faster rate of 19.2 per cent in 2004, well above the 9.3 per cent growth realized in 2003. Imports of textile fabrics for garment exports, which constitute the largest component of intermediate imports, grew rapidly. Capital goods imports also registered substantial growth with all subsectors including building materials, transport equipment and machinery, and other equipment contributing to this growth. Higher oil prices were among the factors raising import expenditures, along with higher prices for other goods such as wheat, sugar and milk products. Not unexpectedly, the trade deficit widened in 2004 and, despite enhanced earnings from increased tourist arrivals and greater inflows of migrant worker remittances, the current account deficit increased in 2004.

Higher oil prices boosted export revenues in the Islamic Republic of Iran

In the Islamic Republic of Iran, the value of merchandise exports expanded at double-digit rates in 2002 and 2003, averaging nearly 19 per cent annually. Oil and gas exports constitute around 80 per cent of the country's total exports and higher oil prices coupled with enhanced production helped to increase exports from this sector by 18 per cent in 2003. However, non-oil exports expanded at a much faster rate of 27 per cent in that year. The expansion of agricultural and traditional goods exports exceeded 30 per cent owing in large part to the increase in the export of fresh and dried fruits. Exports of carpets and industrial products also registered substantial gains. The recent surge in oil prices was expected to increase the value of merchandise exports 27.3 per cent in 2004 with oil and gas exports expanding 31 per cent.

Merchandise imports, which grew at rates exceeding 20 per cent in 2001-2002, surged 30.7 per cent in 2003. Imports of industrial products in particular increased sharply while imports of agricultural and essential goods, including wheat, rice, sugar, meat, edible oil and fertilizer, slowed as compared with the previous year. Foreign trade liberalization and deregulation, such as the elimination of foreign exchange surrender requirements, the granting of credit facilities in domestic currency and foreign exchange to the foreign trade sector and the gradual elimination of trade barriers played a major role in accelerated import growth. Merchandise import growth slowed but remained high at 24.6 per cent in 2004. The trade surplus widened in 2004, contributing to a current account surplus of 4.6 per cent of GDP in 2004, up from 1.5 per cent in 2003.

Very high growth rates for both exports and imports in Turkey

In 2003, the growth in merchandise exports more than doubled to 31 per cent in Turkey and remained close to this level in the first 10 months of 2004. Low unit labour costs, a decrease in the cost of borrowing and an increase in export prices contributed to higher export revenues. The appreciation of the euro against the United States dollar played an important role in augmenting the dollar value of exports to the EU. In 2003, manufacturing exports, which comprise 94 per cent of total exports, expanded 30 per cent mainly on the strength of exports of automobiles and parts, knitted clothing, apparel, boilers, machinery and mechanical equipment.

Merchandise import expenditure has grown even faster, expanding by 34.5 per cent in 2003 and by nearly 40 per cent in the first 10 months of 2004. Imports of industrial goods increased by over 30 per cent in

2003 and increased capacity utilization necessitated new investment, with capital goods imports also expanding at a similar rate. However, consumer goods imports grew particularly rapidly, by about 44 per cent in 2003. Higher oil prices contributed to more than 18 per cent growth of oil imports in value terms. The trade deficit widened in 2004 and the current account deficit reached 4.9 per cent of GDP in that year as compared with 3.3 per cent in 2003.

Capital flows and exchange rates

Foreign exchange reserves continued to rise in India and Pakistan

India's external trade and payments situation in recent years has been marked by a noticeable structural change towards a more stable and sustainable balance of payments. In the capital account, there was a major shift in favour of long-term and non-debt-creating financial flows such as FDI and portfolio investment. Foreign investment inflows (including both FDI and portfolio investment) increased substantially from $4.5 billion in 2002 to $14.5 billion in 2003 attracted by the sound macroeconomic environment in India, the stability of the exchange rate of the rupee, further liberalization of foreign investment policies and relatively high returns on investment compared with other host countries. FDI inflows witnessed a sharp increase in 2004. However, portfolio investment decreased.

Foreign exchange reserves have been building up rapidly, by $17 billion in 2002 followed by another substantial increase of $31.4 billion in 2003 and $30.5 billion in 2004 owing to private transfers on the current account and sustained foreign investment inflows on the capital account. The stock of foreign exchange reserves stood at $131 billion at the end of December 2004 and was estimated to increase to $133 billion, equivalent to 16.7 months of imports, at the end of March 2005. During 2004, the value of the Indian rupee continued to fluctuate against the United States dollar. For the year as whole, the rupee appreciated marginally (figure II.18). The real effective exchange rate of the rupee depreciated 2.4 per cent in 2002-2003 but appreciated somewhat in 2004 owing to widening price differentials between India and its major trading partners.

In Pakistan, the balance of payments recorded a surplus amounting to $887 million in 2004, which was around 80 per cent lower than what had been achieved in the previous year. Both the current and capital accounts contributed to the lowering of the surplus. The deterioration in the capital account was mainly the result of a large, one-off prepayment of expensive external debt. Both FDI and portfolio investment registered increased inflows; FDI was around $900 million in 2004 as against $711 million in 2003. Foreign exchange reserves increased to $12.3 billion at end-June 2004 compared with $10.7 billion a year earlier. Many factors contributed to this comfortable reserve position, the most important being higher export proceeds, substantial large private inflows, grant assistance provided by development partners, stability in the exchange rate and enhanced investor confidence leading to higher FDI inflows.

Figure II.18. Index of exchange rates against the United States dollar of selected South and South-West Asian economies, 1996-2004

(1996 = 100)

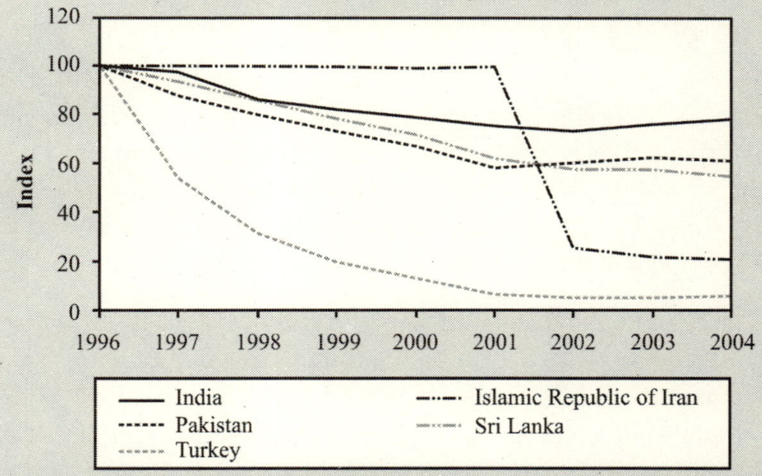

Sources: IMF, *International Financial Statistics*, vol. LVII, No. 10 (Washington, IMF, October 2004); and *The Economist*, various issues.

Note: Figures for 2004 are estimates.

Pakistan exited from the IMF Poverty Reduction and Growth Facility programme in December 2004 and did not voluntarily utilize the final tranche of $262 million available to it under the programme. Tighter macroeconomic policies and structural reforms have resulted in a stronger external position, a lower public debt burden, renewed access to international capital markets and a revival in growth. IMF commended Pakistan on the successful completion of its arrangements under the programme. Pakistan will now have to place more reliance on domestic and international capital markets to meet its financing needs. The Pakistan rupee strengthened against the United States dollar in the first half of fiscal year 2004 but depreciated in the second as the current account surplus narrowed. The central bank defended the rupee aggressively to slow its depreciation so as to allow the economy to adjust gradually to the changing exchange rate environment. For the year as whole, the average value of the rupee was stable against the dollar. In line with the dollar, the rupee depreciated against other major currencies, particularly the Japanese yen, Australian dollar, pound sterling and euro.

Net capital and financial inflows to Sri Lanka decreased

Net inflows under the capital and financial account were not sufficient to finance the widening current account deficit in Sri Lanka in 2004. Therefore, the overall balance of payments was in deficit after recording surpluses in the previous three years. Total foreign exchange reserves decreased by $56 million from December 2003 to reach $3.2

billion in August 2004. FDI inflows were estimated at $190 million in 2004, a level similar to that achieved in the previous year. Net inflows of credit to the Government, mostly on concessional terms, were estimated to have decreased to $327 million in 2004 from $550 million in 2003 owing to lower programme financing. The drop in foreign loan disbursements in 2004 was partly the result of delays in implementing projects and structural reforms.

During 2004, the Sri Lanka rupee depreciated against the dollar by about 5 per cent owing to the widening current account deficit and the slowdown in programme loans to the Government. Aid inflows in the wake of the tsunami disaster strengthened the rupee against the dollar at the beginning of 2005.

Foreign exchange reserves rose in the Islamic Republic of Iran

In the Islamic Republic of Iran, the capital and financial accounts recorded a large surplus in 2003 partly owing to higher FDI inflows mainly in the energy sector. FDI in 2003 was over $1 billion and portfolio investment stood at $643 million. Similar high levels of FDI and portfolio investment were expected in 2004. Gross official reserves increased by $3 billion to $24.4 billion in 2003 and a further large increase is also expected in 2004. The exchange rate of the Iranian rial against the United States dollar remained relatively stable in 2004. The rial's average real effective exchange rate depreciated 8.8 per cent in 2003, in part owing to expansionary monetary policy and appreciation of the euro against the dollar.

Large net inflows of FDI and portfolio investment in Turkey

The capital and financial account generated a surplus of $1.9 billion in 2003 in Turkey. However, the net inflow of FDI was only $76 million in that year owing to large FDI outflows while net portfolio investment inflows amounted to $2.6 billion. During the first 10 months of 2004, net FDI flows surged to $1.7 billion and portfolio investment climbed to $4.5 billion. The appreciation of the Turkish lira against the United States dollar, which began in mid-2002, continued until the end of the first quarter of 2004. There was also some appreciation against the euro at the same time but to a much lesser extent. In April-May 2004, the lira depreciated against the dollar, remaining relatively stable subsequently. For the year as a whole, the lira appreciated marginally against the dollar.

Foreign debt

External debt ratios show marked improvement in India's indebtedness

The trends in various debt indicators, such as the ratio of debt to GDP and debt-service ratios, indicate a marked improvement in India's external indebtedness. India's external debt, consisting of both short-term and long-term liabilities on government and non-government accounts, increased from $105.4 billion at the end of March 2003 to $111.8 billion at the end of March 2004 and was expected to increase further to $114.5 billion at the end of March 2005. The share of short-term debt has declined continuously in recent years, standing at 4.4 per cent of total external debt in 2004. The changing composition of the capital account in favour of non-debt financial flows led to an impressive improvement in debt indicators. The external debt-to-GDP ratio declined continuously from 38 per cent in 1991 to 18.3 per cent in 2003 and further to 16.1 per cent in 2004.

Pakistan attempting to prepay its expensive foreign debt

The total external debt of Pakistan declined marginally to $33.3 billion at the end of fiscal 2004 from $33.4 billion a year earlier. Pakistan made large prepayments of public and private loans in 2004 but their impact was offset by the disbursement of fresh inflows, interest capitalization and, most important, the revaluation impact on the stocks of debt not denominated in United States dollars. The Government prepaid $1.17 billion of a costly ADB loan in January 2004. While the stock of external debt did not change much in 2004, the prepayments contributed to a significant reduction in the outstanding stock of expensive external debt and liabilities.

In Sri Lanka, debt-service payments as a percentage of the exports of goods and services and income were estimated to increase to around 11.8 per cent in 2004 from 11.6 per cent in 2003 owing to an increase in loan repayments. In the wake of the tsunami, a moratorium on debt repayment announced by donors will improve debt-service ratios at least for the period of the moratorium.

Stock of external debt low in the Islamic Republic of Iran but growing in Turkey

The external debt of the Islamic Republic of Iran continues to be low. In 2003, this stock amounted to $12.1 billion, or 9.2 per cent of GDP. Debt servicing in the same year was 1.2 per cent of GDP and 4.5 per cent of exports. The amount of external debt and the debt ratios were not expected to change much in 2004. Turkey's external debt expanded from $131 billion in 2002 to $147 billion in 2003. Short-term debt constituted around 16 per cent of total external debt in 2003 and over 60 per cent of the total was held by the public sector. The debt-service ratio, calculated as the ratio of the principal and interest payments on external debt to revenues in foreign exchange, declined from 47 per cent in 2002 to 36 per cent in 2003 as a result of higher exports as well as a decline in external debt service.

Policy issues

Strong growth momentum needs to be maintained to tackle the problem of poverty

Most countries in the subregion have achieved high growth rates in the past few years. This strong growth momentum needs to be maintained if poverty is to be reduced further. Despite significant progress, the incidence of poverty remains high in several countries of the subregion. Economic growth is necessary for sustained poverty reduction, and growth that is broadly based generates employment opportunities from which the poor also benefit. Economic growth enhances government revenues, which can be used to improve the quantity and quality of education, health, water supply, sanitation and other services. Sound macroeconomic policies, the main elements of which include fiscal discipline, appropriate monetary and exchange rate policies and prudent debt management, are key to sustained economic growth. Agriculture and the housing and construction sectors, as well as SMEs, have more potential for generating pro-poor growth. Therefore, placing the emphasis on the growth of those sectors can help in rapid poverty reduction.

While the recent tsunami in Asia devastated many countries, India and Sri Lanka were the hardest hit in this subregion. The dead or missing in India are more than 16,000 and in Sri Lanka over 36,000. The number of those injured and displaced is very much higher. People living in coastal areas and dependent on fisheries suffered huge losses in terms of damaged fishing boats and other equipment and the loss of entire fishing communities. People dependent on the tourism industry in the affected areas have lost their jobs and earnings. Since this terrible calamity happened during the peak tourist season, many people were deprived of a major part of their earnings for the entire year. All this will add to the incidence of poverty in the affected countries. Rehabilitation of the poor families affected should be vigorously pursued through targeted programmes. The Government of India's fiscal budget for the current year, announced on 28 February 2005, brought some new initiatives and expanded several existing targeted programmes to mount an assault on poverty and unemployment. The budget also contains various measures for the development of employment intensive industries such as textiles, food processing and construction. More emphasis will be placed at improving rural infrastructure. By the time of the announcement of the budget, the Government had approved relief packages amounting to Rs. 36.44 billion to help the victims of the tsunami.

Efforts to reduce public debt should be strengthened

High public debt continues to be a serious challenge for most countries in the subregion. In addition to external debt, a substantial part of total debt consists of domestic debt. Public debt servicing consumes a major part of government budgets in the subregion. Funds that could have been used to build infrastructure and provide social services to tackle the problem of poverty go instead for servicing debt. A high overhang of public debt poses significant challenges for debt management as it puts pressure on interest rates, crowds out private investment and creates problems for future debt servicing. Countries need to use periods of strong growth to reduce fiscal imbalances and lower fiscal vulnerabilities. It is useful to note that countries' efforts in this regard are visible in declining fiscal deficits as a percentage of GDP in most countries of the subregion in recent years. Moreover, some countries in the region have made noteworthy progress in putting their debt ratios on a declining path.

In Pakistan, the public debt-to-GDP ratio declined to 70 per cent in 2004 after reaching 89 per cent in 2001. In India, the debt of the central Government as a percentage of GDP declined from 69 per cent in 2002 to 66 per cent in 2003. The public debt-GDP ratio was expected to remain unchanged in 2004.

Further fiscal consolidation and debt reduction have to be an integral part of a more comprehensive, coherent and multipronged strategy consisting of tax and expenditure reforms. Revenues need to be raised through broadening of the tax base, further rationalization of rate structures, removal of exemptions, continued improvement in tax administration, introduction of a comprehensive value-added tax and further widening of the service tax base. In addition, expenditure needs to be rationalized by reducing subsidies and wage bills. Disinvestment of government equity in public enterprises can be expedited and a part of the privatization receipts should be used for prepayment of more expensive public debt, restructuring of weak public enterprises and high-priority social expenditures.

Better management of water resources to mitigate the effects of adverse weather conditions

Agriculture is the backbone of most economies in the subregion. It provides employment to large numbers of people, particularly in the rural areas. Moreover, agriculture provides raw materials for many manufacturing industries and contributes significantly to exports, both directly and indirectly. With all this, agricultural output remains highly dependent on weather conditions. Bad weather can seriously damage economic growth and worsen the incidence of poverty. The high growth rates achieved in some countries in 2003 were partly dependent on the good performance of agriculture, which benefited from good weather conditions in that year. In contrast, a shortfall in rain in 2004 led to negative growth in the agricultural sector in Sri Lanka and much slower growth in India and Pakistan. Overall GDP growth rates slowed in India and Sri Lanka, mainly because of bad weather conditions. This cycle of good and bad weather is immutable and better water management is essential to overcome water shortages as well as flooding. Investment in building dams of appropriate sizes, with due consideration for protecting the environment, can help in storing water for agricultural purposes as well as generating electricity. Appropriate pricing of water can help to minimize waste and lead to its efficient use. Governments can provide technical and financial assistance to develop underground water resources. Investment in water resources should be given top priority for rapid and sustained economic growth.

Phasing out of the Agreement on Textiles and Clothing may hurt some economies

The Agreement on Textiles and Clothing was phased out at the beginning of 2005. Exports of textiles and clothing account for a major share of the total exports of Pakistan (66 per cent), Sri Lanka (50 per cent), Turkey (33 per cent) and India (20 per cent). The fear is that increased competition from countries such as China may hurt exports of textiles and clothing by Sri Lanka and Turkey. Available studies show that high-end producers of garments already compete in a non-quota market and cater for niche markets. Moreover, the phasing-out process began in 1994 and many major players in the garment industry have by now become adjusted to competing in a quota-free world in terms of modernizing plants and machinery. However, some small- and medium-scale firms could face difficulties. Such firms will have to enhance productivity and competitiveness to remain in business. India and Pakistan may benefit from the phasing out of the Agreement since their firms will have unrestricted access to world markets and because of their domestic raw materials and textile base, particularly in cotton.

Comprehensive structural reform agenda in the fourth five-year development plan of the Islamic Republic of Iran

The fourth five-year development plan, covering fiscal years 2005-2009, which was recently approved in the Islamic Republic of Iran, contains ambitious macroeconomic targets and a comprehensive structural reform agenda. The new plan targets real GDP growth of 8 per cent per annum compared with 5.7 per cent in the previous plan. Inflation is projected to decelerate to 9.9 per cent per annum on average during the plan period from an estimated 14.4 per cent in 2004. On the fiscal side, dependency on oil revenues will be reduced and growth in current expenditure contained. The reform agenda includes the introduction of VAT in 2006, a reduction in tax exemptions, a gradual phasing out of implicit energy subsidies and other explicit subsidies and an overhaul of benefits and contributions under the current social security system. Other elements include the assignment of a central role to the private sector and market forces, downsizing of the public sector, institutional and governance reforms, completion of the reform of the financial sector, privatization of most public enterprises, labour market reforms, completion of the ongoing trade and tariff reforms and capital account liberalization.

Ambitious fiscal decentralization initiative being planned in Turkey

To cater for local needs better, the Government of Turkey has decided to introduce an ambitious fiscal decentralization reform in order to transfer major spending powers to special provincial administrations and to metropolitan and other municipalities. New regional development agencies will be established to coordinate infrastructure projects and lead local development initiatives. While fiscal decentralization has many advantages, costs and risks are also involved. The Government seems to be cognizant of this and is seeking to contain them. One of the major risks is poor fiscal discipline at the local government level, which can lead to higher fiscal deficits. Limits can be placed on local government borrowing and the responsibilities of local governments in terms of the provision of basic and other services should be clearly defined and adequate revenues provided to meet those responsibilities. Capacity-building of local government officials should be a top priority so that they can fulfil their responsibilities. The experiences of other countries suggest that the full implementation of fiscal decentralization can take a long time and, therefore, it should be pursued with adequate preparation.

B. Least developed countries in the subregion

Overview

With the exception of Afghanistan, economic growth improved modestly in the least developed countries in South and South-West Asia in 2004 and ranged from 3.7 per cent in Nepal to 8.8 per cent in Maldives (figure II.19). However, the outlook for GDP growth in several of these countries may be less rosy. Maldives, which had earlier projected the highest rate of growth among these countries, was hit particularly hard by the Indian Ocean tsunami in December 2004, which is expected to adversely affect tourism and fisheries, its two principal industries. Meanwhile, the expiration of the MFA is likely to lower growth in the manufacturing sector in Bangladesh, Maldives and Nepal, where garments have been a key export.

Figure II.19. Rates of GDP growth in least developed countries in South and South-West Asia, 2001-2004

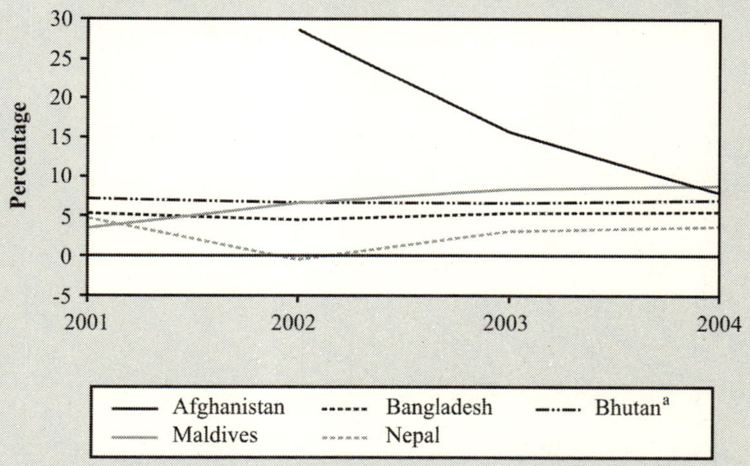

Sources: ESCAP, based on national sources; IMF, *IMF Executive Board Concludes 2004 Article IV Consultation with the Islamic State of Afghanistan,* Public Information Notice (PIN) No. 05/9 (27 January 2005); Bangladesh Bank web site <www.bangladesh-bank.org>, 18 November 2004; Royal Monetary Authority of Bhutan, *Selected Economic Indicators* (CD-ROM), September 2004; and Nepal Rastra Bank, *Economic Survey 2003/04* (Kathmandu, July 2004).

Note: Growth rates for 2004 are estimates.

[a] GDP at factor cost. Fiscal years for Afghanistan, Bangladesh and Nepal.

Inflationary pressures were also rather modest in the least developed countries of the subregion in 2004, partly owing to relatively stable exchange rates (figures II.20 and II.21). Maldives, which had experienced deflation in 2003, was expected to show some increase in consumer prices in 2004. However, the continuing increase in oil prices is a concern in all South and South-West Asian least developed countries, as its impact on both the transport and energy sectors will feed into higher prices elsewhere in their economies.

With the expiration of the MFA, diversification of exports and markets has become increasingly important to the least developed countries of the subregion. However, those countries need to ensure that poor macroeconomic management does not adversely affect the competitiveness of the external sectors and that supply capacities are enhanced.

Figure II.20. Inflation[a] in least developed countries in South and South-West Asia, 2001-2004

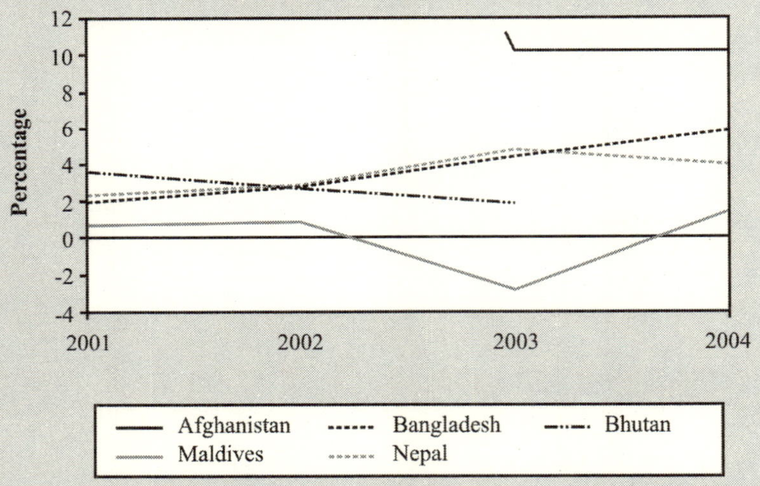

Sources: ESCAP, based on national sources; IMF, *IMF Executive Board Concludes 2004 Article IV Consultation with the Islamic State of Afghanistan*, Public Information Notice (PIN) No. 05/9 (27 January 2005); Bangladesh Bank web site <www.bangladesh-bank.org>, 18 November 2004; Royal Monetary Authority of Bhutan, *Selected Economic Indicators* (CD-ROM), September 2004; Nepal Rastra Bank, Economic Survey 2003/04 (Kathmandu, July 2004); and ADB, *Key Indicators of Developing Asian and Pacific Countries 2004* (Manila, ADB, 2004).

Note: Inflation rates for 2004 are estimates.

[a] Changes in the consumer price index in main urban areas by fiscal year.

Figure II.21. Index of exchange rates against the United States dollar of least developed countries in South and South-West Asia, 1996-2004

(1996 = 100)

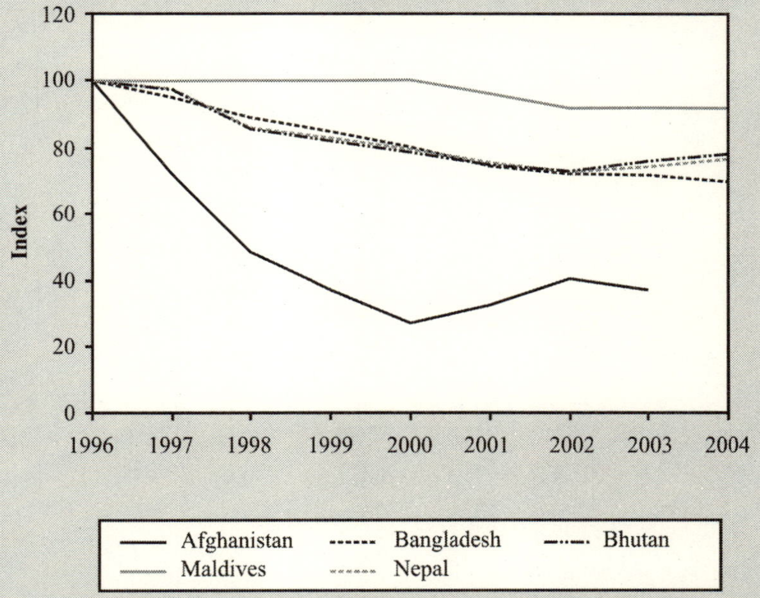

Sources: IMF, *International Financial Statistics*, vol. LVII, No. 10 (Washington, IMF, October 2004); and *The Economist*, various issues.

Note: Figures for 2004 are estimates.

Growth performance

Strong growth in Afghanistan despite lingering drought

As a result of lower than anticipated agricultural output owing to lingering drought in some regions, growth in real GDP in Afghanistan was revised downwards from 23 to 15.7 per cent in 2003, excluding opium production (table II.24). The drought reduced production of hydroelectricity but construction and services benefited from donor assistance. According to the United Nations Office on Drugs and Crime, the opium economy in Aghanistan is valued at $2.8 billion, equivalent to 60 per cent of non-drug GDP in 2003. Opiates produced in Afghanistan are consumed by an estimated two thirds of opiate abusers worldwide. Despite a decline in yields from crop disease and adverse climatic conditions, poppy production increased by 64 per cent in 2004 from the level in 2003. Although a broad strategy focusing on education, alternative livelihoods, interdiction, eradication and legal reforms is being implemented, eradication of opium production is expected to have a significant impact on the most vulnerable segment of the population. As a result of the effects of adverse weather conditions

Table II.24. Least developed countries in South and South-West Asia: growth rates, 2001-2004

(Percentage)

		Rates of growth			
		Gross domestic product	*Agriculture*	*Industry*	*Services*
Afghanistan	2002	28.6	27.7	21.1	39.5
	2003	15.7	..	..	..
	2004	8.0	..	..	..
Bangladesh	2001	5.3	3.1	7.4	5.3
	2002	4.4	0.0	6.5	5.4
	2003	5.3	3.1	7.3	5.4
	2004	5.5	2.7	7.7	5.7
Bhutan[a]	2001	7.1	3.2	13.8	7.6
	2002	6.7	2.6	17.9	−2.3
	2003	6.5	4.0	7.3	7.8
	2004	7.0	..	..	..
Maldives	2001	3.4	5.0	8.0	2.4
	2002	6.5	15.9	10.4	4.7
	2003	8.4	1.9	7.5	9.6
	2004	8.8	2.9	9.9	9.4
Nepal	2001	4.7	5.5	2.7	5.3
	2002	−0.6	2.2	−2.8	−1.4
	2003	3.1	2.5	2.3	3.3
	2004	3.7	3.7	1.8	4.2

Sources: ESCAP, based on national sources; IMF, *IMF Executive Board Concludes 2004 Article IV Consultation with the Islamic State of Afghanistan,* Public Information Notice (PIN) No. 05/9 (27 January 2005); Bangladesh Bank web site <www.bangladesh-bank.org>, 18 November 2004; Royal Monetary Authority of Bhutan, *Selected Economic Indicators* (CD-ROM), September 2004; and Nepal Rastra Bank, *Economic Survey 2003/04* (Kathmandu, July 2004).

Notes: Growth rates for 2004 are estimates. Industry comprises mining and quarrying; manufacturing; electricity, gas and power; and construction. In the case of Maldives, agriculture includes coral and sand mining. Fiscal years for Afghanistan, Bangladesh and Nepal.

[a] GDP at factor cost.

on agricultural production, real GDP was projected to rise by only 8 per cent in 2004, even with several important agricultural and manufacturing projects coming on stream. Growth in the construction, power and transport sectors remained strong in the first half of 2004. Afghanistan has taken steps to rationalize the public enterprise sector and create an environment conducive to private sector-led growth. Growth, employment and exports hinge on creating an environment conducive to both domestic and foreign investment through enforcement of property rights, bankruptcy laws, contract enforcement and a transparent and effective judicial system.

High oil prices and floods lower projected real GDP growth in Bangladesh

Overall real GDP growth in Bangladesh rose from 5.3 per cent in 2003 to an estimated 5.5 per cent in 2004. There was positive growth in all sectors of the economy in Bangladesh in 2004, led by industry at 7.7 per cent, followed by services at 5.7 per cent and agriculture at 2.7 per cent. Growth in crops and horticulture declined substantially in 2004 from the level reached the previous year, owing in part to floods. Industrial output continued to rise in 2004, led by manufacturing, construction and power, gas and water supply. The sharp rise in international steel prices had a negative impact on construction, which was partly cushioned by lower tariffs. Growth in mining and quarrying slowed from the previous year. The output of the service sector rose, owing to gains in wholesale and retail trade, hotels and restaurants and social services, including health and education. Slower growth in agriculture, however, dampened growth in transport, storage and communications. The service sector accounted for nearly half of GDP in 2004, while agriculture contributed slightly less than one quarter and industry accounted for 27.8 per cent. The forecast rate of GDP growth in fiscal 2005 has been revised downwards from 6.0 to 5.2 per cent in view of the increase in oil prices as well as the floods in mid-2004. Losses in assets and output from the floods have been tentatively estimated at 2.3 and 1.5 per cent of GDP. Medium-term growth projections are modest, muted by risks and uncertainties regarding apparel exports post-MFA.

With revived international interest in Bhutan, tourism increased substantially

Real GDP growth in Bhutan declined from 6.7 per cent in 2002 to 6.5 per cent in 2003, owing to a slowdown in electricity and construction, which comprise nearly one third of GDP. Sales of electricity continued to increase throughout the period as the lower-stage Basochu project commenced hydropower generation in September 2004 but the Kurichhu project was affected by flash floods in eastern Bhutan. Growth in the agricultural sector, which accounted for slightly less than a third of GDP, improved to 4.0 per cent in 2003. Led by growth in construction, manufacturing and transport, real GDP is expected to grow around 7 per cent in 2004. Both tourist arrivals and tourism revenues doubled in the third quarter of 2004 over the same period in 2003 as a result of renewed international interest in Bhutan. The current five-year plan, which runs from July 2002 to June 2007, accords high priority to infrastructure development and improving the quality of social services in the country.

Tsunami highlights Maldives' vulnerability as a small economy heavily reliant on tourism and fisheries

Real GDP growth in Maldives was estimated at 8.4 per cent in 2003 and projected to reach 8.8 per cent in 2004 prior to the tsunami at the end of the year. The primary sector was projected to grow 2.9 per cent in 2004, as growth in agriculture, fisheries and sand mining increased during the period. Liberalization and restructuring of the fishing sector resulted in significant growth in exports. Growth in the secondary sector, led by double-digit growth in electricity, water supply and construction, was projected to increase to 9.9 per cent in 2004, but the closure of garment factories will lower growth in manufacturing in 2005. A marginal decline in projected growth in the tertiary sector to 9.4 per cent reflects a slowdown in tourism. Maldives announced plans to allow private sector participation in telecommunications and implemented measures to enhance competition in the financial sector. The passage of the amended Land Act is expected to reduce impediments to bank lending and enable the creation of a functioning housing and commercial property market essential for private sector development.

Tsunami-related infrastructure repairs needed in Maldives

Despite the good economic performance, the vulnerability of Maldives, stemming from its heavy reliance on tourism and fisheries, was highlighted as tsunamis displaced more than 40 per cent of the total population, devastated 20 of the 199 inhabited islands and severely damaged another 53 islands in December 2004. Total damages in the Maldives were estimated to be approximately $470 million, or close to 62 per cent of GDP. In proportionate terms, Maldives was among the countries worst affected by the disaster and is likely to face the highest per capita reconstruction costs. Infrastructure repairs, estimated at $1.3 billion, are twice the country's annual GDP. Damage to the fisheries sector was severe as a quarter of the islands lost their entire fishing fleets. Recovery of the tourism sector, which accounts for a third of GDP and a significant portion of foreign exchange earnings, will also be essential. Initial estimates suggest that 4 percentage points may be lost from GDP growth in 2005.

End of armed conflict could enable growth envisaged in Nepal's PRSP

In Nepal, real GDP growth increased from 3.1 per cent in 2003 to 3.7 per cent in 2004 owing to stronger growth in agriculture and services. The agricultural sector, which accounts for about 40 per cent of GDP, grew 3.7 per cent in 2004 owing to a favourable monsoon, increased road connectivity and smooth supply of fertilizers following private sector involvement in fertilizer distribution. Growth in the industrial sector slowed to 1.8 per cent in 2004, owing in part to an increasing lack of security in rural areas, which dampened construction activity. Quantitative restrictions placed by India on its preferential export facility led to declining output of vegetable ghee and garment production slowed owing to weaker exports. The electricity sector continued to grow rapidly but its share in industrial output remained very small. The trade, restaurant and hotel sector, as well as the transport and communication sector, benefited from a ceasefire during part of 2004 as private airlines and communication services expanded. Community and social services benefited from increased activities of the non-government sector. Financial services performed poorly in 2004 owing to low private sector demand for bank credit, restructuring of State-owned banks and the state of insecurity.

High petroleum prices, the ending of the MFA and continued armed conflict within the country have led to projected growth in real GDP of 4.0 per cent in 2005, below the 6.2 per cent growth rate envisaged in Nepal's PRSP. However, if external shocks are temporary and armed conflict is resolved, higher growth could be possible given the country's current physical, institutional and financial infrastructure.

Inflation and exchange rates

Willingness to accept the afghani increased

Consumer price inflation, as measured by changes in the CPI in Kabul, was estimated at 10.3 per cent in 2003 as housing, education, health and transport costs all rose (table II.25). Acceleration in the rate of inflation in the first quarter of 2004, owing to seasonal and tax-related factors as well as higher spending on rent and other non-traded goods by the donor community, was offset in the second quarter as food prices declined, and the rate of inflation projected for the full year is 10.2 per cent. Growth of domestic currency in circulation, which jumped to 40.9 per cent in 2003, double the growth rate of the previous year, declined slightly to 38.0 per cent in 2004. The exchange rate appreciated somewhat in 2003 owing to the increased willingness of the population, especially in rural areas, to accept the currency as a medium of exchange and store of value and of donors to make payments in the currency. Administrative measures, including a requirement that goods be priced in afghanis, as well as the stable exchange rate have also ensured greater use of the currency.

Table II.25. Least developed countries in South and South-West Asia: inflation and money supply growth (M2), 2001-2004

(Percentage)

	2001	2002	2003	2004
Inflation[a]				
Afghanistan	..	52.3	10.3	10.2
Bangladesh	1.9	2.8	4.4	5.8
Bhutan	3.6	2.7	1.8	..
Maldives	0.7	0.9	−2.9	1.5
Nepal	2.4	2.9	4.8	4.0
Money supply growth (M2)				
Afghanistan	..	20.1	40.9	38.0
Bangladesh	16.6	13.1	15.6	13.7
Bhutan	7.6	28.5	0.4	4.1[b]
Maldives	9.0	19.3	14.6	23.0[c]
Nepal	15.3	4.4	9.8	13.5

Sources: ESCAP, based on national sources; IMF, *IMF Executive Board Concludes 2004 Article IV Consultation with the Islamic State of Afghanistan,* Public Information Notice (PIN) No. 05/9 (27 January 2005); Bangladesh Bank web site <www.bangladesh-bank.org>, 18 November 2004; Royal Monetary Authority of Bhutan, *Selected Economic Indicators* (CD-ROM), September 2004; Nepal Rastra Bank, *Economic Survey 2003/04* (Kathmandu, July 2004); and ADB, *Key Indicators of Developing Asian and Pacific Countries 2004* (Manila, ADB, 2004).

Note: Figures for 2004 are estimates.

[a] Changes in the consumer price index in main urban areas by fiscal year.
[b] January-June.
[c] January-July.

Inflation continues to rise in Bangladesh owing to higher food prices

During fiscal 2004, the 12-month average CPI inflation for Bangladesh rose to 5.8 per cent from 4.4 per cent in 2003. Inflation increased further to 6.2 per cent in October 2004, owing largely to flood-related agricultural output losses as well as higher prices of rice, wheat and sugar in international markets. Pressure on food prices was expected to ease with new harvests but upward revision of managed domestic fuel oil prices was expected to exert upward pressure on the non-food component and the CPI inflation projected for 2005 was raised to 6.8 per cent. Owing to the large volume of formal and informal imports from India, inflation trends in India have a significant impact on inflation in Bangladesh. The market-based, floating exchange rate of the taka against the dollar remained quite stable during the first 5 months of 2004. Pressure on the exchange rate heightened significantly in the period to mid-2004 with a sharp rise in payments for the import of ships for scrapping and again in late 2004 as payments for fuel oil imports increased.

Inflation in Bhutan drops to a historical low

In Bhutan, where price developments closely track those in India, inflation dropped to a historically low rate of 1.3 per cent in December 2003. The quarterly CPI was revised, starting in the third quarter of 2004 and using the third quarter of 2003 as the new base. The weight of food items in the consumer basket was reduced from more than half to less than a third while rent was added to the commodity basket. Based on the new CPI, inflation stood at 4.6 per cent for the third quarter of 2004. Since no quarterly price indices were calculated prior to the third quarter of 2003, the year-on-year changes in the CPI for the second half of 2003 and the first half of 2004 were not calculated. Parity between the ngultrum and the Indian rupee continues to be maintained as it contributes to macroeconomic stability and facilitates trade with India, which accounts for 80 per cent of Bhutan's external trade.

Inflation in Maldives remained subdued

A sharp deflation of 2.9 per cent in 2003, owing to falling prices for locally produced food, gave way to positive inflation of 1.5 per cent in 2004 in Maldives, as measured by the CPI in Male. The rise in petroleum prices, which affected transport and fuel prices, was largely responsible for the increase. The policy of pegging the rufiyaa to the United States dollar, recently reaffirmed by the authorities, strengthened the competitive position of Maldives as the dollar depreciated against the euro in recent years.

Lower food and commodity prices lead to drop in inflation in Nepal

In Nepal, the average annual rate of inflation, as measured by the National Urban Consumer Price Index, declined from 4.8 per cent in 2003 to 4.0 per cent in 2004 owing to an easing of price pressures on food, which comprises over half the weight of the CPI, lower international commodity prices and an appreciating nominal exchange rate of the Nepalese rupee. Production of foodgrains was satisfactory and imported grain prices remained low. Prices of education- and health-related services increased moderately but fuel, light, water and transport charges rose more markedly owing to higher oil prices. Despite an upward adjustment in administered petroleum prices in 2004, domestic prices of petroleum at the pump are still low compared with international prices, adding to losses at the Nepal Oil Corporation. The rate of inflation is projected to increase to 5.5 per cent in 2005 owing to higher prices for foodgrains and sugar and upward adjustment in petroleum prices. In line with the movement of the Indian rupee, to which it is pegged, the Nepalese rupee appreciated against the dollar by 4 per cent in 2003 and another 1.7 per cent in 2004. Despite nominal appreciation of the Nepalese rupee, the real exchange rate remains broadly competitive.

External sector

Afghanistan reconciles debts incurred by previous administration with external creditors

Although reliable balance-of-payments figures for Afghanistan are not available, the external current account, excluding grants, is estimated to have deteriorated in 2003 owing to a surge in imports related to reconstruction and rising consumer demand. Exports, including re-exports, were projected to rise from an estimated $1.7 billion in 2003 to over $1.8 billion in 2004, while imports were projected to increase from nearly $3.8 billion to over $4.1 billion during the period. As a result of the significant transit trade through Afghanistan, the amounts of both domestic exports and retained imports are estimated to be much lower (tables II.26 and II.27 and figures II.22 and II.23). A high-level donors' conference held in 2004 resulted in new pledges seen as adequate to meet Afghanistan's development needs over the next few years. External loans contracted by Afghanistan in 2004 were on highly concessional terms and disbursements have been limited. In order to manage external debts prudently, Afghanistan has made progress in identifying debts incurred by previous administrations and reconciling them with external creditors. A full and detailed inventory of external loans

Table II.26. Least developed countries in South and South-West Asia: merchandise exports and their rates of growth, 2001-2004

	Exports (f.o.b.)				
	Value (millions of US dollars)	*Annual rate of growth (percentage)*			
	2003	*2001*	*2002*	*2003*	*2004*
Afghanistan	209	−37.7	11.5	109.4	42.6
Bangladesh	6 492	12.6	−7.6	9.5	15.9
Bhutan	121	3.0	2.3	12.1	..
Maldives	152	1.4	20.1	14.9	3.9
Nepal	644	6.0	−19.2	5.0	11.3

Sources: IMF, *Direction of Trade Statistics* (CD-ROM), February 2005; and national sources.

Notes: Growth rates for 2004 refer to January-July for Afghanistan and January-June for Maldives. All growth rates are annual. Figures for Bangladesh and Nepal in fiscal years. Maldives includes re-exports.

Table II.27. Least developed countries in South and South-West Asia: merchandise imports and their rates of growth, 2001-2004

	Imports (c.i.f.)				
	Value (millions of US dollars)	*Annual rate of growth (percentage)*			
	2003	*2001*	*2002*	*2003*	*2004*
Afghanistan	1 599	−8.9	76.7	56.9	23.0
Bangladesh	8 707	11.4	−8.7	13.1	13.0
Bhutan	224	−6.0	−13.4	35.5	..
Maldives	414	1.3	−0.4	20.2	30.7
Nepal	1 893.3	1.1	−11.1	14.4	18.0

Sources: IMF, *Direction of Trade Statistics* (CD-ROM), February 2005; and national sources.

Notes: Growth rates for 2004 refer to January-July for Afghanistan and January-June for Maldives. All growth rates are annual. Figures for Bangladesh and Nepal in fiscal years. F.o.b. value for Bangladesh.

Figure II.22. Growth rates in merchandise export earnings of least developed countries in South and South-West Asia, 2001-2004

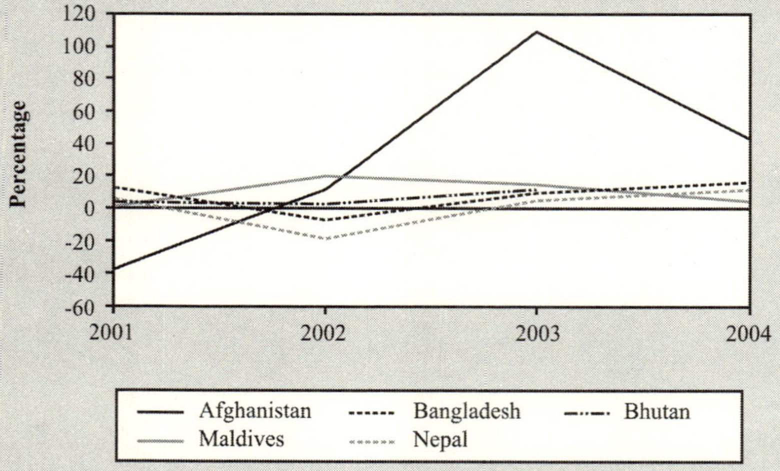

Sources: IMF, *Direction of Trade Statistics* (CD-ROM), December 2004; and national sources.

Notes: Growth rates for 2004 refer to January-July for Afghanistan and January-June for Maldives. All growth rates are annual. Figures for Bangladesh and Nepal in fiscal year. Maldives includes re-exports.

Figure II.23. Growth rates in merchandise import spending of least developed countries in South and South-West Asia, 2001-2004

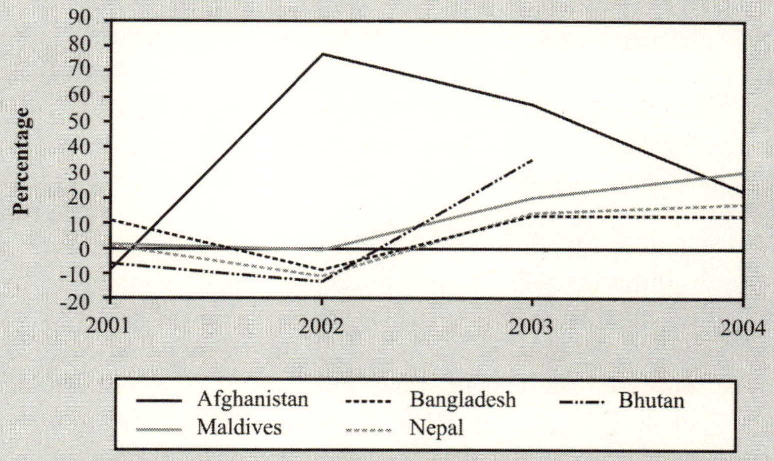

Sources: IMF, *Direction of Trade Statistics* (CD-ROM), December 2004; and national sources.

Notes: Growth rates for 2004 refer to January-July for Afghanistan and January-June for Maldives. All growth rates are annual. Figures for Bangladesh and Nepal in fiscal year.

verified by external creditors is expected to be available by the beginning of 2005. Generous debt relief is being sought from bilateral creditors to ensure fiscal sustainability in the medium and long terms. Gross international reserves are expected to rise from an estimated $815 million at the end of 2003 to $977 million at the end of 2004.

Rising cotton imports signal growing backward linkages in textile production in Bangladesh

In Bangladesh, exports increased by nearly 16 per cent to $7.5 billion while imports increased by 13 per cent to $9.8 billion in 2004. Exports of woven garments and knitwear comprise three quarters of total exports and, along with frozen fish and leather, were robust in 2004, but exports of jute goods and raw jute declined. There appears to be widespread optimism that the apparel-exporting sector, used to surviving on thin margins at the lower end of the global market, will not experience a drastic fall in market share in the post-MFA world; however, it may suffer further erosion in prices. The resolution of quality certification issues for frozen fish is expected to stabilize demand and permit steady growth. A strong increase in exports of items such as vegetables and non-jute agricultural products and light engineering products in recent years suggests increased export diversification and reduced dependence on apparel exports. Imports of inputs for domestic processing, including textiles, yarn, cotton and staple fibres for the apparel-export sector, as well as crude and refined petroleum, rose in 2004 while growth of capital goods imports remained modest. The increase in imports of cotton and staple fibres suggests more extensive backward linkages in textile and apparel production.

Although the trade deficit widened, the increase in the inflow of current transfers, mainly remittances from migrant workers, led to a higher current account surplus in Bangladesh. The overall balance-of-payments surplus fell from $815 million in 2003 to $184 million in 2004 reflecting the sharp decline in grants and concessional loans from multilateral and bilateral donors from $1.4 billion in 2003 to $679 million in 2004. With the Government's fiscal programme heavily reliant on these inflows, fiscal stability could be undermined. Net FDI increased marginally from $376 million in 2003 to $385 million in 2004. Gross foreign exchange reserves rose to $2.7 billion at the end of June 2004 from $2.5 billion a year earlier. Official external debt outstanding increased somewhat to $17.2 billion at the end of June 2004, about 31.7 per cent of GDP. Since most of the debt is concessional, debt-service liabilities are manageable and the debt-service ratio declined to 7.5 per cent of exports in 2004.

Commissioning of Tala hydropower project will boost Bhutan's exports

In 2002, Bhutan's overall trade deficit decreased to 13.1 per cent of GDP owing to a reduction in imports. Inflows of aid, concessional loans and FDI offset the trade deficit and contributed to the overall balance-of-payments surplus. Exports to India, Bhutan's largest trading partner, increased over 20 per cent in 2003 but imports rose 70 per cent. The commissioning of the Tala hydropower project in 2005 is, however, expected to boost electricity exports to India and narrow the trade deficit. Electricity, base metals and chemicals comprised 70 per cent of Bhutan's exports to India in 2003, while machinery and mechanical appliances, mineral products and base metals comprised 60 per cent of imports from that country. Vegetables and fruits comprised more than 60 per cent of exports to countries other than India in the same year while over 70 per cent of imports from those countries consisted of machinery, mechanical appliances, base metals and electronic items. Bangladesh is the second-most important export destination for Bhutan while Japan, Singapore and Thailand largely account for the rest of its imports. Bhutan acceded to the World Customs Organization in 2003 and joined Bangladesh-India-Myanmar-Sri Lanka-Thailand Economic Cooperation (BIMST-EC) in 2004, becoming a signatory to the BIMST-EC Free Trade Area. It also signed the Framework Agreement on SAFTA in an effort to diversify its export markets and link transport infrastructure.

Bhutan's stock of external debt outstanding at the end of 2003 amounted to $472 million, or 67 per cent of GDP. Of this total, 41 per cent is convertible currency debt. External borrowings were expected to fund 15 per cent of the Government's total capital outlay in 2004. Since the entire convertible debt stock is highly concessional, the debt-service ratio in 2003 was 3.5 per cent of total exports. FDI accounted for less than 3 per cent of transactions in the capital and financial account that year. Reserves declined to $349 million in the third quarter of 2004, the equivalent of 17 months of imports; four fifths of the total was in convertible currencies and the balance in Indian rupees.

Decline in loan concessionality parallels fall in the quantity of aid to Maldives

Exports, including re-exports, from Maldives totalled $152 million while imports totalled $414 million, leading to a widening trade deficit in 2003. A much higher trade deficit is expected in 2004. Marine products, mainly tuna shipped to Sri Lanka and Thailand, constituted half the value of merchandise exports, while garments destined primarily for the United States constituted another quarter. Consumer goods, petroleum products and capital goods, primarily from Singapore, Sri Lanka and India, accounted for the major share of imports to Maldives. Narrowing tariff dispersion, eliminating non-tariff barriers and reducing the number of exemptions are expected to liberalize trade further in Maldives in coming years. Non-factor services contributed $296 million to the income surplus, leading to an external current account deficit equivalent to 6.5 per cent of GDP in 2003. Inflows of private capital, largely to the tourism sector, were estimated to be $56.8 million in 2003. A fall in the quantity of aid to Maldives in recent years has been accompanied by declining loan concessionality. However, reserves improved to the equivalent of 3.4 months of goods and non-factor service imports in 2003. External debt has been steady at 40 per cent of GDP while debt service declined to 4.3 per cent of domestic exports at the end of 2003.

Official grants as well as remittances and pensions from abroad rise in Nepal

Growth in the value of total merchandise exports rose from 5.0 per cent in 2003 to 11.3 per cent in 2004 in Nepal, where India's share of total trade continued to rise from less than 40 per cent a decade previously to 58.8 per cent in 2004. Zinc sheets, jute goods and polyester yarn and thread were major exports to India while woollen carpets, handicrafts and tanned skins were exported to other countries, but exports of ready-made garments and pashmina shawls have declined. Growth in the value of merchandise imports increased from 14.4 per cent in 2003 to 18 per cent in 2004. Petroleum products, iron and steel products and vehicles and spare parts were the principal imports from India while chemical fertilizer, thread, zinc ingots, machinery and parts, crude palm oil, raw wool and telecommunication equipment were imported from other countries.

The merchandise trade deficit widened in Nepal. However, the peace talks initiative resulted in improved security and increased receipts from travel led to higher services income in 2004. The transfer account also rose owing to a sharp increase in official grants as well as growth in remittances and pensions from abroad. The current account surplus, equivalent to 2.4 per cent of GDP, was supplemented by net capital inflows in the form of official aid in 2004. External debt outstanding was equivalent to 49.5 per cent of GDP at the end of 2004 while debt service as a percentage of merchandise exports was 10.8 per cent. Approved FDI totalled $35 million in 2004 but the actual volume is unavailable owing to lack of a proper reporting system; it is estimated to be low, however. The surplus on the balance of payments increased to 3.3 per cent of GDP in 2004 and foreign exchange reserves rose to the equivalent of over 11 months of merchandise imports. Foreign currency liabilities created in the generation of hydropower are, however, putting pressure on foreign exchange reserves and the balance-of-payments surplus is projected to decline in 2005 owing to lower garment exports.

Policy issues and responses

Broadening revenue base essential for fiscal sustainability

In all countries, broadening of the revenue base is essential in order to accommodate increases in public expenditure. Meeting revenue targets in Afghanistan requires concerted efforts by ministries and provincial authorities to address deficiencies in collection, particularly of customs revenues in the provinces. Afghanistan is also committed to customs and tax reforms as well as elimination of tax holidays and concession agreements. In Bangladesh, efforts to increase government revenue are focused on expanding the net of direct income and profits taxes as well as VAT, while reducing dependence on import-related tariffs. To reduce the current dependence of government revenues on the tourism sector, Maldives is considering the introduction of a business profits tax on all sectors and a property tax on land, along with increased fees and administrative charges. The setback caused to development efforts in the Maldives by the tsunami highlights the fragility of the least developed countries and illustrates the need for a smooth transition strategy for such a country at the time of its graduation from the least developed category (box II.2)

Strengthening and deepening banking and financial sectors

A number of least developed countries in South and South-West Asia are engaged in strengthening and deepening the banking and financial sectors. The central bank of Afghanistan completed the licensing procedure for State-owned banks as well as private commercial banks, which have a large degree of foreign investment and management. The introduction of a short-term capital note also allowed for development of a domestic credit market necessary for bank intermediation and investment. Bangladesh focused on reforming nationalized commercial banks by stemming the flow of NPLs and implementing strategies to resolve long-standing challenges resulting from unrestricted net lending and large unsyndicated loans. Measures include restrictions on net lending as well as large non-syndicated loans and expedited loan recoveries. Establishment of the Maldives Finance Leasing Company to provide medium- and long-term equipment finance has facilitated long-term equipment financing in tourism, construction, transport and fisheries. A housing finance institution was also established in Maldives to extend housing loans on more favourable terms than commercial banks. In Nepal, two State-owned banks, which accounted for two fifths of transactions, as well as State-owned development banks specializing in agriculture and industry, were being restructured.

Box II.2. Smooth transition for countries graduating from the list of least developed countries

Graduation from the least developed category reflects the success of a country's development efforts. Support from development partners in the form of trade preferences, ODA and technical cooperation has often been critical to achieving success. Yet, while the list of countries that are least developed has expanded over the years, only Botswana has managed to graduate from the list of least developed countries. While endorsing the decision of the Committee on Development Policy at its sixth session in 2004 on the graduation of Cape Verde and Maldives from the list of least developed countries, the Economic and Social Council recognized the need for a smooth transition for graduating countries to ensure that graduation from the list does not disrupt their development.

Graduation implies reduction, or even loss, of financial and technical assistance that has enabled these countries to develop both economically and socially. As the recent impact of the tsunami in Maldives vividly illustrates, the stock of human assets and economic resources in most of these countries, even in the best of circumstances, remains fragile and the loss of concessions from development partners could set back development efforts. It is therefore evident that a smooth transition strategy, which includes both actions to be taken domestically and continued support from development partners for an adequate period of time post-graduation, is critical for the future success of graduated countries.

To ensure a smooth transition, a vulnerability profile will be prepared for a country identified by the Committee on Development Policy as meeting the criteria for graduation from the list for the first time. The Committee will review the profile at its subsequent triennial review and if the graduation of the country is reconfirmed, the Committee will submit a recommendation to the Economic and Social Council. The Council, in turn, will take action on the Committee's recommendation at its first substantive session following the triennial review of the Committee, and will transmit its decision to the General Assembly. Graduation will become effective three years after the General Assembly's decision to take note of the recommendation of the Committee on Development Policy.

During the three-year period, the graduating country will prepare a transition strategy in consultation with its bilateral and multilateral development and trading partners to adjust to the phasing out of the benefits associated with least developed country status and identify actions to be taken by the graduating country itself and its partners to that end.

All development partners will be invited to support the implementation of the transition strategy and avoid abrupt reductions in either ODA or technical assistance provided to the graduated country, including under the Integrated Framework for Trade-Related Technical Assistance to Least Developed Countries, and to consider extending or reducing trade preferences previously made available as a result of least developed country status in a phased manner. Members of WTO will also be invited to consider extending the existing special and differential treatment and exemptions available to least developed countries to a graduated country.

Trade liberalization for sustained growth and poverty reduction in small economies

Trade liberalization is the key to improved resource allocation, economic growth and poverty reduction in small economies since outward-looking, market-oriented policy reforms stimulate trade and economic growth. Although exports from least developed countries in South Asia have generally risen in recent years, the share of those countries in global trade still remains very low. Export competitiveness is hindered by factors such as high production and transit costs and limited market access. To overcome these factors, improvements are required in infrastructure, ICT, product development and non-reciprocal market access, as well as an environment conducive to investment and trade.

Interventions to build supply-side capabilities need to parallel trade policy reforms

Openness and liberalization alone are of limited effectiveness in diversifying exports and promoting broad-based economic growth. Least developed countries in the subregion generally have a comparative advantage in the production of labour-intensive goods, often based on agriculture and natural resources. To ensure a supply response to trade policy reforms, strategic interventions to build supply-side capabilities in these sectors are essential. Competitiveness is also affected by the macroeconomic policy regime. Fiscal, exchange rate and monetary policies need to ensure that taxes on exports, imperfect financial markets and high interest rates do not adversely affect competitiveness. Accountability, transparency and good governance are also important in maintaining an environment that attracts sustained inflows of long-term investment.

Diversification of markets could provide stable export growth

To increase opportunities through trade, South and South-West Asian least developed countries have recently signed a number of bilateral and multilateral preferential trade and free trade agreements. Nepal joined the global trading regime through WTO membership while both Bhutan and Nepal became signatories to regional trading regimes under SAFTA and BIMST-EC. With the expiration of the MFA, Bangladesh was looking to other countries in Asia, where exports have hitherto been low, as possible markets for apparel and other exports. Diversification of markets could provide stability to export growth and reduce dependence on apparel exports to Europe and North America. Creating access to new markets, however, requires negotiation skills as well as technical assistance and policy support from multilateral institutions.

Transport and transit costs need to be reduced

Integration into the global economy also requires reduction of transport and transit costs. Limitations in transport and trade infrastructure raise transaction costs and erode competitiveness in the least developed countries in the subregion, three of which, Afghanistan, Bhutan and Nepal, are landlocked. In addition to having limited access to the sea, landlocked countries must cover the cost of transit to ports in neighbouring countries in order to conduct international trade. The establishment of an inland container depot in Nepal is expected to reduce transit costs by at least one third. Special economic zones are being established in places adjacent to the depot to facilitate export processing. A competition law is being drafted to eliminate industrial, transport and other service monopolies and reform of custom procedures is also being undertaken in Nepal.

Potential fiscal consequences of high oil prices

The prevailing high price of oil is expected to increase the value of merchandise imports in all the least developed countries in South and South-West Asia. Imports of petroleum products, which accounted for 9 per cent of Nepal's total imports in 2001, accounted for nearly 16 per cent of the total in 2004. Since demand for such imports is inelastic, the oil import bill is expected to rise substantially with continued high international oil prices. To avoid an increase in consumer price inflation in Bangladesh, the administered domestic prices of oil have not fully reflected the rise in import prices. An adjustment of oil prices through a reduction of the tariff element in domestic prices cushioned the impact on consumers but also adversely affected the finances of the State-owned petroleum corporation.

South-East Asia

A. Developing countries in the subregion

Overview

Generally stronger growth in the subregion supported by domestic and external demand

GDP growth improved in most developing countries of South-East Asia in 2004 (figure II.24), the exceptions being Brunei Darussalam, where output in the crucial oil and gas sector was affected by maintenance, and Thailand, where economic growth in 2003 had been unusually vigorous. Growth was broadly based in most countries. Growth in the agricultural sector boosted GDP in Indonesia and the Philippines, despite some typhoon damage in the case of the latter. Drought, aggravated by a poor monsoon, lowered output in that sector in Thailand and Viet Nam. Several economies in the subregion were carried along by the strong upturn in the electronics cycle, which, however, appeared to have passed its peak in the second half of the year. Other manufacturing industries, such as vehicles, chemicals, plastics and biomedical products, also performed strongly. The service sectors benefited from increased trade, renewed consumer confidence and a sharp revival in tourism after the SARS scare of 2003.

Figure II.24. Rates of GDP growth in selected South-East Asian economies, 2001-2004

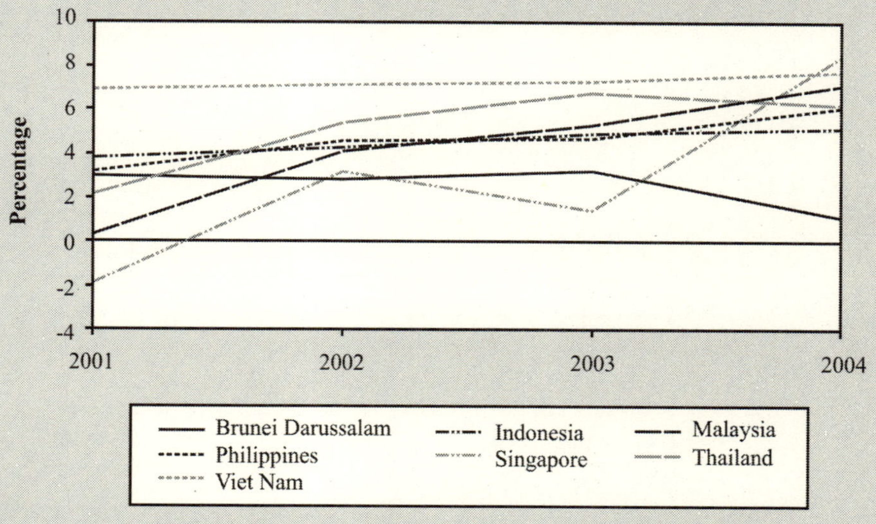

Sources: ESCAP, based on national sources; and ADB, *Key Indicators of Developing Asian and Pacific Countries 2004* (Manila, ADB, 2004).

Note: Growth rates for 2004 are estimates.

External demand played a very significant role in most South-East Asian economies, although Indonesia seemed to lag its neighbours to some extent. Many countries found their trading links with other economies in Asia and the Pacific strengthening and deepening owing to regional production networks and strong growth in China. Private consumption revived very strongly in Singapore as confidence returned and continued to be robust in Indonesia, Malaysia and Viet Nam, although it flagged somewhat in the Philippines and Thailand. One encouraging note is the strong growth of private investment in Indonesia, Malaysia, Singapore, Thailand and Viet Nam, although business confidence remained depressed in the Philippines and Brunei Darussalam. The outlook for growth in 2005 for most developing countries in the subregion is for a slowdown, as the external environment becomes less favourable. The effects of the tsunami of 26 December 2004 on tourism and fisheries in Thailand will slow growth further in that country. Despite the tsunami, strong investment is expected to continue boosting growth in Indonesia, as well as Viet Nam.

With the exception of Indonesia, rates of inflation picked up in developing countries in South-East Asia (figure II.25) generally owing to higher food and oil prices. Many countries resorted to fuel subsidies to

Figure II.25. Inflation[a] in selected South-East Asian economies, 2001-2004

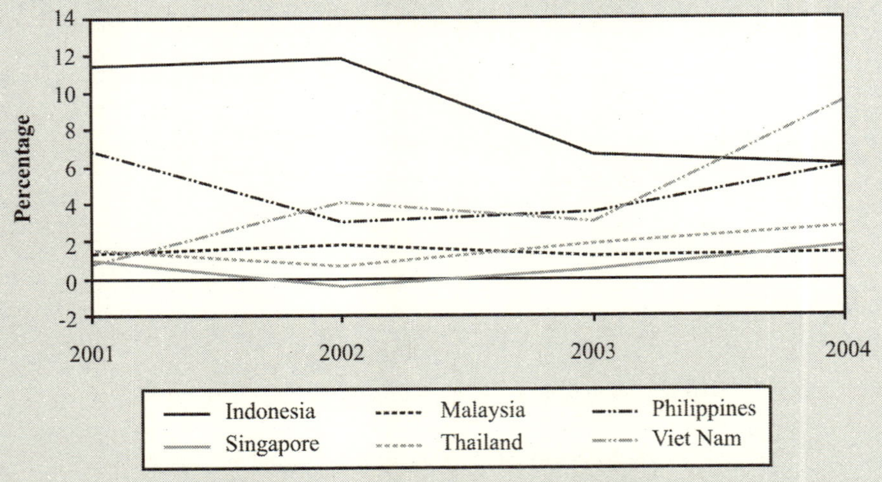

Sources: ESCAP, based on national sources; ADB, *Key Indicators of Developing Asian and Pacific Countries 2004* (Manila, ADB, 2004); and EIU, *Country Forecasts* (London, EIU, 2004), various issues.

Note: Inflation rates for 2004 are estimates.

[a] Changes in the consumer price index.

contain inflation, but not Singapore. However, budgetary pressures prevented the Philippines from doing so to the same extent and led to subsidies being partially removed in Thailand and Viet Nam towards the end of the year. Monetary policy was tightened in response to the pickup in inflation in most countries of the subregion and the rising trend in global interest rates, although the Malaysian central bank maintained a prudent but accommodative stance. Fiscal policies also moved in a more prudent direction in 2004 and public debt continued to fall as a percentage of GDP.

High-tech products and commodities lift exports from the subregion and tourism revives

With the exception of Brunei Darussalam, all the developing countries of South-East Asia took advantage of the surge in external trade in 2004, with double-digit rates of growth of merchandise exports and imports in most cases (figures II.26 and II.27). Electronics, vehicles and other high-tech products as well commodities were the principal exports. Imports tended to be broadly based between consumer, intermediate and

Figure II.26. Growth rates in merchandise export earnings of selected South-East Asian economies, 2001-2004

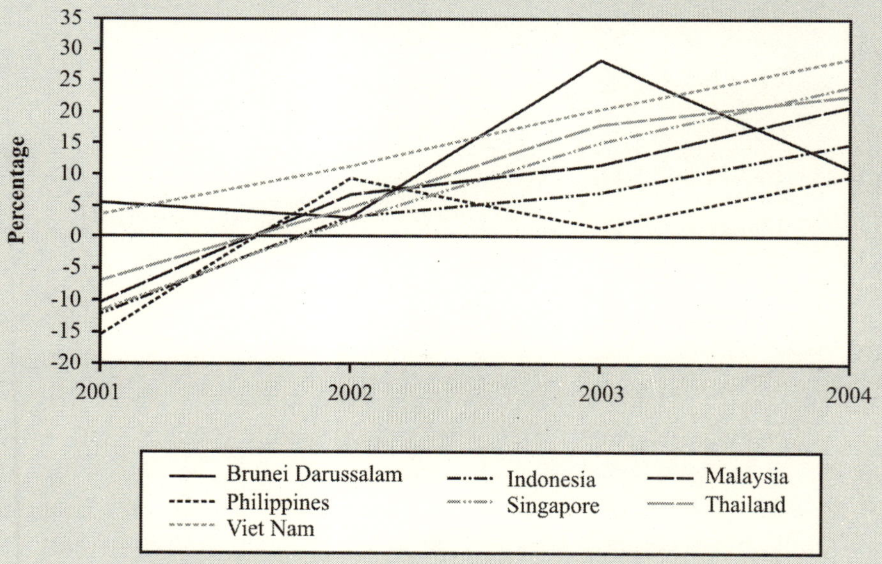

Sources: IMF, *Direction of Trade Statistics* (CD-ROM), February 2005; Bank Indonesia web site <http://www.bi.go.id>, 10 January 2005; Malaysia Economic Planning Unit web site <http://www.epu.jpm.my/>, 7 January 2005; Philippines National Statistics Office web site <http://www.census.gov.ph>, 11 January 2005; Bank of Thailand web site <http://www.bot.or.th>, 18 November 2004; and national sources.

Notes: Growth rate for 2004 compared with the corresponding period of 2003. Growth rate for 2004 refers to the whole year, except that for Indonesia it refers to January-October, Malaysia and the Philippines to January-November and Brunei Darussalam to January-September.

Figure II.27. Growth rates in merchandise import spending of selected South-East Asian economies, 2001-2004

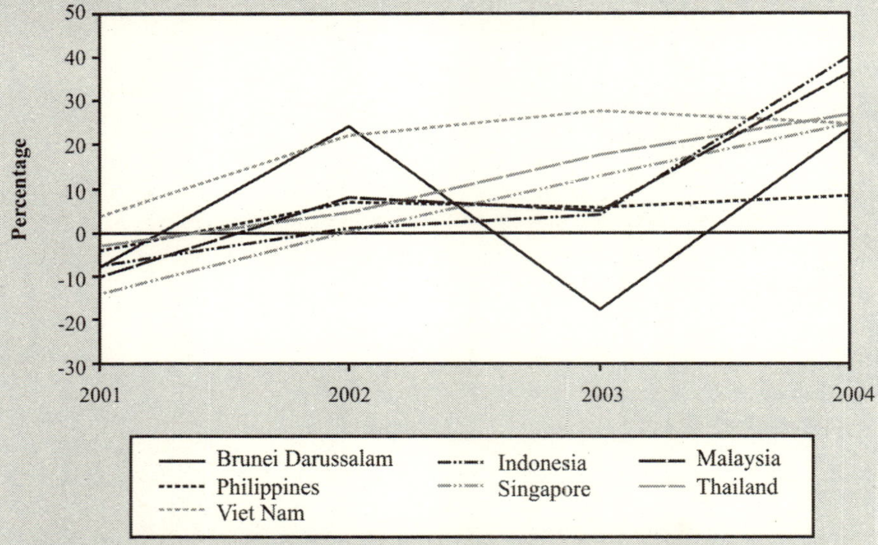

Sources: IMF, *Direction of Trade Statistics* (CD-ROM), February 2005; Statistics Indonesia web site <http://www.bps.go.id>, 7 January 2005; Malaysia Economic Planning Unit web site <http://www.epu.jpm.my/>, 7 January 2005; Philippines National Statistics Office web site <http://www.census.gov.ph>, 11 January 2005; Bank of Thailand web site <http://www.bot.or.th>, 18 November 2004; and national sources.

Notes: Growth rate for 2004 compared with the corresponding period of 2003. Growth rate for 2004 refers to the whole year except that for Indonesia it refers to January-October, Malaysia and the Philippines to January-November and Brunei Darussalam to January-September.

capital goods. Tourism also revived sharply after the SARS scare of the previous year. Current account surpluses narrowed as a percentage of GDP in most cases, except in the Philippines, where the surplus widened, and Viet Nam, where there was a smaller deficit. FDI inflows picked up in most countries in the subregion in 2004, except for the Philippines, but remained relatively low. Official reserves also increased in most countries, very substantially in Malaysia and Singapore, but declined in the Philippines despite heavy government borrowing. The exchange rate picture is mixed within the region (figure II.28).

Better job creation and faster income growth helped to reduce poverty incidence further in 2004 in many developing countries of South-East Asia but Indonesia and the Philippines face significant challenges in those areas. Increasing the competitiveness of domestic economies is another issue of concern to policy makers in the subregion.

Figure II.28. Index of exchange rates against the United States dollar of selected South-East Asian economies, 1996-2004

(1996 = 100)

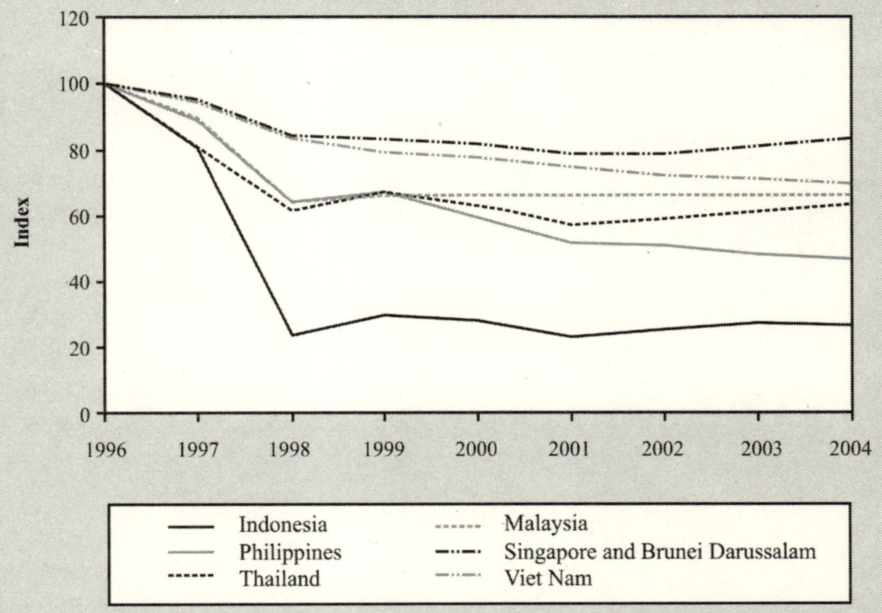

Sources: IMF, *International Financial Statistics*, vol. LVII, No. 10 (Washington, IMF, October 2004); and *The Economist*, various issues.

Notes: Figures for 2004 are estimates. The currency of Brunei Darussalam is set at par with the Singapore dollar.

GDP performance and outlook

Growth in Singapore comes surging back

Singapore was the fastest-growing economy in South-East Asia in 2004 (table II.28). GDP growth was 8.4 per cent for the year, a vast improvement over the modest 1.4 per cent growth in 2003 but substantially down from the 12.5 per cent year on year recorded in the second quarter. The economy decelerated in the second half of the year as manufacturers cut back on electronics production to clear inventories. A decline in biomedical output in the third quarter of 2004, following changes in the industry's production mix[1] also contributed to the deceleration, but growth in the sector improved in the last quarter. Transport engineering and chemicals continued to perform strongly. Construction

[1] Essentially, the withdrawal of the drug Vioxx by the Merck Corporation led to the company's production facilities going offline until they could be geared up to produce other drugs.

remained in the doldrums owing to lingering excess supply in the property market and cutbacks in public construction. Robust entrepôt trade and stronger retail sales, as well as the recovery in tourism following the SARS scare in 2003, boosted the service sector.

Table II.28. Selected South-East Asian economies: growth rates, 2001-2004

(Percentage)

		Rates of growth			
		Gross domestic product	*Agriculture*	*Industry*	*Services*
Brunei Darussalam	2001	3.0	..	..	..
	2002	2.8	..	..	..
	2003	3.2	..	..	..
	2004	1.1	..	..	..
Indonesia	2001	3.8	4.1	2.7	5.0
	2002	4.3	2.8	4.4	4.7
	2003	4.9	3.1	3.6	6.2
	2004	5.1	4.0	3.9	7.0
Malaysia	2001	0.3	–0.9	–3.8	6.1
	2002	4.1	3.0	3.9	4.2
	2003	5.3	5.5	7.0	3.9
	2004	7.1	2.6	8.6	4.9
Philippines	2001	3.2	3.7	1.3	4.4
	2002	4.6	3.5	4.1	5.4
	2003	4.7	3.8	3.8	5.8
	2004	6.1	4.9	5.3	7.3
Singapore[a]	2001	–1.9	–5.9	–9.1	2.4
	2002	3.2	–5.6	3.2	3.2
	2003	1.4	–0.7	0.5	1.8
	2004	8.4	11.4	9.9	7.8
Thailand	2001	2.2	3.2	1.7	2.4
	2002	5.3	1.0	6.9	4.8
	2003	6.9	8.7	9.4	4.0
	2004	6.1	–4.4	8.2	6.2
Viet Nam	2001	6.9	3.0	10.4	6.1
	2002	7.1	4.2	9.5	6.5
	2003	7.3	3.6	10.5	6.5
	2004	7.7	3.5	10.2	7.5

Sources: ESCAP, based on national sources; ADB, *Key Indicators of Developing Asian and Pacific Countries 2004* (Manila, ADB, 2004), and EIU, *Country Forecasts* and *Country Reports* (London, EIU, 2004), various issues.

Notes: Growth rates for 2004 are estimates. Industry comprises mining and quarrying; manufacturing; electricity, gas and power; and construction.

[a] Agriculture also includes quarrying.

External demand, which expanded at rates in excess of 20 per cent in the second and third quarters of 2004, fuelled by the upturn in the electronics cycle, was the driving force behind the improved growth performance in Singapore but domestic demand also played a role. Private consumption, which was depressed in 2001-2003 owing to the weak economy, revived strongly in 2004. Consumer confidence benefited from falling unemployment and better job creation, as well as rising real wages. Investment also picked up, especially in the private sector, after three successive years of contraction. The investment ratio rose to 15.3 per cent in 2004, almost 2 percentage points higher than in the previous year, but still relatively low for Singapore (table II.29). Looking ahead, real GDP growth is expected to moderate as growth in Singapore's main export markets softens along with demand for IT products. The Government expects GDP growth to be in the 3-5 per cent range in 2005. However, the accumulation of inventories has been much less in this electronics cycle than in the previous one and growth is not expected to be depressed for long.

Table II.29. Selected South-East Asian economies: ratios of gross domestic savings and investment to GDP, 2001-2004

(Percentage)

	2001	*2002*	*2003*	*2004*
Savings as a percentage of GDP				
Indonesia	26.4	24.7	23.5	22.4
Malaysia	42.3	41.9	42.9	45.0
Philippines	18.1	19.5	20.1	20.4
Singapore	44.0	43.9	46.7	47.4
Thailand	32.2	32.8	33.1	31.6
Viet Nam	28.8	28.7	27.4	28.3
Investment as a percentage of GDP				
Indonesia	21.5	20.2	19.8	19.5
Malaysia	24.0	23.6	21.8	22.5
Philippines	20.6	19.3	18.7	19.6
Singapore	24.9	21.2	13.4	15.3
Thailand	24.1	23.9	25.2	27.8
Viet Nam	31.2	33.2	33.8	35.5

Sources: ESCAP, based on national sources; and ADB, *Key Indicators of Developing Asian and Pacific Countries 2004* (Manila, ADB, 2004).

Note: Figures for 2004 are estimates.

High and steady growth in Viet Nam

Viet Nam was the second-fastest-growing nation in South-East Asia in 2004 with a GDP growth rate of 7.7 per cent, the first time that this rate has been within the 7.5-8.0 per cent range for annual growth targeted in the 2001-2005 five-year plan. The rate of growth averaged 7.1 per cent in 2001-2003. The marginal slowdown in the agricultural sector, to 3.5 per cent in 2004 from 3.6 per cent a year earlier, disguises a sharp fall in agriculture owing to the effects of a drought brought on by a weak monsoon, an unusually severe winter and avian influenza. Fisheries output increased strongly in 2004 as a result of the vigorous expansion of aquaculture and a greater number of harvests. Despite being hit by anti-dumping duties imposed by the United States on shrimp and catfish exports, which are being challenged, Vietnamese producers have responded by vigorously and successfully pursuing new markets. Value added in the industrial sector grew by a stellar 10.2 per cent in 2004, slightly slower than in 2003. Growth was dampened in manufacturing by the higher costs of imported inputs, particularly steel and oil, which also cooled activity in construction. The service sector performed very strongly, expanding by 7.5 per cent in 2004, 1 percentage point above the 2003 growth rate. Tourism, in particular, boomed with a 20 per cent increase in visitor numbers as compared with the previous year as Viet Nam benefited from being perceived as a safe destination and the Government reduced the time and costs associated with obtaining a visa. Wholesale and retail trade also expanded strongly.

Viet Nam's strong growth performance was sustained by both domestic and external demand. Household final consumption expenditure grew an average annual 7.5 per cent in 2002-2004. At the same time, the savings ratio rose from 27.4 per cent of GDP in 2003 to 28.3 per cent in 2004 largely as a result of increased household savings. A substantial portion of household savings remains outside the banking system. The investment ratio increased from 33.8 per cent in 2003 to 35.5 per cent in 2004. Around 56 per cent of all investment came from the State-invested sector in 2003-2004, with another 27 per cent representing private investment and 17 per cent FDI. Export performance was particularly strong in 2004, owing to the electronics revival as well as to higher international prices for oil and other commodities. The target for economic growth in 2005 has been set to accelerate to 8.5 per cent to meet the goals of the 2001-2005 five-year plan.

Strong external and domestic demand sustain Malaysian growth

Despite signs of a slowdown in the second half of the year in Malaysia, the growth in GDP is expected to be 7.1 per cent for the year as a whole, above the 6-6.5 per cent forecast earlier and well above the 5.3 per cent recorded in 2003. Strong private consumption expenditure, sustained by higher disposable incomes following robust export earnings as well as credit availability and low interest rates, was the principal driver of growth. A bonus for civil servants in the 2005 budget helped to boost consumption further. Public consumption was subdued as the Government focused on fiscal consolidation and net exports were negative as strong export growth was more than matched by imports. Private investment expenditure, on rebuilding inventories as well as on fixed capital, also made a significant contribution to growth in 2004. However, the increase in the savings ratio, from 42.9 per cent in 2003 to 45 per cent in 2004, outpaced that in the investment ratio, which increased to 22.5 per cent in 2004 from 21.8 per cent the previous year. Nevertheless, improved corporate profitability, capacity utilization rates in excess of 80 per cent and generally high levels of business confidence as well as favourable financing conditions suggest that the long-awaited revival in investment is under way.

Economic growth in Malaysia in 2004 was broad-based. Export-oriented manufacturing industries, in particular electronics and electrical products and chemical products such as plastics and resins, grew strongly while growth in domestic-oriented industries was lead by fabricated metal products, beverages and transport equipment. Strong consumer demand and a revival of trade and tourism sustained growth in both intermediate and final services. In agriculture, commodities such as palm oil, rubber and forestry products grew strongly in response to higher world prices, but production also expanded significantly in fisheries, vegetables and fruits. The mining sector was sustained by increased crude oil production but the construction sector declined as government spending on infrastructure slowed. Despite heightened external risks in 2005, the diversified nature of the Malaysian economy is expected to help the country to attain a respectable GDP growth rate of 6 per cent. Demand will continue to be driven by the private sector, particularly as interest rates are likely to remain low.

Some deceleration in growth in Thailand

The Thai economy continued to perform well in 2004 despite some deceleration in growth to 6.1 per cent from 6.9 per cent in 2003. Private consumption expenditure slowed owing to higher retail prices, especially for petrol, slower growth in farm incomes and diminished consumer confidence owing to the avian influenza outbreak and troubles in some provinces in the South. Private investment also slowed, despite rising capacity utilization, as investor confidence declined for similar reasons, but growth remained in double digits at around 15 per cent in the first 9 months of 2004. Public expenditure increased, in part owing to previous fiscal stimulus measures and higher public investment, and the investment ratio increased by over 2.5 percentage points between 2003 and 2004 to 27.8 per cent. Unanticipated expenditure, including compensation for farmers hit by the avian influenza outbreak and outlays for increased security and development in the violence-affected southern provinces, also added to government outlays. Robust external demand showed signs of slowing in the second half.

Agricultural production declined 4.4 per cent in 2004 in Thailand, a sharp fall from the nearly 9 per cent growth in 2003, as renewed outbreaks of avian influenza took their toll on poultry farming and shrimp production fell following the imposition of preliminary anti-dumping tariffs by the United States. In addition, a prolonged drought aggravated by a weak monsoon affected the output of rice and other grains. Growth in industrial production slowed to 8.2 per cent in 2004, down from the robust 9.4 per cent the previous year, as manufacturing output eased owing to slower growth in food processing, weakening exports of electronics and electrical appliances and excess inventories of steel and steel products. The construction sector was sustained by higher public construction while residential construction slowed. The service sector rebounded sharply as tourism recovered from the SARS scare and business and financial services registered robust growth.

Tsunami destroyed assets and livelihoods but growth outlook remains strong

The Indian Ocean tsunami disaster struck Thailand too late to affect 2004 performance but will certainly have an impact on GDP in 2005. Apart from the devastating human toll, preliminary estimates indicate that the tourism and fisheries industries lost around B 30.8 billion and B 2 billion in assets respectively. Damage to public utilities, roads and the power grid will add to overall losses. The Bank of Thailand (BOT) has estimated that tourism industry revenues will decline B 40 billion in 2005, as visitor arrivals are expected to fall by 1.2 million, and that the fishing industry will lose B 3.1 billion in income. Together, losses in those two sectors could shave 0.8 per cent off GDP growth in 2005. In compensation, the injection of State funds, soft loans and donations is expected to raise growth by 0.3 per cent, leaving a net 0.5 per cent reduction in GDP growth in 2005. An additional consideration is that the effect of higher world oil prices has not as yet been fully felt in Thailand owing to the Government's fuel price subsidies, which have now been removed from petrol but remain on diesel at least until early 2005. The current forecast is for GDP growth in the 5.5-6.5 per cent range in 2005.

Surprisingly strong growth in the Philippines

The economy of the Philippines proved to be remarkably resilient in 2004 with a performance that exceeded government expectations despite rising oil prices, slowing global demand, fragile investor confidence, political uncertainty and a series of typhoons that hit the country in the latter part of the year. GDP growth for the year as a whole at 6.1 per cent was well above the 4.7 per cent recorded in 2003 and higher than the Government's target range of 4.9-5.8 per cent. Strong external demand sustained growth, supported by domestic spending. Private consumption was particularly strong in the first half of the year, slowing somewhat thereafter as consumer prices rose but supported by an increased flow of remittances from overseas workers in the second half. The savings ratio also grew modestly to 20.4 per cent in 2004, continuing the slight upward trend of recent years. Public consumption was cut back in the second half of the year, following the election, in order to meet fiscal targets. Although there was a strong revival in investment in 2004, investment in durable equipment slowed to 4.4 per cent from 8.5 per cent the previous year. The investment ratio increased to 19.6 per cent in 2004 but it remains relatively low and the World Bank reports that the capital-labour ratio has fallen in the Philippines, unlike in other economies in the subregion.

Typhoons lower growth in the Philippines but call centres boost telecommunications

The service sector was a key factor in the strong performance of the Philippines, with growth accelerating to 7.3 per cent in 2004 from an average 5.6 per cent in 2002-2003. This can be attributed largely to the telecommunications sector, where investment related to call centre activity and other business process outsourcing, as well as software development, mushroomed. Agriculture benefited from extraordinarily productive harvests of the two food staples, rice and maize, although cash crops such as coconut and pineapple and forestry also performed well. However, losses estimated to be equivalent to 1.7 per cent of the sector's fourth quarter output resulting from four typhoons that hit Luzon in late-November to early-December pulled overall growth in agriculture down to 4.9 per cent in 2004, still an improvement on the average annual 3.7 per cent growth in 2002-2003. The typhoons shaved 0.35 percentage points off fourth-quarter GDP growth. Growth in the industrial sector surged in the first half of 2004, sustained by a strong recovery in construction from the contraction in 2003, but cutbacks in public construction led to a slowdown in the second half. Nevertheless, somewhat stronger growth in manufacturing and double-digit growth in mining, in response to higher commodity prices, led to an overall growth rate for the industrial sector of 5.3 per cent in 2004, well above the 4.0 per cent on average in 2002-2003. GDP growth is expected to slow to 5.3 per cent in 2005 as the external environment becomes less favourable.

Growth picks up in Indonesia but remains low

Robust private consumption and a strong revival in investment underpinned the pickup in GDP growth to 5.1 per cent in 2004 in Indonesia, matching the Government's forecast and continuing the modest upward trend observed since 2001. Consumers' expenditure was boosted by interest rates at six-year lows, as well as election-related spending. Demand for vehicles was particularly strong. Fixed investment grew 11.3 per cent year on year in the first 9 months of 2004, reflecting not only continued strong growth in housing investment but also increased spending on machinery and transport equipment. However, both the savings and investment rates continued to decline. In the first half of the year, export growth was modest, whereas imports soared, and Indonesia did not appear to benefit to the same extent as other countries from the surge in trade until the second half of the year. Public consumption was, however, constrained by budgetary pressures.

Growth was generally broad-based, with all sectors except mining expanding. The lack of investment in the mining sector, which has affected oil production negatively, was responsible for the poor performance. On a more positive note, transport and communications grew very strongly in 2004, as did construction and wholesale and retail trade. A revival in tourism along with strong private domestic consumption led to a recovery in the hotel and restaurant sector, and renewed strength in financial services was demonstrated by continued expansion, particularly in the second half of the year. Agriculture improved its performance through the year, helped by an import ban on rice, and in November 2004 the Ministry of Agriculture announced that Indonesia had regained self-sufficiency in rice production after nearly 10 years, taking a major step towards food security.

Aceh province hardest hit by the tsunami but GDP outlook still positive for Indonesia

The ending of political uncertainty in Indonesia following the elections in October 2004 boosted consumer and business confidence and GDP growth is expected to accelerate to 5.5 per cent in 2005 despite the destruction caused by the tsunami of 26 December 2004. The province of Aceh, which bore the brunt of the destruction, accounts for around 2 per cent of Indonesia's economic output. Although there has been a substantial loss of human and physical capital, other key economic assets in the province, such as coal and copper mines and oil and gas operations, appear to be largely intact. The economic aid and reconstruction following the disaster may also offset the disaster-related reduction in economic activity. Indonesia hopes to attain 7 per cent per annum growth, needed for a consistent reduction in unemployment and poverty, by 2009 but, in the opinion of the World Bank, this growth rate could be attained two years earlier given sufficient investment.

Repairs and upgrades to oil and gas sector slow growth in Brunei Darussalam

GDP growth has been moderate in Brunei Darussalam in recent years, averaging around 3 per cent per annum in 2001-2003. However, repairs and upgrades to oil and gas production facilities constrained growth in 2004. Output in the oil and gas sector, which accounts for around 40 per cent of GDP, is estimated to have declined by 5.4 per cent year on year in the first half. The non-oil and gas sector performed strongly, expanding at 3.9 per cent year on year in the second quarter of 2004, owing to a surge in forestry output, garments, roofing materials and switchboard production, as well as wholesale and retail trade. The restaurant and hotel sector, however, contracted quite sharply as hotel occupancy rates and restaurant sales both declined. Overall GDP growth for the year is estimated at 1.1 per cent but is expected to double to 2.2 per cent in 2005 and to rise further to 3 per cent in 2006.

Inflation and monetary policy

Fuel subsidies restrain inflation in Indonesia and Malaysia

The slowdown in inflation observed in 2003 in Indonesia continued into 2004 (table II.30) despite some acceleration in the second and third quarters, and the rate of inflation for the year was 6.1 per cent. An abundant rice harvest, fuel subsidies and a strengthening rupiah in the latter half of the year were all factors that helped to contain prices. Continuing low capacity utilization rates, of around 55-60 per cent, and declining wage demands were other contributing factors. Although lower oil prices could help to moderate inflation in 2005-2006, the Government has raised its inflation forecast for 2005 from 5.5 to 7 per cent because it expects transport costs to rise as fuel subsidies are reduced. Bank Indonesia raised reserve requirements for commercial banks at mid-year and announced that it would maintain a monetary policy with a tight bias, seeking to support the rupiah without major increases in interest rates so as to encourage economic growth and avoid adverse consequences for the Government's debt servicing. M2 growth between 2003 and 2004 is estimated at 10.5 per cent. The benchmark rate on one-month Bank Indonesia Certificates rose somewhat to 7.43 per cent in December but commercial bank lending rates were significantly higher despite abundant liquidity, reflecting continued risk aversion.

Table II.30. Selected South-East Asian economies: inflation and money supply growth (M2), 2001-2004

(Percentage)

	2001	*2002*	*2003*	*2004*
Inflation[a]				
Indonesia	11.5	11.9	6.6	6.1
Malaysia	1.4	1.8	1.2	1.4
Philippines	6.8	3.0	3.5	6.0
Singapore	1.0	−0.4	0.5	1.7
Thailand	1.6	0.7	1.8	2.7
Viet Nam	0.8	4.0	3.0	9.5
Money supply growth (M2)				
Indonesia	13.0	4.7	8.1	10.5
Malaysia	2.2	5.8	11.1	9.8
Philippines	3.6	10.4	3.6	4.0
Singapore	5.9	−0.3	8.1	6.2
Thailand	4.2	2.6	4.9	5.4
Viet Nam	25.5	17.6	24.9	..

Sources: ESCAP, based on national sources; ADB, *Key Indicators of Developing Asian and Pacific Countries 2004* (Manila, ADB, 2004); IMF, *International Financial Statistics,* vol. LVII, No. 6 (Washington, IMF, June 2004); and EIU, *Country Forecasts* (London, EIU, 2004), various issues.

Note: Figures for 2004 are estimates.

[a] Changes in the consumer price index.

Annual consumer price inflation edged up through 2004 in Malaysia to reach 1.4 per cent, compared with 1.2 per cent in 2003. Prices of food, beverages, tobacco, fuel and power all rose, largely owing to higher transport costs following two increases in the price of petroleum, in May and October, and to increased excise duties. Nevertheless, high prices for crude oil have had only a limited impact on inflation so far owing to the Government's fuel subsidies. Wage cost pressures were largely absent as labour productivity appears to have grown substantially faster than real wages per employee. The outlook for inflation in 2005 is for a further pickup to 2.2 per cent as the Government reduces fuel subsidies in line with its commitment to fiscal consolidation.

Bank Negara Malaysia continued with its accommodative but prudent monetary policy in 2004 and M2 growth was 9.8 per cent in 2004. In a step towards further interest rate liberalization, a new indicator rate, the overnight policy rate (OPR), was introduced in April 2004 and will be maintained close to the overnight interbank rate. The OPR was unchanged at 2.7 per cent during the rest of the year but banks and finance companies lowered lending rates owing to ample liquidity. The Bank has indicated that as the outlook for the Malaysian economy remains favourable, it intends to maintain the current stance of monetary policy and interest rates are unlikely to rise in the near future. The performance of the banking system remained sound with the risk-weighted capital ratio at 13.8 per cent and the net NPL ratio at 5.9 per cent, the lowest level since the 1997-1998 financial crisis, by December 2004.

Inflation accelerates on supply shocks in the Philippines

The rate of inflation in the Philippines slowed to an annual average of 3.2 per cent in 2002-2003. However, the inflation rate picked up significantly in 2004 to reach 6.0 per cent, above the central bank's target range, largely as a result of supply shocks to particular commodities, mainly food and energy items. Higher oil prices on world markets were reflected in higher domestic fuel, energy and transport charges as budget constraints prevented the Government from shielding consumers to the same extent as in neighbouring countries. Bango Sentral ng Filipinas (BSP) is in the process of finalizing inflation targets for 2005 and 2006. Indications are that the target range will be raised to 5-6 per cent using the 2000-based CPI but inflation may go even higher if oil prices continue to rise.

BSP had raised liquidity reserve requirements by 2 percentage points to 10 per cent in February 2004 in response to the upward trend in inflation. It did not, however, tighten monetary policy further in 2004, maintaining the overnight borrowing rate at 6.75 per cent, as it believed that any increase in key policy rates would have limited success in containing inflationary pressures that emanated largely from supply factors. However, if signs emerge of more generalized inflation, policy rates may then be increased. Some progress was made in 2004 in improving asset quality in the banking system in the Philippines. The NPL ratio has been on a downward trend and was reported to be 13.6 per cent in November. This is still high compared with economies that were more directly affected by the 1997 financial crisis as the Philippines has never had a centralized asset management corporation. Take-up under the special-purpose vehicle law, which provided incentives for the disposal of NPLs, has been weak and steps may be taken to extend the validity of the law beyond its scheduled expiry date in April 2005. The capital adequacy ratio of the commercial banking system was 17.8 per cent in September, well above the 10 per cent figure required by BSP, but credit demand is stagnant and bank profitability weak.

Higher food and energy prices in Singapore

The significant pickup in the rate of consumer price inflation in 2004 in Singapore, to 1.7 per cent from 0.5 per cent in 2003, was partly a reflection of higher international oil and other commodity prices as well strong economic growth above the long-term potential rate. Domestic prices of oil-related items such as electricity tariffs and petrol registered significant increases. Food prices also rose in the aftermath of a ban on poultry imports at the end of August owing to avian influenza concerns. There were also very substantial increases in the costs of education and health-care services. The outlook for inflation in 2005 is related to developments in commodity prices, particularly for oil. Currency appreciation and continued weakness in the housing market could moderate price pressures but retail prices may rise in response to improved consumer sentiment.

Singapore has a small, open economy, and its monetary policy is focused on managing the exchange rate, which is permitted to fluctuate within an undisclosed band. Against the background of more favourable economic growth and rising inflationary pressures, the Monetary Authority of Singapore tightened monetary policy somewhat in April 2004, shifting from a stance of 0 per cent appreciation of the trade-weighted nominal effective exchange rate to a policy of modest and gradual appreciation with no change in the slope or width of the policy band. The policy was reaffirmed in October for a further 6 months to reduce the risk of imported inflation while safeguarding the economy's competitiveness. Domestic interest rates have risen in tandem with the United States federal funds rate, the 3-month interbank rate rising from 0.75 per cent at the end of 2003 to 1.44 per cent by December 2004.

Fuel subsidies restrain inflation in Thailand but food prices rise

The rate of inflation accelerated in Thailand from 1.8 per cent in 2003 to 2.7 per cent in 2004 largely as a result of a sharp rise in food prices, reflecting higher demand and reduced agricultural output, and the increase in world oil prices. The Government's fuel subsidies, which will not be fully removed until March 2005, have prevented the full impact of the oil price hike from being reflected in the rate of inflation. Furthermore, an agreement between the Government and 80 suppliers of consumer products not to increase prices for 6 months from September 2004 has kept the price level in check. This suggests that there could be a further sharp pickup in consumer prices during the course of 2005.

The central bank moved to tighten monetary policy during 2004 in Thailand. After being maintained at an all-time low level of 1.25 per cent since June 2003, the benchmark 14-day repurchase rate was raised three times beginning in August 2004 in steps of 25 basis points to 2 per cent in December. BOT was concerned that growth momentum remained strong and that any reduction in inflationary pressures from currency appreciation or lower oil prices could be temporary. BOT has also expressed the view that continued negative real deposit rates discourage savings and lead to increased household debt and it would like to see interest rates return to neutral levels. M2 growth picked up somewhat to 5.4 per cent year on year in December 2004 from 4.9 per cent a year earlier. The overall health of the banking system continued to improve with the NPL ratio down to 11.6 per cent in September 2004 from 13.5 per cent in January and the capital adequacy ratio at around 12 per cent. The Thai Asset Management Corporation estimates that around 69 per cent of debt restructuring has been completed and BOT has introduced tighter provisioning rules against NPLs and moved decisively to curb excess lending by a large State-owned bank. Commercial banks are expected to comply with Basel II by 2008.

Sharp acceleration in the rate of inflation in Viet Nam

The rate of inflation more than tripled in Viet Nam in 2004, accelerating to 9.5 per cent from 3 per cent in 2003 as a result of successive supply shocks. Prices of food and foodstuffs, the largest item in the CPI, rose 15.6 per cent owing to problems in the agricultural sector and a 46 per cent increase in international fertilizer prices. Fuel subsidies were introduced by the Government earlier in 2004 to shield consumers from the effects of rising oil prices, but were withdrawn from petrol in September. At that time, prices of other fuels were capped, forcing suppliers to absorb higher costs. The authorities also lowered tariffs on petroleum and steel products to contain prices. The rate of inflation is expected to slow to 6-7 per cent in 2005 assuming lower oil and food prices. M2 growth has been rapid in recent years, in part reflecting the ongoing monetization, and credit growth accelerated in 2004, led by State-owned banks. In response to rising inflation, the State Bank of Viet Nam increased reserve requirements from 2 to 5 per cent on short-term deposits in July and doubled them on other types of deposits at the same time. However, it has kept the prime lending rate for dong loans unchanged at 7.5 per cent since May 2003. Other administrative measures are being taken to rein in lending, reduce public expenditure and lower production and distribution costs, while tightening enforcement of price controls.

Inflation has remained very subdued in Brunei Darussalam, with the CPI increasing by only 0.7 per cent year on year in the second quarter of 2004, reflecting higher prices for food and non-alcoholic beverages, transport and recreation and entertainment. Low inflation is likely to continue in the near future as commodity prices stabilize and the currency peg with the Singapore dollar is maintained. Although M2 is estimated to have expanded by nearly 10 per cent in the first half of 2004 as compared with a year earlier, private sector credit, principally in the form of personal loans, has expanded slowly. The prime lending rate has remained unchanged at 5.5 per cent since September 2000. NPLs in the banking system have fallen sharply, from 15.9 per cent at the end of June 2003 to 11.8 per cent at the end of the same month in 2004. The establishment of the Brunei Currency and Monetary Board in February 2004 will assist in greater financial market development and improve regulation in the banking sector.

Fiscal policy and public debt

Fuel subsidies weigh on Indonesia's budget

In Indonesia, the deficit target was revised upwards to 1.3 per cent in 2004 in the light of higher oil prices and projected expenditure, mainly on fuel subsidies and revenue-sharing with the regions, were raised. The actual deficit reached 1.4 per cent (table II.31) as fuel subsidy costs are

Table II.31. Selected South-East Asian economies: budget and current account balance as a percentage of GDP, 2001-2004

(Percentage)

	2001	*2002*	*2003*	*2004*
Budget balance as a percentage of GDP				
Indonesia	−2.8	−1.7	−1.9	−1.4
Malaysia	−5.5	−5.6	−5.3	−4.5
Philippines[a]	−4.0	−5.2	−4.6	−3.8
Singapore[b]	1.6	−1.1	−1.6	−0.6
Thailand[c]	−2.4	−1.4	0.4	0.1
Viet Nam[d]	−5.0	−4.5	−5.6	−4.9
Current account balance as a percentage of GDP				
Indonesia	4.8	4.5	3.7	2.8
Malaysia	8.3	8.5	13.0	10.2
Philippines	1.8	5.4	4.3	4.8
Singapore	16.8	17.7	29.2	26.1
Thailand	5.4	5.5	5.6	4.5
Viet Nam	2.1	−1.7	−4.8	−3.2

Sources: ESCAP, based on national sources; ADB, *Key Indicators of Developing Asian and Pacific Countries 2004* (Manila, ADB, 2004); EIU, *Country Forecasts* (London, EIU, 2004), various issues; and web site of the Ministry of Finance of Singapore <www.mof.gov.sg/budget_2004/fiscal_overview/>, 24 September 2004.

Note: Figures for 2004 are estimates.

[a] Including grants.

[b] Budget surplus/deficit computed from government operating revenue minus government operating expenditure minus government development expenditure.

[c] Referring to a government cash balance comprising the budgetary balance and non-budgetary balance.

[d] Including net lending.

estimated to have been nearly $7.5 billion in 2004. The Government plans to reduce the cost of subsidies in 2005 by raising petrol prices while retaining subsidies on diesel and kerosene, used as a cooking fuel by the poor. Fuel subsidies will be eliminated by 2010 as the domestic energy market is gradually liberalized. The Government hopes to continue the process of fiscal consolidation and reduce the deficit to 0.8 per cent of GDP in 2005, assuming that oil prices average $24 per barrel, and to balance the budget by 2007. Greater attention will also be given to spending on infrastructure and social programmes to stimulate employment and soften the effect of higher fuel prices on the poor. Government debt is now around 50 per cent of GDP, down from 67 per cent at the end of 2003. However, the impact of the tsunami disaster on the Government's budget has yet to be assessed. Debt relief will reduce interest payments in the short term and aid inflows will go some way towards meeting the costs of reconstruction. However, there may have to be a diversion of government expenditure from other programmes to rebuilding infrastructure in Aceh.

Slower fiscal consolidation in Malaysia

The process of fiscal consolidation that began in 2004 in Malaysia was reaffirmed in the 2005 budget, which seeks to reduce the budget deficit from 4.5 per cent of GDP in 2004 to 3.8 per cent of GDP in 2005. Much of the reduction is to be achieved by higher revenues but development spending will continue to fall as private investment revives. Spending will also be redirected towards boosting the agricultural sector to become the third growth pole while supporting smallholders. SMEs, new entrepreneurs and infrastructure are also to receive increased support. The goal of balancing the budget by 2006 now appears to be remote but the planned introduction of a VAT in 2007 gives credence to it being achieved soon thereafter. Slower fiscal consolidation will raise debt-service charges but federal government debt as a percentage of GDP is expected to be around 50 per cent in 2004, down from an average 53.6 per cent in 1998-2003.

Greater fiscal discipline in the Philippines

In the Philippines, the fiscal deficit narrowed to 4.6 per cent of GDP in 2003, from 5.2 per cent in 2002, as stronger growth led to higher tax revenues. The deficit target for 2004 was lowered to 4.2 per cent of GDP but fell even more sharply to 3.8 per cent. The better out-turn reflects greater fiscal control, stronger GDP growth and higher power charges, among other factors. Non-financial public sector debt in the Philippines is around 110 per cent of GDP and interest expense some 40 per cent of revenues, raising concerns about debt sustainability and vulnerability to external shocks. However, the Philippines medium-term development plan envisaged a very gradual reduction in the fiscal deficit with the budget balanced only in 2010. As interest rates are likely to rise in the future, there is pressure on the Government to frontload deficit reduction. Tax and customs revenues remain well below potential as tax evasion and corruption continue to be major problems. The Government had proposed eight legislative measures designed to increase tax revenues but only two of these measures, a specific excise levy on alcohol and tobacco and a measure to reward good performance by tax collectors, have been passed, although there has been some progress on two others. The National Power Corporation is to be privatized and one coal-fired facility was auctioned off in December 2004. The Government is forecasting a budget deficit equivalent to 3.5 per cent of GDP in 2005.

A return to fiscal prudence in Singapore

In its efforts to support economic activity in 2003, the Government of Singapore had introduced two off-budget packages to counter the effects of SARS and a reduction in employers' contributions to the Central Provident Fund, in addition to the budget for that year. As a result, the budget deficit rose to 1.6 per cent of GDP but is expected to fall to 0.6 per cent of GDP in 2004 as the Government has returned to a more prudent fiscal position, tightening operating expenditures in particular. Tax receipts have also been rising as a result of the improved economy but have still to recover from the drop in income in 2003. The budget is expected to return to a surplus in 2005 as growth continues although the corporate income tax rate is to be cut 2 per cent and individuals are to be offered tax exemptions on foreign-sourced and investment income.

Unexpected outlays reduce the budget surplus in Thailand

Strong economic growth in Thailand in 2003 led to a small budget surplus equivalent to 0.4 per cent of GDP in that year. Unexpected outlays as a result of avian influenza, the security situation in the South and the increased cost of fuel subsidies narrowed the surplus to 0.1 per cent of GDP in 2004. The Government had hoped for a balanced budget in the current fiscal year, earlier than the original target date of 2008, but the slowing economy, the rising cost of the universal health-care system and tsunami-related expenditure may push the budget into deficit. However, the partial reduction of fuel subsidies will reduce expenditures. Off-budget liabilities accumulated by the Government, mainly loans from State-owned banks to SMEs, continue to be of some concern. Total public sector debt has been on a declining trend and reached 47.8 per cent of GDP by the end of 2004, down from 48.9 per cent in December 2003.

Robust growth in budgetary revenues in Viet Nam

Budget revenues, particularly tax revenues, increased robustly in 2004 in Viet Nam, surpassing targets. This was despite a reduction in the enterprise income tax rate from 32 to 28 per cent. Profits of State-owned oil-producing companies added to non-tax revenue sources. Revenues from trade taxes decreased owing mainly to tariff reductions on oil and steel imports and only partly to Viet Nam's implementation of its AFTA commitments. Budgetary expenditure also increased strongly but there was a decrease in capital expenditure. The budget deficit decreased as a percentage of GDP from 5.6 per cent in 2003 to 4.9 per cent in 2004, in line with the Government's target of 5 per cent.

Helped by higher oil prices and expenditure restraint, the budget returned to a surplus in the second quarter of 2004 in Brunei Darussalam after recording a small deficit in the first quarter. Ensuring the long-term sustainability of public expenditure continues to be an important issue in Brunei Darussalam, where the oil and gas sector contributes around 80 per cent of government revenues. A related issue is the need to deal with fiscal deficits in a manner that does not compromise growth and diversification in the medium term. Under the eighth national development plan from 2001 to 2005, the Government is committed to spending B$ 1 billion annually on financing public investment in infrastructure. However, in 2002 and 2003 only 43 and 26 per cent respectively of the allocated amount were spent.

Foreign trade and external transactions

External trade

After the surge in the value of total exports in 2003 in Brunei Darussalam, due largely to increased revenues from exports of oil and gas, export growth in the first 9 months of 2004 was much slower at 11.1 per cent on an annual basis on diminished production (table II.32). Japan

Table II.32. Selected South-East Asian economies: merchandise exports and their rates of growth, 2001-2004

	Exports (f.o.b.)				
	Value (millions of US dollars)	*Annual rate of growth (percentage)*			
	2003	*2001*	*2002*	*2003*	*2004*
Brunei Darussalam[a]	4 422	5.5	3.1	28.6	11.1
Indonesia[b]	63 450	−12.3	3.1	7.2	15.1
Malaysia[c]	104 969	−10.4	6.9	11.6	21.3
Philippines[c]	35 750	−15.6	9.5	1.5	9.9
Singapore	144 126	−11.8	2.8	15.3	24.6
Thailand	78 105	−7.1	4.8	18.2	23.0
Viet Nam	20 176	3.7	11.2	20.8	28.9

Sources: IMF, *Direction of Trade Statistics* (CD-ROM), February 2005; Bank Indonesia web site <http://www.bi.go.id>, 10 January 2005; Malaysia Economic Planning Unit web site <http://www.epu.jpm.my/>, 7 January 2005; Philippines National Statistics Office web site <http://www.census.gov.ph>, 11 January 2005; Bank of Thailand web site <http://www.bot.or.th>, 18 November 2004; and other national sources.

[a] Growth rate for 2004 refers to January-September 2004 compared with the corresponding period of 2003.
[b] Growth rate for 2004 refers to January-October 2004 compared with the corresponding period of 2003.
[c] Growth rate for 2004 refers to January-November 2004 compared with the corresponding period of 2003.

remains the principal export market. Imports grew very strongly at 23.5 per cent in the first 9 months of 2004, reversing the decline registered in 2003 (table II.33). Other countries in ASEAN are the principal suppliers of imports to Brunei Darussalam.

Table II.33. Selected South-East Asian economies: merchandise imports and their rates of growth, 2001-2004

	Value (millions of US dollars)	*Imports (c.i.f.) Annual rate of growth (percentage)*			
	2003	*2001*	*2002*	*2003*	*2004*
Brunei Darussalam[a]	1 341	−7.8	23.9	−17.7	23.5
Indonesia[b]	32 551	−7.6	1.1	4.0	40.0
Malaysia[b]	83 617	−10.0	8.2	4.8	36.3
Philippines[c]	37 448	−4.2	7.2	5.7	8.2
Singapore	131 335	−13.9	0.4	12.9	24.7
Thailand	74 346	−3.0	4.6	17.4	27.0
Viet Nam	25 227	3.7	22.1	27.8	24.5

Sources: IMF, *Direction of Trade Statistics* (CD-ROM), February 2005; Statistics Indonesia web site <http://www.bps.go.id>, 7 January 2005; Malaysia Economic Planning Unit web site <http://www.epu.jpm.my/>, 7 January 2005; Philippines National Statistics Office web site, <http://www.census.gov.ph>, 11 January 2005; Bank of Thailand web site <http://www.bot.or.th>, 18 November 2004; and other national sources.

[a] Growth rate for 2004 refers to January-September 2004 compared with the corresponding period of 2003.
[b] Growth rate for 2004 refers to January-November 2004 compared with the corresponding period of 2003.
[c] Growth rate for 2004 refers to January-October 2004 compared with the corresponding period of 2003.

Import growth outpaces exports in Indonesia

Export growth in the first half of 2004 in Indonesia was modest, particularly for non-oil and gas exports, but there was an apparent surge in exports in the second half of the year, in part owing to a switch to a computerized data collection system and in part to commodity exports to China and India. Exports are estimated to have increased over 15 per cent year on year in the first 10 months of 2004. Some two thirds of exports in 2003 were from the industrial sector, which has, however, been losing competitiveness as utility prices and wage rates have risen. Imports expanded very strongly, by 40 per cent year on year in January-November 2004. Nearly 80 per cent of imports were intermediate goods and only around 12 per cent were capital goods, half the share of the pre-crisis years. However, an encouraging sign of the revival of investment is that capital goods imports appear to have expanded very rapidly in 2004. The trade balance remained strongly positive in the first three quarters of 2004 but was some 20 per cent below its value in the same period in 2003. The deficit on the services account, which widened sharply in 2003 as tourism fell on fears of terrorism and SARS, narrowed somewhat in the first half of 2004 and tourist arrivals increased 28 per cent on an annual basis in the first 9 months of the year. The current account surplus as a percentage of GDP declined in 2004 to 2.8 per cent (table II.31).

Electronics and electrical products boost trade in Malaysia

The value of merchandise exports and imports soared, by 21.3 and 36.3 per cent respectively, in the first 11 months of 2004 in Malaysia but there were indications of a slowdown in export growth in the second half of the year, mainly of electronics and electrical products to China. Exports to other ASEAN nations, China, the EU, Hong Kong, China, Japan and the United States, which together absorb nearly 80 per cen of Malaysia's exports, all expanded sharply in 2004. Electronics and electrical products dominated total exports, with a share that hovered around 50 per cent. Chemicals and chemical products, crude petroleum and palm oil each contributed over 5 per cent to total exports. The strength of the growth in imports in 2004 was remarkable, as was its broad-based nature. Consumer, capital and intermediate goods imports all expanded at rates well in excess of 20 per cent, with the bulk of imports consisting of parts and components used in the manufacture of electronic and electrical goods. Despite the rapid import growth, the trade balance remained robust during the year. Although tourism revived, higher transport costs led to a widening of the deficit on services, which contributed to a projected narrowing in the current account deficit to 10.2 per cent of GDP in 2004 from 13 per cent in 2003.

Relatively slow export growth in the Philippines

The value of merchandise exports from the Philippines rebounded from low growth in 2003 to expand 9.9 per cent in January-November 2004, relatively slow compared with most of its neighbours. Around 67 per cent of exports are electronic products, mainly semiconductors, destined for Japan and exports of those products accounted for nearly three quarters of the increase as ICT companies built up inventories. Signs of a slowdown were emerging towards the end of the year, suggesting that export growth could be more modest in 2005. Earnings from garment exports declined for much of 2004 and, despite a sharp rebound in November, the trend is likely to continue as the MFA ends. Growth in the value of merchandise imports was slower than export growth, at 8.2 per cent in January-October 2004. Imports of consumer goods outpaced both capital and intermediate goods; the latter contracted towards the end of the year, particularly electronics products. High oil prices led to a sharp increase in imports of mineral fuels and lubricants. The trade deficit narrowed significantly from $1.3 billion in the first 11 months of 2003 to $924 million in the same period of 2004. Increased revenues from tourism and travel together with a bounce-back in migrant remittances in the second half of the year contributed to a surplus on the services and income account. The current account surplus as a percentage of GDP increased somewhat to 4.8 per cent in 2004 from 4.3 per cent in 2003.

Vigorous broad-based export growth in Singapore

The value of merchandise exports in Singapore grew a robust 24.6 per cent in 2004 fuelled by strong growth in non-oil domestic exports, particularly electronics products such as integrated circuits, telecommunications equipment and personal computer parts. Pharmaceuticals, petrochemicals and specialized machinery also performed strongly. The growth in non-oil domestic exports to the EU averaged around 30 per cent in the first half of 2004, much of it representing pharmaceutical exports from European multinationals based in Singapore. Exports to the United States were somewhat sluggish, picking up later in the year, but regional demand for Singapore's exports was very strong, particularly from China. Export growth to that country in each of the first three quarters of 2004 was in the 39-57 per cent range, with electronics exports expanding 60 per cent in the third quarter. The value of merchandise imports surged 24.7 per cent in 2004 as more inputs were needed for exports and retail sales picked up, helped by larger tourist numbers. The trade surplus narrowed in the first half of 2004 before widening again while the small surplus on the services account was rather volatile. The current account surplus had increased sharply as a percentage of GDP to 29.2 per cent in 2003 reflecting weak internal and strong external demand and it narrowed to 26.1 per cent in 2004 as domestic demand revived.

High-tech products lead export growth in Thailand but traditional exports also do well

External performance strengthened in 2004 in Thailand compared with 2003, as the value of merchandise exports increased 23 per cent, up from 18.2 per cent the previous year. High-tech manufactured goods expanded strongly, led by computers and parts, integrated circuits and parts and vehicles, parts and accessories. Exports of traditional labour-intensive products, such as textiles, and resource-based products, such as agricultural and petroleum products, also recorded robust growth, the latter benefiting from higher global commodity prices. The shares of traditional markets such as the United States and Japan in Thailand's exports continued to decrease as the shares of other countries in the Asian and Pacific region, such as fellow members of ASEAN and China, were on an upward trend, particularly in the case of the latter.

Merchandise imports expanded strongly in Thailand in 2004, growing 27 per cent and exceeding the 2003 rate by nearly 10 percentage points. All categories of imports registered robust growth, particularly capital goods. In line with the growth in exports, inputs for the electronics and electrical goods industries expanded strongly. Robust domestic consumption led to higher imports of durable and non-durable consumer goods, and imports of vehicles and parts expanded strongly. The value of fuel and lubricants rose on the back of higher oil prices. The trade surplus fell in 2004 and although the surplus on the services and transfers account surged with the recovery in earnings from tourism, the current account surplus narrowed to 4.5 per cent of GDP, down from the average 5.5 per cent in 2001-2003.

Foreign-invested enterprises major contributors to Viet Nam's export performance

The value of merchandise exports increased by a record 28.9 per cent in 2004, 8 percentage points higher than the growth in 2003. Exports from foreign-invested enterprises increased over 40 per cent year on year in 2004 and those enterprises have accounted for over 50 per cent of total exports in recent years. Exports of crude oil increased around 50 per cent on the back of high international oil prices, while exports of rubber increased 46 per cent. Electronics products and computers expanded over 57 per cent and wooden furniture products grew an astonishing 88 per cent. Exports of garments and textiles were hit by a reduction in the United States quota over a rules-of-origin discrepancy while exports of seafood faced anti-dumping tariffs in that country on shrimp and catfish, reducing export growth in the sector. The EU has now become Viet Nam's largest trading partner and exports to Japan and China have been growing fast while the United States has declined in importance. Non-traditional markets, such as in Africa, are also growing.

The value of merchandise imports grew at a somewhat slower rate than exports in 2004 in Viet Nam, expanding 24.5 per cent, down on the 27.8 per cent growth rate recorded in 2003. Refined oil, steel and steel ingots, plastic raw materials and electronic spare parts were the principle imports, reflecting export and investment growth. While the EU, the United States and Japan remained important sources of imports, China has become the third most important supplier.

The trade deficit widened to around $5.5 billion in 2004 in Viet Nam, an increase of roughly $0.5 billion over 2003. The services account benefited from a surge in tourism in the country. There has also been a steady expansion in overseas remittances to Viet Nam in recent years, which are estimated to have reached $3 billion in 2004. The current account deficit as a percentage of GDP declined from 4.8 per cent in 2003 to 3.2 per cent in 2004.

Capital flows and exchange rates

Higher FDI inflows into Brunei Darussalam

Between 2002 and 2003, FDI inflows into Brunei Darussalam doubled to $2 billion, making the country the ninth largest recipient of FDI among developing Asian nations. An increase in investment in the oil industry and in construction services contributed to the rise in FDI, as did improved economic conditions and a better investment climate. Official international reserves increased substantially in 2002-2003, reversing a decline in the previous two years, to reach $480 million. Brunei Darussalam also holds some $30 billion in foreign assets. The Brunei dollar is exchangeable at par with the Singapore dollar and, in line with the latter, has been appreciating against the United States dollar since 2002.

Net FDI outflows from Indonesia amounted to nearly $600 million in 2003, continuing the trend observed since the 1997-1998 crisis, but net inflows were over $460 million in the first half of 2004. However, FDI approvals contracted some 11 per cent year on year in January-October 2004. Foreign exchange reserves reached $35.8 billion in December 2004, somewhat higher than in the previous year. The ratio of external debt to GDP has fallen to around 53 per cent and IMF stated in September that the level was sustainable and further debt rescheduling was unlikely to be needed. However, Indonesia along with other tsunami-affected countries has been offered a debt moratorium by the Paris Club. The rupiah, which averaged Rp 8,577 to the dollar during 2003, was more volatile in 2004, ending the year at Rp 9,307.5 = $1. Nevertheless, greater confidence in the country was reflected in ratings upgrades by Standard and Poor's in December 2004 to B+ from B and by Fitch Ratings in January 2005 to BB- from B+ for long-term foreign currency sovereign debt.

Substantial net inflows of FDI into Malaysia but little new investment

The financial account surplus in Malaysia in 2004 was helped by a surge in net portfolio investments in the first quarter and by substantial net inward FDI, which totalled M$ 8.9 billion in the first half of the year. A large part of this inflow, however, consisted of unrepatriated profits of multinational corporations rather than new investment. Official reserve assets jumped from $44.2 billion at the end of December 2003 to $66.7 billion at 31 December 2004. Total external debt as a percentage of GDP is expected to decline to 44.3 per cent at the end of 2004 from 47.3 per cent a year earlier. Much of the decline was due to the reduction in medium- and long-term public sector debt. The ringgit's peg to the United States dollar ensured that the currency depreciated against the euro in 2004 but its performance was mixed against other regional currencies. The view of the central bank, endorsed by IMF, is that the value of the ringgit is in line with fundamentals and the peg is likely to remain given current global macroeconomic imbalances and oil price volatility. Greater international confidence in Malaysia was reflected in ratings upgrades for its sovereign long-term foreign currency debt by Moody's and Standard and Poor's to A3/A- with a stable outlook.

The peso comes under pressure in the Philippines

Net FDI and portfolio flows were -$56 million and -$524 million respectively in the first half of 2004 in the Philippines, reversing surpluses of $86 million and $221 million in the same period in 2003. Although the capital account was sustained by heavy government borrowing through bond issues, the overall balance of payments was in deficit and gross international reserves fell to $16.1 billion at the end of December 2004, down $813 million from a year earlier. The peso came under pressure during the year, despite the general weakness of the dollar, averaging P 56.04 to the dollar compared with P 54.20 in 2003. Total external debt, mostly medium- and long-term, amounted to $57.4 billion at the end of 2003, 72 per cent of GDP. The total had fallen to $55.6 billion by September 2004 owing largely to a reduction in the public debt stock, which accounted for two thirds of the total. Reflecting concerns over the prospects for fiscal policy adjustment, Fitch Ratings lowered the outlook on the Philippines' long-term sovereign debt to negative. Standard and Poor's downgraded the foreign currency rating to BB- from BB, three levels below investment grade while Moody's down-graded it two notches to B1 from Ba2, the lowest level since 1993. Nevertheless, the Philippine Government sold $1.5 billion in bonds in January 2005, its largest single bond issue. The size of the issue was increased 50 per cent in response to keen investor interest.

Singapore attracted S$ 8.3 billion in FDI in 2004 in manufacturing, of which S$ 4.6 billion was in electronics and another S$ 2.3 billion in services. While the United States, the EU and Japan continue to be the principal sources of investment, the country is also receiving increased flows of FDI from other economies in the Asian and Pacific region. There were significant inflows of net direct investment in the first half of 2004 before the direction was reversed in the third quarter. Net portfolio investment outflows were sustained in the first three quarters of the year, contributing to a narrowing in the overall balance-of-payments surplus. Official foreign exchange reserves soared to $112.8 billion by December 2004, an increase of $16.5 billion from the previous year. The improvement in the economy, which began in the second half of 2003, has led the Monetary Authority to permit a gradual appreciation of the Singapore dollar. Against the United States dollar, the currency has risen from S$ 1.70 = US$ 1.00 at the end of 2003 to S$ 1.63 = US$ 1.00 at the end of 2004.

Machinery and transport equipment attract most FDI in Thailand

In Thailand, net inflows of FDI dropped to $537 million in the first 7 months of 2004, down from $842 million a year earlier. FDI inflows in the same period were $4.2 billion, slightly higher than in 2003. There was a net inflow from Japan and a small net outflow with other members of ASEAN. The machinery and transport equipment sector attracted most inflows. Thailand's external debt continued to decline in 2004 to a projected 28.6 per cent of GDP from 36.2 per cent in 2003 mainly owing to the Government's efforts to reduce public external debt. Of total external debt outstanding, less than one quarter is short-term. The overall balance of payments was in surplus to the extent of $5.7 billion in 2004 and gross official reserves increased from around $42 billion at the end of 2003 to $49.8 billion at the end of 2004. The baht was in the B 38.87-41.70 range per dollar in 2004 and averaged 40.28, an appreciation of 3 per cent from the average in 2003.

Commitments of FDI have been growing in Viet Nam and are expected to reach $4 billion in 2004, an increase of one third from a year earlier. FDI disbursed is estimated to have been $2.9 billion in 2004, up from $2.4 billion in 2003. ODA commitments increased to $3.4 billion in 2004 from $2.8 billion the previous year. ODA disbursement, however, decreased from $1.7 billion in 2003 to $1.5 billion in 2004 owing to delays in the implementation of some large-scale projects. The overall balance-of-payments surplus amounted to just under 2 per cent of GDP in 2004, lower than the 5.4 per cent achieved in 2003. Viet Nam's international reserves amounted to $5.6 billion, equivalent to nine weeks of imports, at the end of 2003 and increased to $6.2 billion by April 2004. Total external debt is estimated at around 38 per cent of GDP in 2003-2004 but the debt-service ratio declined from 7.5 per cent in 2003 to 6.3 per cent in 2004. The Vietnamese dong depreciated against the United States dollar by 2.2 per cent in 2003 and by 2.0 per cent in 2004 as dollar weakness slowed the fall.

Policy issues and responses

Poverty and unemployment

Good progress in poverty reduction in Indonesia but challenges remain

The proportion of the population below the national poverty line is estimated to have fallen to 17.4 per cent in 2003 in Indonesia, finally below pre-crisis levels. It is likely to have fallen further in 2004 but is unlikely to have reached the Government's target of 14 per cent. However, vulnerability and regional disparities remain high. The Government is seeking to address these concerns and has decided to integrate its poverty reduction strategy paper into the medium-term development plan 2004-2009, which is a major step forward in bringing a poverty focus to all of the Government's work. According to ADB, poverty in Aceh province, which was severely damaged by the earthquake and tsunami disaster, was already rising in recent years and poverty incidence was estimated at 30 per cent in 2003. Nearly 12 per cent of the population of the province lives in coastal areas and civil conflict has led to a large number of displaced people. The disaster will add many more to their number. Although social infrastructure was thought to be good before the disaster, physical infrastructure was already in poor condition. Aid flowing in for relief and reconstruction provides the Government with an opportunity to make significant progress in poverty reduction in the province if the civil conflict can be kept at bay (box II.3).

Box II.3. Post-tsunami reconstruction in Aceh and North Sumatra

The 26 December 2004 earthquake and tsunami in the Indian Ocean, described as the worst natural disaster in living memory, struck the Indonesian provinces of Aceh and North Sumatra extremely hard. The Government of Indonesia has estimated that at least 94,000 people died and 132,000 are missing. Many thousands more were injured. About 11 per cent of the population in the affected areas, or 500,000 persons, have been displaced. Total damage from the tsunami is estimated at $4.5 billion, roughly equal to Aceh's GDP. Apart from the physical infrastructure, the tsunami swept away entire communities, taking with it local administrations, schools, hospitals and all other components of social infrastructure. Fortunately, the world was galvanized into action by the tsunami, responding to the challenge of providing immediate humanitarian relief with great generosity and speed. Funds are still being collected to help the tsunami victims but now the focus has to shift to longer-term recovery and reconstruction.

The Consultative Group on Indonesia, at its meeting in Jakarta on 19 and 20 January 2005, had before it two papers dealing with the tsunami and its aftermath prepared jointly by the Indonesian National Development Planning Agency (BAPPENAS) and the international donor community, one dealing with the task of assessing the damage and the second with issues related to reconstruction.[a] The document on reconstruction draws on international experience to make recommendations for the formulation of a "coherent, credible and comprehensive" reconstruction strategy for Aceh and North Sumatra. The Indonesian Government itself has set out six key principles for a national recovery and reconstruction strategy. First, it should be a people-centred and participative process; second, it should take a holistic approach; third, there should be effective coordination; fourth, there should be a distinction between rehabilitation, i.e. achieving minimum standards, and reconstruction, with a clear strategy for each; fifth, the focus should be on services and institutions rather than projects; and, sixth, it should incorporate fiscal transparency and effective monitoring. The need for effective coordination was particularly stressed as the scale and scope of the disaster were such that virtually all key ministries and State agencies are likely to be involved. In addition, a large number of official donor agencies, multilateral institutions and local and international NGOs, as well as private individuals, responded to the tragedy and many were present in Aceh. Furthermore, Aceh itself presents a challenging environment for reconstruction as it is a conflict zone. In addition, the destruction of local communities and dispersion of remaining members makes consultation that much more difficult, a process rendered even more complex by the ongoing decentralization in Indonesia.

The document points out that a balance has to be struck between rapid response and broad participation. For example, the need for people to get back to work and for children to return to school is more or less immediate, whereas people will need more time to think about rebuilding homes and businesses. Thus, the right balance has to be found based on needs assessments and strategies for specific sectors and programmes need to be appropriately phased in.

As set out in the document, a successful recovery strategy for Aceh should have five basic goals, which build one upon another:

- Restoring people's lives by providing them with clean water, roads to reach clinics, shelter and sources of income to support their families;

- Restoring the economy by creating jobs, rehabilitating markets for buying and selling daily necessities and providing credit and microfinance;

---

[a] "Indonesia: preliminary damage and loss assessment, the December 26, 2004 natural disaster (January 2005) and Indonesia: notes on reconstruction, the December 26 natural disaster (January 2005).

- Rebuilding communities to give them social stability and a sense of orientation and to foster local solidarity;
- Restoring the system of local government to represent people's aspirations and guide development;
- Re-establishing the province as politically stable and economically vibrant so that it can become a growth pole for the country and become resilient and protected against other disasters.

To restore people's lives, labour-intensive public works would be a first step. Household microenterprises should be recapitalized with grants and communities need to be educated to know what aid is available to them. Credit and microfinance are also vital to restarting the economy, to meet demand from SMEs and larger firms. Apart from banks, non-commercial credit sources, such as cooperatives and microfinance institutions, will need to re-establish operations. Transport infrastructure has to be rehabilitated, focusing on infrastructure that is vital to improve access to markets and using labour-intensive methods where possible. Entrepreneurship needs to be encouraged. Rebuilding communities will involve repairing and reconstructing houses but as land has to be cleared and issues such as land titles have to be resolved, temporary shelter may initially be needed. This should be as close to the original community as possible and preferably community-built. Coastal communities need particular attention to rebuild sustainable livelihoods. Host communities that have taken in displaced persons also need support. For rebuilding local governance, local and village councils should coordinate and lead the next stage of assessing local needs and planning local reconstruction. Basic public administration and security functions have to be re-established and financial information should be shared with the public. Finally, a regional development plan for long-term growth in the province of Aceh should be formulated once the social and economic situation has been stabilized. Successful implementation of a reconstruction strategy for the province will require clear and well-designed mechanisms for channelling multiple financing sources, managing the extensive range of activities involved and governing the use of funds.

BAPPENAS in association with Government ministries and agencies as well as the donor community is working on an overall rehabilitation and reconstruction plan, which is to be completed in March 2005. It expects the relief phase, focusing on humanitarian relief including the construction of temporary shelter and emergency repair to infrastructure to last six months. Rehabilitation, focusing on restoring minimum levels of public services and economic facilities, such as banking and financial institutions, securing land rights and establishing law and order, as well as continued work on temporary shelter, is expected to last two years. Reconstruction, which will focus on rebuilding the region through investment in the economy, infrastructure, social and cultural systems, housing and institutional capacity could take at least five years.

Slow growth relative to potential in Indonesia has also resulted in inadequate job creation. According to ADB, some 2.5 million workers enter the labour force each year but in 2002-2003 only 1 million jobs were created annually. In June 2004, the national labour force survey carried out in 2003 was published and indicated that employment in manufacturing, construction, trade and the retail sector had contracted sharply, with displaced workers being pushed back into agriculture or the informal sector. Open unemployment rose to 9.5 per cent of the labour force in 2003, up from 9.1 per cent in 2002, with many more workers underemployed. Labour regulations and rising labour costs contributed to the rise. The outlook for employment is further clouded by Malaysia's intention to expel around 1 million illegal Indonesian workers and by the effect of ending the quotas on the Indonesian textile and garment industry, which could result in some 150,000 workers losing their jobs according to an employers' association. The proposed Jakarta minimum wage was increased 6 per cent in 2004 but still remains below the official cost of living.

The unemployment rate declined somewhat in Malaysia in 2004 to a projected 3.4 per cent of the labour force, from 3.5 per cent in 2003. Strong growth in manufacturing appears to have been the principal factor behind increased employment and rapid growth in wages and salaries in 2004 compared with 2003, although the pace slowed in the second half. Poverty incidence is relatively low in Malaysia and the share of the population with income below $2 per day was 4 per cent in 2002. Nevertheless, the Government is committed to reducing poverty further to 0.5 per cent and to eliminating hard-core poverty by 2009. Socio-economic development is an integral part of the 2005 budget and ensuring the well-being of the population through an improved quality of life is one of its four key strategies. Public expenditure will be directed towards smaller projects that benefit the grass roots.

High poverty incidence and low job growth in the Philippines

Poverty alleviation remains the overriding socio-economic concern in the Philippines. According to the National Statistical Coordination Board, poverty in the Philippines declined from 27.5 per cent in 2000 to 24.7 per cent in 2003 based on the family income and expenditure survey carried out in 2003. However, significant regional variations exist in the proportion of families living in poverty. Poverty incidence was highest in three regions in Mindanao, where the proportion ranged between 44.1 and 47.3 per cent, and lowest in three regions in Luzon, where the proportion was between 5 and 14.9 per cent. Measured in terms of the food poverty line, 1.7 million families in 2003 did not have enough income to provide for their basic food requirements, slightly less than the 1.8 million families in a similar situation in 2000.

The task of reducing poverty in the Philippines is hampered by economic growth that has failed to generate enough jobs for the growing labour force. According to the October 2004 labour force survey, the economy generated an estimated 976,000 jobs in 2004, a clear upturn from the 574,000 jobs added in 2003, but well short of the 1.29 million new entrants to the labour force in 2004, double the number that entered in 2003. The Government's target for annual job creation in the medium-term development plan 2004-2010 is 1.38-1.65 million jobs. Most of the jobs created were in the formal sector, with little change in self-employment and a substantial fall in unpaid family work. Nearly 68 per cent of the new jobs were in services and the balance was equally divided between agriculture and industry. Not surprisingly, the average unemployment rate in 2004 edged up to 11.8 per cent compared with 11.4 per cent in 2003. To generate more jobs, the Philippines clearly needs more pro-poor growth but both consumer and investor confidence have been falling, in part owing to the parlous state of public finances, political instability, corruption and poor infrastructure. High debt-service costs have prevented increased budget allocations for much-needed improvements in infrastructure and social services. As mentioned earlier, the Government exercised considerable fiscal discipline in 2004 and some of its proposed measures to increase revenues have been passed but it remains to be seen if these measures will be enough to lift the low growth path the economy has been on.

Clear improvement in the labour market in Singapore

In 2001-2003, the economy of Singapore lost 35,900 jobs but preliminary estimates indicate that it more than made up for the losses in 2004, adding 66,200 to total employment, principally in services and manufacturing. Construction continued to shed jobs. There have been clear signs of improvement in the labour market since the last quarter of 2003, when the unemployment rate started to decline, in part owing to a reduction in the labour force. The unemployment rate fell to 4 per cent in 2004 from 4.7 per cent the previous year. Average monthly nominal earnings grew over 4 per cent, faster than the rate of inflation, in the first half of 2004 helped also by overtime work, but earnings growth slowed in the second half. The Government believes that despite strong job creation the unemployment rate is not likely to return to the pre-crisis 2 per cent level as structural changes in the Singapore economy have shifted production to more capital-intensive industries. The structurally unemployed, defined as older and less educated workers, are estimated to have risen from 30 per cent of the unemployed before the 1997-1998 financial crisis to 35 per cent in 2003. To address these concerns, the Government has established various funds to promote retraining and skills upgrading as well as an agency to enhance the life-long employability and competitiveness of job seekers in Singapore. Steps are also being taken to increase flexibility in setting wages. The Government outlined some principles regarding social safety nets in the 2004 budget indicating that a balance has to be achieved between providing assistance to those in need and eroding the work ethic. Assistance schemes should be carefully targeted and means-testing will therefore be an important component in the provision of public services and social assistance. Demographic pressures resulting from Singapore's low birth rate and increased longevity may also lead to the retirement age being raised from 62 years as at present.

Higher commodity prices, especially for rice, boost farm incomes in Thailand

Farm incomes have risen sharply in Thailand since 2002, helped by higher world commodity prices. According to the World Bank, the agricultural terms of trade have improved, lifting consumption among rural farm households and reducing poverty. The proportion of the population living below the national poverty line was 9.8 per cent in 2002. One fifth of the poor are rice farmers, most of whom live in the North-East region, where two thirds of the poor reside, and they have benefited particularly from the 15 per cent increase in the price of rice in 2004, following a 3 per cent increase the previous year. In addition, the National Poverty

Eradication Centre announced new measures to assist poor people that had registered with it and caravans of experts and advisers were sent out in November 2004 to meet each registered family to assist in solving problems contributing to their poverty. Five State-owned financial institutions were requested to assist poor families with debt relief and other grass-roots financial schemes have been put in place, again with the support of some of these institutions. The Government's target is to reduce poverty incidence to less than 4 per cent by 2009. According to the labour force survey compiled by the National Statistical Office, total employment rose 4.7 per cent year on year in the second quarter of 2004 in Thailand. Unemployment fell to 2.3 per cent in the same quarter from 2.5 per cent a year earlier. Despite the problems in the agricultural sector, employment in that sector rose sharply and services employment also picked up, particularly in wholesale and retail trade. Employment in manufacturing was little changed. Real wages are reported to have risen 0.3 and 0.7 per cent in the first and second quarters of 2004 respectively.

Robust job creation in Viet Nam and reduced underemployment in rural areas

The rapid rates of GDP growth in Viet Nam in recent years have generated a substantial number of new jobs. An estimated 1.53 million jobs were created in 2003 and 1.56 million in 2004. The urban unemployment rate fell from 6.4 per cent in 2000 to 5.6 per cent in 2004 and underemployment in rural areas is also thought to have decreased sharply. The number of migrants going abroad in search of work decreased from 75,000 in 2003 to 67,500 in 2004. Nevertheless, the pressure to find jobs remains strong, especially among the young. Rising employment and incomes have contributed to falling poverty levels in the country. Viet Nam exited from a three-year Poverty Reduction and Growth Facility arrangement with IMF in April 2004, during which good progress was made on poverty reduction. The number of households falling below the national poverty line is estimated to have decreased from 17.2 per cent in 2000 to 11 per cent in 2003 and further to 8.3 per cent in 2004.

During the December 2004 meeting of the Consultative Group for Viet Nam, donors pledged a record $3.4 billion in ODA for 2005, in line with the Monterrey Consensus, whereby funds are channelled mainly to countries that formulate and follow a clear policy of economic growth accompanied by poverty reduction. Viet Nam received praise for its consistently high rates of growth, accompanied, by and large, by macroeconomic stability, high rates of investment, improved aid utilization and the pro-poor orientation of much public investment.

Maintaining competitiveness

Diversifying the economy through private sector development has been the long-standing aim of the Government of Brunei Darussalam. The Brunei Economic Development Board is pursuing a strategy of attracting

FDI through developing Sungai Liang into an industrial site meeting top international standards and constructing a deep-water port facility at Pulau Muara Besar. Progress has been made in developing the country into a hub for Islamic banking.

Insufficient investment erodes competitiveness in Indonesia

Indonesia's export performance has lagged that of its neighbours in South-East Asia. Much of the problem lies in the lack of investment in plant and equipment and in infrastructure in the country following the 1997-1998 financial crisis and in issues related to corruption. In a report released in December 2004, Transparency International ranked Indonesia as the tenth most corrupt country in the world. Corruption is also behind the low tax effort of Indonesia, reducing revenues available for economic and social development. Eradicating corruption is one of the main planks of the new Government with the announcement of the strengthening of the Corruption Eradication Commission.

The white paper adopted in September 2003 in Indonesia had three principal sections: macroeconomic stability; financial sector restructuring; and investments, exports and employment. Considerable progress was made in passing legislation under the first two headings and the last bank to remain in the hands of the Indonesian Bank Restructuring Agency was put up for sale in 2004. Indonesia's banks will be implementing the Basel II accord by 2008. Progress under the last heading has been somewhat slower. In this regard, greater flexibility and clarity in laws and regulations affecting the labour market will be necessary if investment and employment are to increase. The Government's intention to reorient public expenditures towards infrastructure and human development will require success in reducing politically sensitive fuel subsidies, which the Government has started to do.

Shifting to a higher value-added economy in Malaysia

Faced with increased competition in electronics markets as well as for FDI, the Government of Malaysia is seeking to boost overall competitiveness further to ensure medium- and long-term growth. Domestic private sector-led growth is being promoted while FDI is being sought to develop sectors such as services so as to diversify the economy. Three key strategies outlined in the 2005 budget were enhancing effectiveness and efficiency of financial management and service delivery in the public sector, accelerating the shift towards a higher value-added economy and developing human capital as a catalyst of growth by addressing skills shortages. As a result of earlier reforms, the performance of the corporate and banking sectors has greatly improved. Steps are also being taken under the financial sector master plan to continue strengthening and deepening the financial sector while moving towards greater liberalization.

Three quarters of the 40 government-linked companies in Malaysia are to be restructured and all such companies are to adopt programmes to monitor performance indicators by 2005 and to link executive compensation to them. Malaysia reduced import duties on vehicles and parts made in other ASEAN nations with effect from 1 January 2005 in line with its commitment under AFTA. Tariffs on vehicles and parts made in non-ASEAN countries will also be reduced to a lesser extent. However, excise duties will be increased on vehicles and local manufacturers are to be offered fiscal incentives. The net effect will be to reduce the pricing gap between locally manufactured cars and parts and those imported from other ASEAN countries in particular, which will increase pressure on local manufacturers such as Proton Holdings and Perodua. Malaysia has completed feasibility studies for possible FTAs with Australia and New Zealand and has started negotiations for bilateral FTAs with India, Japan and the United States.

Philippines' comparative advantage under threat

An issue the Philippine economy will have to address in the medium term is the high concentration of exports in a limited number of commodities and services. While this is not in itself a matter of concern, the nature of the economy's comparative advantage in those activities makes it so. Semiconductors and electronics account for over 70 per cent of total merchandise exports from the Philippines and the country's comparative advantage has been in its competitive wages. Here, the emergence of China with its large labour supply poses a distinct threat. A similar situation exists in business outsourcing, where proficiency in the English language provides Filipinos with a comparative advantage that can easily be eroded by India and even by China as it continues to develop. A crucial issue in this context is the friendliness of the business climate in the Philippines to companies seeking to lower costs by locating abroad or outsourcing.

In this regard, the disinterest shown by foreign investors in the Philippines recently is worrying. The Government is seeking to improve the economy's competitiveness by keeping the costs of wage goods low through greater productivity and by reducing transport and distribution costs through improved infrastructure and logistics. Reform of the power sector should also reduce power rates. Upgrading knowledge in the labour force, simplifying procedures and fighting corruption are other actions that the Government is hoping to take. Agreement was reached in November 2004 on the overall terms of a bilateral free trade agreement with Japan, the second-most important market for the Philippines, which is due to be finalized and come into effect in 2005. An important aspect of this agreement is that Filipino caregivers and nurses have been given access to the Japanese market, under certain conditions.

To reduce its vulnerability to both economic and non-economic shocks and carve out a niche for itself in a regional landscape increasingly overshadowed by the emergence of China and India, Singapore embarked some time ago on a multipronged strategy to diversify its economy and enhance competitiveness. Part of this strategy involves strengthening

Singapore's external linkages to position the country as an essential part of regional production networks and as the ideal platform from which to do business with the rest of the region and the world. Several FTAs have been concluded and negotiations are ongoing for several other agreements, the most important involving the Republic of Korea and India.

Singapore focuses on reducing the costs of doing business

The Government is also focused on improving Singapore's ability to attract FDI through reducing the costs of doing business. In 2004, 3,664 new high-tech businesses, of which 624 were foreign, were set up in Singapore. The corporate income tax rate will be cut from 22 to 20 per cent effective 2005 and various tax rebates and concessions will be offered to sectors seen as having the potential to accelerate growth in high value-added items and to foster entrepreneurship. The top marginal personal income tax rate is targeted for reduction in two steps from 22 to 20 per cent by 2006. Government red tape is also to be cut and fees and charges set at cost. Singapore's economy is heavily reliant on manufactured exports and the Government is trying to increase the contribution of the service sector through market liberalization in banking, telecommunications and legal services. Steps are also being taken to boost tourism with a package introduced in December to boost stopovers by transit passengers as visitor numbers topped a record 8 million in 2004. To meet competition from other regional ports and support the transport engineering and tourism sectors, the Maritime and Port Authority slashed port fees from 1 January 2005 for vessels undergoing ship repairs, bunkering and cruises. It will also reduce rates for car carrier operators to encourage trans-shipment of cars through Singapore.

Public investment in infrastructure set to expand in Thailand

Private investment, particularly net FDI, slowed in Thailand in 2004 and one quarter of the investment that took place was in residential construction. There are signs that capacity constraints may be appearing in some manufacturing industries. This is a matter of some concern as Thailand may find itself losing competitiveness in traditional, labour-intensive products such as textiles in the post-MFA world and exports of foods such as chicken and shrimp are facing health-related and other non-tariff barriers. The country's export success in the post-crisis period has been dependant on private investment that has enabled it to shift towards high value-added export items such as machinery and vehicles and parts for them. Trade liberalization helped this trend and Thailand's interest in pursuing FTAs both bilaterally and through ASEAN testifies to this. The Government hopes to improve competitiveness through investment in infrastructure and for the first time since the 1997-1998 crisis, public investment by both central and local governments and SOEs began to expand in 2004 as large infrastructure projects were initiated. The Government has announced ambitious plans for a five-year programme of infrastructure development, which could total B 1-1.5 trillion over the next four years. Full details are still to be worked out. Several other measures were taken in 2004 to enhance competitiveness. These include steps taken by the National Competitiveness Committee to develop business clusters, improve logistics, enhance skills and promote "green productivity". The Ministry of Finance has provided tax incentives to promote the competitiveness of SMEs, encourage investments abroad, support industrial estates and promote long-term savings and investment. The National Economic and Social Development Board has proposed an infrastructure strategy to increase competitiveness, including developing Bangkok as a regional business hub, improving the transport and communications systems and increasing energy and water security.

WTO accession critical to long-term growth and poverty reduction in Viet Nam

Sustaining strong growth and poverty reduction in Viet Nam in the longer term requires structural reforms as well as the maintenance of macroeconomic stability. The reforms hinge on restructuring SOEs and banks, further development of the private sector and securing accession to WTO. While progress on trade liberalization has been impressive and talks on WTO accession are moving forward, progress on the other issues has been somewhat slower. During 2003-2005, around 3,000 SOEs were scheduled for restructuring but by September 2004, only 1,560 had been restructured, of which 1,098 were equitized. The State-owned banking sector remains fragile with weak supervision and continues to favour SOEs. Although steps have been taken to improve the business environment, obstacles such as the lack of a transparent legal system, complex legislation governing taxation and investment, highly regulated imports and corruption remain. To improve the business climate, the Government cut the corporate tax rate levied on newly established enterprises in industrial zones to 10-20 per cent, from 28 per cent, with effect from August 2004. The Government has also commenced work on preparing a unified law for all types of enterprises as well as a unified investment law so as to enhance transparency and simplify procedures, as well as to improve corporate governance. Attempts have been made to lower business costs, particularly in telecommunications.

Viet Nam has fulfilled nearly all its commitments under AFTA but has agreed to compensate Thailand for delaying tariff reduction on motorcycles and parts until 2008. As Viet Nam is not a member of WTO, it will face intense competition in the post-MFA world since it will continue to be subject to quotas. The Government has set itself the target of end-2005 for completing the accession process and in the meanwhile it has been seeking to negotiate increases in garment quotas with the EU and the United States. The former removed quotas on garment and textile exports from Viet Nam with effect from 1 January 2005. Viet Nam successfully completed the ninth round of negotiations for entry into WTO in December 2004, during which the first draft report of the working group on Viet Nam's accession was discussed. Agreements have been reached with the EU and with Argentina, Brazil, Cuba, Chile and Singapore as part of the entry process.

B. Least developed countries in the subregion

Overview

Economic growth generally higher in 2004

With the exception of Cambodia, the least developed countries of South-East Asia achieved economic growth in 2004 that was generally higher than in 2003 (figure II.29) Growth rates were low in most cases, although the Lao People's Democratic Republic continued its comparatively strong performance, helped by strong investment and exports and a recovery in tourism. For other countries, regional and global factors such as the prevalence of bird flu adversely affected both agriculture and tourism, while the anticipated expiration of the MFA had a substantial impact on both the manufacture and export of garments. Greater emphasis is being placed on agricultural development to ensure that these countries achieve sustained economic growth and meet internationally agreed development goals. This requires not only greater investment in the sector but also in transport infrastructure, private sector development, financial services and the social sector.

Figure II.29. Rates of GDP growth in the least developed countries in South-East Asia, 2001-2004

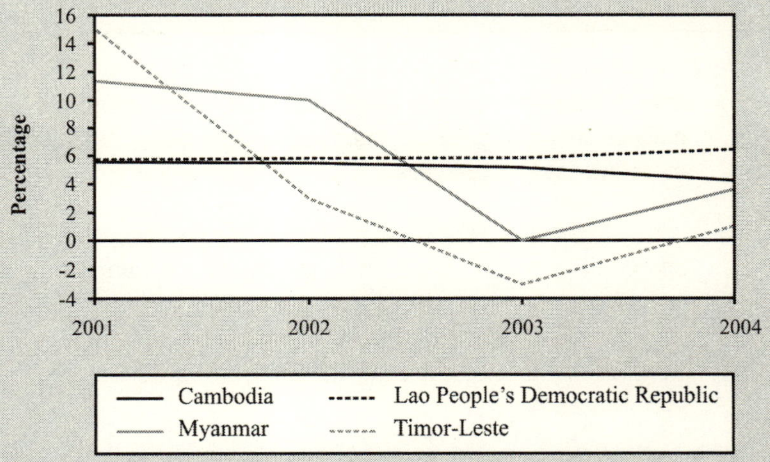

Sources: ESCAP, based on national sources; ADB, *Key Indicators of Developing Asian and Pacific Countries 2004* (Manila, ADB, 2004); IMF, *Democratic Republic of Timor-Leste: 2004 Article IV Consultation*, IMF Country Report No. 04/321 (October 2004) and *Cambodia: Statistical Appendix,* IMF Country Report No. 04/330 (October 2004); and other international sources.

Notes: Growth rates for 2004 are estimates. Fiscal year for Myanmar.

Inflation declined or remained low in three of the four least developed countries in the subregion, with the exception of Myanmar (figure II.30). This was partly due to the implementation of prudent fiscal

Figure II.30. Inflation[a] in the least developed countries in South-East Asia, 2001-2004

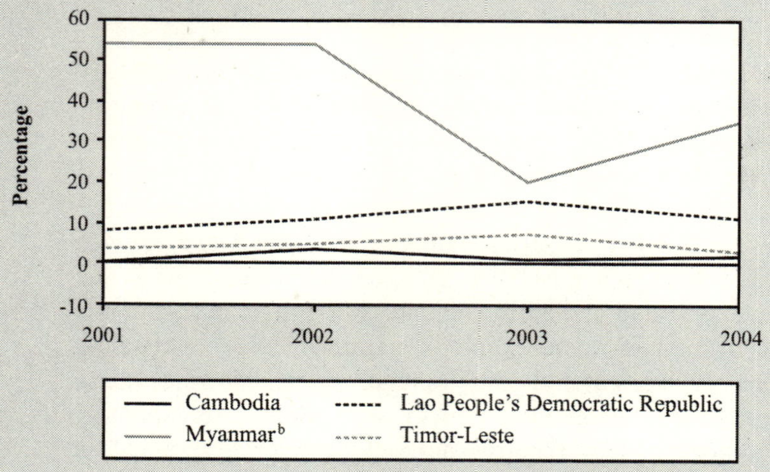

Sources: ESCAP, based on national sources; ADB, *Key Indicators of Developing Asian and Pacific Countries 2004* (Manila, ADB, 2004); IMF, *Democratic Republic of Timor-Leste: 2004 Article IV Consultation*, IMF Country Report No. 04/321 (October 2004); and other international sources.

Note: Inflation rates for 2004 are estimates.

[a] Changes in the consumer price index in main urban areas.

[b] Inflation at the end of the period.

and monetary policies and partly to low rates of inflation in trading-partner nations. Stable exchange rates also contributed greatly to the fall in inflationary pressures.

Measures to increase revenue from domestic sources through broadening of the tax base and improved revenue collection were recently introduced in least developed countries of the subregion. The expected resolution of debt arrears in Cambodia and the Lao People's Democratic Republic was expected to facilitate long-term economic growth in these two countries.

Growth performance

Growth in the agricultural and industrial sectors falls in Cambodia

Economic growth in Cambodia has been slowing in recent years. Despite slower growth in the non-agricultural sectors owing to the SARS-related drop in tourism and election year uncertainties in 2003, real GDP grew by 5.2 per cent, down from an average 5.6 per cent in 2001-2002, owing to a strong rebound in agricultural production (table II.34). Growth in real GDP was projected to decline further to 4.3 per cent in 2004, owing to a weaker performance in agriculture, and to less than 2 per cent in 2005 owing to weaker growth in the industrial sector following the expiry of the MFA.

Table II.34. Least developed countries in South-East Asia: growth rates, 2001-2004

(Percentage)

		Rates of growth			
		Gross domestic product	*Agriculture*	*Industry*	*Services*
Cambodia	2001	5.7	2.2	12.9	4.2
	2002	5.5	–2.7	17.7	4.5
	2003	5.2	9.2	6.7	1.6
	2004	4.3	0.4	..	..
Lao People's Democratic Republic	2001	5.7	3.8	10.1	5.7
	2002	5.9	4.0	10.3	5.7
	2003	5.9	2.6	11.1	7.1
	2004	6.5	3.5	11.4	7.4
Myanmar	2001	11.3	8.7	21.8	12.9
	2002	10.0	4.2	32.8	12.5
	2003	0.0	3.0	–3.4	-3.4
	2004	3.6	4.0	3.0	3.0
Timor-Leste	2001	15.0	..	..	..
	2002	3.0	..	..	..
	2003	–3.0	..	..	..
	2004	1.0	..	..	..

Sources: ESCAP, based on national sources; ADB, *Key Indicators of Developing Asian and Pacific Countries 2004* (Manila, ADB, 2004); IMF, *Democratic Republic of Timor-Leste: 2004 Article IV Consultation,* IMF Country Report No. 04/321 (October 2004) and *Cambodia: Statistical Appendix,* IMF Country Report No. 04/330 (October 2004); and other international sources.

Notes: Growth rates for 2004 are estimates. Industry comprises mining and quarrying; manufacturing; electricity, gas and power; and construction. Fiscal year for Myanmar.

The output of the agricultural, fisheries and forestry sector, which accounted for a third of GDP, rose by a robust 9.2 per cent in 2003 as reduced rainfall exposed a larger area of arable land along the Mekong. Growth in the sector was estimated to be a more modest 0.4 per cent in 2004 as a result of the bird flu outbreak, a smaller fish catch and lower crop production. The agricultural sector, focused mainly on paddy production, is constrained by the limited land available for cultivation and lack of property rights. Permanent cropland comprises only 1 per cent of the land area and only 7 per cent of this is irrigated. Most farmers are hesitant to engage in long-term investment, especially in irrigation, as only one tenth have formal titles to agricultural land and they have no access to collateralized lending. Inadequate rural roads, weak marketing systems, lack of modern farming techniques, limited access to formal financial services and barriers to public health also contribute to the limited growth in the agricultural sector. Community-based forestry is being considered as a means to safeguard livelihoods in rural areas as unsustainable logging has destroyed a source of income and contributed to soil erosion.

Output from the industrial sector, which had exhibited double-digit growth during the previous four years, rose by a more moderate 6.7 per cent in 2003, as rudimentary infrastructure and high wages have kept operating costs high. Manufacture of textiles, apparels and footwear accounted for approximately half of industrial output while construction accounted for another quarter. In anticipation of the expiration of the MFA in January 2005, growth in the garment sector slowed over the past two years and output was expected to contract substantially in 2005 (see box II.4). The quota removal is, however, expected to have a modest impact on the balance of payments as most inputs are imported and profit remittances are expected to fall. Depreciation of the currency is likely to have a limited impact in the industrial sector since most costs, including wages, are denominated in dollars. The high minimum wage, relative to average wages, applied to all industries in the formal sector has reduced employment further. Administrative impediments to investment as well as informal fees need to be addressed in order to stimulate the industrial sector, which accounts for a quarter of GDP, and to promote export diversification. The service sector, which accounts for more than a third of GDP, grew by a marginal 1.6 per cent in 2003 owing to the SARS-related drop in tourism and election-related uncertainties.

Real GDP in the Lao People's Democratic Republic rose from 5.9 per cent in 2003 to an estimated 6.5 per cent in 2004 as higher private and public investment, a recovery in tourism and a robust export performance fuelled by growth in China, Thailand and Viet Nam mitigated the adverse impact of higher crude oil prices on domestic production. Real GDP was targeted to grow between 6.5 and 7 per cent in 2005, as large investment projects in mining and tourism are completed.

Rice cultivation in the Lao People's Democratic Republic expected to increase with effective use of irrigation

The share of GDP held by the agricultural sector decreased to less than half while the shares of the industrial and service sectors each increased to more than a quarter of GDP in 2004. Growth in the agricultural sector, which employs more than three quarters of the population, rose from the drought-affected 2.6 per cent in 2003 to an estimated 3.5 per cent in 2004, despite the bird flu outbreak, which inflicted losses on poultry farmers. Owing to problems with irrigation systems and difficulties in obtaining fertilizer, the harvest of dry-season rice was expected to fall, as cultivation was possible on only three quarters of the available land. With more effective use of existing irrigation infrastructure, rice cultivation should increase over time. Non-rice crops, such as corn, beans and eggplants, for which production costs are lower, are increasingly being produced during the dry season. Cash crop production is being expanded to include rubber and cashew nuts, as well as coffee, in the northern and southern regions, and cassava in the central plains. Production in the industrial sector rose marginally from 11.1 per cent in 2003 to an estimated 11.4 per cent in 2004 as a result of strong hydropower and mining exports. As in Cambodia, the phasing out

Box II.4. Phase-out of the Multifibre Arrangement and least developed countries in the Asian and Pacific region

Trade in textiles and clothing (T&C) is one of the earliest forms of trade, with a long history of protectionism based to a large extent on a bilateral quota system – the so-called Multifibre Arrangement. With the abolition of the MFA on 31 December 2004, T&C trade is now free from all quantitative restrictions and is governed by prevailing WTO rules.

Several of the smaller and poorer countries in the Asian and Pacific region, including a number of least developed countries, built up their T&C export-oriented sectors relying on exports guaranteed under the MFA quota system. The underutilization of quotas in those countries attracted FDI, which played a major role in the development of their T&C industries. As can be seen from the table below, T&C today constitute an important portion of the total exports of several least developed countries in Asia.

Exports of textiles and clothing of selected least developed countries in Asia as a percentage of total exports, 2003

Bangladesh	84.4
Cambodia	87.1
Lao People's Democratic Republic	48.3
Maldives	32.0
Myanmar	25.9
Nepal	50.6

Source: Secretariat calculations based on the World Integrated Trade Solution.

Notes: "Textiles and clothing" defined as HS 50-63. Partner country import data used where export data not available.

While providing opportunities to smaller suppliers which had consistently underutilized quotas, the MFA system also artificially repressed the exports of highly competitive countries that had the capacity to supply T&C in larger quantities than quotas permitted. With the removal of quotas, market forces will determine T&C trade to a much larger extent. This will work to the advantage of a small number of major suppliers that can withstand competitive pressures. These suppliers are located mainly in China but also in India and a few other countries where low wage rates and integrated industries lend a comparative advantage. However, least developed countries and other smaller exporters of T&C, such as Sri Lanka, will face severe difficulties competing in this new trading environment. With women forming an important part of the largely low-skill workforce in the T&C sector in developing countries, the social costs of job losses and factory closures could be high.

Action will certainly be required at the national level to provide social safety nets and introduce training and labour readjustment programmes but, at the same time, many countries in the region, particularly the least developed, will have difficulty coping with long-term structural unemployment without assistance from the international community.

In April 2004, the IMF Executive Board approved the so-called Trade Integration Mechanism (TIM), designed to assist countries in overcoming balance-of-payments problems arising from trade liberalization, including the abolition of MFA, and Bangladesh became the first country to activate the Mechanism in July 2004. While there are

(Continued overleaf)

(Continued from preceding page)

concerns, inter alia, with regard to the fact that it is a lending facility and could increase debt burdens, the Mechanism nevertheless represents a collective recognition that trade liberalization can expose countries to adverse impacts, which if not addressed in a timely and comprehensive manner can result in escalating adjustment costs. Other financial mechanisms to assist countries experiencing adjustment challenges arising from trade liberalization should also be considered.

Some member countries of WTO have further argued that an additional solution to the problem could be found within the organization itself. The pace, depth and scope of additional market access negotiated in the Doha Round will play a key role. The time seems ripe for least developed countries to be given the bound duty- and quota-free market access that has been on the agenda since 1996. In a submission[a] by a number of countries to the WTO membership, it has been proposed that the WTO secretariat undertake a study identifying adjustment-related issues and costs, paying particular attention to the impact on least developed countries and other small and vulnerable economies that will lose from quota elimination, and that a work programme be established in WTO to discuss and find solutions to problems identified by concerned parties. Turkey, a major T&C exporter, made a similar proposal.[b]

These initiatives raise an interesting question regarding negotiating strategies: should least developed countries continue to seek compensation through increased market access or should they be seeking compensation through direct forms of financial assistance? While WTO has traditionally eschewed any possible linkage to financial compensation, such linkages do exist and they appear to be increasing in regional trade agreements and bilateral trade agreements.[c]

Entering into free trade agreements with neighbouring countries is, indeed, one possible option open to least developed countries to help them to maintain at least some segments of their T&C industries. More specifically, the larger developing countries in the region, China and India in particular, could do much to strengthen South-South solidarity by assisting the least developed countries, inter alia, through providing full and free market access to those countries. The issue of financial compensation should also be given further thought at the regional level by exploring the feasibility of establishing a regional financial facility to assist countries adversely affected by the elimination of quotas, particularly the least developed among them.

Mitigating factors

Finally, some mitigating factors could come into play that may prevent, or at least slow down, the domination of the global T&C industry by China and other large suppliers. Given the long history of protectionism in this sector, it is highly possible that developed countries will increasingly resort to new forms of barriers, such as safeguard duties, anti-dumping duties and more stringent labour standards to undercut the competitive edge of developing countries and thus protect their less efficient domestic T&C industries. It is also worth noting that as part of the terms of China's accession to WTO, members of WTO have the right to impose safeguard measures under certain conditions specifically against imports from China until 2008. This being said, the potential hardships that could be faced by several countries in the region, especially the least developed, remain of great concern and continued support and attention from the international community will be required to cushion the negative effects of quota elimination and find an appropriate solution to the problem.

---

[a] "Post-ATC adjustment-related issues" (G/C/W/496/Rev.1).

[b] "Turkey's contribution to the debate on post-ATC related issues" (G/C/W/497).

[c] A more detailed discussion can be found in the theme study for the sixty-first session of ESCAP.

of the MFA is expected to undermine garment exports, but the granting of normal trading relations status by the United States, as well as tax concessions by China for imports of more than 200 items produced in the Lao People's Democratic Republic, are expected to ameliorate the adverse impact. Growth in the service sector rose from 7.1 per cent in 2003 to an estimated 7.4 per cent as foreign tourist arrivals, especially from China, Singapore and Viet Nam, increased dramatically despite the outbreak of bird flu and heightened security concerns. Telecommunications and trade-related services rose but weaknesses in the banking sector hampered growth in financial services.

Constraints on imported inputs, structural rigidities and sanctions continue to affect Myanmar adversely

In Myanmar, growth in real GDP in 2002[2] was estimated at 10.0 per cent, owing to the substantial expansion of industrial production reflected in increased electricity consumption, cement production and the number of licensed motor vehicles. Although the Government expected growth of real GDP to continue at a similar rate in 2003, it is generally projected to have been flat, owing to a decline in industrial production, services and trade. Constraints on imported inputs, structural rigidities as well as the delayed effects of earlier sanctions and the banking crisis continue to affect economic growth adversely. Real GDP was expected grow 3.6 per cent in 2004, led by steady growth in the agricultural sector following the implementation of the revised rice trade regime. Agricultural output consists primarily of paddy, sugar cane, pulses, groundnuts, maize and sesame. Agriculture, manufacturing and processing, livestock and fisheries, and construction accounted for more than two thirds of GDP in 2002. Industrial development is being encouraged with the establishment of 18 industrial zones.

Income from oil and gas in Timor-Leste projected to rise

After contracting by an estimated 3 per cent in 2003 as the presence of international staff and peacekeepers was reduced and agricultural production fell owing to a drought, Timor–Leste's real GDP is projected to grow by 1 per cent in 2004. Agricultural production is expected to recover with the return of normal weather conditions. In order to achieve the 5 per cent annual real GDP growth envisaged in the national development plan, the agricultural sector needs to be developed further through improved productivity and expansion of cash crop production. Agriculture, forestry and fisheries accounted for a quarter of total GDP in 2003, while the industrial sector accounted for another 18 per cent. Income from the exploitation of oil and gas resources in the Timor Sea was projected to rise from 9 per cent of GDP in 2003 to nearly 13 per cent of GDP in 2004. The service sector accounted for 57 per cent of total GDP in 2003, with public administration and defence accounting for nearly two thirds of the subtotal.

---

[2] National account statistics are available only annually in Myanmar and revised after the start of the following year. A large informal sector, including much of the border trade, is not captured in official statistics while the use of official exchange rates for conversion purposes results in understatement of external trade and foreign exchange.

Enactment of legislation to establish a framework for business activity, development of an independent judiciary and completion and implementation of sector investment programmes to improve infrastructure are necessary for the further development of the private sector. A commercial code and a company law were enacted as initial steps to establish a legal and regulatory framework for business activity. A policy paper on private investment was prepared for public consultation and draft domestic and foreign investment laws were submitted to the Council of Ministers. Following the enactment of a basic law on land ownership in 2003, the Council of Ministers is reviewing draft laws on the leasing of private and public land and land and property dispute mediation.

Inflation and exchange rates

Inflation wanes in 2004

Helped by low inflation in its trading partners, inflation in Cambodia rose by only 1.1 per cent in 2003 (table II.35). Prudent monetary and fiscal policies also contributed to this relative price stability, as M2 growth slowed to 14.9 per cent from 31.1 per cent in 2002 and the budget deficit was held at 7 per cent of GDP in 2003, close to the average of 6.5 per cent in 2001 and 2002 (table II.36). Higher prices for

Table II.35. Least developed countries in South-East Asia: inflation and money supply growth (M2), 2001-2004

(Percentage)

	2001	*2002*	*2003*	*2004*
Inflation[a]				
Cambodia	0.2	3.4	1.1	2.0
Lao People's Democratic Republic	7.8	10.6	15.5	11.2
Myanmar[b]	53.8	54.0	20.0	35.0
Timor-Leste	3.6	4.8	7.1	3.0
Money supply growth (M2)				
Cambodia	20.4	31.1	14.9	14.1
Lao People's Democratic Republic	13.7	37.6	20.1	18.1
Myanmar	43.9	34.6	1.4	11.0[c]
Timor-Leste	155.5	6.8	32.4	37.9[c]

Sources: ESCAP, based on national sources; ADB, *Key Indicators of Developing Asian and Pacific Countries 2004* (Manila, ADB, 2004); IMF, *International Financial Statistics,* vol. LVII, No. 8 (Washington, IMF, August 2004) and *Democratic Republic of Timor-Leste: 2004 Article IV Consultation,* IMF Country Report No. 04/321 (October 2004); and other international sources.

Note: Figures for 2004 are estimates.

[a] Changes in the consumer price index in main urban areas.
[b] End of period.
[c] January-March.

Table II.36. Least developed countries in South-East Asia: budget and current account balance as a percentage of GDP, 2001-2004

(Percentage)

	2001	2002	2003	2004
Budget balance as a percentage of GDP				
Cambodia	−6.4	−6.5	−7.0	−6.1
Lao People's Democratic Republic[a]	−7.6	−8.3	−7.8	−9.2
Myanmar[b]	−5.9	−4.1	−4.5	−5.9
Timor-Leste[c]	−5.5	−6.1	−4.4	−2.4
Current account balance as a percentage of GDP				
Cambodia	−1.2	−1.2	−2.4	−3.3
Lao People's Democratic Republic	−4.7	−1.7	−3.1	−3.8
Myanmar	..	..	..	..
Timor-Leste[d]	13.9	11.6	12.6	12.0

Sources: ESCAP, based on national sources; ADB, *Key Indicators of Developing Asian and Pacific Countries 2004* (Manila, ADB, 2004) and *Asian Development Outlook 2004 Update* (Manila, ADB, 2004); EIU, *Country Reports* (London, EIU, 2004), various issues; IMF, *Democratic Republic of Timor-Leste: 2004 Article IV Consultation,* IMF Country Report No. 04/321 (October 2004); and other international sources.

Note: Figures for 2004 are estimates.

[a] Fiscal year.
[b] Including grants.
[c] On the basis of fiscal year (July-June); for example, 2000 relates to FY2000/01.
[d] Including official transfers.

transport, communications and housing were offset by a decline in the prices of clothing, recreation and medical care. Price developments in its trading partners were, however, expected to increase inflationary pressures in 2004. Since the foreign exchange market is shallow and exchange rate policy has a limited effect on competitiveness, Cambodia stabilizes inflation at a low level by maintaining a broadly stable exchange rate (figure II.31). The official exchange rate, which applies to all external transactions conducted by the Government and State enterprises, is adjusted daily to maintain a spread of less than 1 per cent against the market rate, which applies to all other transactions.

Inflation in the Lao People's Democratic Republic in 2004 has been kept reasonably well under control and exchange rates have been relatively stable. Annual average inflation declined from 15.5 per cent in 2003 to an estimated 11.2 per cent in 2004 as most CPI categories registered smaller increases. Declining food prices, which comprise nearly half of the total CPI basket, as a result of improved rice and other crop production during the second half of 2004 offset the increase in the cost of construction materials, including steel bars and cement, as well as higher petroleum prices, which exerted upward pressure on housing, transport and production and distribu-

Figure II.31. Index of exchange rates against the United States dollar of least developed countries in South-East Asia, 1996-2004

(1996 = 100)

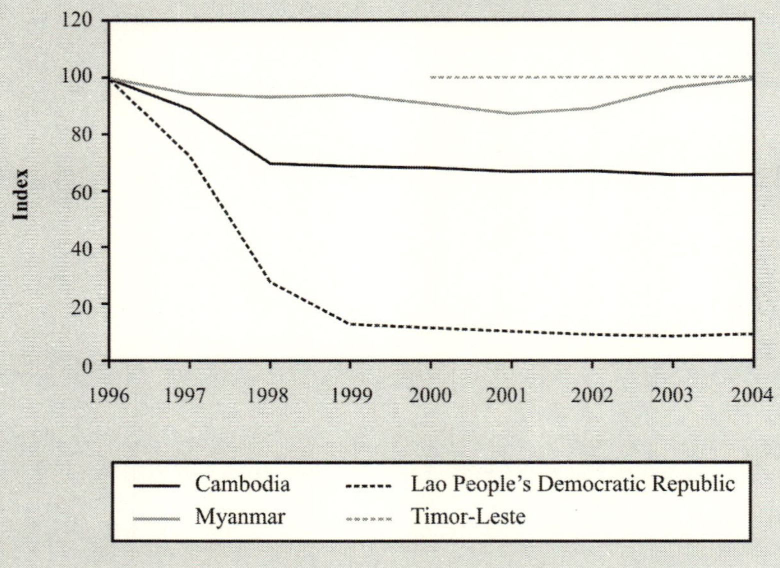

Sources: IMF, *International Financial Statistics*, vol. LVII, No. 10 (Washington, IMF, October 2004); and *The Economist*, various issues.

Notes: Figures for 2004 are estimates. In the case of Timor-Leste, base year 2000=100.

tion costs. The exchange rate of the kip against the dollar remained relatively stable throughout 2004. As in Cambodia, the Lao People's Democratic Republic has adopted a policy of maintaining a spread of less than 1.5 per cent between the parallel market and official exchange rates to reduce the volume of transactions occurring outside the banking sector. Steady fiscal and monetary policies to ensure macroeconomic stability have also contributed to exchange rate stability, although the projected budget deficit, excluding grants, is expected to widen to 9.2 per cent of GDP in 2004.

In Myanmar, the rate of inflation averaged 54 per cent in 2001 and 2002 as the fiscal deficit was monetized and private sector lending rose sharply. Nevertheless, low nominal interest rates and high inflation kept the domestic debt burden fairly stable. The rate of inflation is estimated to have fallen to 20 per cent in 2003, but is projected to have accelerated again to 35 per cent in 2004. The CPI for urban areas comprises 135 consumption items using new weights from a 1997 survey and includes a wider coverage of items at market prices as well as imported goods. The kyat has been losing its value in the parallel exchange rate market broadly in line with inflation. The dual exchange rate regime distorts relative prices, affects investment and production decisions adversely and imposes additional costs on the economy. A gradual move towards a flexible, unified exchange rate regime would improve the allocation of resources.

Inflationary pressures in Timor-Leste have been waning in recent months, with CPI inflation declining to 3 per cent in 2004 from 7.1 per cent the previous year, when drought created a scarcity of agricultural goods. The commodity basket and weighting scheme for the CPI were revised in 2003 to reflect household expenditure more closely. Looser monetary and fiscal policies may affect the outlook for inflation in coming years.

Foreign trade and other external transactions

Garment exports accounted for four fifths of Cambodia's merchandise exports in 2003

The value of Cambodia's merchandise exports is projected to expand by 7.4 per cent in 2004, substantially slower than the 18.7 per cent growth in 2003, to reach $2.2 billion (table II.37). Retained merchandise imports are projected to slow somewhat from the rapid 12.9 per cent growth registered in 2003 to 11.8 per cent in 2004, when the value of those exports could total $2.9 billion (table II.38). Garment exports accounted for more than four fifths of all merchandise exports in 2003. After the inclusion of official transfers, the current account deficit is projected at 3.3 per cent of GDP in 2004 (table II.36). However, high petroleum prices are expected to add another 0.5 per cent to this estimate. Official gross international reserves are expected to have increased to $782 million, slightly less than 2.8 months of imports of goods and services, by

Table II.37. Least developed countries in South-East Asia: merchandise exports and their rates of growth, 2001-2004

	Exports (f.o.b.)				
	Value (millions of US dollars)	*Annual rate of growth (percentage)*			
	2003	*2001*	*2002*	*2003*	*2004*
Cambodia[a]	2 076	12.1	11.3	18.7	7.4
Lao People's Democratic Republic[b]	359	0.3	–10.1	20.7	19.9
Myanmar[c]	2 127	39.4	24.1	–26.0	–0.3
Timor-Leste[d]	7	–20.0	50.0	16.7	14.3

Sources: IMF, *IMF Concludes 2004 Article IV Consultation with the Democratic Republic of Timor-Leste,* Public Information Notice (PIN) No. 04/118 (12 October 2004) and *Cambodia: 2004 Article IV Consultation,* IMF Country Report, No. 04/328 (October 2004); and EIU, *Country Reports* (London, EIU, 2004), various issues.

[a] Figure for 2004 is a projection.
[b] Figure for 2004 is an EIU estimate.
[c] Figures for 2002, 2003 and 2004 are EIU estimates.
[d] All figures are estimates.

Table II.38. Least developed countries in South-East Asia: merchandise imports and their rates of growth, 2001-2004

	Imports (c.i.f.)				
	Value (millions of US dollars)	*Annual rate of growth (percentage)*			
	2003	*2001*	*2002*	*2003*	*2004*
Cambodia[a]	2 613	8.0	10.5	12.9	11.8
Lao People's Democratic Republic[b]	482	−1.4	−18.3	11.8	18.0
Myanmar[c]	1 880	19.5	−19.6	−9.6	4.5
Timor-Leste[d]	203	11.7	−6.3	−19.1	−17.7

Sources: IMF, *IMF Concludes 2004 Article IV Consultation with the Democratic Republic of Timor-Leste,* Public Information Notice (PIN) No. 04/118 (12 October 2004) and *Cambodia: 2004 Article IV Consultation,* IMF Country Report, No. 04/328 (October 2004); and EIU, *Country Reports* (London, EIU, 2004), various issues.

[a] Import value in f.o.b.; figure for 2004 is a projection.
[b] Figure for 2004 is an EIU estimate.
[c] Imports value f.o.b.; figures for 2002, 2003 and 2004 are EIU estimates.
[d] All figures are estimates.

the end of 2004. Cambodia is seeking preferential duty treatment from the United States on the same terms as applied to African countries under the African Growth and Opportunity Act. Following the adoption of the WTO accession package by the National Assembly, Cambodia is required to strengthen its legal and judicial system. Accession requires the adoption and implementation of 46 pieces of legislation ranging from judicial reform to trade-related property rights over the next several years. In accordance with its commitment under ASEAN, Cambodia reclassified tariff lines to the ASEAN Harmonized Tariff Nomenclature, with the unweighted average tariff remaining unchanged at 15 per cent.

Technical assistance and food aid comprise bulk of aid flows to Cambodia

Large aid inflows have financed domestic investment and spurred construction activities. In view of the weak administrative capacity, technical assistance and investment comprised 45 and 39 per cent respectively of total aid flows in 1999-2003. Budgetary support and food aid comprised only 8 and 7 per cent respectively during the same period. A review of the current allocation of aid is under way and should ensure that poverty alleviation and long-term growth, especially in the agricultural sector, are addressed. After an initial increase from 34 per cent of GDP in 2004 to 35 per cent of GDP in 2006, Cambodia's stock of public debt is projected to decline to 16 per cent by 2023 on the assumption that the ratio of revenues to GDP expands from the current 11 per cent so as to maintain a sustainable debt-to-revenue ratio. Cambodia's total external public debt of $3 billion, or 71 per cent of GDP, at the end of 2003 was considered to be sustainable. A dialogue is being conducted with both the Russian Federation and the United States, which together account for 64 per cent of total external debt, to reach agreements on debt rescheduling. The proposal by the Russian Federation involves cash payments up front and substantial debt cancellation.

In the Lao People's Democratic Republic, merchandise exports totalled $359 million while merchandise imports totalled $482 million, leading to a trade deficit of $123 million in 2003. Exports are forecast to expand just under 20 per cent in 2004, slightly less than in 2003, as improved weather conditions contributed to a substantial increase in exports of agricultural and forest products as well as electricity. The growth in imports is forecast to accelerate to 18 per cent in 2004 from 11.8 per cent the previous year owing to increased imports of equipment and machinery for large mining-related investment projects, raw materials for manufacturing, including garments, and oil and gas. In 2004, the external current account, including ODA grants, is expected to show a deficit of 3.8 per cent of GDP, owing to an increase in investment-related imports. Official gross international reserves are expected to increase to $224 million, close to four months of imports, by the end of 2004.

Lao People's Democratic Republic meets its external debt-service obligation

The total external debt stock, of which about 89 per cent is public debt, is projected to rise from $2.17 billion in 2003 to $2.27 billion in 2004. In addition to concessional borrowings from multilateral donors, the stock of public debt reflects borrowings from the Russian Federation. Public debt service, both amortization and interest payments, rose from 7.2 per cent of exports of goods and services in 2003 to 13.4 per cent in 2004, but is expected to fall gradually as mining and hydropower exports rise. Despite the high level of external public debt, the Lao People's Democratic Republic has met its external debt-service obligations without arrears and has not sought debt relief under the enhanced Highly Indebted Poor Countries (HIPC) initiative. The expected rescheduling of the Russian debt on concessional terms will reduce external debt further to below the HIPC eligibility criteria.

Myanmar's balance of payments strengthens owing to gas exports

After a significant rise in exports in 2002 owing to gas-exporting facilities coming on stream, Myanmar's merchandise exports were projected to fall substantially by 26 per cent in 2003 to $2.1 billion. An earlier ban imposed by the United States on imports from Myanmar resulted in substantial employment losses in the garment industry, while the provision of financial services to Myanmar, including trade facilitation, banking services and money transfers, was prohibited. Merchandise imports were also projected to fall by 9.6 per cent to $1.9 billion in 2003, leading to a small trade surplus. The current account deficit at the official exchange rate was a negligible percentage of GDP in that year. While positive growth is expected for imports in 2004, little change is expected in exports. Thailand, China and India accounted for more than 60 per cent of Myanmar's exports while Singapore, China, Malaysia and Japan accounted for a similar share of imports. Although tariff reforms have been undertaken, non-tariff barriers such as the priority import list and administrative requirements continue to hamper trade. Furthermore, import licences were granted only to exporters against a portion of their export earnings. The balance of payments strengthened owing to gas exports and continued import compression. Official gross international reserves, including a $200 million renewable loan from Malaysia, were estimated to be $783.6 million, equivalent to four months of imports, in 2003.

Myanmar has not received aid in recent years. In the absence of donor support, there are limits to the economic adjustments that can be made without undermining social stability. At $128.7 million, actual FDI disbursed in 2002 was less than a fifth of the level registered in 1998. Four fifths of this amount went to the oil and gas sector. Of total external debt outstanding, amounting to $5.9 billion in 2002, $4 billion consisted of concessional loans, three quarters of which were from bilateral sources; half of the outstanding external debt is estimated to be in arrears.

International assistance to Timor-Leste falls by half from an estimated peak in 2001

In Timor-Leste, exports of goods, excluding border trade and oil and gas revenues, which are recorded as royalties and tax revenues, are projected to rise from $7 million in 2003 to $8 million in 2004, with coffee accounting for the bulk of exports in both years. Merchandise imports, excluding border trade, are projected to decline from $203 million in 2003 to $167 million in 2004 as imports related to international assistance declined from $104 million to $84 million during the period. Despite technical problems, the Bayu-Undan oil and gas project came on stream, contributing an additional $19 million in royalties and interest as well as $24 million in tax revenues in 2004 and paving the way for increased revenues over the coming years. The external current account (excluding official transfers) remains substantially in deficit, but the deficit is narrowing owing to a further reduction in donor-assisted reconstruction activities. International assistance fell from an estimated peak of $347 million in 2001 to a projected $181 million in 2004. Timor-Leste has not tapped concessional loans to fund essential capital investments.

Policy issues and responses

Rural poverty incidence in Cambodia more than double the urban rate

Poverty reduction in least developed countries requires strengthening of the agricultural sector and rural development. As small economies with unused arable land and a large unskilled labour force, their comparative advantage lies in agriculture. Large aid inflows and the boom in the garments and tourism sectors have, however, strengthened the formal sector in urban areas, while rural subsistence farmers have been left behind. Since the income gap between the urban and rural areas remains wide, many young people migrate to urban areas to seek employment in the industrial and service sectors. Poverty in rural areas of Cambodia, where more than fourth fifths of the population lives, was more than double the rate in urban areas, with average household expenditure in 2002 in rural areas estimated to be less than a quarter of the expenditure of households in Phnom Penh. Cambodia has recognized the need for agricultural reforms to improve land use and for redirection of aid to build irrigation and road infrastructure to promote agricultural growth.

Rural sector development in the Lao People's Democratic Republic is constrained by remoteness, mountainous terrain and lack of necessary services, including transport infrastructure. To narrow the disparities in employment opportunities between urban and rural areas, the Lao People's Democratic Republic has provided tax incentives to attract investment projects to rural areas and has allocated greater public investment to rural social development. A village development fund was also established to finance projects for building small-scale infrastructure, creating new employment opportunities for farmers and introducing new techniques to people in rural areas. The country's national growth and poverty eradication strategy stresses fostering economic growth with equity, modernizing social and economic infrastructure and enhancing human resources development. Although defence spending has been declining in both Cambodia and Myanmar, greater resources need to be allocated to social services. Furthermore, to alleviate poverty and safeguard human capital, such expenditure adjustment needs to rely on improved budgetary controls. Reduction in the incidence of poverty in Timor-Leste requires the development of a dynamic private sector, strengthened institutions and capacity to deliver government services in rural areas, as well as effective use of oil and gas wealth and continued international assistance.

To achieve fiscal objectives, revenue from domestic sources needs to rise

In order to achieve their fiscal objectives, all four least developed countries in South-East Asia need to increase revenues from domestic sources. Fiscal revenue collection in Cambodia was lower than expected in 2003 partly owing to delayed payment of taxes. Broadening of the tax base through reduction of exemptions, strengthened enforcement through computerization of revenue departments, passage of the customs law and good management of natural resources are seen as critical to the achievement of the 2004 revenue target of 11.9 per cent of GDP. To attain the targeted revenue of 12.8 per cent of GDP in 2005, the Lao People's Democratic Republic planned to improve the State budget law, strengthen the national revenue administration by centralizing revenues and prepare for the introduction of VAT at a single 10 per cent rate in January 2007. Since persistent fiscal deficits have led to macroeconomic instability in Myanmar, transparent and fair revenue collection through strengthening tax compliance, limiting exemptions and loopholes, assessing import duties based on the market exchange rate and restoring excise and user charges, whose value has been erased by inflation, was expected to increase revenue by 1 to 2 per cent of GDP. Timor-Leste was expected to use part of its oil and gas wealth to meet pressing investment needs for infrastructure and human capital development, with the majority of the wealth saved in financial assets for future generations. Following the commencement of oil and gas production in the Bayu-Undan field, establishment of a petroleum fund, based on a Norwegian model to ensure transparency and accountability in the management of oil and gas savings, was expected by mid-2005. Timor-Leste has avoided external borrowing and lacks access to domestic borrowing under the dollar-based monetary and exchange rate arrangement. Broadening the non-oil tax base is, however, necessary in order to avoid excessive reliance on oil and gas revenues.

Promoting the use of national currencies

The high degree of dollarization in Cambodia, the Lao People's Democratic Republic and Timor-Leste limits the conduct of domestic monetary policies. In addition to the loss of seigniorage, the lack of monetary independence and the central banks' inability to act as lenders of last resort could threaten financial stability. Increased deposits denominated in national currencies, however, reflect greater public confidence as exchange rates and prices stabilize. To address the challenges posed by the circulation of several currencies outside of the banking system, both Cambodia and the Lao People's Democratic Republic have noted the importance of promoting the national currency as a means of payment for all trade in goods and services domestically, while liberalizing currency exchange for all current account payments. In Cambodia, demand for the riel was expanding in rural areas as well as for government transactions, and currency in circulation reached over 5 per cent of GDP in 2003. It is, however, essential that administrative measures be implemented carefully to avoid capital flight. Given the country's institutional and financial constraints, the dollar-based monetary and exchange rate regime is seen as being appropriate for Timor-Leste, but prudent fiscal and wage policies are essential to avoid erosion in its external competitiveness.

Steps to combat money laundering and financing of terrorism

In view of the inherent weakness of the financial sector in many least developed countries, any hint of money laundering or financing of terrorism would be detrimental to the banking sector. In Cambodia, an inter-ministerial working group, headed by the central bank, was charged with preparing a draft anti-money-laundering law while the Lao People's Democratic Republic was in the process of establishing the legal framework to combat money laundering and terrorist financing. Myanmar's efforts to be in compliance with international norms include the introduction of anti-money-laundering legislation in 2003 and collaboration with regional organizations on these issues. Enactment of legislation on money laundering and combating the financing of terrorism is also expected in Timor-Leste.

Restructuring of State-owned enterprises focused on tariff reform

As in other least developed countries in transition to a market economy, restructuring of SOEs is considered an essential complement to the banking reform agenda, since such enterprises account for a large share of credit and non-performing loans. In the Lao People's Democratic Republic and Timor-Leste, restructuring has focused on tariff reform to commercialize large utilities. The installation of prepayment meters and improvement in billing at the power authority in Timor-Leste and gradual upward adjustment of fees for electricity usage in the Lao People's Democratic Republic are aimed at making the companies concerned more commercially viable. Restructuring programmes for three other major enterprises as well as Lao Airlines have been launched in the country with completion expected by the end of 2005. In Myanmar, SOEs, which account for the majority of production in the communications, power, energy and financial sectors, need to operate commercially in order to reduce budgetary costs and free resources for the private sector. This will require exchange rate unification to make the tax and subsidies provided to these enterprises explicit.

DEVELOPED COUNTRIES OF THE REGION

Australia, Japan and New Zealand

Overview

Modest economic recovery in Japan, buoyant growth in Australia and New Zealand

The picture of recent economic growth in Japan has had to be reassessed in the light of the revision of national accounts data carried out by the Government in late 2004, which now makes Japanese GDP estimates more readily comparable with those of other leading OECD economies. Since the previous method for calculating GDP gave an upward bias to the figures, it is not surprising that the revisions suggest recent economic growth was not as strong as previously reported. Nevertheless, it is clear that there was a significant but shallow recovery in 2003, after years of relative stagnation, and that economic growth was very much stronger in 2004, albeit not to the same extent as previously thought (figure II.32). In particular, the recovery in investment was much more subdued.

Figure II.32. Rates of GDP growth in developed countries in the ESCAP region, 2001-2004

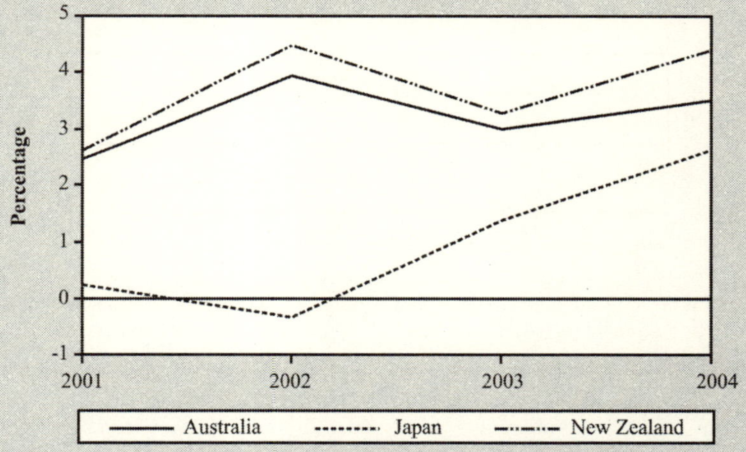

Sources: ESCAP, based on national sources; Cabinet Office, Government of Japan, *Quarterly Estimate of GDP*, at web site <www.esri.cao.go.jp/jp/sna/qe044/men.html>, 17 February 2005; and EIU, *Country Forecasts* (London, EIU, 2004 and 2005), various issues.

Note: Growth rates for 2004 are estimates.

Economic growth also accelerated in New Zealand while remaining substantially unchanged in Australia in 2004, supported by strong domestic demand buoyed by the housing boom, which, however, showed signs of easing during the year. The contribution of net exports to GDP growth in those countries was minimal as currency appreciation in both countries muted export revenues, despite the increase in global commodity prices, while strong domestic demand boosted imports. Against the background of a favourable international environment for much of the year, all three countries experienced falling unemployment and improved business and consumer confidence, particularly in the first three quarters of 2004.

In Australia and New Zealand, the strong housing market and increased resource constraints pushed up prices for non-tradables, although deflationary pressure on the prices of tradables contained consumer price inflation within the authorities' target ranges. Inflation rates remain low in both countries and in Australia the growth in consumer prices continued the downward trend that commenced in 2002 in Australia. Deflationary pressure eased in Japan, although firm evidence that deflation has come to an end is still awaited (figure II.33).

Figure II.33. Inflation[a] in developed countries in the ESCAP region, 2001-2004

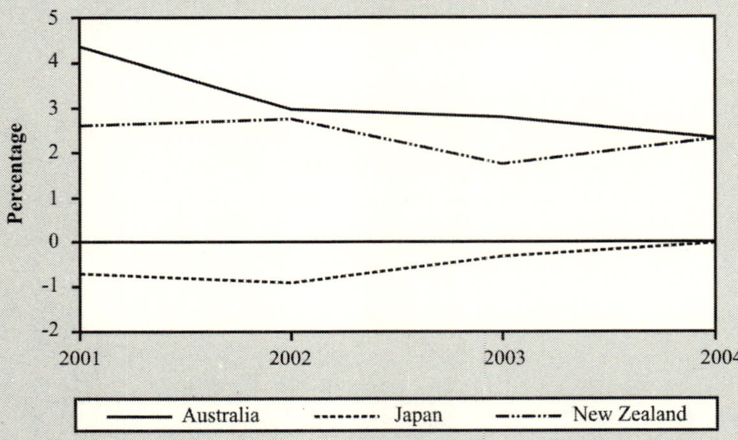

Sources: ESCAP, based on national sources; IMF, *International Financial Statistics*, vol. LVII, No. 8 (Washington, IMF, August 2004); and EIU, *Country Forecasts* (London, EIU, 2004 and 2005), various issues.

Note: Inflation rates for 2004 are estimates.

[a] Percentage changes in the consumer price index.

The Japanese current account surplus widened during 2004 as strong export growth outpaced a significant increase in imports (figures II.34 and II.35). In Australia and New Zealand, import growth has been running well ahead of export growth in recent years, and, although both countries enjoyed a surge in export revenues in the first half of 2004, their current account deficits widened, increasing the debt-service burden. Exchange rate appreciation in those two countries dampened export growth and added fuel to the already strong demand for imports. The exchange rates of all three countries appreciated against the dollar (see figure II.36), principally reflecting uncertainty about the recovery, and concern about the twin deficits, in the United States. The yen was also boosted by greater international confidence in Japan's economic outlook, while the New Zealand dollar has benefited from interest rates that are among the highest in the OECD countries. Concern about Australia's current account deficit and softening economic growth took some pressure off the Australian dollar in the second half of the year.

Figure II.34. Growth rates in merchandise export earnings of developed countries in the ESCAP region, 2001-2004

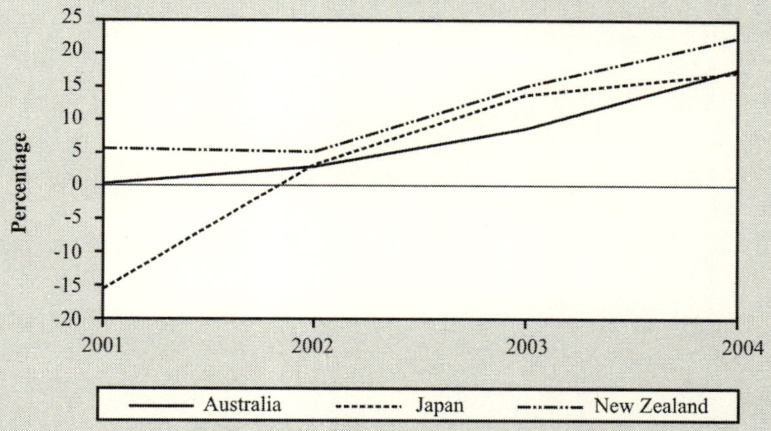

Source: IMF, *Direction of Trade Statistics* (CD-ROM), December 2004.

Note: Growth rate for 2004 refers to January-July 2004 compared with the corresponding period of 2003.

Figure II.35. Growth rates in merchandise import spending of developed countries in the ESCAP region, 2001-2004

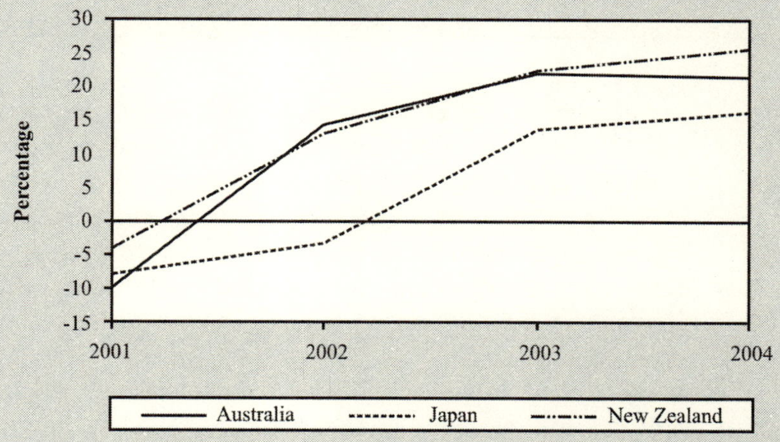

Source: IMF, *Direction of Trade Statistics* (CD-ROM), December 2004.

Note: Growth rate for 2004 refers to January-July 2004 compared with the corresponding period of 2003.

GDP performance and prospects

Has the Japanese economy really recovered?

Despite the revision of national accounts data by the Government in late 2004, in conjunction with the adoption of a different accounting methodology that cast doubt on the widespread view that the Japanese economy had finally recovered from close to a decade of near stagnation, economic growth clearly strengthened in 2003-2004 although there was some loss in momentum in the second half of 2004 (table II.39). GDP growth was 1.4 per cent in 2003, as compared with –0.3 per cent in 2002,

Table II.39. Developed countries of the ESCAP region: rates of economic growth and inflation, 2001-2004

(Percentage)

	2001	*2002*	*2003*	*2004*[a]
GDP growth rates				
Australia	2.5	3.9	3.0	3.5
Japan[b]	0.2	–0.3	1.4	2.6
New Zealand	2.6	4.5	3.3	4.8
Inflation[c]				
Australia	4.4	3.0	2.8	2.3
Japan	–0.7	–0.9	–0.3	0.0
New Zealand	2.6	2.7	1.8	2.3

Sources: ESCAP, based on national sources; Cabinet Office, Government of Japan, *Quarterly Estimate of GDP,* at web site <www.esri.cao.go.jp/jp/sna/qe044/rnen.html>, 17 February 2005; EIU, *Country Forecasts* (London, EIU, 2004 and 2005), various issues; and IMF, *International Financial Statistics,* vol. LVII, No. 8 (Washington, IMF, August 2004).

a Estimates.

b Calendar year basis.

c Percentage changes in the consumer price index.

and accelerated to 2.6 per cent in 2004 despite a slowdown in the second half of the year. The new data downgraded figures for the growth in business investment and private consumption in 2003 and 2004 (table II.40), indicating that the recovery was much weaker than previously reported. Nevertheless, there were growing signs that the export-led economic recovery had been gradually spreading to domestic demand growth although a surge in imports, owing partly to higher oil prices and strong demand for raw materials, and weaker private consumption, owing partly to bad weather, dampened economic activity in the latter part of 2004. Since mid-2003 prospects for improved economic performance have been reflected in the rising stock market, where significant inflows of portfolio investment from abroad have made a substantial contribution. During 2004, turnover reached levels that had not been seen since the late 1980s and the stock market peaked some 30 per cent higher than in 2002.

Table II.40. Developed countries of the ESCAP region: consumption and investment as a percentage of GDP, 2001-2004

(Percentage)

	2001	*2002*	*2003*	*2004*[a]
Consumption as a percentage of GDP				
Australia	77.6	77.9	78.0	77.3
Japan	73.6	74.7	74.5	74.3
New Zealand	76.0	76.9	76.9	76.1
Investment as a percentage of GDP				
Australia	21.8	23.7	24.6	24.6
Japan	25.8	24.2	23.9	23.6
New Zealand	19.5	20.2	21.5	22.9

Sources: ESCAP, based on Economic and Social Research Institute, Government of Japan, *Annual Revision of GDP (GDE) for 2003FY*, at web site <www.esri.cao.go.jp>, 17 January 2005; IMF, *International Financial Statistics,* vol. LVII, No. 8 (Washington, IMF, August 2004); and EIU, *Country Forecasts* (London, EIU, 2004 and 2005), various issues.

[a] Estimates.

The recovery of the Japanese economy was initially driven by strong export demand within the Asian and Pacific region, particularly from China. However, domestic demand, in particular business investment and private consumption, made more of a contribution to growth in 2004. With the gradual reduction in the fiscal stimulus in recent years, the Japanese economy appeared to be on track for a more durable recovery in 2004 than in previous upturns, although there were signs of a softening of consumer and business sentiment towards the end of the year as economic prospects became somewhat more uncertain. The unemployment rate has been declining, falling to 4.5 per cent in November 2004, its lowest level since January 1999, contributing to the improvement in consumer confidence and private consumption. However, this has been tempered by sluggish wage growth as a result of competitive pressures and cost-cutting in the corporate sector. Average monthly wages rose 0.4 per cent in November 2004, the third gain in 10 months and the sixth in 48 months. Nevertheless, the increasingly evident slowdown of the world economy towards the end of 2004 added to uncertainty about the sustainability of the economic recovery, as reflected in the deterioration of corporate sentiment. For the first time in almost two years, the *Tankan* survey of corporate sentiment by the Bank of Japan reported a deterioration in the diffusion index[3] of large manufacturers in October 2004, after it had recorded the highest level since 1991 6 months earlier, although there were signs of a recovery in the index in November.

[3] This measures the difference between the number of firms with optimistic views on the current situation and those with pessimistic views.

Deflationary pressures not entirely eradicated in Japan

Deflationary pressures continued to ease in Japan in 2004 (table II.39). With the narrowing of the output gap, producer prices were on the upward trend, although this was partly a reflection of higher prices of imported commodities such as oil and raw materials. However, despite recent economic growth, consumer price inflation did not move up to positive territory in 2004. Nevertheless, there were some signs of consumer price increases towards the end of the year, as seen in the positive growth of consumer and land prices in the Tokyo area. The slow response of consumer prices to the economic recovery is also partly due to competitive pressures in the markets for consumer products, where increases in commodity prices have not been passed on to consumers. Against this background, the Bank of Japan has given a clear direction with regard to monetary policy, indicating that the current easy-money policy stance will be maintained and ample liquidity will continue to be provided under the quantitative easing framework until deflation has been decisively defeated (table II.41). The recently revealed softness of the economic recovery is likely to reinforce this view.

Table II.41. Developed countries of the ESCAP region: short-term interest rates and money supply growth (M2), 2001-2004

(Percentage)

	2001	*2002*	*2003*	*2004[a]*
Short-term interest rates				
Australia	4.9	4.7	4.9	5.3
Japan	0.1	0.1	0.04	0.03
New Zealand	5.7	5.7	5.4	6.5
Money supply growth (M2)				
Australia	11.4	5.6	10.2	4.5[b]
Japan	2.2	3.4	1.8	3.5
New Zealand	14.7	8.0	4.1	1.2[c]

Sources: ESCAP, based on IMF, *International Financial Statistics,* vol. LVII, No. 10 (Washington, IMF, October 2004); and OECD, *Main Economic Indicators, November 2004,* at web site <http://www.oecd.org/dataoecd/>, 17 January 2005.

[a] Estimates.
[b] January-May.
[c] January-July.

Japan's fiscal position continued to pose a daunting challenge in 2004. While the economic recovery contributed to a slight contraction of the budget deficit, increased public expenditure, largely owing to rising welfare spending, offset higher tax revenues (table II.42) The deficit added to mounting government debt, which is thought to have reached 164 per cent of GDP by the end of 2004. Attempts at fiscal consolidation, such as a recent increase in contributions to the employee pension scheme and a planned reversal of the 1999 income tax cuts, risk dampening consumer confidence in the face of still modest economic growth and sluggish wages; consumer confidence fell in the fourth quarter of 2004 for the first time since the first quarter of 2003. Meanwhile, the Government is planning an overseas marketing mission in early 2005 to solicit additional buyers for the country's bonds, the first such mission in a century. About 60 per cent of the country's bonds are held by Japanese banks and insurance companies, including the postal and insurance systems run by the Government, and only 4 per cent are held by foreign investors, a much lower share than in other developed economies. However, Japan's bond ratings and yields remain low compared with other leading economies.

Table II.42. Developed countries of the ESCAP region: budget and current account balance as a percentage of GDP, 2001-2004

(Percentage)

	2001	*2002*	*2003*	*2004*[a]
Budget balance[b] as a percentage of GDP				
Australia[c]	0.9	1.0	1.2	0.7
Japan	−6.1	−7.9	−7.9	−7.8
New Zealand[d]	1.6	1.7	2.9	4.0
Current account balance as a percentage of GDP				
Australia	−2.4	−4.3	−6.0	−6.2
Japan	2.1	2.8	3.2	3.8
New Zealand	−2.4	−3.3	−4.3	−4.6

Sources: ESCAP, based on IMF, *International Financial Statistics*, vol. LVII, No. 8 (Washington, IMF, August 2004) and *World Economic Outlook: The Global Demographic Transition* (Washington, IMF, September 2004); and EIU, *Country Forecasts* (London, EIU, 2004 and 2005), various issues.

[a] Estimates.
[b] General government fiscal balance.
[c] Data exclude net advances (primarily privatization receipts and net policy-related lending).
[d] Government balance is revenue minus expenditure plus balance of State-owned enterprises, excluding privatization receipts.

Within the financial sector, there is a growing feeling that the worst of the non-performing loan issue is over and profits at most of the major banks returned to positive territory in 2004. However, near-zero nominal interest rates (table II.41) have not succeeded in stimulating credit growth in the economy. Bank loans continued to decline in 2004, although the *Tankan* survey has indicated that corporate sentiment with regard to the availability of credit in the financial sector improved slightly in recent years.

Weak domestic demand continues to undermine sustainability of growth in Japan

There remain several concerns over the sustainability of the economic recovery in Japan. The strength of the Japanese economy continues to rest largely upon foreign demand, in particular from the United States, China and other East Asian countries. Signs of a slower pace of growth in those economies, together with the movement of oil prices into a higher range, add to the uncertainty of the recovery. The sustainability of domestic demand relies on strengthening consumer and business confidence mostly through improved corporate profits, employment and wages. As indicated earlier, confidence may evaporate if wage growth remains sluggish, encouraging consumers to increase precautionary savings and thus further undermining growth in private consumption expenditures. There is also the risk that private investment could diminish in response to slowing external demand. Current forecasts suggest that GDP growth will weaken significantly in 2005 to 1.5 per cent and that growth will be somewhat lower than this in 2006-2007. The rate of inflation is expected to be just barely positive in 2005, picking up somewhat thereafter.

Continued strong economic performance in Australia

The Australian economy benefited from a favourable external environment and higher commodity prices in the first half of 2004, maintaining a solid rate of economic growth and low inflation, although it slowed down towards the end of the year reflecting capacity constraints. The growth rate is projected to have increased to 3.5 per cent in 2004 from 3.0 per cent in 2003. The expansion of economic activity was broad-based, driven also by domestic demand growth. Strong household consumption and private investment were underpinned by a supportive financial environment, as well as employment and income growth, high levels of household wealth backed by increasing housing prices and stock market gains, and strong consumer confidence. Despite the appreciation of the Australian dollar against most major currencies, export growth was driven by strong global demand, leading to increased corporate profits, which, together with increased capacity utilization, provided an incentive for business investment on the one hand and contributed to the growth of employment on the other. The unemployment rate declined to 5.1 per cent in the fourth quarter of 2004, its lowest level in 27 years. However, the direct contribution of net exports to growth has been limited owing to the currency appreciation and much stronger import growth. Reflecting the housing boom, property and business services and construction grew strongly in 2004 while the performance of the manufacturing sector, which has been weak since late 2003, deteriorated in the second half of 2004, contracting in the third quarter.

The rate of inflation continued to decline in 2004, reaching 2.3 per cent, within the 1-3 per cent target band of the Reserve Bank of Australia, but with divergent trends in the prices of non-tradables and tradables. Appreciation of the Australian dollar dampened import prices and, thus, tradables inflation. It also cushioned the impact of the oil price hike that started in 2002, keeping the annual average oil price in the first half of 2004 some 7 per cent below the average in 2003. However, strong demand growth raised the prices of non-tradables, although supply constraints, indicated by high levels of capacity utilization and the low unemployment rate, were somewhat offset by constrained wage growth and improvements in labour productivity.

House price boom in Australia may have passed its peak

Subdued inflation led the central bank to keep interest rates on hold at 5.3 per cent during 2004. As the boom in the housing market appears to have passed its peak, there seems to be no pressing need for a rise in interest rates in the short term. However, the rate of inflation is projected to increase to 3 per cent in 2005, at the top end of the Reserve Bank's target range, before falling back in 2006. The strong expansion of consumer credit, record low unemployment, fiscal easing and fading disinflationary pressure from a stronger exchange rate could point to a tightening of monetary policy in the medium term if inflationary pressures are stronger than expected, which would have to be balanced against the possible impact of higher interest rates on highly indebted households.

Australia's fiscal position remained strong for the year to end-June 2004. During the year, the underlying cash surplus reached $A 8.0 billion, or 1.0 per cent of GDP. The surpluses are projected to continue in the near future, in stark contrast to Japan and other OECD countries, many of which have significant fiscal deficits. The surplus is largely the result of higher corporate tax revenue flowing from the gain in corporate profits supported by high export prices. The revenue increase more than offset the increase in expenditure owing to the Government's election commitments and additional policy measures announced since the 2004 budget, such as tax cuts for high and middle income earners and extra spending on family assistance, health care and education.

Economic growth is expected to moderate in coming years with domestic demand expected to slow, as business investment eases and housing demand unwinds, and export growth returns to more modest levels reflecting slower world economic growth. Economic growth is expected to slow to 3.0 per cent in the next two years, with inflation gradually edging up towards 3.0 per cent, the upper limit of the inflation target range. A weaker growth rate and contraction of residential and business investment in the third quarter of 2004 already indicated a deceleration of the economy. The trend of economic slowdown was even stronger in the fourth quarter. The reported drop in exports in November also implies a loss in competitiveness owing to the strong Australian dollar. Furthermore, given the importance of property investment in GDP growth in Australia since 1999, the peaking of the real estate boom will dampen new investment in property, with knock-on effects on the consumption of property-related consumer goods.

Vigorous growth continued in New Zealand, sustained by domestic demand growth

The economy of New Zealand, which has outperformed the OECD average over the past five years, continued to grow vigorously at a rate of 4.8 per cent in 2004, above the 3.3 per cent recorded in 2003. The strong growth, driven primarily by domestic demand growth and household consumption, has been fuelled by rising household wealth as a low interest rate environment contributed to a strong property market. The housing market remained robust in 2004, although there were growing signs that the boom had passed its peak with house price inflation beginning to slow at the end of 2003. Strong export growth despite the appreciation of the New Zealand dollar was outweighed by exceptionally strong imports, leaving the contribution of net exports to GDP growth in negative territory.

The strength of domestic demand has been buoyed recently by consistent inward migration and the ensuing higher domestic investment, such as in residential construction, has led to a significant rise in job opportunities. In fact, strong employment growth in construction led to the unemployment rate falling to 3.8 per cent in the third quarter of 2004, a 17-year low. Employment growth increased consumer confidence and, thus, consumer spending, while the tightening of the labour market has put increased upward pressure on wages, most noticeably in the property and business sectors. Increasing capacity utilization has stimulated business investment, which has been reflected in higher capital goods imports to take advantage of the stronger currency. On the supply side, the construction sector led the strong growth, driven by the continued boom in housing, in the first half of 2004 but the manufacturing sector decelerated in the same period as the demand for manufactured goods was met from inventories.

The rate of inflation in New Zealand remained within the Reserve Bank of New Zealand's target range of 1 to 3 per cent in 2004. However, as was the case in Australia, the subdued inflation rate masks a significant divergence among the major components of consumer price inflation. Non-tradables inflation has been accelerating in recent years, reaching a rate close to 5 per cent in late 2003, reflecting strong domestic demand and housing cost increases. Housing prices recorded an increase of nearly 25 per cent year on year in July 2004 and, although there has been some deceleration since, the rate of increase was over 15 per cent in October. In stark contrast, there was a deflation in the prices of tradables in 2003 and the first half of 2004 owing to the sizeable appreciation of the New Zealand dollar, offsetting the strong growth in non-tradables prices and leading to subdued consumer price inflation.

The continued strength of domestic demand and growing evidence of capacity constraints, reflected in the historically low unemployment rate, led the central bank to turn to monetary tightening and the official cash rate was raised six times, from 5.0 to 6.5 per cent, commencing in January 2004. The full impact of the monetary tightening is likely to be felt in coming years, in particular in the housing market and on consumer spending.

Buoyant New Zealand tax revenues contribute to widening budget surplus

Budget surpluses have been rising as a percentage of GDP in New Zealand, and the surplus for the fiscal year ending in June 2004, at 4 per cent of GDP, was considerably higher than the budget estimate. The results for 2003/04 reflected higher than expected tax revenues, particularly from the goods and services tax as a result of buoyant consumer spending. Robust growth in employment and corporate profits, as well as the improved performance of SOEs, also contributed to higher revenues. The Government expects to reduce its debt at a slightly faster pace than projected earlier owing to the increased surplus. The current ratio of government debt to GDP of over 25 per cent in 2003/04 is expected to fall to 20 per cent by 2007/08. The surplus is likely to ease in coming years as a result of slower GDP growth and higher planned expenditures.

The economy of New Zealand is forecast to expand at a slower pace in coming years as private consumption slows sharply owing to weaker income growth. Higher interest rates and decelerating migrant flows are likely to lead to a fall in housing demand. In addition, the increase in the debt burden of households as a result of mortgage borrowing in the past few years will also contribute to the expected deceleration in private consumption as households try to improve their net asset positions. However, higher business investment in response to resource constraints and growth in government expenditure will prevent the economy from slowing too sharply. Economic growth is expected to slow to 2.7 per cent in 2005, remaining close to that rate in 2006-2007, while the rate of inflation is expected to accelerate to 3.0 per cent in 2005 before slowing somewhat.

Trade, exchange rate and capital flows

Strong momentum of regional trade, with widening current account imbalance

East and South-East Asian nations, particularly China, have increasingly become important trading partners for Japan, accounting for over 40 per cent of both the country's exports and its imports. In particular, China's share of Japan's exports rose from 5 per cent in 1998 to almost 20 per cent in 2003 as a result of annual double-digit growth in exports. China is now second only to the United States in its importance as a destination for Japanese exports, while it has overtaken the United States as the most important source for imports, supplying one quarter of Japanese imports in 2003.

Largely owing to strong demand from trade partners within the Asia and Pacific region, the growth in the value of merchandise exports from Japan accelerated to 13.7 per cent in 2003 and further to 17.2 per cent in the first half of 2004 after a small recovery in 2002 following the 15.6 per cent plunge during the global slowdown in 2001 (table II.43). Exports to East and South-East Asian countries grew almost 20 per cent in 2003,

Table II.43. Developed countries of the ESCAP region: merchandise exports and their rates of growth, 2001-2004

	Exports (f.o.b.)				
	Value (millions of US dollars)	Annual rate of growth (percentage)			
	2003	2001	2002	2003	2004[a]
Australia	70 793	0.4	2.8	8.6	17.7
Japan	473 911	−15.6	3.3	13.7	17.2
New Zealand	16 271	5.8	5.2	15.0	22.4

Source: IMF, *Direction of Trade Statistics* (CD-ROM), December 2004.

[a] Growth rate of January-July 2004 compared with the corresponding period of 2003.

while the growth in exports to China was a massive 41 per cent. Growth in the value of merchandise imports was also sustained in the first half of 2004 at 16.3 per cent, after expanding 13.6 per cent in 2003 following two consecutive years of decline (table II.44). This was partly a reflection of higher oil prices, which inflated the value of crude oil imports by 30 per cent. Japan's current account surplus widened from 3.2 per cent of GDP in 2003 to 3.8 per cent in 2004 (table II.42) as the higher trade surplus offset the services deficit and the income surplus increased in the wake of greater inflows of portfolio investment from abroad.

Table II.44. Developed countries of the ESCAP region: merchandise imports and their rates of growth, 2001-2004

	Imports (c.i.f.)				
	Value (millions of US dollars)	Annual rate of growth (percentage)			
	2003	2001	2002	2003	2004[a]
Australia	93 202	−10.0	14.4	21.8	21.5
Japan	383 025	−8.0	−3.4	13.6	16.3
New Zealand	18 466	−4.3	13.0	22.3	25.7

Source: IMF, *Direction of Trade Statistics* (CD-ROM), December 2004.

[a] Growth rate of January-July 2004 compared with the corresponding period of 2003.

Capacity constraints hampered non-rural commodity exports from Australia

Notwithstanding the acceleration in the value of merchandise export growth to 17.7 per cent in the first half of 2004, more than double the 8.6 per cent growth in 2003, Australia's trade performance has been affected by the appreciation of its currency and supply constraints on the production side. The severe drought of 2002 constrained exports of agricultural products, which were limited by the need to rebuild stocks at the expense of increases in output. Capacity constraints in Australia hampered non-rural commodity exports somewhat, preventing a fuller response to strong world demand and higher commodity prices, while the firmer exchange rate affected export earnings. However, the strong currency boosted domestic demand for imported capital and consumer goods and the value of merchandise imports expanded at rates above 21 per cent in 2003 and the first half of 2004, widening the trade deficit significantly.

The current account deficit is estimated at 6.2 per cent of GDP in 2004 in Australia, widen from 2003, reflecting the trade deficit as well as the deficit on the income account that is the result of outflows of investment income, rising debt-service costs and the low domestic savings rate. The continuing deficit raises concerns about the persistently high level of net external debt, which worsened from around 40 per cent of GDP in 1998 to over 49.2 per cent in the third quarter of 2004. The negative trend increased the cost of debt servicing, rendering reduction in external debt more intractable, although the debt is concentrated in the private sector and the currency risk is well managed.

New Zealand is a highly trade-dependent economy, with both exports and imports of goods and services amounting to over one third of GDP. The country's three major trading partners, namely, Australia, the United States and Japan, account for almost half of all trade. The sizeable appreciation of the New Zealand dollar has had a significant impact on trade performance. So far, the impact on exports has been cushioned as exporters are becoming more adept at managing currency fluctuations. It is noteworthy that recent surveys of manufactured goods exporters indicated that despite the currency appreciation they had not reduced export activities, unlike during the last peak in the exchange cycle in the mid-1990s. Nevertheless, continued strength of the currency will erode export competitiveness in coming years as hedging arrangements eventually unwind.

The growth in the value of merchandise exports continued to accelerate to 22.4 per cent in the first half of 2004 following the sharp acceleration to 15 per cent growth in 2003, reflecting strong overseas demand and higher commodity prices. Growth in the value of merchandise imports was also exceptionally strong at 22.3 per cent in 2003 and

25.7 per cent in the first half of 2004, as vigorous domestic demand was further stimulated by currency appreciation and oil prices surged. The trade deficit widened as a result of faster import growth in 2004.

As in Australia, the deficit on the income account has been increasing in recent years in New Zealand

New Zealand's current account deficit in 2004, at an estimated 4.6 per cent of GDP, was similar to the level in 2003. In addition to the deficit on trade, the major contributor to the current account deficit was the deficit in the income account, which has increased in recent years for much the same reasons as in Australia. With higher interest rates and rising external debt, the negative trend in the income account is expected to widen in coming years.

Uncertainty over the sustainability of the economic recovery in the United States and the high current account and budget deficits in that country resulted in the currencies of all three developed countries in Asia and Pacific appreciating against the United States dollar (figure II.36). The appreciation was particularly significant in Australia and New Zealand, where the interest rate differential with the United States is positive.

Figure II.36. Index of exchange rates against the United States dollar of developed countries in the ESCAP region, 1996-2004

(1996 = 100)

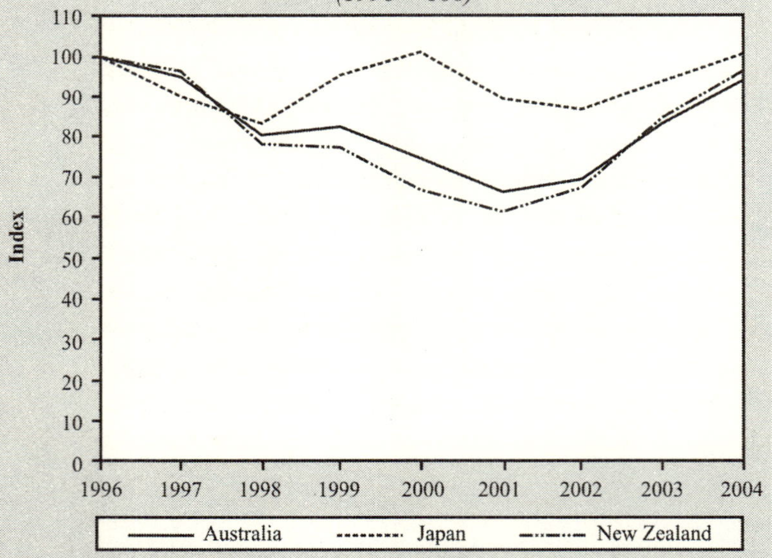

Sources: IMF, *International Financial Statistics*, vol. LVII, No. 10 (Washington, IMF, October 2004); and *The Economist*, various issues.

Note: Figures for 2004 are estimates.

Key policy issues

Japan's structural reform plans moving ahead

The Government of Japan continued to push ahead with a series of structural reform programmes in 2004. However, the interlocking issues of sustainable economic growth, fiscal consolidation and financial sector stability pose daunting challenges for the Government in its efforts to press ahead with reform plans and pursue effective policies to address any one of these issues without jeopardizing the others.

The controversial privatization plan for Japan Post, which is to be finalized during 2005, is one of the major reform plans to which the Government is committed. Under the plan, Japan Post will be divided up into four operations under a State-owned holding company, with the privatization process to be completed by 2007. The economic implications of the privatization are potentially substantial, as the mammoth public institution transforms itself into a private entity and its business operations and flow of financial assets are governed more or less in line with market principles. The potential impacts range from a change in the nation's massive flow of savings; uncertainty as to the future availability of a buyer for government bonds; the entry of a disproportionately large semi-private entity into hitherto competitive markets; and concerns over adverse effects on consumers in economically disadvantaged areas. The privatization plan faces enormous challenges in its implementation in the face of fierce opposition. Some of these challenges are examined in box II.5.

In pursuing reform of the financial system, the Government launched the Programme for Further Financial Reform, which is to be operational in 2005, signalling a shift from emergency measures designed to prevent a systemic crisis towards modernizing and internationalizing the financial system. The launch of the new plan follows an earlier plan, launched in April 2002, which attempted to reduce the bulk of NPLs held by major banks in two years. With a growing sense of relief as most major banks reported significant reductions in NPLs, in the new plan the Government turns its attention to other priorities, such as stabilizing and strengthening regional banks and improving transparency, corporate governance and official supervision, particularly in view of the planned removal of the remaining blanket deposit insurance scheduled for April 2005. However, the new plan is being launched while the basic structure of the system is likely to face fundamental changes owing to the proposed privatization of Japan Post and when the concept of internationalizing the yen is being revisited. Pursuing these objectives in tandem will pose yet another challenge for the Government.

Box II.5. Economic implications of privatizing Japan Post

In 2004, the Japanese Cabinet approved a controversial plan to privatize Japan Post, with enabling legislation to be introduced in March 2005. However, the Government faces enormous challenges in formulating meaningful legislation in the face of fierce opposition to the privatization plan. Difficulties also lie in ensuring that the transition process is completed with minimum upheaval, given the extent of conflicting interests between various segments of society, including consumers, the financial sector, the public sector and, not least, Japan Post itself.

Background

Japan Post is a relatively recent creation that came into existence in 2003 to replace the post office following the restructuring of government ministries that took place in 2001. Although it is meant to be a profit-seeking enterprise, Japan Post is still a public entity with many privileges such as tax exemptions. At present, it has three main businesses, postal services, savings and life insurance, and is a mammoth institution with nearly 25,000 branches across the country[a] and 271,000 employees, about one quarter of the nation's civil servants. The nationwide network of branches and its public status with tax-free privileges have enabled Japan Post to become the custodian of around one quarter of Japan's personal financial assets.[b] However, each business has its own problems. The chronically loss-making postal service operation used to be subsidized by the savings and life insurance operations. The funds collected by the savings and life insurance businesses are directly and indirectly channelled to government projects or semi-government institutions and it is obligatory that a portion be invested in government bonds. While the reform of the Fiscal Investment and Loan Programme (FILP) in 2001 gave the business greater freedom and responsibility in fund management, so far changes have been somewhat limited. A substantial reduction in the direct financing of public sector projects was compensated by an increase in the holdings of public sector bonds, resulting in only a modest change in the flow of funds to the private sector. Criticism that the postal system distorts domestic capital flows in favour of public investment that is often inefficient continues.

Reform plans

Under the basic plan for privatization approved by the Cabinet in September 2004, Japan Post will be divided into four separate businesses under a single holding company, namely, mail delivery, management of post offices, savings deposits and life insurance, and employees will lose their status as civil servants. Privatization will then begin over a 10-year period starting in April 2007. The postal savings and life insurance businesses are to be sold off completely and the remaining businesses will be partially privatized.

The Government argues that the public will benefit from the proposed privatization in several ways. First, the quality of services should improve as a result of greater managerial and operating freedom in all four businesses. Second, the hidden burden borne by taxpayers as a result of the indirect financial support, such as tax breaks, given to the postal business will be removed. Finally, a large part of Japan's substantial domestic savings will be redirected from public sector investment to the private sector, so fostering economic growth.

For those benefits to materialize, the Government's basic privatization plan placed strong emphasis on the following:

- A relaxation in restrictions on the current postal business, providing greater opportunities for expanding the scope of its operations;
- Creating a level playing field for all competitors, with the postal savings and life insurance businesses coming under the same regulatory authority as private sector companies, as well as the removal of tax exemptions and government guarantees for new contracts, among other things;[c]

---

[a] Yomiuri On-Line at <http://www.yomiuri.co.jp/atmoney/special/47/naruhodo175.htm>, 29 September 2004; and *Financial Times*, 9 November 2004.

[b] *The Economist*, 2 September 2004; and *Financial Times*, loc.cit.

[c] The postal savings business, which is no longer under government guarantee, will also have to pay deposit insurance premiums like any other bank. Similarly, the life insurance business will have to pay into the insurance industry's policyholder-protection fund.

- Greater transparency in the operations of each business and the removal of cross-subsidies among the four operations.

Implications for the economy

The economic implications of the privatization could be substantial, as the mammoth public institution transforms itself into a private entity and its business operations and the flow of financial assets held by it are governed more or less in line with market principles. First of all, there are various issues related to the transformation of a disproportionately large, semi-private entity into a profit-oriented business. For the private sector, the entry of a huge, government-backed business with various privileges, nationwide networks and infrastructure into markets that are already highly competitive is clearly threatening. In the mail delivery service, in addition to the privileges given to an official mail delivery institution, Japan Post can take advantage of the cross-subsidized pricing structure established under the universal services principle rather than commercial viability. In financial services, Japan Post is regarded as being "too big to fail", suggesting the continuation of an implicit government guarantee should problems arise in the future. With its nationwide network of branches and around 227 trillion yen in savings deposits, the postal savings business dwarfs even the biggest private bank in Japan.[d] Total private deposits in all major banks amounted to only about one half of those held by Japan Post[e] and none of those banks has more than 600 branches. The dominance of Japan Post is also true in the life insurance sector, where it has a 40 per cent share of the country's total household life insurance assets. Thus, the private sector continues to have strong doubts on how level the playing field will actually be and, in particular, how to ensure that cross-subsidies among the various businesses of Japan Post will in fact be removed.

Second, for Japan Post itself, profitability as the new criterion for survival will be a daunting challenge after the removal of government protection and disallowance of cross-subsidies, given the uncertainties surrounding its operations. How profitable existing and new businesses will be is unclear, while operating costs are sure to rise as a result of new financial burdens such as taxes and deposit insurance payments. Once the savings and insurance businesses are transformed into private financial institutions, they will be subject to a new set of regulations, possibly including meeting international financial standards, which they have never had to face before. Moreover, management flexibility will be limited as the mandate to provide an acceptable standard of service nationwide will continue, so that some loss-making operations will have to be maintained. It may also prove difficult to reduce the number of employees given the size of Japan Post as an employer. Similarly, there is limited scope, at least for the time being, for autonomous decision-making with regard to the current semi-obligatory investment in government bonds and public entities. Customers of Japan Post are also concerned that the provision of universal services may be overruled by market considerations for the sake of profits, to the detriment of economically disadvantaged areas.

Third, whether funds will be effectively redirected to the private sector is still unclear although it is one of the major aims of this reform. As mentioned earlier, the reform of FILP did not lead to a dramatic change in the flow of funds. Furthermore, with the savings and life insurance businesses together holding about one quarter of the total national bonds outstanding, the magnitude of the potential loss from any rise in interest rates becomes increasingly significant with the accumulation of national debt. Yet portfolio decisions are governed not only by profitability considerations but also by an assessment of the impact on the financial markets. While the Government's mid-term strategy is to encourage foreign and domestic private investors to absorb Japanese government bonds as a precursor to postal savings and life insurance institutions that are fully privatized, those institutions would remain the major holders of national bonds for the time being.

Despite widespread opposition in the country, the Government is committed to finalizing the Japan Post privatization plan in early 2005. The current plan suggests potentially significant changes in the structures of the financial and postal delivery markets, as well as in financial flows in the economy. The challenge is to strike a balance between the somewhat conflicting interests of the various parties and still bring about meaningful change.

---

[d] *The Economist*, 2 September 2004.

[e] Japanese Bankers Association, at <http://www.morebank.gr.jp/category_a/02084_genjo84.html>, January 2005. This refers to the situation as at September 2000.

Issues of macroeconomic management in Australia

The Australian economy's sound economic growth over the previous decade is attributed to the transparent and effective monetary and fiscal policy frameworks, healthy public finances and the Government's commitment to carry forward its pro-growth strategy. However, the persistent current account deficit and high level of household debt, estimated at 140 per cent of disposable income in 2003, continue to be potential vulnerabilities in the Australian economy, in particular in the face of recent currency fluctuations. Given the importance of trade in the country's economic activities, monetary policies to balance the needs of the domestic economy and of the external sector against a background of uncertainty are particularly challenging. An increase in interest rates in the near future may be inevitable if the cooling in the housing market remains short-lived, but this will strengthen the currency further and affect exports adversely. Economic data released late in 2004 illustrated this challenge as the pace of domestic demand slackened while the trade deficit widened to its second highest level on record, reflecting a sharp slowdown in exports as a result of currency appreciation and weak overseas demand.

Preparing for an ageing society

Macroeconomic fundamentals remain sound in New Zealand as in Australia. Growth has been fairly strong for a number of years, thanks to a wide-ranging programme of structural reforms initiated more than 20 years ago. Like other industrial countries, New Zealand is not free from significant spending pressures owing to the ageing of its population and attendant rising health-care costs, although the issue is not as imminent as in Japan, allowing the Government to consider these issues over a longer time frame. The New Zealand Superannuation Fund scheme was established to partially pre-fund future pension liabilities. In the longer term, the Government needs to achieve budgetary operating surpluses over the course of the economic cycle sufficient to meet contributions to the Fund, while reducing gross debt and meeting capital spending requirements. The Fund, which is estimated to amount to 4.4 per cent of GDP in the 2004/05 budget, is expected to reach 40 per cent of GDP over the next 20 years. Yet various uncertainties in demographic and economic conditions leave the future possibility of the need for additional measures to contend fully with the long-term fiscal challenges, including further changes in the structural parameters of the pension and health-care systems. Moreover, the accumulation of assets on such a scale poses a challenge to prudent fund management in terms of achieving reasonable average annual and long-term returns without taking on excessive risk, while minimizing the impact on macroeconomic conditions.

III DYNAMICS OF POPULATION AGEING: HOW CAN ASIA AND THE PACIFIC RESPOND?

INTRODUCTION

Ageing, one of the most distinctive demographic events

Population ageing, the process by which older individuals form a proportionately larger share of the total population, was one of the most distinctive demographic events of the late twentieth century.[1] This phenomenon is equally reflective of the Asian and Pacific region despite diverse trends of ageing. The diversity of demographic transition in the region is reflected in having three distinctive sets of countries in relation to population ageing: countries or areas (such as Japan) whose population has already aged; those (such as Armenia, Georgia, Hong Kong, China, Macao, China, the Russian Federation and Singapore) whose population is likely to age very rapidly in the near future; and those (such as Bangladesh, India, Indonesia, Malaysia and Pakistan) whose population is still young and ageing slowly or moderately (table III.1).

Increasing intensity of ageing

The intensity of ageing in the Asian and Pacific region is bound to increase at a faster rate in the next 50 years with the share of population over 60 years of age more than doubling from 9.4 per cent of the total population in 2000 to an estimated 23.5 per cent by 2050.[2] As such, how Governments respond to the challenges now would be a deciding factor in the well-being of not only the current young and the elderly but also future generations. The diversity in the ageing experience in the region would require different policy responses in each set of countries depending on their current and expected levels of ageing and institutional settings. For example, policy responses in developing countries with large informal sectors would be more complex than with those having dominant formal sectors, where statutory provisions for pensions, provident funds and other forms of savings can exist.

---

1 "Older persons" are defined as the population aged 60 years and over. This definition used by the United Nations is consistent with the retirement age of most countries in Asia and the Pacific.

2 *World Population Ageing 1950-2050* (United Nations publication, Sales No. E.02.XIII.3).

Table III.1. Diversity of the demographic characteristics in the region

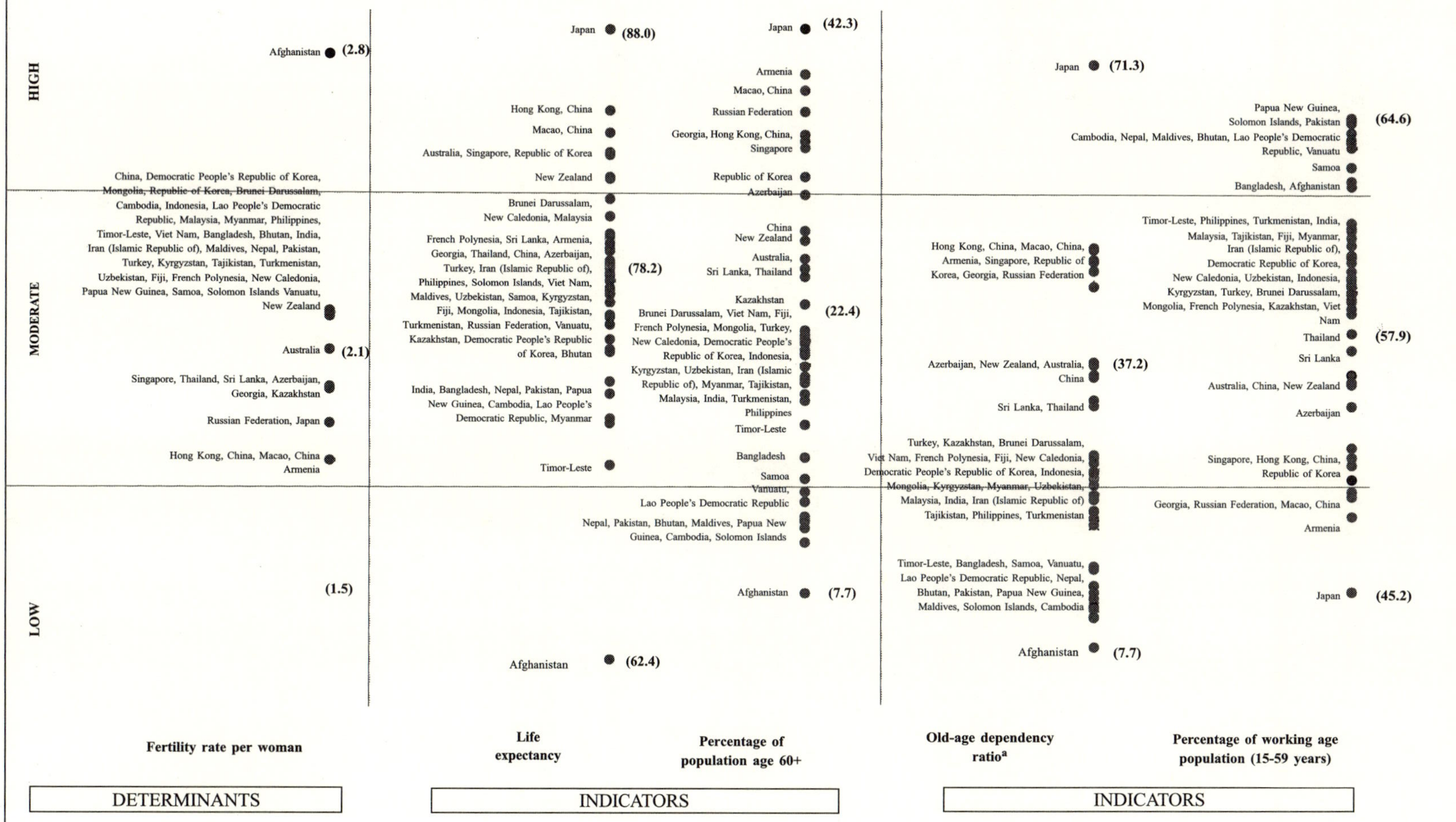

Source: *World Population Ageing 1950-2050* (United Nations publications, Sales No. E.02.XIII.3).

[a] The number of persons 65 years and over per 100 persons 15-64 years.

Countries under pressure to devise innovative mechanisms to handle ageing ...

Governments could be increasingly under pressure not only to devise innovative mechanisms to deal with issues arising from an ageing population but also to undertake market reforms and policy coordination to ensure the long-term viability of social welfare programmes while minimizing the negative effects on the economy. A clear objective is to prevent old age poverty. Handling ageing in the context of the already existing high levels of poverty across age groups will be a challenge and a daunting task. At the same time, for least developed countries with a low level of savings in relation to investment requirements, ageing poses special difficulties.

... but the problem not insurmountable if proper action taken in time

The fact that ageing is not a transitional issue makes it essential to respond to the ageing process in time. The ability to anticipate the demographic transition with a fairly high degree of accuracy provides countries with ample room to better prepare for the challenges posed by ageing and makes it a surmountable problem provided that proper action is taken in time. As different countries have different levels of economic development, market mechanisms, incentive structures and cultures, it is necessary for each country to evaluate the trade-offs of different policy options with the overall objective of improving individual welfare across the age cycle. A package of policies and incentives for countries whose population is already ageing, or likely to age in the near future, would include:

- Boosting labour supply through fine-tuning migration policy and population policy taking into account the complexities involved and expanding women's participation in the labour market
- Increasing labour productivity through technological innovations, capacity-building and training or retraining
- Changing the incentive structure to alter savings and investment behaviour
- Carrying out market reforms, including pension reforms, that ensure a minimum standard of living for the elderly and improved individual welfare
- Bringing about attitudinal change, particularly relating to opportunities for employment in old age, and providing a climate of acceptance to facilitate the integration of older people into mainstream development
- Safeguarding family values in the care of the elderly through incentives while providing institutional care for them in the light of changing family structures

Time-bound opportunity for some countries to reap the "demographic dividend"

Responding to ageing in advance would enable countries to reap the "demographic dividend" produced by reduced fertility rates.[3] It would also give countries where the population is still young a time-bound opportunity to capitalize on their demographic conditions and benefit from ageing in other countries by making productive use of their young labour force. However, benefiting from the demographic dividend would also require appropriate policies to be in place. The major policy areas needing particular attention are an enabling environment that ensures macro stability and at the same time provides opportunities for human development; educational reforms; market reforms, including savings generation and sustainability of pension schemes; labour market reforms to improve productivity and mobility; and the provision of social security to the poor.

Holistic approach needed to respond to ageing

Countries in Asia and the Pacific could learn from other ageing societies both within and outside the region as to how they have responded to emerging health issues, care of the elderly and social security requirements, as well as policies such as those covering labour and capital markets, government budgets and human migration. In this regard, seeing how countries such as Japan and Germany are coping with ageing while maintaining a high level of economic prosperity, including social welfare, would provide important lessons for other countries. Australia's strategic approach to older persons and community care, the United States migration policy to stabilize the working-age population and Chile's pension reforms provide good examples of policy responses to issues relating to ageing. The Australian response to population ageing underscores the need for a holistic approach to ageing with a focus not only on care for the elderly but also on planning retirement, participation in the workforce and staying healthy. An important lesson from the Australian experience is the need for responses to be proactive and forward-looking, with flexibility to change as necessary.

Labour as a regional public good!

Addressing issues arising from ageing goes beyond national boundaries as ageing may lead to increasing levels of human migration in the next few decades. How labour issues are treated in a global or regional context would be a key factor not only in making productive use of excess labour in some countries by allowing people to migrate to countries with a shortage of labour but also in containing the destabilizing effects of uncontrolled emigration on labour markets in labour-exporting developing countries. The increasing interdependency of labour markets in a regional context would imply that it is an opportune time for treating labour as a regional public good. These complexities call not only for bilateral and regional cooperation for the orderly use of labour but also for

---

[3] For example, the East Asian "economic miracle" shows how reduced fertility can help to create conditions for robust economic growth (see D. Bloom, D. Canning and J. Sevilla, *The Demographic Dividend: A New Perspective on the Economic Consequences of Population Change* (RAND, 2002), <http://www.rand.org/publications/MR/MR1274/>).

a fresh look at the existing global frameworks, such as Mode 4 of the WTO General Agreement on Trade in Services, to widen the scope of such initiatives for human migration, just as in the case of trade in services.

The objective of this chapter is to analyse the dynamics of population ageing in the Asian and Pacific region giving particular attention to considering the socio-economic implications of ageing and the policy responses required to face the current and future challenges posed by the demographic changes.

POPULATION DYNAMICS

More than half of the world's older population live in Asia and the Pacific and the share will continue to increase in the next 50 years

The dynamics of population ageing differs from country to country depending on the level of economic and social development as well as the policies adopted in the past. Population ageing has taken place at a rapid rate in the Asian and Pacific region during the past 50 years and is likely to continue at a faster pace during the next 50 (figure III.1). The region is already home to more than half of the world's older persons and its share will continue to increase in the next 50 years. Further, population dynamics have created several gender-related issues which could worsen the welfare situation, particularly of women.

Determinants of population ageing

The demographic transition witnessed in the Asian and Pacific region is underlined by declines in mortality and fertility rates, mainly owing to improved health conditions and family planning, respectively.

Figure III.1. Proportion of population aged 60 and over

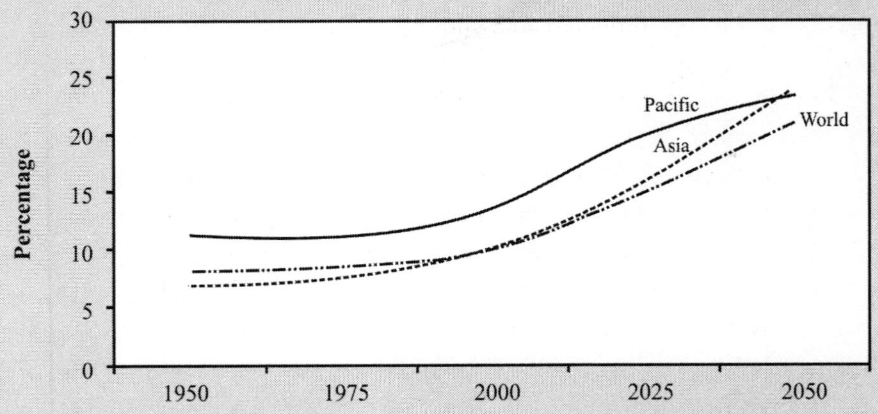

Source: World Population Ageing 1950-2050 (United Nations publication, Sales No. E.02.XIII.3).

Decline in mortality

Declining mortality a key determinant

The decline in the mortality rate has been the main trigger at the initial stage of demographic transition. Advances in the medical field and improved access to health services have led to a sharp reduction in infant mortality along with maternal and adult mortality. Aggressive campaigns to control infectious diseases such as malaria and tuberculosis, along with the successful control of frequent epidemics of smallpox, cholera and yellow fever, contributed positively to improvements in the mortality rate as early as the 1920s. For example, the mortality rate fell sharply in Sri Lanka when public health programmes and campaigns for sanitation were undertaken, particularly to eradicate malaria, which led to an increase in life expectancy by 14 years between 1947 and 1954.[4] Similar trends were seen in countries such as India and Pakistan after the Second World War.

Table III.2. Changes in infant mortality rate and total fertility rate in developing countries

	1950-1975	*1975-2000*	*2000-2025*
Infant mortality rate (percentage)	−58	−41	−42
Total fertility rate (percentage)	−27	−29	−27

Source: *World Population Ageing 1950-2050* (United Nations publication, Sales No. E.02.XIII.3).

Life expectancy in Asia and the Pacific remains high ...

As reflected in table III.2, the decline in the mortality rate has been a common feature in developing countries. For example, the infant mortality rate declined by 58 per cent in the period 1950-1975 and by a further 41 per cent in 1975-2000 in developing countries. This trend is expected to continue in the next quarter of a century. Reflecting these improvements in the mortality rate, life expectancy increased by 26 years, or 63 per cent, to 67.4 years in Asia and by 13.5 years, or 22 per cent, to 74.4 years in the Pacific during the last half century. As shown in figure III.2, life expectancy in the Asian and Pacific region stood above the world average, while it had been below the world average 50 years before.

[4] M. Cosio-Zavala, "Demographic transition and social development in low-income countries", in *Population Growth and Demographic Structure* (United Nations publication, Sales No. E.99.XIII.7).

Figure III.2. Life expectancy and fertility trends

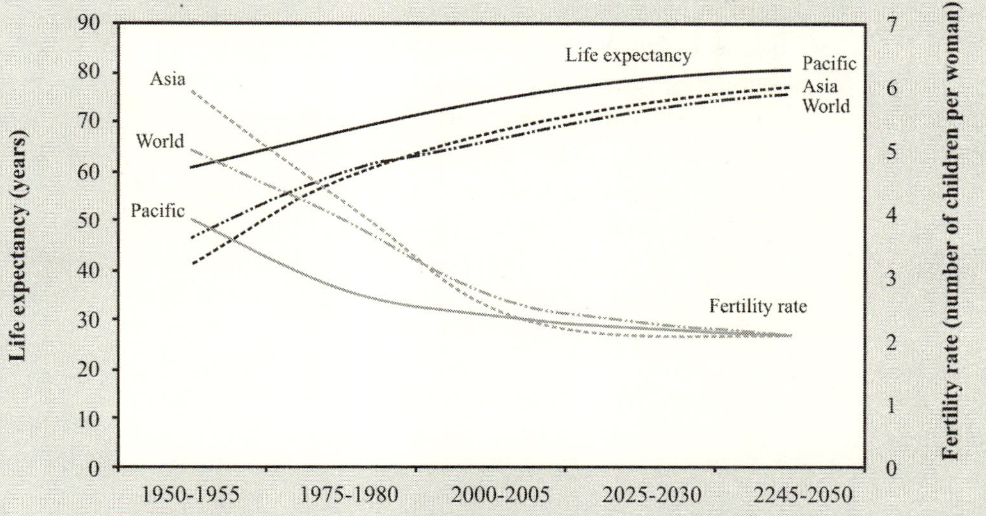

Source: World Population Ageing 1950-2050 (United Nations publication, Sales No. E.02.XIII.3).

Decline in the fertility rate

... while the fertility rate declines to close to replacement level

Fertility rates in many countries in Asia exceeded 6 children per woman until the mid-1960s owing to very early nuptiality and an increase in fertility since 1956 in several countries in the region. As a whole, Asia had a high fertility rate of 5.9 children per woman during the period 1950-1955, while that in the Pacific was 3.9. Thus, fertility played a marginal role in the demographic transition in many developing countries in the region in its initial phase.

Table III.3. Total fertility rate

	1950-1955	*1975-1980*	*2000-2005*	*2025-2030*	*2045-2050*
Asia	5.9	4.2	2.5	2.1	2.1
percentage drop		−28.8	−40.5	−16.0	–
Pacific	3.9	2.8	2.4	2.2	2.1
percentage drop		−28.2	−14.3	−8.3	−4.5

Source: World Population Ageing 1950-2050 (United Nations publication, Sales No. E.02.XIII.3).

However, as shown in table III.3, the total fertility rate in the region declined by 29 per cent between 1950-1955 and 1975-1980. The Asian region, in particular, witnessed a sharp decline of 40 per cent in the fertility rate during the last quarter of the twentieth century. In countries such as Japan, the fertility rate has dropped well below the replacement rate. Several socio-economic factors have contributed to this decline. Foremost among these are the population control policies adopted by Governments either through family planning programmes or fertility control measures, such as the "one child" policy in China,[5] as a response to dealing with poverty. Individual family planning, even in the absence of State-sponsored family planning programmes, especially among the educated, in response to economic pressure is also a major contributory factor in the declining fertility rate.

Socio-economic challenges in a changing global environment exert pressure on nuptiality control

Nuptiality control, characterized by a delay in the age of first marriage in response to cultural changes and socio-economic challenges in a changing global environment, is increasingly becoming a major force in population control. Among educated women, there is an increasing tendency to give more priority to career development and independence than to marriage.[6] This has been the case particularly in countries where the wage gap between men and women has narrowed over the years. The difficulty of reconciling work with child-rearing is another reason. A further contributory factor is the steady improvement in pension schemes over the years, which has reduced the need to rely on the traditional sources of old-age support, such as children. The likelihood of using children as old-age support has also declined over the years owing to rural-urban migration and declining fertility rates. As a result of these changes, the fertility rate in the Asian and Pacific region has declined to below the world average (see figure III.2). The sharp decline in the fertility rate since the mid-1960s has made it the driving force behind the demographic transition during the past quarter of a century.

Another important development is the increasing life expectancy at older ages, which is expected to continue during the next 50 years. For example, life expectancy at age 60 in Asia is expected to increase from 18.1 in 2000 to 21.8 years by 2050, while that in the Pacific is expected to increase from 21.5 to 23.9 years.

---

[5] F.D. McCarthy and K. Zheng, "Population ageing and pension systems: reform options for China", World Bank Policy Research Working Paper No. 1607 (1996).

[6] For example, in Japan, as women acquire education their salaries increase, which in turn raises the opportunity cost of withdrawing from the labour force to rear children (see D.E. Horlacher and L. MacKellar, "Population ageing in Japan: policy lessons for South-East Asia", *Asia-Pacific Population Journal,* vol. 10, No. 1, June 2003). Another study reveals that 25 per cent of ethnic Chinese women in Singapore and Malaysia were still single by the time they reached 30 years (see G. Jones and K. Ramdas, eds., *(Un)tying The Knot: Ideal and Reality in Asian Marriage,* Asia Research Institute, Singapore, 2004).

Scale and speed of ageing

By 2050, Asia and the Pacific will be home to over 1.2 billion people aged over 60 years ...

Many countries in the Asian and Pacific region have experienced rapid ageing of their populations during the past 50 years and the intensity of ageing is expected to increase at a faster rate during the next 50 years. For example, the number of persons aged 60 and over increased from 104 million in 1950 to 351 million in 2000, registering an over threefold increase within half a century. An even higher rate is expected during the next 50 years, raising the number of people aged 60 and over to more than 1.2 billion by 2050 (table III.4). The older population as a share of the total population in the region increased from 7 per cent in 1950 to 9.4 per cent in 2000. This share is expected to rise sharply to 15.4 per cent by 2025 and to 23.5 per cent by 2050.

Table III.4. Population aged 60 and over

(Millions)

	1950	*2000*			*2050*		
	Population aged 60 and over	*Population aged 60 and over*	*Percentage increase*	*Share of total population*	*Population aged 60 and over*	*Percentage increase*	*Share of total population*
World	205	606	195	10.0	1 964	224	21.1
Asia-Pacific	104	351	237	9.4	1 238	253	23.5
China	42	129	210	10.1	437	239	29.9
India	20	77	282	7.6	324	322	20.6
Indonesia	5	16	226	7.6	70	331	22.3
Japan	6	30	359	23.2	46	57	42.3

Source: *World Population Ageing 1950-2050* (United Nations publication, Sales No. E.02.XIII.3).

... and this will account for 63 per cent of the world total

The speed of ageing in the region is such that the share of the population aged 60 and over in Asia and the Pacific, which stood at 50.7 per cent of the world total in 1950, increased to 57.9 per cent by 2000, surpassing the rest of the world. The region's share of older persons is expected to increase to a staggering 63.0 per cent by 2050 (figure III.3).

Four countries in the region, China, India, Indonesia and Japan, accounted for 71.6 per cent of the region's older persons and for 41.5 per cent of the total older population in the world in 2000. The increase in the region's share in the world total to 63 per cent by 2050 from the current level of 58 per cent partially reflects the expected rapid pace of ageing in other countries in the region during the next 50 years.

Figure III.3. Distribution of 60+ population in selected economies, 2000 and 2050

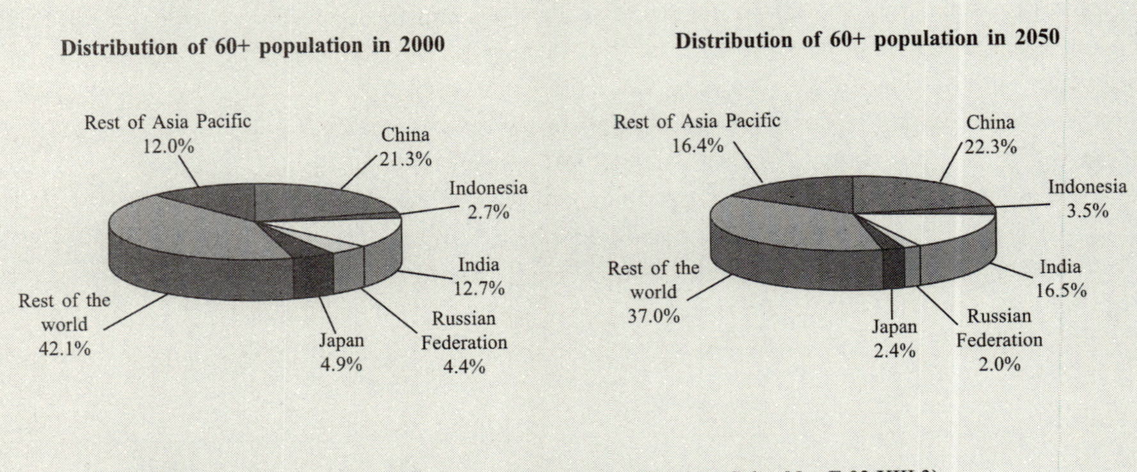

Source: *World Population Ageing 1950-2050* (United Nations publication, Sales No. E.02.XIII.3).

Ageing, a challenge for still developing economies

Table III.5 provides a classification of countries in the region according to the rate of ageing. According to this classification, many countries of East and North-East Asia, North and Central Asia, and all developed economies in the region, are ageing rapidly. An interesting feature of demographic transition in the next half century will be the rapid ageing in countries such as China, Sri Lanka, Thailand and several North and Central Asian countries which are still developing. Such a rapid evolution of demography could pose serious challenges for these countries in the immediate future.

The demographic dividend wasted

One positive sign is the still moderate rate of ageing in large economies such as India and Indonesia, which have ample room to benefit from the current wave of rapid ageing in the rest of the world by effective utilization of their labour force, as well as to prepare to face the challenges posed by the ageing of their populations well in advance. However, despite these opportunities, the Asian and Pacific region has 80 million unemployed youth, indicating that it has yet to make the demographic dividend effective so as to be able to address its high unemployment rate.

Ageing of the older population

Share of the over 80 age group increasing

Relative ageing of the older population itself is becoming a notable feature of the ageing process in the Asian and Pacific region (figure III.4). A larger proportion of the older population in the world is living in the Asian and Pacific region and is growing faster. For example, the share of the 80 and over age group in the region is expected to increase from 51.7

Table III.5. Speed of ageing of 60+ population

	Slow	*Moderate*	*Rapid*
East and North-East Asia			
		Democratic People's Republic of Korea	China
		Mongolia	Republic of Korea
			Hong Kong, China
			Macao, China
South-East Asia			
	Cambodia	Malaysia	Thailand
	Lao People's Democratic Republic	Myanmar	Singapore
	Timor-Leste	Indonesia	
	Philippines	Viet Nam	
		Brunei Darussalam	
South and South-West Asia			
	Afghanistan	India	Sri Lanka
	Maldives	Iran (Islamic Republic of)	
	Bhutan	Turkey	
	Nepal		
	Pakistan		
	Bangladesh		
North and Central Asia			
	Turkmenistan	Tajikistan	Kazakhstan
		Kyrgyzstan	Azerbaijan
		Uzbekistan	Georgia
			Russian Federation
			Armenia
Pacific			
	Solomon Islands	New Caledonia	
	Papua New Guinea	French Polynesia	
	Vanuatu	Fiji	
	Samoa		
Developed economies			
			Australia
			New Zealand
			Japan

Source: *World Population Ageing 1950-2050* (United Nations publication, Sales No. E.02.XIII.3).

Notes: Slow - percentage of 60+ population in 2050 less than 20 per cent.
Moderate - percentage of 60+ population in 2050 between 20 and 25 per cent.
Rapid - percentage of 60+ population in 2050 greater than 25 per cent.

per cent of the world's total in 2000 to 61.5 per cent by 2050 (figure III.5). Four countries in the region, China, India, Indonesia and Japan, accounted for 65.7 per cent of the region's population aged 80 and over in 2000, and this is expected to rise to 74.8 per cent in 2050.

Figure III.4. Total 80+ population by ESCAP subregions and the rest of the world

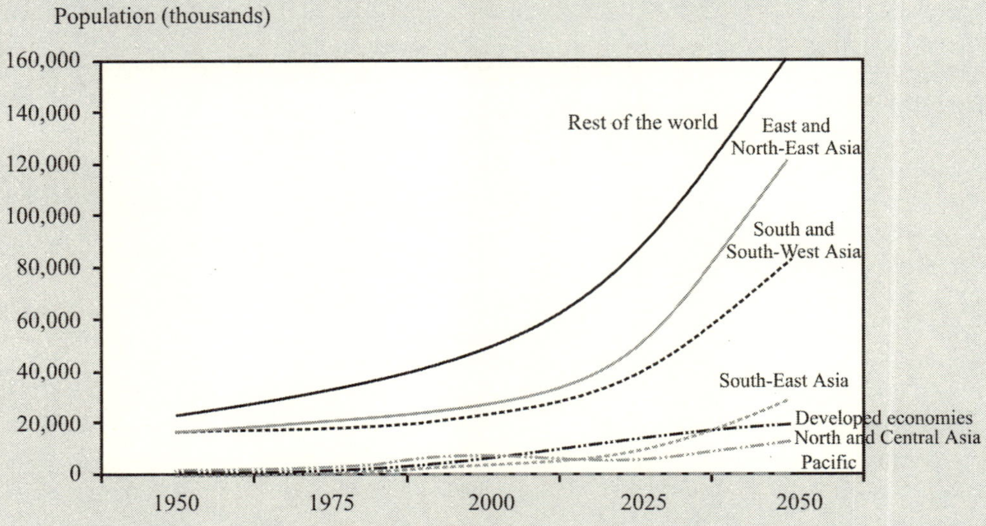

Source: *World Population Ageing 1950-2050* (United Nations publication, Sales No. E.02.XIII.3).

Figure III.5. Distribution of 80+ population in selected economies, 2000 and 2050

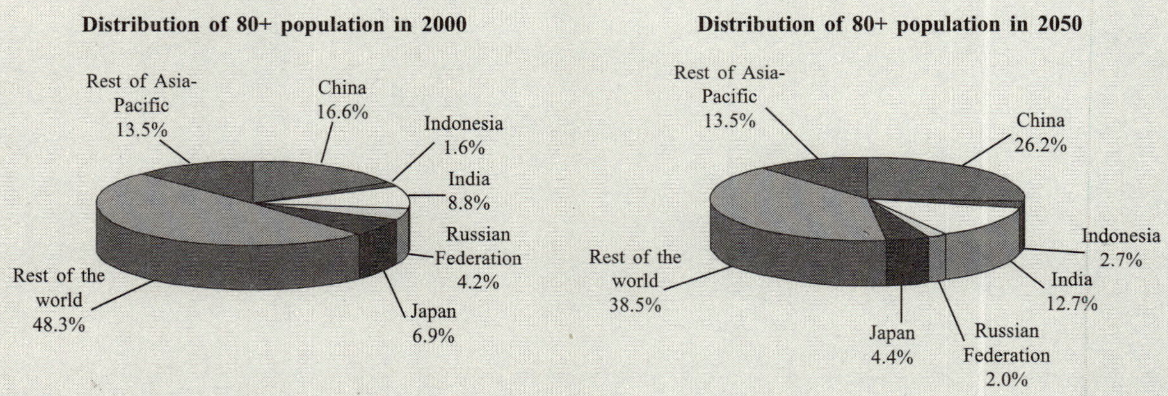

Source: *World Population Ageing 1950-2050* (United Nations publication, Sales No. E.02.XIII.3).

Is ageing a gender issue?

More women in the older age groups

An important dimension of the ageing process is the rising number of women in the older age groups. Ageing has been a progressively gendered experience in the Asian and Pacific region (see figure III.6). The share of women in the 60 and over age group is expected to increase from 5 per cent of the total population in 2000 to 12.4 per cent by 2050. In contrast, the share of men in that age group would rise from 4.3 to 10.8 per cent during the same period. A similar pattern is observed in the 80 and over age group, with a sharp increase in the share of women over 80 years predicted during the second quarter of the twenty-first century. This phenomenon is underlined by the higher life expectancy of women owing to their better survival chances in old age for biological reasons.

Figure III.6. Share of male and female population aged 60+ and 80+ of Asian and Pacific economies in the total population, 1950-2050

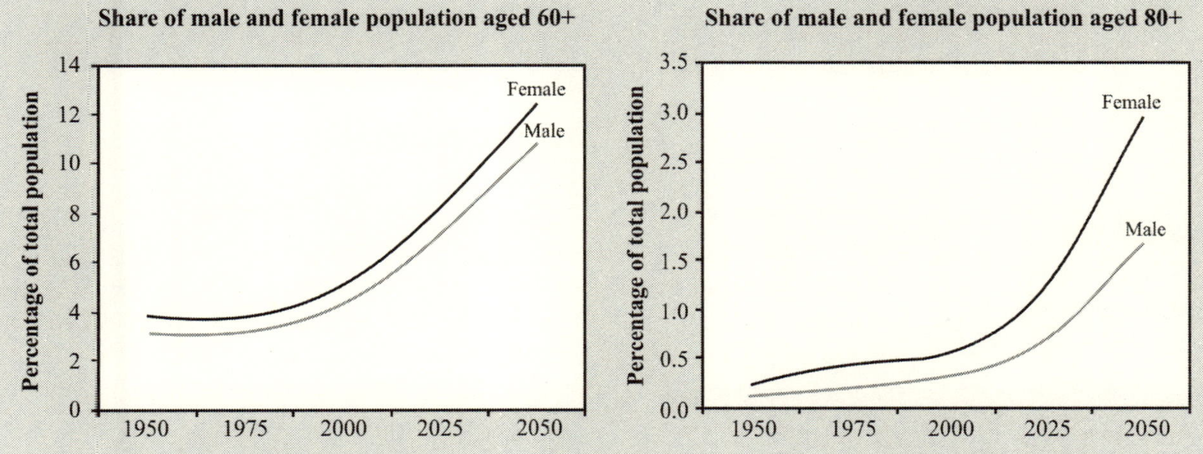

Source: World Population Ageing 1950-2050 (United Nations publication, Sales No. E.02.XIII.3).

IMPLICATIONS OF POPULATION AGEING

Ageing may shift consumption and savings behaviour and labour productivity

Population ageing could have profound implications for the economies as well as societies experiencing a rapid increase in the share of older persons in the total population. While the rising demand for medical services in old age and high medical costs could impose pressure on government and family budgets, an ageing population could lead to a drastic shift in the consumption and savings behaviour of people. Labour markets may also experience a shift in the supply of labour with implications for labour productivity. However, ageing can also lead to the emergence of social welfare and gender-related issues. The combined effect of these changes could have an impact on economic growth and thereby the welfare of the people. These issues are discussed below in detail.

Fiscal implications

Possible shrinking of the tax base amid growing expenditure

The demographic changes that would be experienced by countries are likely to have a significant influence on public expenditure, in particular on the provision of pensions and health care. Since expenditure on pensions and health care is a major component of government budgets, pressures arising from demographic changes would have adverse effects on the budget deficit or surplus. The expected decline in the share of the working-age population in the region from 62.4 per cent in 2025 to 57.9 per cent in 2050, as well as the possible drop in output, could lead to a shrinkage in the tax base and thereby tax revenues in the second quarter of this century. The fiscal implications of ageing would be felt strongly and much earlier in such countries as Armenia, Australia, China, Georgia, Japan, New Zealand, the Republic of Korea, the Russian Federation, Singapore, Sri Lanka and Thailand, where the population is ageing rapidly and the working-age groups will decline in the first quarter of the century.

Public pensions

Unsustainable pay-as-you-go pension schemes

In many countries of the Asian and Pacific region, public pension schemes are unfunded and operate on a pay-as-you-go system. In most cases the pension benefits are defined. With the number of workers per pensioner declining rapidly, as reflected in the predicted sharp rise in the old-age dependency ratio in the Asian and Pacific region during the next 50 years (see figure III.7), the financial burden on Governments to provide

Figure III.7. Old-age dependency ratio in Asia and the Pacific and selected economies

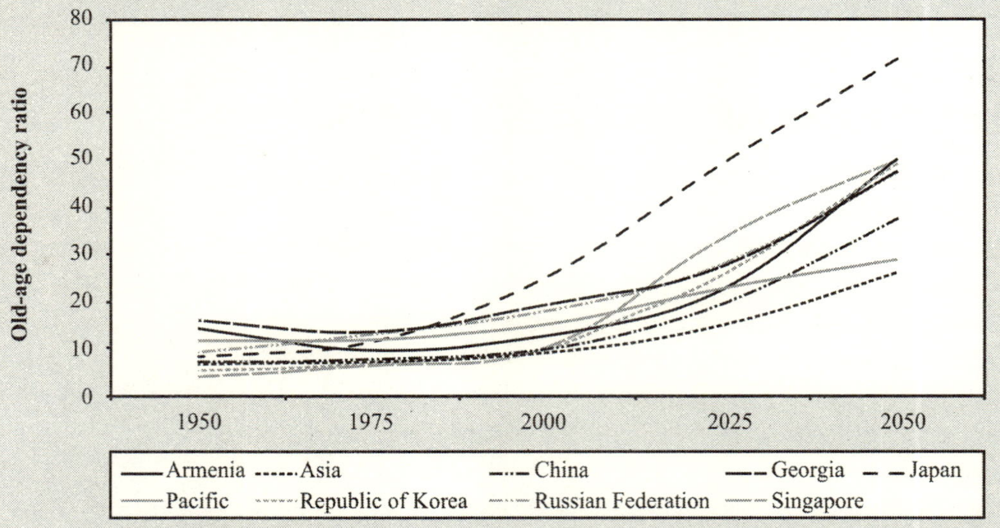

Source: World Population Ageing 1950-2050 (United Nations publication, Sales No. E.02.XIII.3).

adequate public pensions under the existing defined benefit pension schemes could be substantial. Such systems also lead to wider intergenerational inequality of burden-sharing.[7]

In the absence of increased contributions to compensate for the declining workforce or policy changes, an increase in public pension expenditure could lead to large budget deficits.

Health care

Increasing demand for health services likely

The rapid ageing of the population in the region, in particular the ageing of the older population, would increase expenditure on public health, for three reasons. First, older people and, in particular, those of advanced age, are more prone to diseases.[8] The older population group is expected to expand more than fourfold during the next 50 years and is bound to increase the demand for health services on a substantial scale. Second, health care for older persons is on average more expensive than that for younger people. Finally, the declining trend in the number of families operating as caretaking institutions for older persons owing to the decrease in the size of family units may result in a shift in health financing from family-financed to publicly financed health services. For example, money transfers by children as a source of income of older people declined from 72.4 per cent of their total income in 1980 to 56.3 per cent in 1995 in the Republic of Korea, while those in Japan declined from 18.7 to 6.6 per cent during the same period, reflecting the declining role of the family as a source of income for older persons.[9]

Implications for the labour market

Decline in the working-age population in some countries ...

Population ageing could have implications for both the supply of and the demand for labour, leading to a labour market mismatch. On the supply side, the share of the working-age group (15-59 years) in the Asian and Pacific region is expected to drop from 61 per cent in 2000 to 58 per cent by 2050. The expected drop would imply that the labour force could

---

[7] For example, in Japan, the intergenerational inequality of burden-sharing under the existing public pension system is so large that the young decline to pay their contributions to the national pension system (see K. Iwata, "Japan's economy under demographic changes", summary of the speech given at the Australia-Japan Economic Outlook Conference, Sydney, 7 December 2004, <http://www.boj.or.jp/en/press/04/ko0412c.htm>).

[8] For example, industrial country data suggest that older people consume almost three times more medical services than those aged 0-14. The results also suggest that there is a positive link between medical cost and age (see P.S. Heller, "Aging in the Asian 'Tigers': challenges for fiscal policy", IMF Working Paper No. WP/97/143).

[9] H.S. Phang, "Rapid ageing and labour force changes in Korea", paper presented at the International Seminar on Low Fertility and Rapid Ageing, organized by the Korea National Statistical Office and the Population Association of Korea, Seoul, 31 October 2003.

shrink in many countries in the region within the next 50 years. In countries such as Japan, the share of this most productive age group in the population may drop from 62.1 per cent in 2000 to 52.8 per cent by 2025 and further to 45.2 per cent by 2050. Countries such as China, the Republic of Korea and Sri Lanka may follow suit, albeit to a lesser extent, during the second quarter of the twenty-first century (see figure III.8).

Figure III.8. Dynamics of the working-age population in selected economies: population aged 15-59 for selected Asian and Pacific economies as a percentage of the total population, 1950-2050

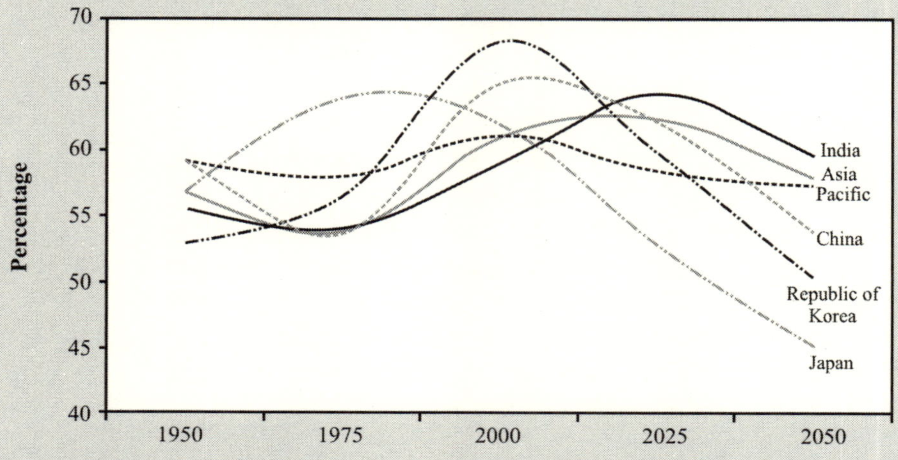

Source: World Population Ageing 1950-2050 (United Nations publication, Sales No. E.02.XIII.3).

... but hope remains alive in others

On the demand side, there will be a growing demand for labour-intensive services such as old-age health-care, institutional, social and home-care services during the next 50 years. The demand for educational services could drop as the population of school-age is expected to decline in the next few decades. The demand for labour in the former category, however, may not be met domestically as long as the labour force is shrinking and there is no excess labour. However, countries with moderate ageing and high unemployment rates would be in a position to meet their labour demand and benefit from the ageing processes, but the migration of labour in response to changes in immigration policies in more advanced economies in the face of rapid ageing in those economies may eliminate that advantage unless a coordinated approach to immigration policies is adopted in labour-importing and -exporting countries.

Negative impact of the shift in the age structure on productivity ...

The expected sharp increase in the median age during the next 50 years implies that many countries in the region will have an ageing labour force, which may have the following adverse implications:

(1) *A structural change in production owing to a shift in demand towards services and products for older people and the resulting frictional unemployment if labour mobility remains restricted.* Such frictional unemployment could widen the qualification gap, producing a situation in which the highly qualified are in short supply and the poorly qualified are out of work.

(2) *A possible change in labour productivity, although research in this area is not conclusive.* While older workers are likely to have a positive attitude, be more reliable and possess better skills than the average workers, they are also more expensive in terms of health-care costs and lack flexibility in accepting new assignments and training.[10]

Savings and investment

... and on savings and investment

According to the life-cycle theory of savings, individuals make a choice between present consumption and savings for future consumption. Assets accumulated during their working years are spent during their retirement. This is particularly the case when there are no or limited retirement benefit schemes to smooth out consumption during retirement. However, empirical evidence in support of the life-cycle hypothesis is mixed.[11] While some studies provide support for a strong link between demographic changes and private savings,[12] others find only a weak relationship between them.

Ageing could have a negative impact on savings in many developing countries in the region because retirement benefits are inadequate to support living in old age and additional years of life expectancy, particularly of the older groups, as retirees would involve greater consumption.

---

[10] M.C. Barth and others, "Corporations and the ageing workforce", in Philip J. Mirvis, ed., *Building the Competitive Workforce* (John Wiley and Sons, 1993).

[11] For example, in a study of major industrial economics, it is estimated that an increase of 1 percentage point in the dependency ratio causes a commensurate fall in the savings ratio (see P.R. Masson and K.W. Tryon, "Macroeconomic effects of projected population aging in industrial countries", IMF Working Paper No. 90/5). With the old-age dependency ratio in the region rising to 26.2 per cent by 2050 from 9.2 per cent in 2000, this would imply that, everything else remaining constant, the region's savings rate could drop by 17 percentage points by 2050.

[12] For example, Ando and others projected a drop in Japanese savings rates to 10 per cent by 2040 (see A. Ando and others, "Dynamics of demographic development and its impact on personal savings: case of Japan", *Richerche Economiche*, September 1995).

The severity of the drop in savings could be offset to some extent if young workers had prior knowledge of increases in life expectancy which could prompt them to save more for future consumption.

The drop in savings would ultimately lead to a contraction in investment in countries that are ageing, unless compensated by investment from abroad. As the demand for homes, recreation, transport and schooling drops as a result of the shift in the relative age structure and preferences, investment in such areas may be particularly affected.

Public debt

Many countries have large implicit pension debts

The pressures arising from an ageing population on public expenditure on pensions and health care, particularly in the absence of reforms in pensions and health services, could lead to a build-up of public debt in developing countries in the region. Countries with weak tax systems and high levels of public debt and fiscal deficits could be at a particular disadvantage unless specific policy actions are in place to broaden the tax base, and efficiency in tax administration and debt management improved. The expected drop in savings would impose additional pressure on public debt as the increasing demand for pensions and health care could compel Governments to depend on borrowing to finance increasing expenses. The unfunded pension schemes in a majority of countries could lead to large implicit pension debts, undermining the sustainability of such systems (see box III.1).

Impact on capital markets

A negative impact on domestic capital markets ...

The dominance of the pay-as-you-go systems in the provision of pensions in many countries in the region and the rapid ageing of populations would require substantial reform of public pension schemes, leaning more towards defined contributory pension schemes. Such a policy change could have important implications for both the domestic and international capital markets and their governance behaviour.

The possible emergence of prefunded public and private pension systems and insurance schemes would enable the development of capital markets in developing countries in the region whose population is ageing, provided that proper incentives for innovations and efficient regulatory structures are in place and Governments refrain from manipulating the public pension funds for budgetary purposes.

However, the lower propensity of the older generation to save could have a negative impact on capital markets, in particular stock markets. This effect would be heightened by the ageing of the baby boomers beginning in 2010.[13]

---

[13] IMF, *World Economic Outlook, September 2004* (Washington, 2004).

Box III.1. Growing implicit pension debt

Implicit pension debt (IPD),[a] which refers to the benefit promises a pension scheme makes to workers and pensioners, is perhaps the largest single unreported liability in the public sphere. Such implicit liabilities have grown rapidly with the proliferation of publicly managed, defined benefit pension plans during the twentieth century. Estimates of IPD for selected countries in the Asian and Pacific region are given in the following table.

Implicit pension debt in selected countries

	IPD as a percentage of GDP		*IPD as a percentage of GDP*		*IPD as a percentage of GDP*
Australia	115	Kazakhstan	88	Republic of Korea	33
China	94	Kyrgyzstan	185	Turkey	72
Japan	162	Philippines	107		

Source: Wang and others and Holzmann and others (see note[a] below).

The above estimates show that unfunded pension liabilities are large even in developing countries such as Kyrgyzstan and the Philippines where the population is still young. A similar pattern can be expected for other countries in the region as most countries have pay-as-you-go pension systems. IPD liabilities will become larger and heavier as the population ages. The rapid ageing in the Asian and Pacific region, as well as the dominance of a publicly funded pension scheme, would add an additional burden to the existing levels of IPD. Such large implicit liabilities will have serious implications for the intertemporal budget constraints as such liabilities become due in the future. The design and implementation of pension reform, as well as fiscal policy, would be influenced very much by the level of IPD.

---

[a] IPD is measured by adding the present value of benefits that have to be paid to current pensioners plus the present value of pension rights that current workers have already earned and would have to be paid if the system were terminated today (see Wang and others, "Implicit pension debt, transition cost, options and impact of China's pension reform: a computable general equilibrium analysis", World Bank Working Paper No. 2555 and R. Holzmann and others, "Implicit pension debt: issues, measurement and scope in international perspective", World Bank Social Protection Discussion Paper No. 0403).

Economic growth

... and on growth

The rising dependency ratio in the Asian and Pacific region could have a major impact on economic growth as the output is produced by a declining labour force. The drop in labour force and investment could affect economic growth adversely unless factor productivity improves commensurately or the drop in the labour force is matched by migrant labour. However, the negative impact of slow output growth on per capita income would be mitigated to some extent by the declining population growth. For example, the level of real GDP in Japan is estimated to drop by a cumulative 20 per cent over the next century owing to a shrinking population and associated lower employment levels while per capita GDP is expected to drop by about 5 per cent.[14] Real economic growth rates could also drop in Hong Kong, China, the Republic of Korea, Singapore and Taiwan Province of China during the third quarter of the twenty-first century.[15] Developing countries which experience ageing at early stages of their development could be at a particular disadvantage as they are resource-constrained, are subject to labour outflows owing to migration and lack initiatives for productivity gains.

Care of older persons

Familial care is still a deep-rooted social norm, but changing family structures are putting pressure on the tradition

Familial care of older persons is a deep-rooted social norm in most parts of Asia and the Pacific. Caring for older people has been a moral obligation of children and as a result only a small proportion of older people in the region live alone. However, with the changing family structure and composition in the face of urbanization, industrialization, migration and the increasing trend towards nuclear families coupled with declining fertility and increasing longevity, the ability of families to take care of older persons is gradually declining. The extent to which the family will remain the primary source of care for older people will have important implications for formal arrangements for the care of older persons.

Poverty, isolation and discrimination

Older persons are often afflicted by poverty owing to a host of factors, including lack of skills or skills mismatch, lack of resources, ill-health and social prejudices. Poverty among the rural elderly, in particular older women, tends to be severe owing to the lack of formal or informal social security in old age. As reflected in figure III.6, women tend to live longer than men and rapid urbanization, resulting from the migration of mostly youth to urban areas, leads to the isolation particularly of rural women in old age. With the expected decline in the potential support ratio[16] from 10.9 per cent in 2000 to 3.8 per cent by 2050, the poverty aspects of ageing could become worse in the next few decades, underscoring the need for formal social support and care of older persons. Discriminatory treatment of older people, particularly in relation to job recruitment, promotion and training, creates stigma and social exclusion.

---

[14] H. Faruqee and M. Mühleisen, "Population aging in Japan: demographic shock and fiscal sustainability", IMF Working Paper No. WP/01/40, <http://www.imf.org/external/pubs/ft/wp/2001/wp0140.pdf>.

[15] This is against a baseline simulation with a stationary population (see IMF, *Finance and Development*, <http://www.imf.org/external/pubs/ft/fandd/2001/03/mahleise.httn>).

[16] The number of persons aged 15-64 per every person aged 65 or older.

In order to eliminate such discriminatory attitudes, a climate of acceptance must be provided so that older people can be integrated into mainstream development.[17]

POLICY RESPONSES

Fundamental changes in policy design in pension and health systems necessary

The rapid ageing of populations, unless managed in a proactive manner, could impose serious challenges for policy makers in Asian and Pacific countries. The severity and complexity of such challenges would depend on the level of economic development, the stage of ageing and the level of preparedness. Rapid ageing in the region and the resulting socio-economic implications would require Governments to take corrective action to minimize the negative effects of ageing in a host of areas, including fiscal operations and social welfare provision for older persons. These measures may also cover market reforms, institutional reforms, economic policy responses and initiatives for regional cooperation. Fundamental changes in policy design, particularly in health and pension systems, would be necessary to minimize the pressures on public expenditure and the overall growth potential of the economy. Countries experiencing a shift from a relatively young to an ageing population at a rapid pace while their economies are still not sufficiently mature to manage such shocks would face a daunting task in putting in place such policies and institutional changes. However, the effective implementation of national and regional action plans established in line with the Shanghai Implementation Strategy for the Madrid International Plan of Action on Ageing 2002 could provide an enabling and supportive environment for ageing.

Pension reforms

As indicated earlier, in many countries of the region public pension schemes are pay-as-you-go systems with the financial burden accumulating over time. Rapid ageing of the population with a shrinking labour force would put pressure on public pension expenditure on two counts. First, an ageing population along with increasing life expectancy implies that the share of retirees who receive public pensions would become larger in the next half century. Second, the share of contributors to pension funds would become smaller with the declining share of the working-age population. This would have a negative impact on pension funds unless corresponding adjustments are made in contribution rates and new solutions found to address this issue. Under these circumstances, drastic policy changes would be inevitable to sustain such pension schemes to prevent poverty in old age. The policy options available for Governments are as follows.

---

[17] For a discussion on the situation of older persons in the region, see *Policies and Programmes for Older Persons in Asia and the Pacific: Selected Studies,* United Nations Social Policy Paper No. 1, 2001 (United Nations publication, Sales No. E.02.II.F.6).

Converting pay-as-you-go pension systems to funded schemes vital

(a) *Converting unfunded pension schemes to funded pension systems.*

A move towards the actuarial neutrality of old-age pension systems through prepayment as against unfunded schemes would not only reduce the financial burden on Governments but also ensure the sustainability of such schemes.

The advantage of moving towards funded pension schemes is that it enables Governments to minimize the economic costs of restoring long-run fiscal sustainability in the face of ageing-related pressures by spreading the required adjustment over a long period.[18] The Latin American experience shows not only that fully or partially funded, privately managed pension systems can be more effective provided that adequate regulatory and supervisory mechanisms are in place, but also that pension reform is possible under very different economic, political and social conditions.[19]

Parametric changes to pension systems required

(b) *Increase in the age of retirement*

In the majority of countries the mandatory retirement age is 60 years and workers are given the option of early retirement at age 55. The fact that a substantial number of retirees enjoy a healthy life, especially during the first five to seven years after retirement, would make extending the retirement age to 65 or 67 years, depending on the existing retirement age, an effective and practical option.[20]

Although such an option would not be feasible in countries having high unemployment rates, the mismatch in the labour supply and demand in the years ahead would make such an approach a justifiable and productive one. The impact of such an increase in the retirement age on unemployment could be offset to some extent by implementing pension reforms along with labour market reforms to increase the flexibility of the labour market. Prolonging working lives, along with the move towards funded pension schemes, would reduce the scale of money transfers and minimize the long-term economic costs. Older workers may have to be trained or retrained to ensure that they are equipped with the necessary skills and competence and their specific needs have to be met so as to achieve efficient outcomes of this policy option.

---

[18] D. Carey, "Coping with population ageing in the Netherlands", OECD Economics Department Working Paper No. 325.

[19] M. Queisser, "The second-generation pension reform in Latin America", OECD Working Paper No. AWP 5.4.

[20] This is also supported by the fact that many rural elderly people continue to work despite being over 60 years of age. Shortage of labour in rural areas owing to rural-to-urban migration of the younger cohorts makes it necessary for the elderly to continue to work (see L.J. Domingo, "Ageing and women in developing countries: examination of issues from a cohort perspective", in *Population Growth and Demographic Structure* (United Nations publication, Sales No. E.99.XIII.7)). In the Republic of Korea, older persons tend to remain in the work-force as the majority are either self-employed or act as employers (Phang, loc.cit.).

(c) *Remove incentives to early retirement*

Incentives to early retirement could nullify the effectiveness of parameters of pension schemes

Along with the above policy measures, reforms are also needed in the public pension systems, taxation policy and social transfer programmes to remove financial incentives for early retirement and disincentives for late retirement. Incentives for early retirement have become a major policy option for countries facing high unemployment rates and removing such incentives in those countries may be counterproductive in the short run. However, future trends of a declining labour force would make such a policy option an effective one as it would not only enable the retention of productive workers in the labour force without undue impact on unemployment rates but also reduce the fiscal burden on Governments.

(d) *Providing adequate social security coverage to the poor through a multi-pillar pension scheme*

An evaluation of the existing pension schemes in selected Asian countries, along with possible policy options, is given in table III.6.

Increasing efficiency in the health-care sector

Lack of an efficient regulatory mechanism could undermine the very objectives of a multi-pillar system

The demand for health services is bound to increase substantially in the next few decades with the rising share of older age groups in the society. Older people are usually prone to diseases, especially at older ages, and will require services for the specific needs of their age group. Policy options for addressing the emerging health needs of older persons will also need to take into account resource requirements, present and future institutional constraints and the sustainability of such policy measures.

Healthy ageing

A healthy lifestyle key to healthy ageing

Health promotion throughout the life course is a key factor for a healthy life in old age. The promotion of healthy diets, physical activity, the prevention of unhealthy and risky behaviour and health education could be as important as improving the efficiency of health service delivery at both the local and national levels and investing in health infrastructure and human resources development. Several countries and areas in the region have introduced health promotion campaigns aimed at healthy lives in old age. For example, in 2001 Hong Kong, China, introduced the Healthy Ageing Campaign to effect a cultural change in the society's mindset in the longer term, so that ageing is seen in a more positive manner and there is greater awareness in the community of the need to adopt a healthy lifestyle from an early age in order to achieve active and healthy ageing.

Table III.6. Common features of pension schemes in the Asian region and policy options

Common features	*Policy options*
Low coverage: Coverage is below 20 per cent in most countries.[a] The vast majority in the informal sector are not covered by any social security and rely mostly on family support.	Increase coverage by introducing multi-pillar structures consisting of: (i) Mandated publicly managed defined benefits scheme for redistributive and coinsurance objectives; (ii) Privately managed and funded defined contribution scheme for savings; (iii) Retirement provisions on a voluntary basis for those who would like more protection in their old age.[b]
High replacement rates: Formal public sector schemes are relatively generous making them fiscally unsustainable in the long run when such schemes mature and the potential support ratio declines.	Move towards notional defined contribution pension schemes and link benefits to contributions. Limit early retirement windows. Shift the indexation of pensions to prices rather than wages.[c]
Low rate of return: Publicly managed pension schemes governed by mandates and limitations on investments result in a lack of portfolio diversification. These are mostly tied up with government bonds with low return for budgetary needs.	Move away from politically determined investment decisions by giving autonomy in decision-making to fund managers. Reduce administrative costs.
Limited investment options: Statutory restrictions on investment abroad and shallow capital markets limit investment options.	Shift towards independently managed systems along with reforms of the capital market, providing opportunities for innovation in market instruments. Care needs to be taken to protect the interests of the account holders through regulatory mechanisms and oversight procedures. Another option would be the establishment of pension protection funds, as in the United Kingdom. Foster the development of government bond markets to provide a term structure which serves as a benchmark for the private sector.
Non-portable: Impedes labour mobility between sectors and creates obstacles to reforms.	Make pensions portable and improve labour market flexibility.

[a] Coverage in countries such as Singapore and Malaysia exceeds 50 per cent. India has recently switched to a defined contributory pension system.

[b] Such a system would address not only short- and long-term sustainability issues of pension systems but also economic and distributive concerns. For a detailed account of the multi-pillar system for pensions, see World Bank, *Averting the Old Aged Crisis: Policies to Protect the Old and Promote Growth* (Washington, World Bank and Oxford University Press, 1994).

[c] H. Polackova, "Population ageing and financing of government liabilities in New Zealand", World Bank Policy Research Working Paper No. 1703.

Health insurance

Pooling of risks through the promotion of health insurance

The increasing public health expenditure would make health insurance an effective mechanism for financing the health-care needs of older persons. However, at present private prepaid health insurance is almost non-existent in most developing countries in the Asian and Pacific region. In many countries, health-care expenditure is borne either by the Government or by individuals themselves. More advanced economies, such as the Republic of Korea and Singapore, provide substantial coverage under medical insurance programmes funded largely by a combination of employer and employee contributions, budgetary transfers and direct co-payments by patients. Japan provides a separate system of health care for older people. Private prepaid health insurance plans are being developed in Indonesia, the Philippines, the Republic of Korea and Thailand.

Institutional arrangements for care of the elderly

Greater requirement for institutional care of the elderly

An important implication of the declining fertility rate to replacement or even below-replacement level for care of the elderly is the pressure on family caregiving. This demographic change would result in a 2-2-4 (or 1-2-4) family structure, that is, a middle-aged couple would have to support their two children (or one child as in the case of China's one-child policy) as well as four old parents (grandparents of the children). Such a family structure would compel present and future generations to look for alternative arrangements for taking care of older parents. For example, the gradual weakening of the residual mechanism for care of the elderly in Sri Lanka has led to an increase in the demand for institutional support by the elderly.[21] One way of meeting such demand is the public provision of institutional care for the elderly. The other option would be to create an environment conducive to the not-for-profit organizations providing such services. Residential and community care constitutes a key element of Australia's strategic approach to population ageing (see box III.2). The establishment of international retirement centres in low-income countries, which would be beneficial not only for retirees but also for the host country, is another option in dealing with the rising cost of care of the elderly.

Promotion of familial care of the elderly

"Asian values" of familial care drastically reduce the burden of institutional care of the elderly

Despite the pressures arising from the changing socio-economic environment, familial care continues to be the main support system for older persons in the Asian region, reflecting the affection of children for

---

[21] This argument is supported by the growing number of homes for the aged and also by the long waiting lists of persons requesting admission to them (see K.A.P. Siddhisena and K. Ratnayake, "Ageing of population and elderly care in Sri Lanka", *Sri Lanka Journal of Population Studies*, vol. 1, No. 1, 1998).

Box III.2. Responding to rapid ageing in Australia: a strategic approach[a]

The proportion of people aged 60 years and over in Australia is predicted to reach 28.4 per cent by 2050, reflecting the rapid ageing of the Australian population. Such rapid ageing will have important ramifications for both the economy and society at large. Recognizing these potential implications, Australia has adopted a strategic approach in addressing issues relating to the ageing of its population. The main elements covered in the strategy are:

- Encouraging the continued participation of older persons in the workforce.
- Supporting retirement planning, which covers financial and social or lifestyle issues.
- Encouraging people to stay healthy and active and continue to participate in their community as they age.
- Improving the health and care services for older persons.

Key aspects of old-age and community care

- Family and other informal care arrangements play a significant role in enabling older people to remain in the community and avoid premature admission to residential old-age care.
- A national needs-based planning framework for residential and community old-age care places has been introduced, ensuring that growth in care services is controlled and targeted to areas of greater need.
- A national needs-based assessment mechanism has been introduced at an individual level to control access to services by the needy on a priority basis.
- A national accreditation framework has been established for residential old-age care services to ensure high standards of care and for eligibility of government funding.

Key lessons

The key lessons learned from Australia's experience in developing a response to population ageing include the need to:

- Develop a strategic and holistic response to population ageing.
- Maintain national leadership and direction in developing a response to such a complex policy area.
- Engage all stakeholders in the process.
- Ensure coordination of activities and collaboration between Governments, businesses, other organizations and the community.
- Ensure that responses are proactive and forward-looking with flexibility to incorporate the required changes as they arise.
- Maintain a strong evidence base to inform policy responses to population ageing.

---

[a] For a detailed account, of Australia's approach to ageing, see *Ageing in Asia and the Pacific: Emerging Issues and Successful Practices,* Social Policy Paper No. 10 (United Nations publication, Sales No. E.03.II.F.13).

their parents. Such "Asian values" underscore the importance of the quality of interpersonal relationships between generations as an effective way of care of the elderly. How can Governments promote the filial responsibility of taking care of older people? Some Governments use social and fiscal policies to achieve these goals. For example, in Singapore, the Government promotes filial responsibility through government policies on housing, health and infrastructure. In Malaysia, institutional care is considered a last resort. The National Welfare Policy formulated in 1990 calls for the welfare of older persons to be safeguarded with the support of the family and the community. To this end, tax deductions for medical expenses incurred by parents have been proposed. The Plan of Action for Older Persons introduced in 1998 recognizes community-based programmes as one of the feasible approaches for meeting current and future challenges.

Market reforms

One of the most important aspects of policy design to face the challenges of rapid ageing would be regulatory and market reforms that would provide an enabling environment for promoting higher levels of efficiency in both the public and private sectors and raising the growth of factor productivity. Macroeconomic stability, increased competition in an open market setting, transparency and accountability would ensure the sustainability of the dynamic gains from such reforms with a positive impact on growth and welfare.[22] Such reforms could help countries to transform the ageing problem into opportunity (see box III.3).

Labour market reforms

Reforms in the labour market are required to face the challenges and opportunities of population ageing. Liberalization of the labour market would need to focus on the effect of the declining labour force, productivity, migration and the adaptability of older workers to the existing working environment.

Labour market reforms critical

Implementing measures that would increase the efficiency of the economy could offset the adverse effects of population ageing to a large extent. Initiatives to improve total factor productivity at both the local and national levels through technological innovation and more efficient allocation of resources could be the most important strategy, particularly in countries where the labour force is likely to shrink owing to an ageing population. This would allow countries experiencing rapid ageing of their populations to sustain their current levels of economic growth.

Liberalization of the labour market would also enable countries to face the possible adverse effects of increasing labour migration. The threat of large-scale migration would be inevitable, particularly in developing countries in the face of a declining labour force and in countries

---

[22] Regulatory and market reforms are probably the most important as the gains could have a permanent positive influence on growth and living standards (see Dave Turner and others, "The macroeconomic implications of ageing in a global context", OECD Economics Department Working Paper No. 193, <http://www.oecd.org/eco/eco>).

Box III.3. Population ageing: from problem to opportunity

The cost of ageing populations is becoming a serious concern for policy makers in countries in the Asian and Pacific region where the population is ageing rapidly. The adverse implications of rapid ageing could be reflected in slow growth and deterioration in social welfare. Contrary to these pessimistic views, the paradigm shift in population dynamics could be transformed into an opportunity for both economies with a young population and those with an older population provided that the right incentives are in place and opportunities are seized in time.

For economies whose population is still young, the "demographic dividend" is derived mainly on four counts:

- *The increasing labour force* could be an impetus to higher growth. For example, large countries such as India and Indonesia, whose population is ageing moderately, and countries such as Bangladesh, Pakistan and the Philippines, whose population is ageing slowly, could benefit from their still young workforce. These countries would be competitive at the labour-intensive end of manufacturing for several decades to come.
- Those economies whose population is ageing slowly would benefit more from a "consumption dividend" than those whose population is ageing rapidly such as Japan, as they would be better placed to invest less and still maintain a given level of per capita output during the next two to three decades.
- *Higher return to capital in economies* whose population is young could attract foreign direct investment. The relative scarcity of capital in developing economies where the population is ageing slowly would drive up the rate of return on capital in these economies. Such high rates of return could induce capital flows from economies in which the population is ageing and where capital is abundant while the rate of return is low.
- *Increasing opportunities to export labour to economies with a rapidly ageing population.* The still growing labour force and excess labour would enable these economies to export labour to countries with a labour shortage. For example, countries such as India, which has one of the largest stocks of skilled human capital in the world, while having limited opportunities in the domestic market, would be in a better position to exploit the evolving global labour market conditions, including the acceleration in outsourcing in services and manufacturing.

The realization of these opportunities in the face of generally favourable demographic trends, however, depends critically on the progress made with the closely intertwined tasks of fiscal consolidation and structural reforms, educational reforms to suit the changing environment in a globalized world, development of infrastructure, provision of legal protection and adoption of an effective migration policy.

Economies with a rapidly ageing population could also benefit from an ageing population. The following are key areas:

- *Productivity growth.* A relative shortage of workers would increase the incentives for developing labour-saving technologies which would spur technological development.[a] Economic incentives such as patent rights could provide a boost for technological innovation.
- *Increasing the purchasing power of older persons.* Unlocking the purchasing power of older persons as a consumer force could yield growth as the demand for health-care and recreation services could increase in an ageing population. Older people could also constitute a productive power as they have good work ethics and are experienced and knowledgeable.

---

[a] One reason that the United States surpassed the United Kingdom in the early nineteenth century as the leader in technological innovation was the relative scarcity of labour in the United States (see the Testimony of Chairman Alan Greenspan before the Special Committee on Aging, Senate, <http://www.federalreserve.gov/boarddocs/testimony/2003/20030227/default.htm>).

which are experiencing rapid ageing.[23] A flexible labour market would enable migrant labour to return to their home countries after their short-term contracts abroad are completed, a process necessary to avoid transforming short-term labour migration into permanent migration.

An important source of labour for many countries in the region would be the unemployed and underemployed women themselves in home countries. In many countries in the region the participation of women in the labour force is constrained by factors such as lack of flexibility in career and child-rearing, the lack of day-care facilities for children, the lack of home care for older persons and social norms which lead to gender bias in education and employment. Removal of these constraints alone could neutralize a large part of the negative impact of ageing on labour markets.

Labour markets should also respond to the needs of older persons

Labour markets should also respond to the needs of older workers as the older workforce will become an important component of the labour force in the years to come. Job redesign, the reorganization of the division of labour and the provision of a flexible working environment to meet the aspirations of older persons and make the best use of a growing number of older workers could be effective policy responses to an ageing workforce.

Migration policy

Critical role of international migration in stabilizing labour markets ...

The historical movement of natural persons indicates that international migration can play an important role in offsetting many of the consequences of population ageing and labour shortages. How can migration policy be fine-tuned to cope with the adverse effects of ageing in labour-importing countries, while minimizing the negative effects of the "brain drain" on labour-exporting countries?

The fact that international human migration is a transnational phenomenon makes handling migration for the benefit of both the home and host countries a global issue. Formal arrangements between labour-exporting countries and labour-importing countries through bilateral or regional cooperation could benefit all parties, as such arrangements could solve the unemployment problem in the exporting country while meeting the supply shortages in the importing country. The following are some proposals for consideration.

... and a greater need for a global framework for the orderly flow of persons

- Explore the possibilities of bringing international human migration under a global framework to ensure an orderly and rule-based flow of persons. A fresh look at the existing global

---

23 Immigration or temporary worker flows have already proved important in Malaysia and Thailand. For example, foreign workers account for 25 per cent of Malaysia's labour force (see Heller, op. cit.).

frameworks, such as Mode 4 of the WTO General Agreement on Trade in Services, for widening the scope of such initiatives for human migration, just as in the case of trade in services, would be a starting point.[24]

- Facilitate return migration and introduce compensation systems for countries of origin to recover the cost of education, lost innovation and creativity in the event that temporary migration becomes permanent.
- Make efforts to integrate migrants into local society along with measures to protect the rights of migrants and meet their obligations.

However, as elaborated in box III.4, international migration by itself may not be able to offset completely the effects of population ageing on the labour market. For certain countries, a migration policy may not be an option at all as cultural identities and values may compel them to focus on alternative choices, such as productivity improvement and market reforms.[25]

Population policy

What size population is affordable?

Just as the population policies of the past have played some role in the present-day demographic dynamics, population policy could also be used to reverse rapid fertility declines. Increase in fertility, removing restrictions on having large families and promoting early marriage could reverse the future demographic trend. Some countries have already taken steps in this direction. For example, countries such as Singapore provide incentives such as housing priority for large and multigeneration families, flexitime for mothers to nurture their children, cash and fiscal incentives, child-care subsidies and enhanced child relief in income taxation.

Population policies need to be carefully planned

However, changing the hard-earned gains of low fertility may not be a good choice for certain countries as overcrowding could create serious problems. What size population can be affordable? Even with declining fertility rates, the world population is projected to increase to over 9 billion by 2050. Overcrowding in countries which already have high

---

[24] A similar argument was put forward in *World Economic and Social Survey 2004* (United Nations publication, Sales No. E.04.II.C.3).

[25] For example, Japan is taking initiatives such as support measures for the balancing of work and child-raising instead of receiving migrant workers. The House of Lords of the United Kingdom, in its report to the Select Committee on Economic Affairs on *Aspects of the Economics of an Ageing Population,* <http://www.parliament.the-stationery-office.co.uk/pa/ld200203/ldselect/ldeconaf/179/179.pdf>, concludes that it is neither appropriate nor feasible to attempt to counter the trend towards a more aged society in the United Kingdom through a manipulation of immigration policy.

Box III.4. Migration policy: a cushion for the ageing process?

The Asian and Pacific region constitutes both labour-importing and labour-exporting countries. For example, Bangladesh, India, Indonesia, Pakistan, Sri Lanka, Thailand and Viet Nam serve as a pool of migrant workers for countries experiencing labour shortages. The number of migrant workers deployed from these countries had increased from 1 million in 1990 to 2.4 million by the end of 2000. About 5.5 million foreign workers are estimated to be living in main areas of destination in East and South-East Asia.[a] With rapid ageing, economies such as Japan, the Republic of Korea and Singapore are expected to experience severe shortages in labour supply in the coming decades.

In these circumstances, would immigration be a promising cushion for the ageing process in the region? The current debate provides support for answering both yes and no.

On the positive side are the following factors:

- Higher net migration may mitigate the negative fiscal consequences of an ageing society because of the expected age distribution of migrants, who are more likely than the resident population to be of working age.[b] Migrant workers are on average younger than non-immigrants and are likely to contribute more in taxes than they receive in services.
- The imbalance between labour supply and demand and the resulting labour market mismatching could be avoided to some extent with migrant labour, thereby sustaining growth.[c]

On the negative side are the following factors:

- The amount of migration required to prevent a decline in the working-age population may be larger than exporting countries can afford owing to its adverse implications for the labour markets in the countries of origin. For example, if Japan wished to keep the size of its population at the level attained in 2005, the country would need 17 million net immigrants up to 2050, or an average of 381,000 immigrants per year between 2005 and 2050. By 2050, 30 per cent of the population would be immigrants and their descendents. Similarly, the Republic of Korea may need an average of 100,000 immigrants per year between 2035 (the population will peak in 2035) and 2050 although migration is already taking place.[d] It is unlikely that such large flows can happen in these countries in the foreseeable future.
- In most of the ageing economies, labour markets are not sufficiently flexible to absorb migrant workers and offer the requisite training on a large scale.[e]

The above arguments underscore the fact that immigration alone may not be an effective solution for labour market distortions arising from an ageing population. It has to go hand in hand with reforms in labour markets and social insurance. However, the evolving dynamics of population ageing would provide an opportunity for a collaborative effort by both the labour-exporting and -importing countries to exploit the labour market conditions to their advantage. An understanding on a common migration policy framework at the regional and multilateral levels and bilateral negotiation within such a framework would enable mitigation of the labour shortages in ageing economies, while allowing countries of origin to benefit from such initiatives without disrupting the labour markets in home countries. Labour market flexibility, the portability of pensions and restricting such migration to a fixed term or mechanisms for compensation for the countries of origin would be key ingredients of such a framework.

---

[a] J.W. Huguet, "International migration and development: opportunities and challenges for poverty reduction", in *Fifth Asian and Pacific Population Conference: Selected Papers,* Asian Population Studies Series No. 158 (United Nations publication, Sales No. E.03.II.F.27).

[b] H. Polackova, "Population ageing and financing of government liabilities in New Zealand", World Bank Policy Research Working Paper No. 1703.

[c] Y. Katsumata, "The impact of population decline and population ageing in Japan from the perspectives of social and labour policy", paper presented at the Expert Group Meeing on Policy Responses to Population Ageing and Population Decline, New York, 16-18 October 2000.

[d] United Nations, *Replacement Migration: Is It a Solution to Declining and Ageing Populations?* (ESA/P/WP.160).

[e] Axel Boersch-Supan, "Labor market effects of population ageing", National Bureau of Economic Research Working Paper No. 8640, <http://www.nber.org/papers/w8640>.

population densities could have serious repercussions in the long run, undermining the well-being of future generations. Thus, such changes should be implemented only through a carefully planned population policy.

Fiscal policy

Fiscal consolidation and overall macroeconomic stability vital

The most important policy issue arising from an ageing population from the Government's perspective is the fiscal burden of rising public pension and health-care expenditure. Many developing countries in the region already have large budget deficits and the fiscal demands arising from an ageing population would be an additional burden on them. The challenges facing the developing countries with ageing populations may thus become more difficult in the years ahead.

In this context, effective fiscal consolidation would become an important policy goal for developing countries in the Asian and Pacific region. While maintaining macroeconomic stability should be a primary goal, policy coordination to ensure the coherence and consistency of policies would be essential. Taxation could be an important policy instrument in financing social security. For example, a consumption tax earmarked for social security and care of the elderly would be an effective means of raising funds in developing countries, although this mechanism may be counterproductive in countries that are struggling to recover from economic downturns. Efforts to reduce the public debt burden would be necessary not only to absorb future shocks but also to prevent the country from falling into a debt trap in the face of rising public expenditure. The provision of an environment conducive to saving more is another option which would lessen the pressure on the budget. While the negative impact of pensions on the budget could be minimized by linking pension benefits to contributions, that arising from health-care expenditure could be reduced to a certain extent by introducing privately managed health-care systems.

Role of the private sector

Strategic public-private partnerships necessary to narrow the gap between the rich and the poor

The rapid ageing of populations in many countries in the region would open the door for the private sector, including NGOs, to play an important role in addressing issues relating to ageing. The diminishing role of Governments and the increasing influence of the private sector on society in a globalized world and the increasing gap between rich and poor would necessitate strategic partnerships between the Government and the private sector, as no single sector or organization can address issues relating to ageing on its own.[26]

---

[26] J.E. Austin, *The Collaboration Challenge: How Nonprofits and Businesses Succeed through Strategic Alliances* (Jossey-Bass, 2000).

The increasing demand for health insurance, annuities and savings instruments and institutionalized care services for older persons would provide ample opportunities for the private sector to expand its services while contributing to easing the pressure on the public sector. The role of NGOs would be critical in providing community-based support systems for older persons and covering gaps in public and private services.

CONCLUSION

Anti-poverty family planning playing an important role in ageing

Many countries in the Asian and Pacific region are experiencing rapid ageing of their populations, reflecting declines in mortality and fertility rates. The intensity of population ageing in the region is bound to increase rapidly during the next 50 years with the share of the population aged 60 and over predicted to more than double to 23.5 per cent by 2050. A distinctive feature of ageing in the region is the rapid ageing of populations in economies which are still developing. For example, the implementation of family planning as an anti-poverty measure had a significant impact on the demographic structures of countries such as China, India, Indonesia, Malaysia, Singapore and Sri Lanka.

The rapid ageing of populations in developing countries could have profound implications for their economies and societies. The rising demand for health-care services in old age and increasing pension liabilities, particularly in the face of declining potential support ratios, would place the fiscal implications of ageing at the forefront. Labour markets could experience a shift in the supply of labour, with adverse implications for labour productivity. The changing age structure could also induce a shift in the consumption and savings behaviour of people. The combined effect of these changes would have adverse implications for capital markets, growth and social welfare.

More complex challenges for developing economies

In many countries a large proportion of older persons are poor and work in the informal sector, without any support from formal pension schemes in old age. In many countries, effective institutions, procedures, rules and regulations for addressing issues relating to older persons are not in place. Moreover, the changing family structure and composition in the face of urbanization, globalization and migration would have a negative impact on social norms in familial care, imposing pressure on the provision of formal residential care for older persons. As a result, the challenges faced by developing economies in the region with an ageing population in the years to come would be more complex than those faced by developed economies with an ageing population.

A balanced and holistic approach, taking into account both economic and social considerations with a view to achieving improved individual welfare, would be necessary to respond effectively to the challenges of ageing. On the economic front, fundamental changes are needed in policy design, particularly in health and social security systems, to minimize the pressures on public expenditure which would have an impact on the potential for overall growth. Pension schemes in many countries in the region are pay-as-you-go systems with the financial burden accumulating over time, resulting in an intergenerational transfer of liabilities and a disproportionate reduction of welfare for future generations. The implementation of multi-pillar social security structures consisting of mandated, publicly managed defined benefit schemes on an equity basis, privately managed and funded defined contributory schemes for the working class and additional retirement schemes for voluntary contributions would constitute an effective and sustainable approach in addressing old-age social security. Such an approach would not only make pension schemes financially sustainable but also function as an anti-poverty measure.

Regulatory and market reforms to provide an enabling environment for promoting a higher level of efficiency in both the public and private sectors and the provision of incentives for innovation would be important aspects in addressing issues relating to ageing. The liberalization of labour markets to make them more flexible and boost labour supply, fiscal consolidation and policy coordination, while maintaining macroeconomic stability to withstand the pressures on social expenditures and negative effects on the economy, should be key elements in such a policy agenda.

The Millennium Development Goals could be a benchmark in responding to ageing

On the social front, the promotion of health throughout life and the creation of an environment conducive for the private sector to develop alternative social security schemes such as health insurance and annuity schemes are important policy options to consider. While the promotion of family care for the elderly by providing incentives should be a priority, the development of institutional care for the elderly by both the public and private sectors would also be necessary, particularly in the light of the changing family structures and their negative impact on familial care. The fundamental thrust of both economic and social policies should be avoiding the elderly becoming poor, isolated and discriminated against while maintaining the socio-economic conditions of the public in general. The Millennium Development Goals could provide a benchmark for both the economic and social policies required to face the challenges of ageing.

Fresh look at Mode 4 of the WTO General Agreement on Trade in Services needed

Regional and global actions could also play a key role in responding to ageing. For example, how migration is treated at the regional and global levels would have important implications for both ageing and non-ageing economies. Treating labour as a regional public good and measures for the orderly flow of labour would be necessary, particularly in the light of increasing international human migration in the coming decades. To the extent that population ageing could pose risks, particularly for the future labour supply, and international migration could play an important role in minimizing such risks, regional cooperation on human migration could be a key vehicle for harmonizing labour resources in the region. It is thus important to explore the possibilities of bringing international human migration within a global framework to ensure the orderly and rule-based flow of persons. In this regard, a fresh look at the existing frameworks, such as Mode 4 of the WTO Agreement, would be a starting point.

SPECIAL FEATURE TO MARK THE INTERNATIONAL YEAR OF MICROCREDIT, 2005[1]

MICROFINANCE IN POVERTY REDUCTION – ASIA-PACIFIC CHALLENGES

"The International Year of Microcredit 2005 underscores the importance of microfinance as an integral part of our collective effort to meet the Millennium Development Goals. Sustainable access to microfinance helps alleviate poverty by generating income, creating jobs, allowing children to go to school, enabling families to obtain health care, and empowering people to make the choices that best serve their needs... Together, we can and must build inclusive financial sectors that help people improve their lives." (United Nations Secretary-General Kofi Annan)

INTRODUCTION

In marking the International Year of Microcredit, this special feature reviews some of the issues associated with the opportunities created and the challenges faced by microfinance initiatives in becoming a more effective and potent instrument to serve the multidimensional needs of the poor.

Microfinance initiatives initially emerged as small loans known as microcredit provided by NGOs with a strong focus on poverty reduction. Subsequently, an increasingly wider range of financial services to the poor came to be provided by various types of organizations, termed microfinance institutions (MFIs). The services they rendered generally related to small-scale financial services such as loans, savings, insurance and money transfer services provided to poor and low-income people. MFIs have become increasingly diverse in organizational types and their associated objectives, methodologies, products, target groups and scales of operation.

Poverty reduction

The role of microfinance has gained strong acceptance as an effective tool for poverty reduction. General Assembly resolution 59/246 of 22 December 2004 on the role of microcredit and microfinance in the eradication of poverty recognizes the following points:

- The importance of microfinance in providing access to capital for people living in poverty
- The need to create inclusive financial sectors to facilitate microfinance for the poor, and particularly women, in order to mitigate their vulnerability

[1] The United Nations General Assembly designated 2005 as the International Year of Microcredit to highlight and promote recognition of the role of microfinance in the eradication of poverty and its contribution to social development.

- The importance of sharing good practices and enhancing financial sector support to pro-poor financial services in scaling up microfinance to reinforce development impact and sustainability
- The importance of collaborative efforts among all the stakeholders, including Governments, NGOs, international organizations, the private sector and civil society, in raising public awareness and knowledge of microfinance
- The potential contribution of microfinance to the achievement of development goals including the Millennium Development Goals
- The role of Governments in upscaling microfinance through, among others, developing mechanisms to promote sustainable access to financial services, removing institutional and regulatory obstacles and providing incentives to MFIs
- The role of government in the development of regulatory frameworks to ensure good governance, transparency and accountability in MFIs

Microfinance and the Millennium Development Goals[2]

Numerous experiences in the region have indicated that providing the poor with access to microfinance directly addresses the poverty eradication goal of the Millennium Development Goals by increasing opportunities to generate income and building capacity to smooth consumption flows. For instance, it has been reported that 90 per cent of Bank Rakyat Indonesia clients surveyed on the island of Lombok in Indonesia have moved above the poverty line, with average income increases of 112 per cent, while in India, clients of the Society for Helping and Awakening Rural Poor through Education (SHARE) had, in addition to increased economic well-being, a marked shift from irregular, low-paid daily labour to more diversified sources of income.[3] A study on the Grameen Bank in Bangladesh found that the incomes of the participants in the programme (members) were higher than those of non-participants. Its members were reportedly able to rely more on savings and their own funds in crises rather than borrowing from moneylenders.

Income growth in turn facilitates access to crucial services addressed in the Millennium Development Goals, such as health care and education. Some studies, including those on the Grameen Bank, the Bangladesh Rural Action Committee and the Self-Employed Women's Association in India, found that children of MFI clients were more likely to go to school for a longer time and a higher level of education, with lower dropout rates.

Thus, access to a small loan which enables the poor to take advantage of economic opportunities, to plan and expand their business opportunities, to pay school fees or to bridge a cash-flow gap can be a first step in breaking the cycle of poverty and moving out of the poverty trap. Similarly, the ability to access a safe and convenient savings account enables them to save in order to meet unexpected expenses and plan for future investments, in such areas as inventories for

---

2 Examples in this section draw upon Elizabeth Littlefield, Jonathan Morduch and Syed Hashemi, "Is microfinance an effective strategy to reach the Millennium Development Goals?", <http://www.cgap.org/docs/FocusNote_24.html>.

3 Microfinance Gateway, <http://www.microfinancegateway.org/>.

their small businesses, children's education and housing improvements. Moreover, access to financial services by poor women has reportedly empowered them in many instances as they play a larger role in income-earning activities.

REACHING OUT TO THE POOR

Microfinance initiatives have evolved over time to be more responsive to the needs of the poor, but a major issue in the promotion of microfinance initiatives remains how to extend the proven benefits of micro-level intervention to a larger and poorer population.

Supply-driven poverty lending approach

The emergence of microfinance initiatives in poverty reduction is aimed at bridging the gap between the reluctance of the formal financial sector to provide financial services to the poor and the unmet demand of the poor, which can otherwise only be met through an informal system, which is often inconvenient, insecure or exorbitantly expensive.[4] As exemplified by microcredit experiences in South Asia and Latin America in the 1970s, this poverty lending approach focuses on poverty reduction through the provision of microcredit and other complementary services without collateral to those denied access to formal financial services, particularly poor women. Successful experiences with microcredit initiatives have provided evidence contrary to the conventional view of the formal financial sector that there is no demand for financial services among the poor and that the risk associated with the poor is high since they have neither collateral nor proven capacity to repay loans and interest. The noteworthy experience of the Grameen Bank in Bangladesh has been replicated in many countries in the region.

Demand-driven and financial system approach

It has become increasingly evident that the supply-driven microcredit approach cannot reach a wide range of potential clients, leaving out many non-microentrepreneurs.[5] It has also become clear that there is effective demand by the poor for access to savings, with an increasing number of institutions mobilizing voluntary savings from low-income households, which in turn increases the ability of financial institutions to provide microfinance services without a subsidy. Against this background, a financial system approach developed as a more market-based concept of microfinance, focusing on demand for financial services on the part of poor borrowers and savers, while setting the price of the services to ensure cost recovery and financing loans from locally mobilized savings and other commercial sources, as exemplified by the transformation of the Bank Rakyat Indonesia Unit system from a channelling agent for subsidized credit for agricultural lending to a microfinance entity serving a wider population. Its commercially successful operations provided more evidence contrary to the conventional perception of the financial sector that small financial schemes for the poor are not profitable as the costs of handling small accounts are high. This approach provided scope for reaching a wider population of poor people while achieving institutional financial self-sufficiency.

---

4 For example, effective interest rates from moneylenders can be as high as 100 per cent per month.

5 E. Littlefield, "Building financial services for the poor", *Finance for the Poor,* vol. 4, No. 2, June 2003.

Breadth and depth of outreach

Breadth of outreach

One of the important challenges throughout the various experiments in microfinance initiatives is to provide access to as many poor people as possible. Although microfinance initiatives have increased their outreach over the years and many MFIs have even shown the potential profitability of financial services for the poor, there is still a large unmet demand for microfinance and an estimated 400-500 million poor and low-income people worldwide still do not have access to microfinance.[6] So far, only a handful of organizations in Asia are serving more than a million poor clients.[7] If microfinance is profitable as is often claimed, why have MFIs not expanded their operations dramatically and why have commercial banks not tapped into the microfinance market more aggressively?

For MFIs one of the constraints in extending outreach is the limited availability of funding resources. To ensure sustainable provision of services as well as expansion of operations, MFIs need an injection of funds from external sources or have to generate funds through their microfinance operations. For institutions which rely on donor funding and subsidies for their finances, the scope for extending the breadth of outreach depends on the availability of additional funds. For many NGO MFIs, the limitation of their scale also relates to the regulatory framework that restricts NGOs to accessing domestic or international capital markets. As NGOs are not permitted to offer savings services in many countries, they cannot mobilize deposits as a way to finance other financial services such as lending. NGO MFIs appear to have achieved significant scale in countries where the regulatory framework has been made suitable for MFIs or has allowed them to flourish unregulated.[8]

The limited scale may also indicate the need for further efforts to match methodology or selection of financial products with the specific needs of potential clients. For instance, the provision of saving services has long been unavailable despite the needs of the poor. For those in remote areas, difficulties in gaining physical access to microfinance facilities may have discouraged potential clients. The poorest reportedly prefer individual loans to group-based schemes packaged with training or regular meetings.[9] Thus, microfinance products and services that respond to the specific needs of the poor would increase the breadth of outreach while they have to be weighed against the cost of delivery.

Moreover, the limited scale may be due to the fact that the effective provision of microfinance to low-income clients is resource-intensive and developing countries do not have enough of the resources required. Human resources, including a capacity for strategic management, may be one of the important resource requirements. Only when management resources are strategically applied to

---

[6] "Implementation of the first United Nations Decade for the Eradication of Poverty (1997-2006) and preparations for the International Year of Microcredit, 2005" (A/59/326).

[7] Based on data provided by the Microcredit Summit Campaign in "Appendix 1: microcredit institutions whose figures on poorest* and total clients as of December 31, 2003 have been verified", <http://www.microcreditsummit.org/pubs/reports/socr/2004/en_app1.pdf>.

[8] Heather Montgomery and John Weiss, "Modalities for microfinance delivery in Asia and Latin America: lessons for the People's Republic of China", <http://www.iadb.org/laeba/downloads/WP_29_2004.pdf >.

[9] N. Fernando, "Microfinance outreach to the poorest: a realistic objective?", *Finance for the Poor,* vol. 5, No. 1, March 2004.

a sufficiently large scale of microfinance operations of any type will microfinance provision be able to cross the threshold and achieve the scale, seen in Bangladesh for example, where some estimates suggest that the number of borrowers at MFIs exceeds 10 per cent of the total population.[10] Thus, for most large commercial banks, the heavy commitment of management time involved in setting up a microfinance programme against the modest financial returns expected[11] may be seen as unattractive compared with other investment options.

Depth of outreach – reaching the poorest – alternative perspective

Another important challenge of microfinance is how to reach the poorest. There are various views on the relevance of microfinance for the poorest and corresponding opinions on how to reach this group effectively.[12]

One view is that microfinance cannot reach the poorest on a sustainable basis. The extreme poor may not benefit from microfinance and would be better served by other poverty reduction and social protection measures.[13] Many of the poorest with no capacity to generate income would require grants, employment and other services, rather than microcredit, which can make the extremely poor even more vulnerable, not less. According to this argument, the cost of providing microfinance to the poorest is so high that MFIs may not be able to sustain the service without cost recovery while the poorest would not be able to afford such a high cost.

This view, however, is contested by the argument that lack of poverty reduction measures and social protection are the core issues of poverty and the required services for the poorest are not readily available.

The above view, which would exclude the poorest from the microfinance target group, contrasts with the view that microfinance can reach and benefit even the poorest of the poor on a sustainable basis and on a large scale. It holds that there is a vast effective demand for microfinance services among the poorest and "…the reality in most poor countries is that the poorest are already saddled with incredible debt at usurious rates from local moneylenders. This is the fundamental predicament that microfinance institutions have effectively addressed for nearly three decades now."[14] This view is supported by the experience of an increasing number of MFIs with a strong focus on reaching the poorest, which have reported successful results in reaching the poorest without jeopardizing financial sustainability. Yet the rapid increase in outreach to the poorest depends on the funding agencies' financial support to those MFIs, as exemplified by the view of the Microcredit Summit that donors should direct more funds to microfinance to reach the poorest.[15]

---

[10] P. Honohan, "Financial sector policy and the poor: selected findings and issues", World Bank Working Paper No. 43, <http://www1.worldbank.org/finance/assets/images/0821359673_Financial_Sector_Policy_and_the_Poor.pdf>.

[11] Ibid.

[12] N. Fernando, loc. cit.

[13] M. Robinson, *The Microfinance Revolution: Sustainable Finance for the Poor* (Washington, World Bank, 2001).

[14] Unpublished letter to the editor in response to the *New York Times* article, "Debate stirs over tiny loans to world's poorest" (29 April 2004, by Celia Dugger), and the ensuing editorial, "Microcredit's limits" (5 May 2004), <http://www.microfinancegateway.org/content/article/detail/19028>.

[15] Sam Daley-Harris, "State of the Microcredit Summit Campaign Report 2004", <http://www.microcreditsummit.org/pubs/reports/socr/2004/SOCR04.pdf>.

However, there is a less optimistic view about large-scale sustainable provision of microfinance for the extreme poor. Reaching the poorest may be inherently more costly, as the size of transactions is much smaller and thus the operational cost per transaction is far higher. Risk factors associated with the poorest may also be higher as they are likely to be exposed to risks stemming from multiple interlocking disadvantages. It is questionable to what extent the poorest can afford to pay a higher price for microfinance services to cover the higher operational costs, although some feel that the poorest can pay, as otherwise they would have to resort to informal sources to finance their needs, which could be expensive. In this view, the scope for sustainable provision of microfinance to the poorest on a large scale is limited, while there is still much room to explore innovative approaches that combine livelihood protection with livelihood promotion to expand the outreach to the poorest, such as the Income Generation for Vulnerable Groups Development programme in Bangladesh,[16] and external financial support can facilitate experiments.

MICROFINANCE INITIATIVES IN THE REGION

Around 2 billion people, or 70 per cent of the world's poor, were living on less than 2 dollars a day in the region in 2001.[17] The region also has a large number of MFIs. Estimates by the Microcredit Summit Campaign indicate that more than half of the MFIs in the world are located in Asia. In 2003, there were 1,600 MFIs in Asia, serving almost 90 per cent of world's MFI clients or 71 million clients consisting of 49 million of the poorest. Among the poorest, more than 80 per cent of clients are women.[18]

The Asia-Pacific region has a wide variety of experiences in microfinance experiments. The successes and challenges of these various experiences have been debated in the light of various criteria and there is no agreed model of microfinance that satisfies all. Thus, this section highlights some experiences in the region to flag the diversity of microfinance initiatives in Asia and the Pacific.

South Asia

South Asia, seen as the birthplace of microfinance, houses a wide range of microfinance institutions, including many large MFIs experimenting with various microfinance schemes.[19]

A hallmark microfinance initiative in the region is the microcredit scheme pioneered by the Grameen Bank in Bangladesh, which demonstrated the possibility of reaching out to the poor on a large scale. Many MFIs, mostly NGO MFIs in the subregion, have either replicated the approach of

---

16 This programme of Bangladesh Rural Action Committee, building on the Government's safety net programme, provided foodgrain to hard core poor women to cater for their immediate consumption needs, packaged with skills training on poultry and livestock raising, etc., as well as a savings and credit service to buy chickens. "Two-thirds of these women have reportedly 'graduated' from absolute poverty to becoming microfinance clients, and have not slipped back into requiring government handouts", <http://www.cgap.org/docs/FocusNote_21.pdf>.

17 See chapter I of this *Survey*.

18 Sam Daley-Harris, loc. cit. Poorest is defined here as those in the bottom half of those living below their country's poverty line or below $1 a day.

19 According to the Microcredit Summit Campaign, out of 179 validated MFIs in Asia, 144 are in South Asia and half of them are in Bangladesh.

the Grameen Bank or developed their own variants with more flexible products and methodologies. In addition to various experiments, many Governments in the subregion have attempted to upscale their microfinance initiatives, for example, through establishing wholesale banks for MFIs and linking microfinance initiatives with the formal financial sector.

The novelty of the Grameen Bank in Bangladesh, which first started as an action experiment in the 1970s, was that it targeted poor women and had a group lending mechanism that allows a number of individuals to provide collateral or guarantee a loan through a group repayment pledge, giving an incentive to repay through peer pressure. In addition to group responsibility for loan repayment, a contribution of savings was one of the conditions prior to the disbursement of loans. The Grameen Bank experience showed the contribution of microfinance to income generation by the poor while achieving a significantly high repayment rate. It had grown to become a specialized commercial bank with 4 million members with outstanding loans of $283.95 million by the end of December 2004.[20]

Many replicators in the country and the region have been inspired by the Grameen Bank experience. For instance, Credit and Savings for the Hard-Core Poor, a network of 20 microfinance organizations in Asia, is explicitly aiming for Grameen Bank-type replications to provide credit and savings programmes targeting poor women. Within Bangladesh itself, several NGOs were induced to innovate on the basis of the Grameen Bank methodology.

Some NGO MFIs have also grown into large scale MFIs with more commercially focused operations. For example, the Bangladesh Rural Action Committee and the Association for Social Advancement (ASA) in Bangladesh have demonstrated that NGO MFIs can achieve financial self-sufficiency while serving a large number of the poor. ASA focuses on individual clients instead of a group approach and emphasizes the mobilization of voluntary savings and pricing its financial products to cover its operational costs.[21] It is reported to have served over 2 million poorest clients by the end of 2003, with an average outstanding loan balance of $90.

While some MFIs have grown into large-scale operations, most MFIs in the subregion remain small. Yet some Governments have begun to link the small-scale microfinance scheme to the formal financial system. For instance, the National Bank for Agriculture and Rural Development in India, an offshoot of the Reserve Bank of India, has played a central role in promoting self-help groups and linking them to the formal banking system through its banks/self-help groups linkages programme, which had served 11 million people by end of 2003.[22] Under the programme the poor organize self-help groups for lending and saving and mature groups are linked to the formal banking system. The Small Industries Development Bank of India has taken a similar approach, working with a close network of NGO partners.[23]

---

20 Grameen Bank monthly update, December 2004, <http://www.grameen-info.org>.

21 S.H. Choudhury and M. Kamal, "ASA: profile of a successful microfinance institution", <http://devnet.anu.edu.au/online%20versions%20pdfs/57/1357Choudhury.pdf>.

22 Sam Daley-Harris, loc. cit.

23 Pascal Marino, "Five years on: the Microcredit Summit Campaign and the development of microfinance in Asia and the Pacific", <http://www.fdc.org.au/publications/20030523_57.html>.

Government initiatives to link formal institutions and microfinance are also found in Bangladesh. With the substantial growth of NGO MFIs in the country, the Palli Karma-Sahayak Foundation was established by the Government as a wholesaler of microfinance funds in the country. It provides loans to partner organizations, around 200 NGO MFIs. By February 2004, it had disbursed a total of about $277 million among 4.55 million poor borrowers through its partner organizations.[24]

In some countries, government initiatives to promote microfinance led to the creation of an MFI to play a leading role in microfinance initiatives, such as the Pakistan Poverty Alleviation Fund, an apex organization to provide wholesale funds/credit lines and grants to NGOs, and Khushali Bank, a microfinance retail bank, in Pakistan. The Government facilitated the establishment of Khushali Bank, which is owned by 2 public sector, 12 private sector and 2 foreign banks[25] and has a major share (95 per cent) in lending. It has a network of 40 branches and 70 service centres across 41 districts.[26]

Private investments in microfinance are another innovation linking private banks with MFIs that is in its nascent stage in many countries. Securitization of loans, guarantees, lines of credit and other instruments are used to promote private capital in microfinance. For instance, in India, ICICI Bank, which is a private bank wholesaling to MFIs, has securitized loans of Bhartiya Samruddhi Finance Limited and SHARE by releasing equity funds for the organizations to lend to clients.

East and South-East Asia

There is a vast diversity of schemes and levels of development of microfinance in East and South-East Asia, while direct credit programmes are also prevalent. The experiences in the region range from large-scale microfinance schemes involving formal financing institutions and initiatives led by central government programmes and associated NGOs to initiatives with a strong NGO presence.

Some examples in this region have shown the potential for formal financial institutions to be involved in microfinance on a large scale. The Bank Rakyat Indonesia Unit system in Indonesia is often viewed as a hallmark example of large-scale, financially sustainable provision of microfinance by a formal financial institution. Its unit desas ("village units"), originally established as a government-subsidized agricultural credit programme, were transformed into full-service rural banks that provide a wide range of flexibly priced products, with profitability the primary criterion of success. They succeeded in attracting a large number of clients, serving 29.9 million savers and 3.1 million borrowers at the end of 2003,[27] although along with the transformation their client base has changed from poor farmers to members of the semi-urban and rural population with regular

---

[24] Palli Karma-Sahayak Foundation, "Microcredit programs in Bangladesh: giving the poor a chance", <http://www.pksf-bd.org/Microcredit_bangladesh.htm> (February 2005).

[25] "The road map for development of microfinance sector in Pakistan", <http://www.adb.org/Documents/others/PRM_Supplement/Microfinance_Development_Road_Map_PAK.asp?p=prmnews>.

[26] State Bank of Pakistan, *The State of Pakistan's Economy - First Quarterly Report 2004-2005,* <http://www.sbp.org.pk/reports/quarterly/FY05/first/index.htm>.

[27] Microfinance Information Exchange, <http://www.mixmarket.org/en/demand/demand.show.profile.asp?ett=93&> (March 2005).

incomes. The Bank for Agriculture and Agricultural Cooperatives in Thailand is another example of a large, financially sustainable and formal institution playing a major role in providing microfinance services. It is owned by the Government and through a reform process shifted its focus from short-term agricultural loans to non-farm micro and small enterprise lending as well as deposit services. It served 2.7 million active loan clients in 2002 and 9.6 million savings accounts and reportedly over 90 per cent of farm households were registered as its clients. The high number of savings and loan accounts compared with low outstanding balances suggests the outreach of its services to the poorer clientele.[28] The experience of rural credit cooperatives in China also shows the potential for large-scale mobilization of small savings by formal financial institutions. The nationwide network of cooperatives, under the control of the central bank, mobilizes significant amounts of rural savings. It reportedly holds deposits amounting to $210 billion or 12 per cent of the total deposits of Chinese financial institutions in 2001. Savings from rural households account for 80 per cent of the deposits in the cooperatives.[29]

In addition to financial assistance to rural areas that has been traditionally provided by government programmes, there have been microfinance initiatives by Governments and associated NGOs drawing on microfinance experiments in other countries. For example, in China, the central bank has initiated programmes that have given selected rural credit cooperatives increased flexibility in such areas as interest rates and their products in order to encourage loans to poorer households. Various levels of the Government have also experimented with lending to households as part of the poverty alleviation programme, applying such microfinance methodologies as group mechanisms and instalment repayments. Official microcredit schemes were reportedly operating in more than 600 counties of 22 provinces by 1998, with the largest programmes reaching over half a million households.[30]

In Viet Nam, the Viet Nam Bank for Agriculture and Rural Development, formerly the agricultural credit arm of the State Bank of Viet Nam, provides loans to poor households and private businesses using joint-liability groups such as the Viet Nam Women's Union or the Farmers' Association and the Viet Nam Bank for the Poor. As an indication of its substantial outreach, it had reportedly provided over 30 per cent of rural households with access to its loans by 1998.

Many microfinance initiatives have been led by NGOs in the subregion. For example, in the Philippines, where the Government actively promotes microfinance initiatives with a supportive legislative environment, a number of NGOs have established MFIs, with some of them transformed into regulated microfinance institutions. The Center for Agriculture and Rural Development (CARD), for instance, transferred part of its loan portfolio to establish CARD Rural Bank (CARD Bank) while it continues to operate as an NGO. The Microfinance Council of the Philippines reports that as at the end of December 2003, its 21 MFI members served a total of 578,000 borrowers, with five large members each serving an average of 62,000 active borrowers.[31]

---

[28] Pascal Marino, loc. cit.

[29] Sun Ruomei, "The development of microfinance in China", <http://topics.developmentgateway.org/chinamicrofinance/rc/filedownload.do~itemId=323395> (February 2005).

[30] Kieran Donaghue, "Microfinance in the Asia Pacific", *Asian-Pacific Economic Literature,* vol. 18, No. 1, pp. 41-61.

[31] Microfinance Council of the Philippines, *Performance Monitoring Report, 2003,* <http://www. microfinancecouncil.org/dload/Performance%20Monitoring%20Report%202003.pdf>.

The role of NGO MFIs is also significant in Cambodia, where the low level of development of the formal commercial system, particularly in rural areas, requires MFIs to play a major role in the financial system. Approximately 55 credit programmes operating in Cambodia reportedly had an outreach of 450,000 households as at February 2002.[32] Some NGO MFIs have been transformed into regulated financial institutions, such as ACLEDA Bank, which has been licensed as a commercial bank, and Ennathian Moulethan Tchonnebat, which has been transformed into a regulated non-bank MFI.

North and Central Asia

The role of microfinance emerged in the subregion as the countries went through the transition process from State-managed economies to market-oriented economies accompanied by increased poverty and unemployment. Thus, the target group for microfinance is the poor, many of them literate and well-educated, who lost their jobs relatively recently in the market transition process and are newcomers to microenterprise, unlike in most of the developing countries, where millions of poor people have traditionally earned a living in small informal businesses.

In regional reviews by the Consultative Group to Assist the Poor, microfinance institutions operating in the subregion are divided into four distinct types; credit unions, NGO MFIs, commercial banks and microfinance banks.[33]

Credit unions, which had a long history of providing financial services to the large segments of society without access to mainstream banks, have been revived and redeveloped as part of the transitional process. They are member-owned and offer savings and credit services to members. In 2001, there were reportedly 62 credit unions in the Russian Federation and 206 in Kyrgyzstan serving 26,000 and 12,500 members respectively.

NGO MFIs emerged in the subregion during the transition process, with growing recognition of the role of microfinance as a tool to reduce the subregion's increasing unemployment and poverty. Most of the NGO MFIs provide low-income micro entrepreneurs and the self-employed, with access to credit and other services, often using group-lending methods. Many NGO MFIs operating in the subregion are relatively small. For example, as at September 2001, about 320 NGO MFIs in six countries (Kazakhstan, Kyrgyzstan, Mongolia,[34] Tajikistan, Turkmenistan and Uzbekistan) were serving 80,000 borrowers and 17,000 depositors, accounting for outstanding loans of $76.5 million and deposits of $2.8 million. Relatively larger-scale NGO MFIs in the subregion, such as FINCA in Kyrgyzstan, the Constanta Foundation in Georgia and the Mercy Corps Women's Microcredit Programme in Kyrgyzstan, still did not serve more than 20,000 borrowers as at the end of 2002.

---

32 NGO statement to the 2002 Consultative Group Meeting on Cambodia, <http://www.ngoforum.org.kh/Development/Docs/ngo-2002/32.htm>.

33 Microfinance Centre, *The State of Microfinance in Central and Eastern Europe and the New Independent States,* <http://www.cgap.org/assets/images/TheStateOfMicrofinance.pdf>.

34 Mongolia is included because of its similar demography and topography although it is not geographically part of Central Asia.

Commercial banks have been providing specialized lending services for micro and small enterprises. This approach was introduced as a potential means of rapidly scaling up microfinance in the subregion using bank networks of retail branches. This "downscaling" approach has not proved to have significant outreach, particularly to low-end clients, partly owing to the timing of its introduction, which coincided with widespread bank restructuring and reform and lower-than-expected profits. One of the few successful examples is Sberbank in the Russian Federation, which has developed a downscaling programme of significant scale, serving 10,000 clients with a gross outstanding loan portfolio of $47.5 million in September 2001. It is reportedly running profitable operations at the branch level.

The microfinance banks are fully regulated, for-profit commercial banks and have been the last to develop in the subregion. Microfinance banks aim to balance both commercial and social goals, offering a broad range of products and services while providing loans to micro and small enterprises as their primary business purpose. For example, Xac Bank in Mongolia transformed itself from an NGO into a regulated microfinance institution serving over 6,500 clients. The Microfinance Bank of Georgia had nearly 16,000 clients with a portfolio of $23 million in September 2001, while KMB-Bank in the Russian Federation had 7,400 clients with a portfolio of $78 million.

Pacific islands

Microfinance in the Pacific island countries is still in the embryonic phase, with no sustained success stories of microfinance initiatives for poverty reduction. Given the dominance of subsistence economies with no pressing need to engage in small-scale production and trading, the strong culture of redistribution within the extended family or community and the dispersed and isolated populations of the island States, the relevance of microfinance to poverty reduction and other development goals is open to debate. Nevertheless, with an increasing incidence of poverty, many parts of the Pacific subregion are developing informal market-based sectors and thus microfinance is becoming increasingly relevant, in particular savings mobilization[35] and loans for consumption smoothing to meet customary obligations and seasonal cash needs without having to sell productive assets necessary for the people's livelihoods.

Microfinance in the Pacific subregion, as elsewhere in the ESCAP region, is provided through a range of formal and informal sources, such as development and commercial banks, government agencies, village banks, self-help groups, NGOs, friends and relatives, and moneylenders.[36] Examples of these microfinance providers exist across the Pacific. There have been attempts by some development banks, such as the Tonga Development Bank, the Cook Islands Development Bank and the Development Bank of Western Samoa, to develop specific lending programmes for borrowers located in isolated regions and the outer islands. Most countries in the Pacific have varying numbers of credit unions in both urban and rural areas. For example, the Bougainville Microfinance Scheme in Papua New Guinea is a savings-based programme built on credit union principles.

---

35 Mobilization of savings is stressed in "Microfinance in the Pacific, lessons learned and directions for future development", <http://www.fdc.org.au/programs/130_microfinance/20041027_101.html>.

36 Pascal Marino, loc. cit.

Some NGOs and government projects are using the Grameen Bank as their microcredit model, including Liklik Dinau Abitore Trust in Papua New Guinea, the Women's Social and Economic Development Programme in Fiji, the Vanuatu Women's Development Scheme,[37] and the Solomon Islands Microcredit Scheme for Disadvantaged Women. Semi-formal microfinance, such as revolving loan fund schemes, has generally been seen in Papua New Guinea and the outer islands of Kirabati, Cook Islands and Tuvalu. Yet the most common forms of microfinance in the Pacific appear to be those in the informal sector, including family and friends, commercial moneylenders, traders and shopkeepers.

There have been some achievements by several organizations in savings mobilization and loan repayment, but not in operational self-sufficiency. In addition to the organizational sustainability of MFIs in the Pacific islands, the distinct environment of isolated island States with low populations and limited market bases suggests that the MFIs need to respond to a demand for microfinance services which are different from those in other parts of the ESCAP region. Thus, effective microfinance methodologies for the Pacific region need to be explored.

CHALLENGES OF MICROFINANCE

Microfinance initiatives have great potential to make a significant contribution to the lives of the poor. As shown in the previous section, the Asian and Pacific region has seen the development of diverse MFIs. Countless good practices of MFIs in various forms across the region have been widely reported,[38] although this paper does not go into detail on those experiences. Instead, in this section it attempts to examine the factors that constrain the microfinance initiative. Despite growing empirical evidence of the promising contribution of microfinance, the scale of operations has remained small in general and has not grown as quickly as many feel it should. What are the challenges in enhancing the contribution of microfinance initiatives to ensure further poverty reduction? The earlier section highlighted the issue of reaching out to the poor, which is the core of the challenges associated with microfinance. This section reviews a number of areas which have a direct bearing on reaching out to the poor.

Sustainability of microfinance

Financial sustainability of microfinance

Sustaining the provision of microfinance services is an important goal of any microfinance operation. Thus, how to achieve institutional sustainability has become an important issue for many MFIs, as reliance on subsidies and donor funding may not continue indefinitely. One of the key questions relates to the balance between the financial sustainability of MFIs and their social goals. Financial sustainability can range from recovery of operational costs and achievement of operational self-sustainability to financial self-sustainability and go further to profitability as in commercial

---

[37] Robyn Cornford, " 'Microcredit', 'microfinance' or 'access to financial services': What do Pacific people need?", <http://www.fdc.org.au/publications/20020307_42.html>.

[38] See, for example, <http://www.microfinancegateway.org/> for various resources on microfinance.

operations. The extent of financial sustainability and profitability, in turn, depends on the cost and price structure of financial products and services, which are determined in the light of each MFI's social goal. Subsidization is certainly an important source of funds, "...but should be not seen (and is not seen by many microfinance enthusiasts) as essential to the health and sustainability of a microfinance industry",[39] in particular if subsidies are designed to support the set-up costs of MFIs or educational and other ancillary programmes provided in connection with microfinance.

One side of the argument is that commercial viability is a practical solution to increase outreach to the poor on a large scale. Some MFIs became "for-profit" institutions and found themselves serving a larger population of the poor, such as the Bank Rakyat Indonesia Unit system, which serves an estimated 3.1 million active clients.[40] Some financially sustainable NGO MFIs were transformed into regulated financial institutions with scope for a sustainable increase in the depth and breadth of outreach by increasing access to lendable funds from commercial sources and permission to offer a broader range of financial services. For instance, SHARE in India has made such a transformation and increased the number of its borrowers more than 10 times in five years.[41]

However, some MFIs view financial sufficiency as a trade-off with their social goals. For instance, "...it is clear that the main reason for Grameen's lack of financial sustainability is its decision not to charge a high enough interest rate (Grameen's rates are lower than those of self-financing MFIs.) ... Despite the higher loan losses experienced in recent years, a high-interest Grameen would surely be potentially sustainable; the current slight-loss-making strategy is a management choice."[42] These MFIs are also concerned that microfinance operations focusing on profitability tend to serve those who are relatively better off and neglect the poorer population.

Commercialization of microfinance

As discussed above, commercialization is increasingly seen as a practical solution to the problem of limited sustainability and outreach. In addition, the introduction of commercial principles in their microfinance activities responds to concerns over the lack of accountability and transparency for which MFIs have often been criticized. These issues are partly attributed to the facts that MFIs often have no owners whose capital is at risk and that NGOs' assets cannot be seized easily in case of default. The result is that this provides little incentive to ensure accountability and little security to lenders.[43] The advocates of the commercialization of MFIs feel that although the term "commercialization" may be interpreted as an anti-poor approach evoking connotations of exploitation and exclusion of the poor, the purpose is simply to ensure good financial practices, efficiency and financial discipline[44] and thus benefit the poor.

---

[39] P. Honohan, loc. cit.

[40] As at end-December 2003 (<http://www.microcreditsummit.org/pubs/reports/socr/2004/en_app1.pdf>).

[41] For transformation of NGO MFIs, see, for example, N. Fernando, *Micro Success Story? Transformation of Nongovernment Organizations into Regulated Financial Institutions,* <http://www.adb.org/Documents/Studies/miorofinance-success/micro-success.pdf>.

[42] P. Honohan, loc. cit.

[43] N. Fernando, loc. cit.

[44] Nimal Sanderatne, "Provocative issues in commercialization of microfinance", *Finance for the Poor,* vol. 3, No. 1, March 2002.

Commercialization would require the establishment of some kind of performance standard relating to portfolio quality, efficiency, sustainability and outreach.[45] It thus raises some concern over the potential impacts on the poor since MFIs may establish standards that can work against the case-specific needs and characteristics of poor clients.

Microfinance as an integral part of the financial system

Microfinance has become more mature and dynamic, offering a wider range of financial services such as loans, savings, insurance and remittances for poor and low-income people. It is increasingly diverse in its organizational types and their associated objectives, methodologies, products, target groups and scales of operation. Along with the growth and evolution of MFIs, formal financial institutions are also becoming increasingly involved in microfinance operations. These developments have led to the view that a strategy for developing microfinance, including a regulatory and monitoring framework, has to be an integral part of the financial sector strategy rather than being treated in isolation to achieve sustainable provision of financial services to a much wider and poorer population.

Impact of microfinance

It is now widely accepted that microfinance makes a positive contribution to poverty reduction efforts. However, access to microfinance does not automatically lead to increased earnings, nor is it a panacea for poverty reduction, since the creation of income-generating opportunities through access to finance assumes a certain economic environment and entrepreneurial capacity of the poor. To what extent has microfinance contributed to poverty reduction then? Qualitative as well as quantitative assessment of both the positive and negative impacts of microfinance would be a particularly challenging task where diverse MFIs themselves are evolving to meet the diverse needs of the poor and make a dent on the poverty situation.

Various studies, in both qualitative and quantitative terms, have attempted to assess the impact of microfinance on the well-being of the poor, with the results generally indicating positive impacts. They support the view that access to finance provides the poor with opportunities to invest in income-generating activities, smooth consumption and thus reduce their vulnerability to income fluctuations during emergencies. Yet there are many uncertainties associated with assessing the impact, such as the extent to which microfinance contributes to pulling people out of poverty on a permanent basis and the extent of outreach to the poorest.[46] The magnitude of the impacts of microfinance on the overall poverty situation is also not clear. For instance, despite the large amount of outreach to the poor reported in Bangladesh, the poverty situation has not improved dramatically. Furthermore, as is the case with quantitative impact assessment in general, the extent of the impacts drawn from various studies is bound to have a number of technical measurement

---

45 Antonino L. Alindogan, Jr., "Commercialization of microfinance", *Finance for the Poor,* vol 3. No. 3, September 2002.

46 For example, the Microcredit Summit (<www.microcreditsummit.org>) has attempted to verify the data reported by its members (MFIs) on the outreach to the poorest clients and the proportion of female clients among the poorest, although its coverage may be limited and there will be a certain amount of self-selection bias in reporting MFIs.

biases, which may make it impossible to draw clear conclusions. For instance, one of the challenges is establishing effective control-group mechanisms that can create a counterfactual, i.e., comparing the situation with microfinance with the situation without it. Moreover, it has been felt that the design of microfinance products would serve as a "self-selection" bias towards the poor, i.e., more attractive to the poor than the well-off, with many of the products characterized by small loan size, higher interest rate than the market rate, short loan duration, weekly repayment and dependence on mutual guarantees. Yet this self-selection process is seen to favour those who are relatively better off and pose a lower risk of default. Thus, despite various efforts to assess the impact of microfinance, the reliability of the impact assessment is still open to debate.

CONCLUSION

Microfinance initiatives have gained importance through their role in poverty reduction efforts. As they aim to increase the depth and breadth of outreach on a significant scale, various questions arise as to what changes are required to achieve such upscaling, what regulatory requirements foster an enabling environment in support of further development of microfinance initiatives, whether MFIs have to be transformed into different entities and how these changes affect the poor and the poorest.

Since the 1957 issue, the *Economic and Social Survey of Asia and the Pacific* has, in addition to a review of the current situation of the region, contained a study or studies of some major aspect or problem of the economies of the Asian and Pacific region, as specified below:

1957: Postwar problems of economic development
1958: Review of postwar industrialization
1959: Foreign trade of ECAFE primary exporting countries
1960: Public finance in the postwar period
1961: Economic growth of ECAFE countries
1962: Asia's trade with western Europe
1963: Imports substitution and export diversification
1964: Economic development and the role of the agricultural sector
1965: Economic development and human resources
1966: Aspects of the finance of development
1967: Policies and planning for export
1968: Economic problems of export-dependent countries. Implications of economic controls and liberalization
1969: Strategies for agricultural development. Intraregional trade as a growth strategy
1970: The role of foreign private investment in economic development and cooperation in the ECAFE region. Problems and prospects of the ECAFE region in the Second Development Decade
1971: Economic growth and social justice. Economic growth and employment. Economic growth and income distribution
1972: First biennial review of social and economic developments in ECAFE developing countries during the Second United Nations Development Decade
1973: Education and employment
1974: Mid-term review and appraisal of the International Development Strategy for the Second United Nations Development Decade in the ESCAP region, 1974
1975: Rural development, the small farmer and institutional reform
1976: Biennial review and appraisal of the International Development Strategy at the regional level for the Second United Nations Development Decade in the ESCAP region, 1976
1977: The international economic crises and developing Asia and the Pacific
1978: Biennial review and appraisal at the regional level of the International Development Strategy for the Second United Nations Development Decade
1979: Regional development strategy for the 1980s
1980: Short-term economic policy aspects of the energy situation in the ESCAP region
1981: Recent economic developments in major subregions of the ESCAP region
1982: Fiscal policy for development in the ESCAP region
1983: Implementing the International Development Strategy: major issues facing the developing ESCAP region
1984: Financing development
1985: Trade, trade policies and development
1986: Human resources development in Asia and the Pacific: problems, policies and perspectives
1987: International trade in primary commodities
1988: Recent economic and social developments
1989: Patterns of economic growth and structural transformation in the least developed and Pacific island countries of the ESCAP region: implications for development policy and planning for the 1990s
1990: Infrastructure development in the developing ESCAP region: needs, issues and policy options
1991: Challenges of macroeconomic management in the developing ESCAP region
1992: Expansion of investment and intraregional trade as a vehicle for enhancing regional economic cooperation and development in Asia and the Pacific
1993: Fiscal reform. Economic transformation and social development. Population dynamics: implications for development
1995: Reform and liberalization of the financial sector. Social security
1996: Enhancing the role of the private sector in development. The role of public expenditure in the provision of social services
1997: External financial and investment flows. Transport and communications
1998: Managing the external sector. Growth and equity
1999: Social impact of the economic crisis. Information technology, globalization, economic security and development
2000: Social security and safety nets. Economic and financial monitoring and surveillance
2001: Socio-economic implications of demographic dynamics. Financing for development
2002: The feasibility of achieving the millennium development goals in Asia and the Pacific. Regional development cooperation in Asia and the Pacific
2003: The role of public expenditure in the provision of education and health. Environment-poverty nexus revisited: linkages and policy options
2004: Poverty reduction strategies: tackling the multidimensional nature of poverty

This publication may be obtained from bookstores and distributors throughout the world. Please consult your bookstore or write to any of the following:

Sales Section
Room DC2-0853
United Nations Secretariat
New York, NY 10017
USA

Tel: (212) 963-8302
Fax: (212) 963-4116
E-mail: publications@un.org

Sales Section
United Nations Office at Geneva
Palais des Nations
CH-1211 Geneva 10
Switzerland

Tel: (41) (22) 917-1234
Fax: (41) (22) 917-0123
E-mail: unpubli@unog.ch

Chief
Conference Management Unit
Conference Services Section
Administrative Services Division
Economic and Social Commission for
Asia and the Pacific (ESCAP)
United Nations Building
Rajadamnern Avenue
Bangkok 10200, Thailand

Tel: (662) 288-1234
Fax: (662) 288-1000
E-mail: likitnukul.unescap@un.org

For further information on publications in this series, please address your enquiries to:

Chief
Poverty and Development Division
Economic and Social Commission for
Asia and the Pacific (ESCAP)
United Nations Building
Rajadamnern Avenue
Bangkok 10200, Thailand

Tel: (662) 288-1610
Fax: (662) 288-1000, 288-3007
Cable: ESCAP BANGKOK

READERSHIP SURVEY

The Poverty and Development Division of ESCAP is undertaking an evaluation of this publication, ***Economic and Social Survey of Asia and the Pacific 2005,*** with a view to making future issues more useful for our readers. We would appreciate it if you could complete this questionnaire and return it, at your earliest convenience, to:

Chief
Poverty and Development Division
ESCAP, United Nations Building
Rajadamnern Avenue
Bangkok 10200, THAILAND

QUESTIONNAIRE

	Excellent	*Very good*	*Average*	*Poor*
1. Please indicate your assessment of the *quality* of the publication on:				
• Presentation/format	4	3	2	1
• Readability	4	3	2	1
• Timeliness of information	4	3	2	1
• Coverage of subject matter	4	3	2	1
• Analytical rigour	4	3	2	1
• Overall quality	4	3	2	1
2. How *useful* is the publication for your work?				
• Provision of information	4	3	2	1
• Clarification of issues	4	3	2	1
• Its findings	4	3	2	1
• Policy suggestions	4	3	2	1
• Overall usefulness	4	3	2	1

3. Please give examples of how this publication has contributed to your work:

....

....

....

....

4. **Suggestions for improving the publication:**

....

....

....

....

5. **Your background information, please:**

Name: ....

Title/position: ....

Institution: ....

Office address: ....

....

Please use additional sheets of paper, if required, to answer the questions.
Thank you for your kind cooperation in completing this questionnaire.